interchange

FIFTH EDITION

1

Teacher's Edition

Jack C. Richards
with Jonathan Hull and Susan Proctor

CAMBRIDGE
UNIVERSITY PRESS

CAMBRIDGE
UNIVERSITY PRESS

University Printing House, Cambridge CB2 8BS, United Kingdom

One Liberty Plaza, 20th Floor, New York, NY 10006, USA

477 Williamstown Road, Port Melbourne, VIC 3207, Australia

314–321, 3rd Floor, Plot 3, Splendor Forum, Jasola District Centre, New Delhi – 110025, India

103 Penang Road, #05-06/07, Visioncrest Commercial, Singapore 238467

Cambridge University Press is part of the University of Cambridge.

It furthers the University's mission by disseminating knowledge in the pursuit of education, learning and research at the highest international levels of excellence.

www.cambridge.org
Information on this title: www.cambridge.org/9781108406062

First published 1990
Second edition 1997
Third edition 2005
Fourth edition 2013
Fifth edition 2017
Fifth edition update published 2021

20 19 18 17 16 15 14 13 12 11 10 9 8 7 6 5 4 3

Printed in Great Britain by CPI Group (UK) Ltd, Croydon CR0 4YY

A catalogue record for this publication is available from the British Library

ISBN 978-1-009-04044-0 Student's Book 1 with eBook
ISBN 978-1-009-04047-1 Student's Book 1A with eBook
ISBN 978-1-009-04048-8 Student's Book 1B with eBook
ISBN 978-1-009-04063-1 Student's Book 1 with Digital Pack
ISBN 978-1-009-04064-8 Student's Book 1A with Digital Pack
ISBN 978-1-009-04065-5 Student's Book 1B with Digital Pack
ISBN 978-1-316-62247-6 Workbook 1
ISBN 978-1-316-62254-4 Workbook 1A
ISBN 978-1-316-62266-7 Workbook 1B
ISBN 978-1-108-40606-2 Teacher's Edition 1
ISBN 978-1-316-62226-1 Class Audio 1
ISBN 978-1-009-04066-2 Full Contact 1 with Digital Pack
ISBN 978-1-009-04067-9 Full Contact 1A with Digital Pack
ISBN 978-1-009-04068-6 Full Contact 1B with Digital Pack
ISBN 978-1-108-40305-4 Presentation Plus Level 1

Additional resources for this publication at cambridgeone.org

CONTENTS

Introduction

Plan of Book 1 iv
Informed by teachers viii
The Fifth Edition of *Interchange* x
Student's Book overview xi
Cambridge One xv
Digital Workbook overview xvi
Workbook overview xvii
Teacher's Edition and Testing Program overviews xviii
Presentation Plus overview xix
Teacher Resources and Video Program overviews xx
Introduction to the CEFR xxi
Essential teaching tips xxii
Classroom language xxiii

Teaching notes

1 Where are you from? T-2
2 What do you do? T-8
Progress check T-14
3 How much are these? T-16
4 Do you play the guitar? T-22
Progress check T-28
5 What an interesting family! T-30
6 How often do you run? T-36
Progress check T-42
7 We went dancing! T-44
8 How's the neighborhood? T-50
Progress check T-56
9 What does she look like? T-58
10 Have you ever been there? T-64
Progress check T-70
11 It's a really nice city. T-72
12 It's important to get rest. T-78
Progress check T-84
13 What would you like? T-86
14 It's the coldest city! T-92
Progress check T-98
15 What are you doing later? T-100
16 How have you changed? T-106
Progress check T-112
Interchange activities T-114
Grammar plus T-132
Grammar plus answer key T-148

Additional resources

Appendix T-151
Language summaries T-152
Workbook answer key T-168
Credits T-184

Plan of Book 1

	Titles/Topics	Speaking	Grammar
	UNIT 1 PAGES 2–7 **Where are you from?** Introductions and greetings; names, countries, and nationalities	Introducing oneself; introducing someone; checking information; exchanging personal information; saying hello and good-bye; talking about school subjects	Wh-questions and statements with *be*; questions with *what, where, who,* and *how*; yes/no questions and short answers with *be*; subject pronouns; possessive adjectives
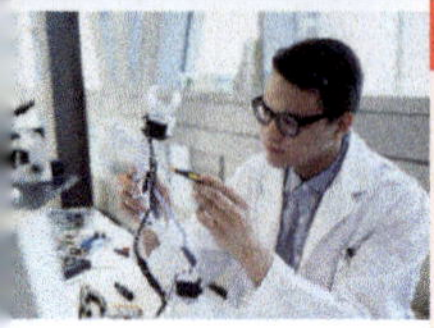	UNIT 2 PAGES 8–13 **What do you do?** Jobs, workplaces, and school; daily schedules; clock time PROGRESS CHECK PAGES 14–15	Describing work and school; asking for and giving opinions; describing daily schedules	Simple present Wh-questions and statements; question: *when*; time expressions: *at, in, on, around, early, late, until, before,* and *after*
	UNIT 3 PAGES 16–21 **How much are these?** Shopping and prices; clothing and personal items; colors and materials	Talking about prices; giving opinions; discussing preferences; making comparisons; buying and selling things	Demonstratives: *this, that, these, those*; *one* and *ones*; questions: *how much* and *which*; comparisons with adjectives
	UNIT 4 PAGES 22–27 **Do you play the guitar?** Music, movies, and TV shows; entertainers; invitations and excuses; dates and times PROGRESS CHECK PAGES 28–29	Talking about likes and dislikes; giving opinions; making invitations and excuses	Yes/no and Wh-questions with *do*; question: *what kind*; object pronouns; modal verb *would*; verb + *to* + verb
	UNIT 5 PAGES 30–35 **What an interesting family!** Family members; typical families	Talking about families and family members; exchanging information about the present; describing family life	Present continuous yes/no and Wh-questions, statements, and short answers; quantifiers: *all, nearly all, most, many, a lot of, some, not many,* and *few*; pronoun: *no one*
	UNIT 6 PAGES 36–41 **How often do you run?** Sports, fitness activities, and exercise; routines PROGRESS CHECK PAGES 42–43	Asking about and describing routines and exercise; talking about frequency; discussing sports and athletes; talking about abilities	Adverbs of frequency: *always, almost always, usually, often, sometimes, hardly ever, almost never,* and *never*; questions: *how often, how long, how well,* and *how good*; short answers
	UNIT 7 PAGES 44–49 **We went dancing!** Free-time and weekend activities	Talking about past events; giving opinions about past experiences; talking about vacations	Simple past yes/no and Wh-questions, statements, and short answers with regular and irregular verbs; past of *be*
	UNIT 8 PAGES 50–55 **How's the neighborhood?** Stores and places in a city; neighborhoods; houses and apartments PROGRESS CHECK PAGES 56–57	Asking about and describing locations of places; asking about and describing neighborhoods; asking about quantities	*There is/there are*; *one, any,* and *some*; prepositions of place; quantifiers; questions: *how many* and *how much*; count and noncount nouns

Pronunciation/Listening	Writing/Reading	Interchange Activity
Linked sounds Listening for names, countries, and school subjects	Writing questions requesting personal information "Is Your Name Trendy?": Reading about popular names	"Getting to know you": Collecting personal information about classmates PAGE 114
Syllable stress Listening to descriptions of jobs and daily routines	Writing a biography of a classmate "My Parents Don't Understand My Job!": Reading about four jobs	"What we have in common": Finding similarities in classmates' daily schedules PAGE 115
Sentence stress Listening to people shopping; listening for items, colors, and prices	Writing about favorite clothes "Online Shopping: The Crazy Things People Buy": Reading about unusual online items	"Flea market": Buying and selling things PAGES 116–117
Intonation in questions Listening for likes and dislikes	Writing text messages "The World's Most Powerful Female Musician": Reading about a famous musician	"Are you free this weekend?": Making plans; inviting and giving excuses PAGE 118
Intonation in statements Listening for family relationships	Writing an email about family "Do Families Spend a Lot of Time Together?": Reading about four families	"Is that true?": Finding out information about classmates' families PAGE 119
Intonation with direct address Listening to people talking about free-time activities; listening to descriptions of sports participation	Writing about weekly activities "Fit and Healthy? Take the Quiz!": Reading about health and taking a quiz	"What's your talent?": Finding out about classmates' abilities PAGE 120
Reduction of *did you* Listening to descriptions and opinions of past events and vacations	Writing a blog post "Awesome Vacations": Reading about different kinds of vacations	"Memories": Playing a board game PAGE 121
Reduction of *there is/there are* Listening for locations and descriptions of places	Writing about neighborhoods "Hip Neighborhoods of the World": Reading about popular neighborhoods	"Where are we?": describing and guessing locations PAGE 122

	Titles/Topics	Speaking	Grammar
	**UNIT 9 PAGES 58–63** **What does she look like?** Appearance and dress; clothing and clothing styles; people	Asking about and describing people's appearance; identifying people	Questions for describing people: *What...look like, how old, how tall, how long,* and *what color*; modifiers with participles and prepositions
	**UNIT 10 PAGES 64–69** **Have you ever been there?** Past experiences; unusual activities	Describing past experiences; exchanging information about past experiences and events	Present perfect yes/no and Wh-questions, statements, and short answers with regular and irregular past participles; *already* and *yet*; present perfect vs. simple past; *for* and *since*
	PROGRESS CHECK PAGES 70–71		
	**UNIT 11 PAGES 72–77** **It's a really nice city.** Cities; hometowns; countries	Asking about and describing cities; asking for and giving suggestions; talking about travel	Adverbs before adjectives; conjunctions: *and, but, though,* and *however*; modal verbs *can* and *should*
	**UNIT 12 PAGES 78–83** **It's important to get rest.** Health problems; medication and remedies; products in a pharmacy	Talking about health problems; asking for and giving advice; making requests; asking for and giving suggestions	Adjective + infinitive; noun + infinitive; modal verbs *could* and *should* for suggestions; modal verbs *can, could,* and *may* for requests
	PROGRESS CHECK PAGES 84–85		
	**UNIT 13 PAGES 86–91** **What would you like?** Food and restaurants	Expressing likes and dislikes; agreeing and disagreeing; ordering a meal	*So, too, neither,* and *either*; modal verbs *would* and *will* for requests
	**UNIT 14 PAGES 92–97** **It's the coldest city!** World geography and facts; countries	Describing countries; making comparisons; expressing opinions; talking about distances and measurements	Comparative and superlative forms of adjectives; questions: *how far, how big, how high, how deep, how long, how hot,* and *how cold*
	PROGRESS CHECK PAGES 98–99		
	**UNIT 15 PAGES 100–105** **What are you doing later?** Invitations and excuses; free-time activities; telephone messages	Talking about plans; making invitations; accepting and refusing invitations; giving reasons; taking and leaving messages	Future with present continuous and *be going to*; messages with *tell* and *ask*
	**UNIT 16 PAGES 106–111** **How have you changed?** Life changes; plans and hopes for the future	Exchanging personal information; describing changes; talking about plans for the future	Describing changes with the present tense, the past tense, the present perfect, and the comparative; verb + infinitive
	PROGRESS CHECK PAGES 112–113		
	GRAMMAR PLUS PAGES 132–150		

Pronunciation/Listening	Writing/Reading	Interchange Activity
Contrastive stress Listening to descriptions of people; identifying people	Writing an email describing a person "The Age of Selfies": Reading about the history of selfies	"Find the differences": Comparing two pictures of a party PAGES 123–124
Linked sounds Listening to descriptions of events	Writing an email to an old friend "Unique Experiences": Reading about four peoples' unusual experiences	"Fun survey": Finding out about a classmate's lifestyle PAGE 125
Can't and *shouldn't* Listening to descriptions of cities, towns, and countries	Writing about hometowns "A Big 'Hello!' From . . . ": Reading about interesting cities	"Welcome to our city!": Creating a guide to fun places in a city PAGE 126
Reduction of *to* Listening to health problems and advice	Writing a blog post "Toothache? Visit the Rain Forest!": Reading about a plant used as medicine	"What should I do?": Give suggestions for situations PAGE 127
Stress in responses Listening to restaurant orders	Writing a restaurant review "To Tip or Not to Tip?": Reading about tipping customs	"Planning a food festival": Creating a menu PAGE 128
Questions of choice Listening to a TV quiz show	Writing an article about a place "Earth's Cleanest Places": Reading about three very clean places	"How much do you know?": Taking a general knowledge quiz PAGE 129
Reduction of *could you* and *would you* Listening to telephone messages	Writing text message requests "Cell Phone Trouble!": Reading about cell phone problems	"Weekend plans": Finding out about classmates' weekend plans PAGE 130
Vowel sounds /oʊ/ and /ʌ/ Listening to descriptions of changes	Writing a plan for a class trip "A Goal Accomplished": Reading about a person's goals	"Our possible future": Planning a possible future PAGE 131

Informed by teachers

Teachers from all over the world helped develop *Interchange Fifth Edition*. They looked at everything – from the color of the designs to the topics in the conversations – in order to make sure that this course will work in the classroom.
We heard from 1,500 teachers in:

- Surveys
- Focus Groups
- In-Depth Reviews

We appreciate the help and input from everyone. In particular, we'd like to give the following people our special thanks:

Jader Franceschi, **Actúa Idiomas,** Bento Gonçalves, Rio Grande do Sul, Brazil

Juliana Dos Santos Voltan Costa, **Actus Idiomas,** São Paulo, Brazil

Ella Osorio, **Angelo State University,** San Angelo, TX, US

Mary Hunter, **Angelo State University,** San Angelo, TX, US

Mario César González, **Angloamericano de Monterrey, SC,** Monterrey, Mexico

Samantha Shipman, **Auburn High School,** Auburn, AL, US

Linda, **Bernick Language School,** Radford, VA, US

Dave Lowrance, **Bethesda University of California,** Yorba Linda, CA, US

Tajbakhsh Hosseini, **Bezmialem Vakif University,** Istanbul, Turkey

Dilek Gercek, **Bil English,** Izmir, Turkey

erkan kolat, **Biruni University, ELT,** Istanbul, Turkey

Nika Gutkowska, **Bluedata International,** New York, NY, US

Daniel Alcocer Gómez, **Cecati 92,** Guadalupe, Nuevo León, Mexico

Samantha Webb, **Central Middle School,** Milton-Freewater, OR, US

Verónica Salgado, **Centro Anglo Americano,** Cuernavaca, Mexico

Ana Rivadeneira Martínez and Georgia P. de Machuca, **Centro de Educación Continua – Universidad Politécnica del Ecuador,** Quito, Ecuador

Anderson Francisco Guimerães Maia, **Centro Cultural Brasil Estados Unidos,** Belém, Brazil

Rosana Mariano, **Centro Paula Souza,** São Paulo, Brazil

Carlos de la Paz Arroyo, Teresa Noemí Parra Alarcón, Gilberto Bastida Gaytan, Manuel Esquivel Román, and Rosa Cepeda Tapia, **Centro Universitario Angloamericano,** Cuernavaca, Morelos, Mexico

Antonio Almeida, **CETEC,** Morelos, Mexico

Cinthia Ferreira, **Cinthia Ferreira Languages Services,** Toronto, ON, Canada

Phil Thomas and Sérgio Sanchez, **CLS Canadian Language School,** São Paulo, Brazil

Celia Concannon, **Cochise College,** Nogales, AZ, US

Maria do Carmo Rocha and CAOP English team, **Colégio Arquidiocesano Ouro Preto – Unidade Cônego Paulo Dilascio,** Ouro Preto, Brazil

Kim Rodriguez, **College of Charleston North,** Charleston, SC, US

Jesús Leza Alvarado, **Coparmex English Institute,** Monterrey, Mexico

John Partain, **Cortazar,** Guanajuato, Mexico

Alexander Palencia Navas, **Cursos de Lenguas, Universidad del Atlántico,** Barranquilla, Colombia

Kenneth Johan Gerardo Steenhuisen Cera, Melfi Osvaldo Guzman Triana, and Carlos Alberto Algarín Jiminez, **Cursos de Lenguas Extranjeras Universidad del Atlantico,** Barranquilla, Colombia

Jane P Kerford, **East Los Angeles College,** Pasadena, CA, US

Daniela, **East Village,** Campinas, São Paulo

Rosalva Camacho Orduño, **Easy English for Groups S.A. de C.V.,** Monterrey, Nuevo León, Mexico

Adonis Gimenez Fusetti, **Easy Way Idiomas,** Ibiúna, Brazil

Eileen Thompson, **Edison Community College,** Piqua, OH, US

Ahminne Handeri O.L Froede, **Englishouse escola de idiomas,** Teófilo Otoni, Brazil

Ana Luz Delgado-Izazola, **Escuela Nacional Preparatoria 5, UNAM,** Mexico City, Mexico

Nancy Alarcón Mendoza, **Facultad de Estudios Superiores Zaragoza, UNAM,** Mexico City, Mexico

Marcilio N. Barros, **Fast English USA,** Campinas, São Paulo, Brazil

Greta Douthat, **FCI Ashland,** Ashland, KY, US

Carlos Lizárraga González, **Grupo Educativo Anglo Americano, S.C.,** Mexico City, Mexico

Hugo Fernando Alcántar Valle, **Instituto Politécnico Nacional, Escuela Superior de Comercio y Administración-Unidad Santotomás, Celex Esca Santo Tomás,** Mexico City, Mexico

Sueli Nascimento, **Instituto Superior de Educação do Rio de Janeiro,** Rio de Janeiro, Brazil

Elsa F Monteverde, **International Academic Services,** Miami, FL, US

Laura Anand, **Irvine Adult School,** Irvine, CA, US

Prof. Marli T. Fernandes (principal) and Prof. Dr. Jefferson J. Fernandes (pedagogue), **Jefferson Idiomass,** São Paulo, Brazil

Herman Bartelen, **Kanda Gaigo Gakuin,** Tokyo, Japan

Cassia Silva, **Key Languages,** Key Biscayne, FL, US

Sister Mary Hope, **Kyoto Notre Dame Joshi Gakuin,** Kyoto, Japan

Nate Freedman, **LAL Language Centres,** Boston, MA, US

Richard Janzen, **Langley Secondary School,** Abbotsford, BC, Canada

Christina Abel Gabardo, **Language House,** Campo Largo, Brazil
Ivonne Castro, **Learn English International,** Cali, Colombia
Julio Cesar Maciel Rodrigues, **Liberty Centro de Línguas,** São Paulo, Brazil
Ann Gibson, **Maynard High School,** Maynard, MA, US
Martin Darling, **Meiji Gakuin Daigaku,** Tokyo, Japan
Dax Thomas, **Meiji Gakuin Daigaku,** Yokohama, Kanagawa, Japan
Derya Budak, **Mevlana University,** Konya, Turkey
B Sullivan, **Miami Valley Career Technical Center International Program,** Dayton, OH, US
Julio Velazquez, **Milo Language Center,** Weston, FL, US
Daiane Siqueira da Silva, Luiz Carlos Buontempo, Marlete Avelina de Oliveira Cunha, Marcos Paulo Segatti, Morgana Eveline de Oliveira, Nadia Lia Gino Alo, and Paul Hyde Budgen, **New Interchange-Escola de Idiomas,** São Paulo, Brazil
Patrícia França Furtado da Costa, Juiz de Fora, Brazil
Patricia Servín
Chris Pollard, **North West Regional College SK,** North Battleford, SK, Canada
Olga Amy, **Notre Dame High School,** Red Deer, Canada
Amy Garrett, **Ouachita Baptist University,** Arkadelphia, AR, US
Mervin Curry, **Palm Beach State College,** Boca Raton, FL, US
Julie Barros, **Quality English Studio,** Guarulhos, São Paulo, Brazil
Teodoro González Saldaña and Jesús Monserrrta Mata Franco, **Race Idiomas,** Mexico City, Mexico
Autumn Westphal and Noga La`or, **Rennert International,** New York, NY, US
Antonio Gallo and Javy Palau, **Rigby Idiomas,** Monterrey, Mexico
Tatiane Gabriela Sperb do Nascimento, **Right Way,** Igrejinha, Brazil
Mustafa Akgül, **Selahaddin Eyyubi Universitesi,** Diyarbakır, Turkey
James Drury M. Fonseca, **Senac Idiomas Fortaleza,** Fortaleza, Ceara, Brazil
Manoel Fialho S Neto, **Senac – PE,** Recife, Brazil
Jane Imber, **Small World,** Lawrence, KS, US
Tony Torres, **South Texas College,** McAllen, TX, US
Janet Rose, **Tennessee Foreign Language Institute,** College Grove, TN, US
Todd Enslen, **Tohoku University,** Sendai, Miyagi, Japan
Daniel Murray, **Torrance Adult School,** Torrance, CA, US
Juan Manuel Pulido Mendoza, **Universidad del Atlántico,** Barranquilla, Colombia
Juan Carlos Vargas Millán, **Universidad Libre Seccional Cali,** Cali (Valle del Cauca), Colombia
Carmen Cecilia Llanos Ospina, **Universidad Libre Seccional Cali,** Cali, Colombia
Jorge Noriega Zenteno, **Universidad Politécnica del Valle de México,** Estado de México, Mexico
Aimee Natasha Holguin S., **Universidad Politécnica del Valle de México UPVM,** Tultitlàn Estado de México, Mexico
Christian Selene Bernal Barraza, **UPVM Universidad Politécnica del Valle de México,** Ecatepec, Mexico
Lizeth Ramos Acosta, **Universidad Santiago de Cali,** Cali, Colombia
Silvana Dushku, **University of Illinois Champaign,** IL, US
Deirdre McMurtry, **University of Nebraska – Omaha,** Omaha, NE, US
Jason E Mower, **University of Utah,** Salt Lake City, UT, US
Paul Chugg, **Vanguard Taylor Language Institute,** Edmonton, Alberta, Canada
Henry Mulak, **Varsity Tutors,** Los Angeles, CA, US
Shirlei Strucker Calgaro and Hugo Guilherme Karrer, **VIP Centro de Idiomas,** Panambi, Rio Grande do Sul, Brazil
Eleanor Kelly, **Waseda Daigaku Extension Centre,** Tokyo, Japan
Sherry Ashworth, **Wichita State University,** Wichita, KS, US
Laine Bourdene, **William Carey University,** Hattiesburg, MS, US
Serap Aydın, Istanbul, Turkey
Liliana Covino, Guarulhos, Brazil
Yannuarys Jiménez, Barranquilla, Colombia
Juliana Morais Pazzini, Toronto, ON, Canada
Marlon Sanches, Montreal, Canada

Additional content contributed by Kenna Bourke, Inara Couto, Nic Harris, Greg Manin, Ashleigh Martinez, Laura McKenzie, Paul McIntyre, Clara Prado, Lynne Robertson, Mari Vargo, Theo Walker, and Maria Lucia Zaorob.

The Fifth Edition of *Interchange*

Interchange, the world's favorite English course, has a long tradition of teaching students how to speak confidently. Millions of people all over the world attest to its effectiveness.

What Makes *Interchange* Special?

Jack C. Richards' communicative methodology: Refined over years and in countless classrooms, the *Interchange* approach is rooted in solid pedagogy.

Flexible units: Instructors can change the order of the activities in each unit, keeping lessons fresh and students engaged. Additional photocopiable activities and a full video program give teachers even more freedom to make *Interchange* their own.

Students speak right from the start: The solid research and winning content give students the confidence to speak early and often.

What's New in the Fifth Edition?

50% new content: Readings, listenings, conversations, and Snapshots have been updated throughout the books.

Improved exercises for listenings and readings: We listened to teachers' requests for greater variety in the activities that accompany the listenings and readings.

Digital Pack: Whether you're teaching remotely or in a classroom, your Digital Pack will help you deliver engaging learning experiences through a range of rich media, tools, and data available in one place on Cambridge One.

Student's Book overview

Every unit in *Interchange Fifth Edition* contains two cycles, each of which has a specific topic, grammar point, and function. The units in Level 1 contain a variety of exercises, including a Snapshot, Conversation, Grammar focus, Pronunciation, Discussion (or Speaking/Role Play), Word power, Listening, Writing, Reading, and Interchange activity. The sequence of these exercises differs from unit to unit. Here is a sample unit from Level 1.

Cycle 1 (Exercises 1–8)

Topic: routine and leisure activities
Grammar: simple past
Function: describe past daily and free-time activities

7

We went dancing!

- Describe past daily and free-time activities
- Describe past vacations

1 SNAPSHOT

Free-time Activities

- check social media
- go dancing
- listen to music
- play video games
- read
- relax
- spend time with friends and family
- watch TV

Check (✓) the activities you do in your free time. List three other activities you do in your free time.
What are your favorite free-time activities? Are there activities you don't like? Which ones?

2 CONVERSATION What did you do last weekend?

A Listen and practice.

NEIL So, what did you do last weekend, Cara?
CARA Oh, I had a great time. My friends and I had pizza on Saturday and then we all went dancing.
NEIL How fun! Did you go to The Treadmill?
CARA No, we didn't. We went to that new place downtown. How about you? Did you go anywhere?
NEIL No, I didn't go anywhere all weekend. I just stayed home and studied for today's Spanish test.
CARA Our test is today? I forgot about that!
NEIL Don't worry. You always get an A.

B Listen to the rest of the conversation. What does Cara do on Sunday afternoons?

44

Snapshot

- Introduces the unit or cycle topic
- Presents vocabulary for discussing the topic
- Uses real-world information
- Provides personalized guided discussion questions

Conversation

- Provides structured listening and speaking practice
- Introduces the meaning and use of the cycle's grammar
- Uses pictures to set the scene and illustrate new vocabulary
- Provides follow-up listening tasks

Grammar focus

- Includes audio recordings of the grammar
- Provides controlled grammar practice in realistic contexts, such as short conversations
- Provides freer, more personalized speaking practice

Pronunciation

- Provides controlled practice in recognizing and producing sounds linked to the cycle grammar
- Promotes extended or personalized pronunciation practice

3 GRAMMAR FOCUS

Simple past

Did you **work** on Saturday?
Yes, I **did**. I **worked** all day.
No, I **didn't**. I **didn't work** at all.

What **did** Neil **do** on Saturday?
He **stayed** home and **studied** for a test.

Did you **go** anywhere last weekend?
Yes, I **did**. I **went** to the movies.
No, I **didn't**. I **didn't go** anywhere.

How **did** Cara **spend** her weekend?
She **went** to a club and **danced** with some friends.

GRAMMAR PLUS see page 132

A Complete these conversations. Then practice with a partner.

1. **A:** ________ you ________ (stay) home on Sunday?
   B: No, I ________ (call) my friend Anna. We ________ (drive) to a nice little restaurant for lunch.
2. **A:** How ________ you ________ (spend) your last birthday?
   B: I ________ (have) a party. Everyone ________ (enjoy) it, but the neighbors next door ________ (not, like) the noise.
3. **A:** What ________ you ________ (do) last night?
   B: I ________ (see) a sci-fi movie at the Cineplex. I ________ (love) it! Amazing special effects!
4. **A:** ________ you ________ (do) anything special over the weekend?
   B: Yes, I ________. I ________ (go) shopping. Unfortunately, I ________ (spend) all my money. Now I'm broke!
5. **A:** ________ you ________ (go) out on Friday night?
   B: No, I ________. I ________ (invite) friends over, and I ________ (cook) spaghetti for them.

regular verbs

work → work**ed**
invite → invite**d**
study → stud**ied**
stop → stop**ped**

irregular verbs

buy → **bought**
do → **did**
drive → **drove**
have → **had**
go → **went**
sing → **sang**
see → **saw**
spend → **spent**

B PAIR WORK Take turns asking the questions in part A. Give your own information when answering.

A: Did you stay home on Sunday?
B: No, I didn't. I went dancing with some friends.

4 PRONUNCIATION Reduction of *did you*

A Listen and practice. Notice how **did you** is reduced in the following questions.

[dɪdʒə]
Did you have a good time?

[wədɪdʒə]
What did you do last night?

[haʊdɪdʒə]
How did you like the movie?

B PAIR WORK Practice the questions in Exercise 3, part A again. Pay attention to the pronunciation of **did you**.

We went dancing! 45

5 WORD POWER Chores and activities

A PAIR WORK Find two other words or phrases from the list that usually go with each verb. Then add one more word or phrase to each verb.

a lot of fun	dancing	a good time	shopping	a bike ride
the bed	chores	the laundry	a trip	a video

do	*my homework*			
go	*online*			
have	*a party*			
make	*a phone call*			
take	*a day off*			

B GROUP WORK Choose the things you did last weekend. Then compare with your partners.

A: I went shopping with my friends. We had a good time. What about you?
B: I didn't have a very good time. I did chores.
C: I did chores, too. But I went dancing in the evening, and . . .

6 DISCUSSION Ask some questions!

GROUP WORK Take turns. One student makes a statement about the weekend. Other students ask questions. Each student answers at least three questions.

A: I went shopping on Saturday afternoon.
B: **Where** did you go?
A: To the Mayfair Center.
C: **Who** did you go with?
A: I went with my friends and my sister.
D: **What time** did you go?
A: We went around 3:00.

7 LISTENING Did you have a good holiday?

A Listen to Andrew tell Elizabeth what he did yesterday. Check (✓) the things Andrew did.

Activities	Reasons
☐ went to the gym	
☐ played soccer	
☐ saw a movie	
☐ watched TV	
☐ went to a baseball game	
☐ spent time with family	

B Listen again. Look at the activities Andrew didn't do. Why didn't he do them? Write the reason.

46 Unit 7

Word power

- Presents vocabulary related to the unit topic
- Provides practice with collocations and categorizing vocabulary
- Promotes freer, more personalized practice

Discussion

- Provides communicative tasks that help develop oral fluency
- Includes pair work, group work, and class activities

Listening

- Provides pre-listening focus tasks or questions
- Develops a variety of listening skills, such as listening for main ideas and details
- Includes post-listening speaking tasks

Cycle 2 (Exercises 9–14)

Topic: vacations
Grammar: past of *be*
Function: describe past vacations

Conversation

- Provides structured listening and speaking practice
- Introduces the meaning and use of Cycle 2 grammar, useful expressions, and discourse
- Uses pictures to set the scene and illustrate new vocabulary

Grammar focus

- Presents examples from the previous conversation
- Provides controlled grammar practice in realistic contexts, such as short conversations

8 INTERCHANGE 7 Memories

Play a board game. Go to Interchange 7 on page 121.

9 CONVERSATION Lucky you!

A Listen and practice.

Leah: Hi, Cody. How was your vacation?
Cody: It was excellent! I went to California with my cousin. We had a great time.
Leah: Lucky you! How long were you there?
Cody: About a week.
Leah: Cool! Was the weather OK?
Cody: Not really. It was pretty cloudy. But we went surfing every day. The waves were amazing.
Leah: So, what was the best thing about the trip?
Cody: Well, something incredible happened. . . .

B Listen to the rest of the conversation. What happened?

10 GRAMMAR FOCUS

Past of *be*

		Contractions
Were you in California?	Yes, I **was**.	was**n't** = was **not**
Was the weather OK?	No, it **wasn't**.	were**n't** = were **not**
Were you and your cousin on vacation?	Yes, we **were**.	
Were your parents there?	No, they **weren't**.	
How long **were** you away?	I **was** away for a week.	
How **was** your vacation?	It **was** excellent!	

GRAMMAR PLUS see page 138

Complete these conversations. Then practice with a partner.

1. **A:** ________ you in New York last weekend?
   B: No, I ________ . I ________ in Chicago.
   A: How ________ it?
   B: It ________ great! But it ________ cold and windy as usual.
2. **A:** How long ________ your parents in Chile?
   B: They ________ there for two weeks.
   A: ________ they in Santiago the whole time?
   B: No, they ________ . They also went to Valparaiso.
3. **A:** ________ you away last week?
   B: Yes, I ________ in Madrid.
   A: Really? How long ________ you there?
   B: For almost a week. I ________ there on business.

We went dancing! 47

11 DISCUSSION Past and future vacations

A GROUP WORK Ask your classmates about their last vacations. Ask these questions or use your own ideas.

Where did you spend your last vacation?
How long was your vacation?
Who were you with?
What did you do?
How was the weather?
What would you like to do on your next vacation?

B CLASS ACTIVITY Who had an interesting vacation? Tell the class who and why.

12 WRITING A blog post

A Read the blog post.

TRAVEL BLOG — Home | About | Posts | Subscribe

Greetings from sunny Puerto Vallarta, Mexico!
I'm having a great time. Yesterday, I took a tour of the old town. The buildings and monuments were amazing! This morning, I went swimming and snorkeling. Then I went shopping at one of the town's open markets. I bought a very beautiful handmade ceramic vase and tried the famous fish on a stick. Delicious!
I'm having a really great vacation!
Casey

B PAIR WORK Write a blog post to your partner about your last vacation. Then exchange posts. Do you have any questions about your partner's vacation?

13 LISTENING I was on vacation.

A Listen to Daniel and Amanda talk about their vacations. Did they have a good time? Check (✓) Yes or No.

	Yes	No
Daniel	☐	☐
Amanda	☐	☐

B Listen again. Complete the chart with information about their vacations.

Daniel's vacation		Amanda's vacation	
Place		Place	
Who with		Who with	
Activities		Activities	

48 Unit 7

Writing

- Provides a model writing sample
- Develops skills in writing different texts, such as blogs and email messages
- Reinforces the vocabulary and grammar in the cycle or unit

Listening

- Provides pre-listening focus tasks or questions
- Develops a variety of listening skills, such as listening for main ideas and details

Reading

- Presents a variety of text types
- Introduces the text with a pre-reading task
- Develops a variety of reading skills, such as reading for main ideas, reading for details, and inferencing
- Promotes discussion that involves personalization and analysis

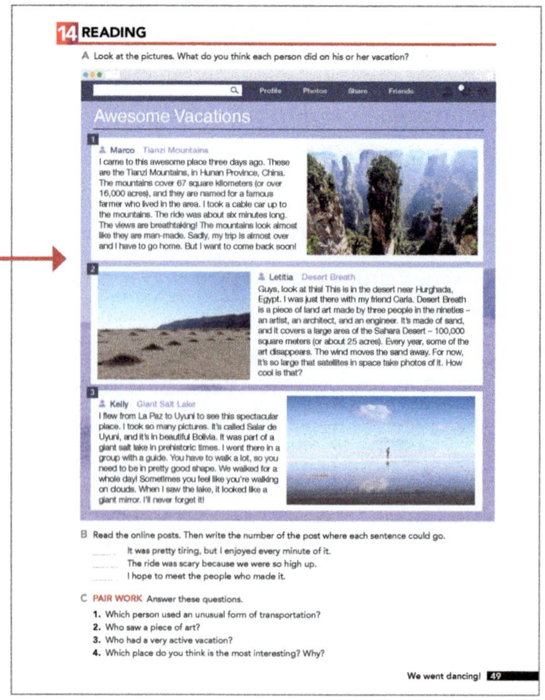

14 READING

A Look at the pictures. What do you think each person did on his or her vacation?

Profile Photos Share Friends

Awesome Vacations

1 Marco Tianzi Mountains

I came to this awesome place three days ago. These are the Tianzi Mountains, in Hunan Province, China. The mountains cover 67 square kilometers (or over 16,000 acres), and they are named for a famous farmer who lived in the area. I took a cable car up to the mountains. The ride was about six minutes long. The views are breathtaking! The mountains look almost like they are man-made. Sadly, my trip is almost over and I have to go home. But I want to come back soon!

2 Letitia Desert Breath

Guys, look at this! This is in the desert near Hurghada, Egypt. I was just there with my friend Carla. Desert Breath is a piece of land art made by three people in the nineties – an artist, an architect, and an engineer. It's made of sand, and it covers a large area of the Sahara Desert – 100,000 square meters (or about 25 acres). Every year, some of the art disappears. The wind moves the sand away. For now, it's so large that satellites in space take photos of it. How cool is that?

3 Kelly Giant Salt Lake

I flew from La Paz to Uyuni to see this spectacular place. I took so many pictures. It's called Salar de Uyuni, and it's in beautiful Bolivia. It was part of a giant salt lake in prehistoric times. I went there in a group with a guide. You have to walk a lot, so you need to be in pretty good shape. We walked for a whole day! Sometimes you feel like you're walking on clouds. When I saw the lake, it looked like a giant mirror. I'll never forget it!

B Read the online posts. Then write the number of the post where each sentence could go.

______ It was pretty tiring, but I enjoyed every minute of it.
______ The ride was scary because we were so high up.
______ I hope to meet the people who made it.

C PAIR WORK Answer these questions.

1. Which person used an unusual form of transportation?
2. Who saw a piece of art?
3. Who had a very active vacation?
4. Which place do you think is the most interesting? Why?

We went dancing! 49

In the back of the book

Interchange activity

- Expands on the unit topic, vocabulary, and grammar
- Provides opportunities to consolidate new language in a creative or fun way
- Promotes fluency with communicative activities such as discussions, information gaps, and games

Grammar plus

- Explores the unit grammar in greater depth
- Practices the grammar with controlled exercises
- Can be done in class or assigned as homework

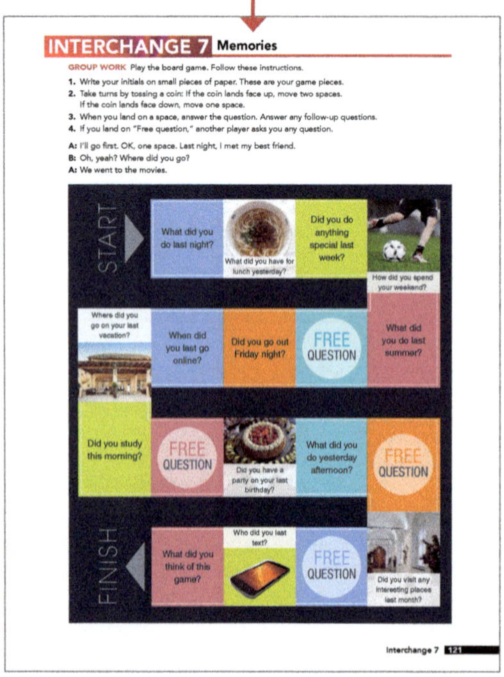

INTERCHANGE 7 Memories

GROUP WORK Play the board game. Follow these instructions.

1. Write your initials on small pieces of paper. These are your game pieces.
2. Take turns by tossing a coin: If the coin lands face up, move two spaces. If the coin lands face down, move one space.
3. When you land on a space, answer the question. Answer any follow-up questions.
4. If you land on "Free question," another player asks you any question.

A: I'll go first. OK, one space. Last night, I met my best friend.
B: Oh, yeah? Where did you go?
A: We went to the movies.

Interchange 7 121

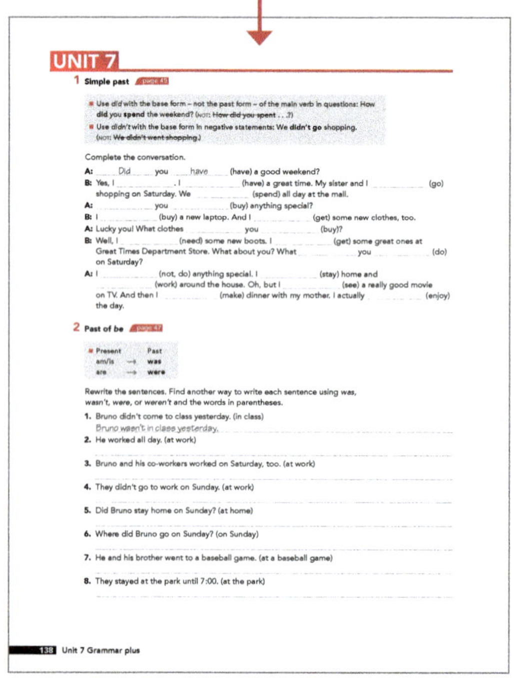

UNIT 7

1 Simple past page 45

- Use *did* with the base form – not the past form – of the main verb in questions: How **did** you **spend** the weekend? (NOT: ~~How did you spent . . .?~~)
- Use *didn't* with the base form in negative statements: We **didn't go** shopping. (NOT: ~~We didn't went shopping.~~)

Complete the conversation.

A: ___Did___ you ___have___ (have) a good weekend?
B: Yes, I ______. I ______ (have) a great time. My sister and I ______ (go) shopping on Saturday. We ______ (spend) all day at the mall.
A: ______ you ______ (buy) anything special?
B: I ______ (buy) a new laptop. And I ______ (get) some new clothes, too.
A: Lucky you! What clothes ______ you ______ (buy)?
B: Well, I ______ (need) some new boots. I ______ (get) some great ones at Great Times Department Store. What about you? What ______ you ______ (do) on Saturday?
A: I ______ (not, do) anything special. I ______ (stay) home and ______ (work) around the house. Oh, but I ______ (see) a really good movie on TV. And then I ______ (make) dinner with my mother. I actually ______ (enjoy) the day.

2 Past of *be* page 47

- Present → Past
  am/is → **was**
  are → **were**

Rewrite the sentences. Find another way to write each sentence using *was, wasn't, were,* or *weren't* and the words in parentheses.

1. Bruno didn't come to class yesterday. (in class)
   Bruno wasn't in class yesterday.
2. He worked all day. (at work)
3. Bruno and his co-workers worked on Saturday, too. (at work)
4. They didn't go to work on Sunday. (at work)
5. Did Bruno stay home on Sunday? (at home)
6. Where did Bruno go on Sunday? (on Sunday)
7. He and his brother went to a baseball game. (at a baseball game)
8. They stayed at the park until 7:00. (at the park)

138 Unit 7 Grammar plus

Cambridge One
Your home for digital learning

Cambridge One is a new digital learning environment providing rich teaching and learning experiences based on years of research and innovation.

Damir
Student

All in one place

Easy access to all teaching and learning materials in one place across multiple devices

Age-appropriate

Engaging design for children, teens and adult learners ensures that students feel motivated and challenged at the right level

Data you can trust

Meaningful, relevant and actionable data with elements of gamification to guide teachers and keep learners motivated

cambridgeone.org

Digital Workbook overview

The *Interchange Fifth Edition Digital Workbook* provides additional activities to reinforce what is presented in the corresponding Student's Book. Each *Digital Workbook* includes:

- A variety of interactive activities that correspond to each Student's Book lesson, allowing students to interact with workbook material in a fresh, lively way.
- Instant feedback for hundreds of activities, challenging students to focus on areas for improvement.
- Simple tools for teachers to monitor students' progress such as scores, attendance, and time spent online, providing instant information.

The *Interchange Fifth Edition Digital Workbooks* can be purchased in two ways:

- as an institutional subscription,
- as part of a Student's Book with Digital Pack.

Interactive exercises

Hundreds of interactive exercises provide hours of

- vocabulary practice
- grammar practice
- listening practice
- speaking practice
- reading practice

Digital Workbook:

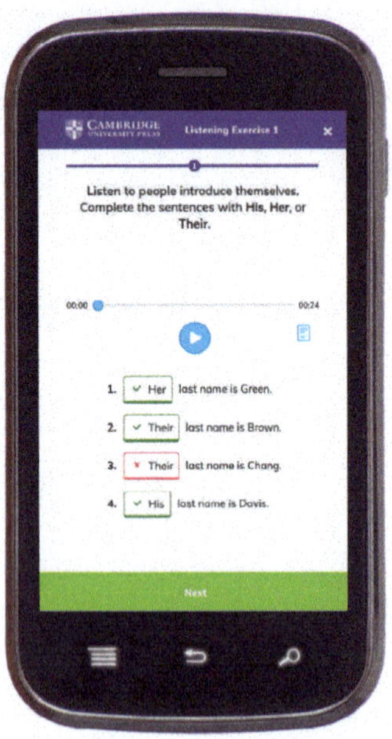

Mobile-friendly activities to practice new language and skills from every unit.

eBook:

Digital version of the Student's Book with audio.

Workbook overview

Interchange Fifth Edition provides students with additional opportunities to practice the language taught in the Student's Book outside of the classroom by using the Workbook that accompanies each level.

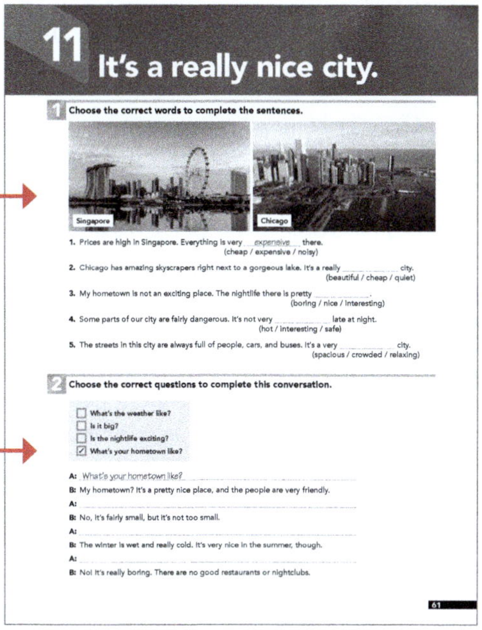

11 It's a really nice city.

1 Choose the correct words to complete the sentences.

Singapore Chicago

1. Prices are high in Singapore. Everything is very *expensive* there. (cheap / expensive / noisy)
2. Chicago has amazing skyscrapers right next to a gorgeous lake. It's a really ______ city. (beautiful / cheap / quiet)
3. My hometown is not an exciting place. The nightlife there is pretty ______. (boring / nice / interesting)
4. Some parts of our city are fairly dangerous. It's not very ______ late at night. (hot / interesting / safe)
5. The streets in this city are always full of people, cars, and buses. It's a very ______ city. (spacious / crowded / relaxing)

2 Choose the correct questions to complete this conversation.

- [ ] What's the weather like?
- [ ] Is it big?
- [ ] Is the nightlife exciting?
- [x] What's your hometown like?

A: *What's your hometown like?*
B: My hometown? It's a pretty nice place, and the people are very friendly.
A: ______
B: No, it's fairly small, but it's not too small.
A: ______
B: The winter is wet and really cold. It's very nice in the summer, though.
A: ______
B: No! It's really boring. There are no good restaurants or nightclubs.

61

Vocabulary

- Provides vocabulary practice based on the unit topic

Grammar

- Reinforces the unit grammar through controlled practice

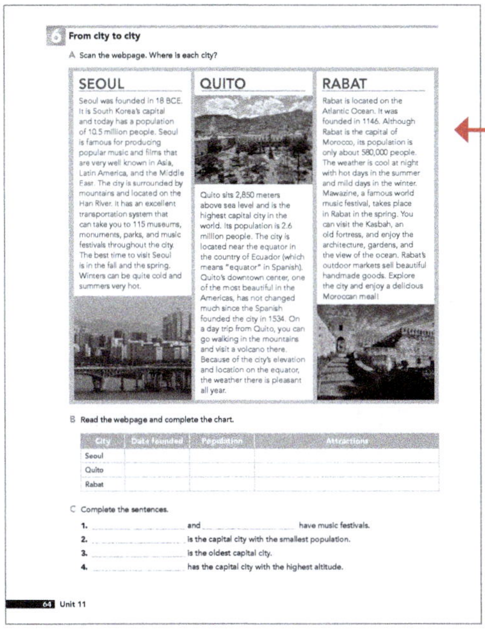

6 From city to city

A Scan the webpage. Where is each city?

SEOUL

Seoul was founded in 18 BCE. It is South Korea's capital and today has a population of 10.5 million people. Seoul is famous for producing popular music and films that are very well known in Asia, Latin America, and the Middle East. The city is surrounded by mountains and located on the Han River. It has an excellent transportation system that can take you to 115 museums, monuments, parks, and music festivals throughout the city. The best time to visit Seoul is in the fall and the spring. Winters can be quite cold and summers very hot.

QUITO

Quito sits 2,850 meters above sea level and is the highest capital city in the world. Its population is 2.6 million people. The city is located near the equator in the country of Ecuador (which means "equator" in Spanish). Quito's downtown center, one of the most beautiful in the Americas, has not changed much since the Spanish founded the city in 1534. On a day trip from Quito, you can go walking in the mountains and visit a volcano there. Because of the city's elevation and location on the equator, the weather there is pleasant all year.

RABAT

Rabat is located on the Atlantic Ocean. It was founded in 1146. Although Rabat is the capital of Morocco, its population is only about 580,000 people. The weather is cool at night with hot days in the summer and mild days in the winter. Mawazine, a famous world music festival, takes place in Rabat in the spring. You can visit the Kasbah, an old fortress, and enjoy the architecture, gardens, and the view of the ocean. Rabat's outdoor markets sell beautiful handmade goods. Explore the city and enjoy a delicious Moroccan meal!

B Read the webpage and complete the chart.

City	Date founded	Population	Attractions
Seoul			
Quito			
Rabat			

C Complete the sentences.

1. ______ and ______ have music festivals.
2. ______ is the capital city with the smallest population.
3. ______ is the oldest capital city.
4. ______ has the capital city with the highest altitude.

64 Unit 11

Reading

- Gives additional reading practice based on the theme of the unit
- Introduces the text with a pre-reading task
- Reinforces reading skills used in the Student's Book

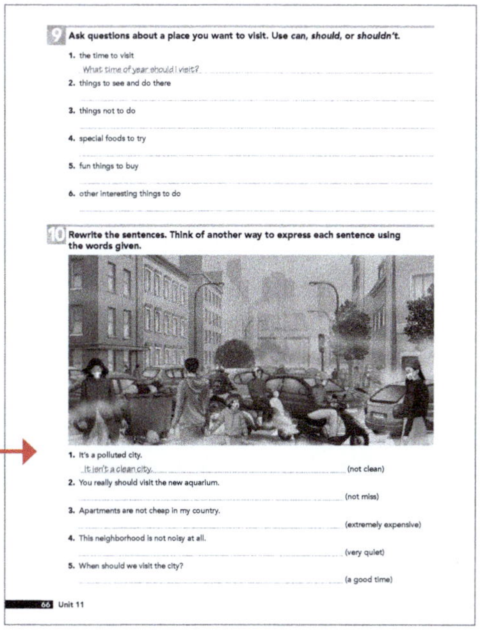

9 Ask questions about a place you want to visit. Use *can*, *should*, or *shouldn't*.

1. the time to visit
What time of year should I visit?
2. things to see and do there
3. things not to do
4. special foods to try
5. fun things to buy
6. other interesting things to do

10 Rewrite the sentences. Think of another way to express each sentence using the words given.

1. It's a polluted city.
It isn't a clean city. (not clean)
2. You really should visit the new aquarium.
______ (not miss)
3. Apartments are not cheap in my country.
______ (extremely expensive)
4. This neighborhood is not noisy at all.
______ (very quiet)
5. When should we visit the city?
______ (a good time)

66 Unit 11

Writing

- Promotes freer, more personalized practice
- Reinforces the vocabulary and grammar in the unit

Teacher's Edition overview

The Teacher's Editions provide complete support for teachers who are using *Interchange Fifth Edition*. They contain Supplementary Resources Overview charts to help teachers plan their lessons (for more information see page xx), Language summaries, Workbook answer keys, Audio scripts, Fresh ideas, and Games. They also include detailed teaching notes for the units and Progress checks in the Student's Books.

Teaching notes

- Learning objectives for each exercise
- Step-by-step lesson plans
- Audio scripts
- Answers and Vocabulary definitions
- Stimulating and fun Games to review or practice skills such as grammar and vocabulary
- Alternative ways to present and review exercises in the Fresh ideas
- Tips that promote teacher training and development
- Options for alternative presentations or expansions
- Suggestions for further practice in other *Interchange Fifth Edition* components and online
- Suggestions for regular assessment using quizzes and tests

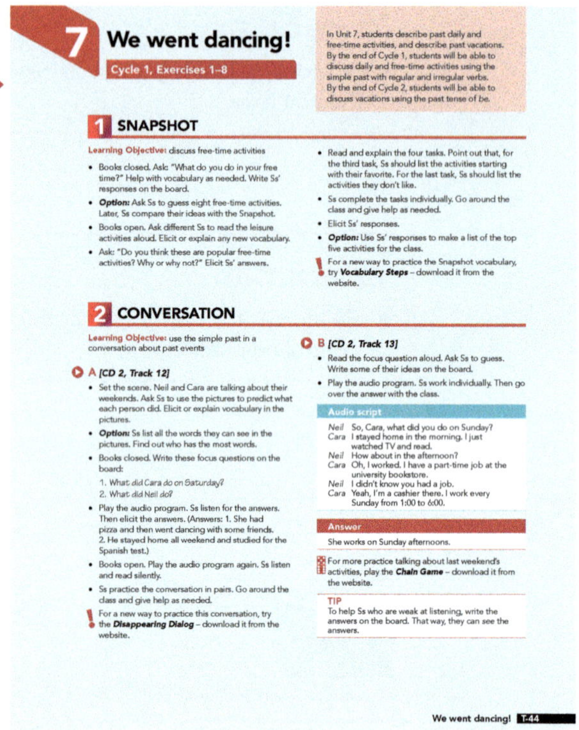

7 We went dancing!

Cycle 1, Exercises 1–8

In Unit 7, students describe past daily and free-time activities, and describe past vacations. By the end of Cycle 1, students will be able to discuss daily and free-time activities using the simple past with regular and irregular verbs. By the end of Cycle 2, students will be able to discuss vacations using the past tense of *be*.

1 SNAPSHOT

Learning Objective: discuss free-time activities

- Books closed. Ask: "What do you do in your free time?" Help with vocabulary as needed. Write Ss' responses on the board.
- ***Option:*** Ask Ss to guess eight free-time activities. Later, Ss compare their ideas with the Snapshot.
- Books open. Ask different Ss to read the leisure activities aloud. Elicit or explain any new vocabulary.
- Ask: "Do you think these are popular free-time activities? Why or why not?" Elicit Ss' answers.
- Read and explain the four tasks. Point out that, for the third task, Ss should list the activities starting with their favorite. For the last task, Ss should list the activities they don't like.
- Ss complete the tasks individually. Go around the class and give help as needed.
- Elicit Ss' responses.
- ***Option:*** Use Ss' responses to make a list of the top five activities for the class.

For a new way to practice the Snapshot vocabulary, try ***Vocabulary Steps*** – download it from the website.

2 CONVERSATION

Learning Objective: use the simple past in a conversation about past events

A *[CD 2, Track 12]*

- Set the scene. Neil and Cara are talking about their weekends. Ask Ss to use the pictures to predict what each person did. Elicit or explain vocabulary in the pictures.
- ***Option:*** Ss list all the words they can see in the pictures. Find out who has the most words.
- Books closed. Write these focus questions on the board:
  1. *What did Cara do on Saturday?*
  2. *What did Neil do?*
- Play the audio program. Ss listen for the answers. Then elicit the answers. (Answers: 1. She had pizza and then went dancing with some friends. 2. He stayed home all weekend and studied for the Spanish test.)
- Books open. Play the audio program again. Ss listen and read silently.
- Ss practice the conversation in pairs. Go around the class and give help as needed.

For a new way to practice this conversation, try the ***Disappearing Dialog*** – download it from the website.

B *[CD 2, Track 13]*

- Read the focus question aloud. Ask Ss to guess. Write some of their ideas on the board.
- Play the audio program. Ss work individually. Then go over the answer with the class.

Audio script

Neil So, Cara, what did you do on Sunday?
Cara I stayed home in the morning. I just watched TV and read.
Neil How about in the afternoon?
Cara Oh, I worked. I have a part-time job at the university bookstore.
Neil I didn't know you had a job.
Cara Yeah, I'm a cashier there. I work every Sunday from 1:00 to 6:00.

Answer

She works on Sunday afternoons.

For more practice talking about last weekend's activities, play the ***Chain Game*** – download it from the website.

TIP
To help Ss who are weak at listening, write the answers on the board. That way, they can see the answers.

We went dancing! T-44

Complete Testing Program

The complete testing program contains oral and written quizzes and tests. It includes PDF and Microsoft Word versions of all quizzes, mid-term and final tests, the placement test program, audio, audio scripts, and answer keys.

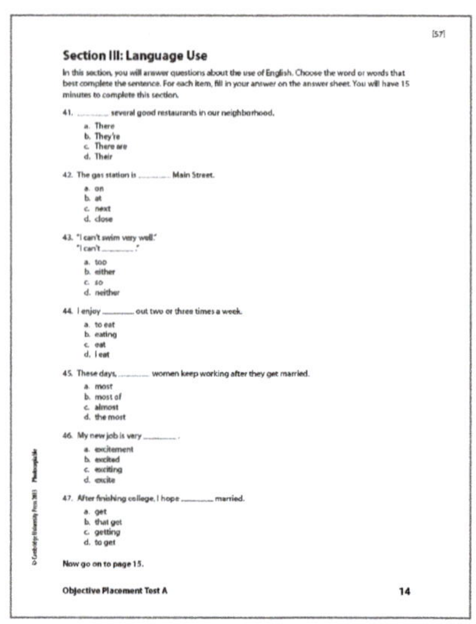

[57]

Section III: Language Use

In this section, you will answer questions about the use of English. Choose the word or words that best complete the sentence. For each item, fill in your answer on the answer sheet. You will have 15 minutes to complete this section.

41. ________ several good restaurants in our neighborhood.
    a. There
    b. They're
    c. There are
    d. Their

42. The gas station is ________ Main Street.
    a. on
    b. at
    c. next
    d. close

43. "I can't swim very well."
    "I can't ________."
    a. too
    b. either
    c. so
    d. neither

44. I enjoy ________ out two or three times a week.
    a. to eat
    b. eating
    c. eat
    d. I eat

45. These days, ________ women keep working after they get married.
    a. most
    b. most of
    c. almost
    d. the most

46. My new job is very ________ .
    a. excitement
    b. excited
    c. exciting
    d. excite

47. After finishing college, I hope ________ married.
    a. get
    b. that get
    c. getting
    d. to get

Now go on to page 15.

Objective Placement Test A 14

Presentation Plus overview

Interchange Presentation Plus is a complete classroom presentation package, combining the contents of the Student's Book, the class audio, and the video program for each level of the series into a convenient one-stop presentation solution. It can be used with all types of interactive whiteboards or with just a projector and a computer to present *Interchange* core materials in the classroom in a lively and engaging way.

Presentation Plus simplifies several of the teaching tasks that take place in the classroom.

You can use Presentation Plus to display the answers for the exercises in an uncomplicated way, zoom in on a page to more efficiently focus students' attention on an activity or image, and even annotate pages for future lessons.

Additional Teacher Resources

Go to cambridgeone.org for a variety of materials to assist with your teaching of the series. Here you will find practical articles, correlations, language summaries, overviews of supplementary materials, ideas for games and extra activities, as well as a number of downloadable worksheets for projects and extra practice of vocabulary, grammar, listening, writing, and speaking.

Supplementary Resources Overviews

Indicate all the activities available in the various ancillary components that can be used after each exercise in the Student's Book units for extra practice, review, and assessment.

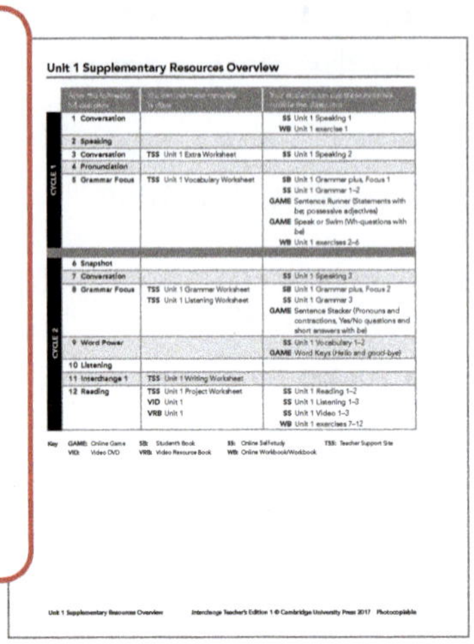

Unit 1 Supplementary Resources Overview

	[illegible]	[illegible]	[illegible]
CYCLE 1	1 Conversation		SS Unit 1 Speaking 1 WB Unit 1 exercise 1
	2 Speaking		
	3 Conversation	TSS Unit 1 Extra Worksheet	SS Unit 1 Speaking 2
	4 Pronunciation		
	5 Grammar Focus	TSS Unit 1 Vocabulary Worksheet	SB Unit 1 Grammar plus, Focus 1 SS Unit 1 Grammar 1–2 GAME Sentence Runner (Statements with be; possessive adjectives) GAME Speak or Swim (Wh-questions with be) WB Unit 1 exercises 2–6
CYCLE 2	6 Snapshot		
	7 Conversation		SS Unit 1 Speaking 3
	8 Grammar Focus	TSS Unit 1 Grammar Worksheet TSS Unit 1 Listening Worksheet	SB Unit 1 Grammar plus, Focus 2 SS Unit 1 Grammar 3 GAME Sentence Stacker (Pronouns and contractions, Yes/No questions and short answers with be)
	9 Word Power		SS Unit 1 Vocabulary 1–2 GAME Word Keys (Hello and good-bye)
	10 Listening		
	11 Interchange 1	TSS Unit 1 Writing Worksheet	
	12 Reading	TSS Unit 1 Project Worksheet VID Unit 1 VRB Unit 1	SS Unit 1 Reading 1–2 SS Unit 1 Listening 1–3 SS Unit 1 Video 1–3 WB Unit 1 exercises 7–12

Key GAME: Online Game SB: Student's Book SS: Online Self-study TSS: Teacher Support Site VID: Video DVD VRB: Video Resource Book WB: Online Workbook/Workbook

Unit 1 Supplementary Resources Overview Interchange Teacher's Edition 1 © Cambridge University Press 2017 Photocopiable

Downloadable worksheets

- Offer extra speaking opportunities
- Provide guidance for projects and extra practice of grammar, vocabulary, listening, and writing

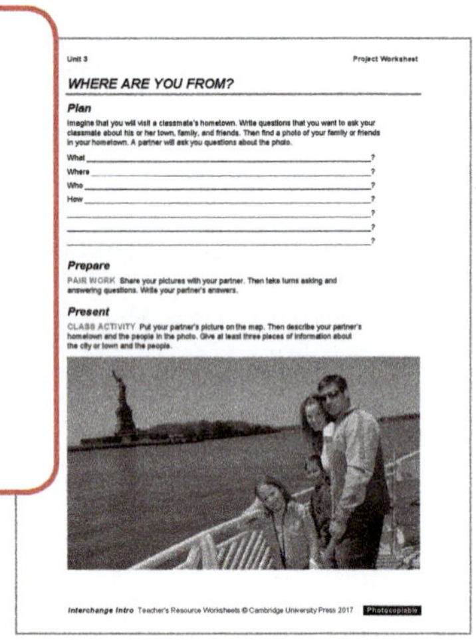

Unit 3 Project Worksheet

WHERE ARE YOU FROM?

Plan

Imagine that you will visit a classmate's hometown. Write questions that you want to ask your classmate about his or her town, family, and friends. Then find a photo of your family or friends in your hometown. A partner will ask you questions about the photo.

What ____________________?
Where ____________________?
Who ____________________?
How ____________________?
____________________?
____________________?
____________________?

Prepare

PAIR WORK Share your pictures with your partner. Then take turns asking and answering questions. Write your partner's answers.

Present

CLASS ACTIVITY Put your partner's picture on the map. Then describe your partner's hometown and the people in the photo. Give at least three pieces of information about the city or town and the people.

Interchange Intro Teacher's Resource Worksheets © Cambridge University Press 2017 Photocopiable

Video Program overview

The *Interchange* Video Program is designed to complement the Student's Books. Each video provides further practice related to the topics, language, and vocabulary introduced in the corresponding unit of the Student's Book.

PROGRAM COMPONENTS

Video

The sixteen videos in each level's video program complement Units 1 through 16 of the corresponding Student's Book. There are a variety of genres: dramatized stories, documentaries, interviews, profiles, and travelogues.

Video Resource Book

The Video Resource Book contains the following:

- engaging **photocopiable worksheets** for students
- detailed **teaching notes** for teachers
- **answer keys** for the student worksheets
- complete **video transcripts**

TEACHING A TYPICAL VIDEO SEQUENCE

The **worksheets** and **teaching notes** for each video are organized into four sections: *Preview*, *Watch the video*, *Follow-up*, and *Language close-up*. The unit-by-unit teaching notes in the Video Resource Book give detailed suggestions for teaching each unit.

Preview

The *Preview* activities build on each other to provide students with relevant background information and key vocabulary that will assist them in better understanding the video.

Watch the video

The carefully sequenced *Watch the video* activities first help students focus on gist and then guide them in identifying important details and language. These tasks also prepare them for *Follow-up* speaking activities.

Follow-up

The *Follow-up* speaking activities encourage students to extend and personalize information by voicing their opinions or carrying out communicative tasks.

Language close-up

Students finish with the *Language close-up*, examining and practicing the particular language structures and functions presented in the video.

Introduction to the CEFR

Introduction to the Common European Framework of Reference (CEFR)

The overall aim of the Council of Europe's Common European Framework of Reference (CEFR) is to provide objective criteria for describing and assessing language proficiency in an internationally comparable manner. The Council of Europe's work on the definition of appropriate learning objectives for adult language learners dates back to the '70s. The influential Threshold series (J. A. van Ek and J. L. M. Trim, Cambridge University Press, 1991) provides a detailed description in functional, notional, grammatical, and sociocultural terms, of what a language user needs to be able to do in order to communicate effectively in the sort of situations commonly encountered in everyday life. Three levels of proficiency are identified, called Waystage, Threshold, and Vantage (roughly corresponding to Elementary, Intermediate, and Upper Intermediate).

The Threshold series was followed in 2001 by the publication of the Common European Framework of Reference, which describes six levels of communicative ability in terms of competences or "can do" statements: A1 (Breakthrough), A2 (Waystage), B1 (Threshold), B2 (Vantage), C1 (Effective Operational Proficiency), and C2 (Mastery). Based on the CEFR descriptors, the Council of Europe also developed the European Language Portfolio, a document that enables learners to assess their language ability and to keep an internationally recognized record of their language learning experience.

Interchange Fifth Edition and the Common European Framework of Reference

The table below shows how *Interchange Fifth Edition* correlates with the Council of Europe's levels and with some major international examinations.

<table>
<tr><th></th><th>CEFR</th><th>Council of Europe</th><th>Cambridge ESOL</th><th>IELTS</th><th>TOEFL iBT</th><th>TOEIC</th></tr>
<tr><td colspan="7">Interchange</td></tr>
<tr><td>Level Intro</td><td>A1</td><td>Breakthrough</td><td></td><td></td><td></td><td>120+</td></tr>
<tr><td>Level 1</td><td rowspan="2">A2</td><td rowspan="2">Waystage</td><td rowspan="2"></td><td rowspan="2"></td><td rowspan="2"></td><td rowspan="2">225+</td></tr>
<tr><td rowspan="2">Level 2</td></tr>
<tr><td rowspan="2">B1</td><td rowspan="2">Threshold</td><td>KET (Key English Test)</td><td rowspan="2">4.0–5.0</td><td rowspan="2">57–86</td><td rowspan="2">550+</td></tr>
<tr><td>Level 3</td><td>PET (Preliminary English Test)</td></tr>
<tr><td colspan="7">Passages</td></tr>
<tr><td>Level 1</td><td>B2</td><td>Vantage</td><td>FCE (First Certificate in English)</td><td>5.5–6.5</td><td>87–109</td><td>785+</td></tr>
<tr><td>Level 2</td><td>C1</td><td>Effective Operational Efficiency</td><td>CAE (Certificate in Advanced English)</td><td>7.0–8.0</td><td>110–120</td><td>490+ (Listening)
445+ (Reading)</td></tr>
</table>

Source: http://www.cambridgeesol.org/about/standards/cefr.html

Essential teaching tips

Classroom management

Error correction

- During controlled practice accuracy activities, correct students' wrong use of the target language right away, either by correcting the error yourself or, whenever possible, by having the student identify and/or correct the error. This way, the focus is on accuracy, and students can internalize the correct forms, meaning, and use of the language.
- During oral fluency activities, go around the room and take notes on errors you hear. Do not interrupt students. Instead, take note of their errors in the use of target language and write these errors on the board. Encourage students to correct them first. Be sure to point out and praise students for language used correctly as well.

Grouping students

It is good to have students work in a variety of settings: individually, in pairs, in groups, and as a class. This creates a more student-centered environment and increases student talking time.

- The easiest and quickest way to put students in pairs is to have two students sitting close to one another work together. This is good for when students need to have a quick discussion or check answers.
- To ensure students don't always work with the same partner and/or for longer activities, pair students by name, e.g., Maria work with Javier.
- One way to put students in groups is to give them a number from 1 to 4, and then have all number 1s work together, all number 2s work together, and so forth.

Instructions

- Give short instructions and model the activity for the students.
- Check your instructions, but avoid asking, Do you understand? Instead ask concept questions such as, Are you going to speak or write when you do this activity?

Monitoring

- Make sure you go around the room and check that the students are doing the activity and offer help as necessary.
- Monitor closely during controlled practice, but don't make yourself too accessible during fluency activities; otherwise, students may rely on you to answer questions rather than focus on communicating their ideas to their partner or group.

Teaching lower-level students

- Teach the Classroom Language on page xxiii and put useful language up in the classroom, so the students get used to using English.
- Don't rush. Make sure all the students have had enough time to practice the material.
- Do a lot of repetition and drilling of the new target language.
- Encourage students to practice and review target language by doing activities in the Workbook and Self-study.
- Elicit answers from your students and involve them in the learning process. Even though they are beginners, they may have a passive knowledge of English. Find out what they already know by asking them questions.
- Use the optional activities within the Teaching Notes and the Supplementary Resources Overview charts at the beginning of each unit in this Teacher's Edition to add variety to your lessons.

Teaching reading and listening

- Reading and Listening texts are meant to help the students become better readers/listeners, not to test them. Explain to your students why they need to read or listen to a text several times.
- Adapt the reading speed to the purpose of the reading. When the students read for gist, encourage them to read quickly. When students read for detail, give them more time.

Classroom Language Student questions

Unit 1 Supplementary Resources Overview

	After the following SB exercises	You can use these materials in class	Your students can use these materials outside the classroom
CYCLE 1	**1 Conversation**		**WB** Unit 1 exercise 1
	2 Speaking		
	3 Conversation	**TR** Unit 1 Extra Worksheet	
	4 Pronunciation		
	5 Grammar Focus	**TR** Unit 1 Vocabulary Worksheet	**SB** Unit 1 Grammar plus, Focus 1 **DW** Unit 1 Grammar 1–2, 4–5 **WB** Unit 1 exercises 2–6
CYCLE 2	**6 Snapshot**		
	7 Conversation		
	8 Grammar Focus	**TR** Unit 1 Grammar Worksheet **TR** Unit 1 Listening Worksheet	**SB** Unit 1 Grammar plus, Focus 2 **DW** Unit 1 Grammar 3, 6–8
	9 Word Power		**DW** Unit 1 Vocabulary 1–2
	10 Listening		
	11 Interchange 1	**TR** Unit 1 Writing Worksheet	
	12 Reading	**TR** Unit 1 Project Worksheet **VID** Unit 1 **VRB** Unit 1	**DW** Unit 1 Reading 1–2 **DW** Unit 1 Listening 1–2 **DW** Unit 1 Video 1–2 **WB** Unit 1 exercises 7–12

Key **SB:** Student's Book **DW:** Digital Workbook **TR:** Teacher's Resources
VID: Video (DW/TR) **VRB:** Video Resource Book (TR) **WB:** Print Workbook

My Plan for Unit 1

Use the space below to customize a plan that fits your needs.

With the following SB exercises	I am using these materials in class	My students are using these materials outside the classroom

With or instead of the following SB section	I am using these materials for assessment

1 Where are you from?

- Introduce oneself and others
- Talk about oneself and learn about others

1 CONVERSATION Please call me Alexa.

Listen and practice.

Arturo: Hello, I'm Arturo Valdez.
Alexa: Hi. My name is Alexandra Costa, but please call me Alexa.
Arturo: OK. Where are you from, Alexa?
Alexa: Brazil. How about you?
Arturo: I'm from Mexico.
Alexa: Oh, I love Mexico! It's really beautiful. Oh, good. Soo-jin is here.
Arturo: Who's Soo-jin?
Alexa: She's my classmate. We're in the same business class.
Arturo: Where's she from?
Alexa: South Korea. Let's go and say hello. Sorry, what's your last name again? Vargas?
Arturo: Actually, it's Valdez.
Alexa: How do you spell that?
Arturo: V-A-L-D-E-Z.

2 SPEAKING Checking information

A **PAIR WORK** Introduce yourself with your full name. Use the expressions in the box. Talk to the classmate sitting next to you and to three more classmates.

A: Hi! I'm Akemi Shimizu.
B: I'm sorry. What's your last name again?
A: Shimizu.
B: How do you spell that?

useful expressions

Hi! I'm . . .
I'm sorry. What's your first / last name again?
How do you spell that?
What do people call you?

B **CLASS ACTIVITY** Tell the class the name of the first classmate you talked to. Make a list of names.

"Her name is Akemi Shimizu. She spells her name . . ."

1 Where are you from?

Cycle 1, Exercises 1–5

In Unit 1, students introduce oneself and others, and talk about oneself and learn about others. By the end of Cycle 1, students will be able to introduce themselves and others using *be* and possessive adjectives, and ask and answer Wh-questions to find out information about others and to state information about themselves. By the end of Cycle 2, students will be able to ask and answer yes/no questions to find out information about others and to state information about themselves.

1 CONVERSATION

Learning Objective: use *be* and possessive adjectives in a conversation about people meeting for the first time

TIP
To learn your Ss' names, have them make name cards. Each S folds a piece of paper in thirds and writes his or her name on one side. Then they place the name cards on their desks.

[CD 1, Track 1]

- Focus Ss' attention on the picture. Ask: "Where are the people? What are they doing? How old are they?" Encourage Ss to make guesses.
- Set the scene. Arturo is meeting Alexa for the first time.
- Books closed. Write these questions on the board:

  1. Where is Alexa from?
  2. Where is Arturo from?
- Play the first part of the audio program. Elicit Ss' answers. (Answers: 1. Brazil 2. Mexico)
- Write this on the board for the next task:

First name	Last name
Alexandra/Alexa	
Arturo	
- Play the first part of the audio program again. Ss listen to find out Alexa's and Arturo's last names. Then elicit the answers and write them on the board. (Answers: Costa, Valdez)
- Books open. Play the first part of the audio program again. Ss listen and read silently. Ss stand up and practice the conversation in pairs. Go around the class and give help as needed.
- ***Option:*** Ss use their own information to practice the first part of the conversation. Before they start, ask Ss to underline the names and countries, so they know what information to substitute.
- Ask: "Where is Soo-jin from?" Play the rest of the audio program and elicit the answer. (Answer: South Korea)
- Ss practice the conversation in pairs.

2 SPEAKING

Learning Objectives: introduce oneself; check information about others

A *Pair work*

- Introduce yourself to the class using your first and last names. Explain that sometimes people misunderstand information like names, so it's important to ask polite questions to check information. Focus Ss' attention on the useful expressions box. Go over each expression. Point out the intonation of the questions.
- Have Ss ask you the questions from the box. Respond with information about yourself. Then model the example dialogue with a strong S, and spell your last name.
- Ss use their own information to ask and answer the questions with the classmate sitting next to them and then with three different classmates.
- ***Option:*** Review the letters of the alphabet.

B *Class Activity*

- Explain the task. Then choose a student and model the task for the class. Tell the class the student's name and how to spell it.
- Ss tell the class about the first person they spoke to in part A.

3 CONVERSATION

Learning Objective: use *be* in a conversation between three people who have just met

A *[CD 1, Track 2]*

- Books closed. Set the scene. Alexa is introducing Arturo to Soo-jin. Ask: "What is Soo-jin's last name?" Play the audio program and elicit the answer. (Answer: Kim)
- Books open. Elicit or explain the meaning of *What's . . . like?* Ask the class: "Where is Arturo from? What's it like?" Ss check answers in the Conversation on page 2. (Answers: Mexico, really beautiful)
- Play the audio program again. Ss listen and read the conversation silently. Then they practice it.

! For a new way to practice this conversation, try ***Look Up and Speak!*** – download it from the website.

B *[CD 1, Track 3]*

- Elicit names of cities in Mexico (e.g., *Mexico City, Acapulco*). Then read the two focus questions.
- Play the audio program. Ss listen to find the answers to the questions. Elicit the answers.

Audio script

Soo-jin	So, Arturo, where are *you* from?
Arturo	I'm from Mexico.
Soo-jin	Really? What city?
Arturo	Puebla.
Soo-jin	Interesting. What's it like there?
Arturo	Well, it's a really beautiful city, and the food there is great!

Answers

Arturo is from Puebla. It's a really beautiful city, and the food is great.

4 PRONUNCIATION

Learning Objective: sound more natural by linking words

[CD 1, Track 4]

- Explain that some English words sound unnatural when pronounced separately. Therefore, native speakers usually link these words.
- Play the audio program. Point out the linked sounds. Ask Ss to practice the sentences.
- ***Option:*** Play the audio program for the Conversation on page 3 again. Then tell Ss to practice linking sounds in selected sentences (e.g., *This‿is‿Arturo.*).

5 GRAMMAR FOCUS

Learning Objectives: make statements/contractions with *be*; use possessive adjectives to describe oneself and others; ask and answer Wh-questions with *be*

[CD 1, Track 5]

***Statements with* be *and contractions of* be**

- Introduce yourself ("I'm . . ."). Explain that it's common to use contractions (e.g., I'm) when speaking. Tell Ss to go around the room and introduce themselves.
- Go over the contractions in the Grammar Focus box. Close your thumb and first finger to show how the pronouns + *be* become contractions. For example, your thumb (*you*) and first finger (*are*) contract to become *you're*.

Possessive adjectives

- Explain the difference between subject pronouns and possessive adjectives by writing this on the board:

<u>I</u> am Arturo.	<u>My</u> name is Arturo.
<u>You</u> are Soo-jin.	<u>Your</u> name is Soo-jin.

- Play the audio program for the first Grammar Focus box.

For more practice with possessive adjectives, try the ***Chain Game*** – download it from the website.

A

- Ss complete the sentences individually or in pairs. Go over answers with the class.

Answers

1. **My** name is Aiko Yoshida. **I'm** from Japan. **My** family is in Nagoya. **My** brother is a college student. **His** name is Haruki.
2. **My** name is Matias. **I'm** from Santiago. **It's** a really nice city. **My** sister is a student here. **Our** parents are in Chile right now.
3. **I'm** Angelica, but everyone calls me Angie. **My** last name is Newton. **I'm** a student at City College. **My** parents are on vacation this week. **They're** in Las Vegas.

3 CONVERSATION This is Arturo Valdez.

A Listen and practice.

Alexa: Hi Soo-jin, this is Arturo Valdez. He's a biology student.

Soo-jin: Nice to meet you, Arturo. I'm Soo-jin Kim.

Arturo: Hi. So, you're from South Korea?

Soo-jin: That's right. I'm from Seoul.

Arturo: Cool! What's Seoul like?

Soo-jin: It's really nice. It's a very exciting city.

B Listen to the rest of the conversation. What city is Arturo from? What's it like?

4 PRONUNCIATION Linked sounds

Listen and practice. Notice how final consonant sounds are often linked to the vowels that follow them.

I'm a biology student. My friend is over there. My name is Alexandra Costa.

5 GRAMMAR FOCUS

Statements with *be*; possessive adjectives

Statements with *be*	Contractions of *be*	Possessive adjectives
I**'m** from Mexico.	I**'m** = I am	my
You**'re** from Brazil.	you**'re** = you are	your
He**'s** from Japan.	he**'s** = he is	his
She**'s** a business student.	she**'s** = she is	her
It**'s** an exciting city.	it**'s** = it is	its
We**'re** in the same class.	we**'re** = we are	our
They**'re** my classmates.	they**'re** = they are	their

GRAMMAR PLUS *see page 132*

A Complete these sentences. Then tell a partner about yourself.

1. ___My___ name is Aiko Yoshida. ________ from Japan. ________ family is in Nagoya. ________ brother is a college student. ________ name is Haruki.
2. ________ name is Matias. ________ from Santiago. ________ a really nice city. ________ sister is a student here. ________ parents are in Chile right now.
3. ________ Angelica, but everyone calls me Angie. ________ last name is Newton. ________ a student at City College. ________ parents are on vacation this week. ________ in Las Vegas.

Wh-questions with *be*

Where's your friend?	He's in class.
Who's Soo-jin?	She's my classmate.
What's Seoul **like**?	It's a very exciting city.
Where are you and Vanessa from?	We're from Brazil.
How are your classes?	They're pretty interesting.
What are your classmates **like**?	They're really nice.

GRAMMAR PLUS *see page 132*

For a list of countries and nationalities, see the appendix at the back of the book.

B Complete these questions. Then practice with a partner.

1. **A:** ___Who's___ that?
   B: Oh, that's Mrs. Adams.
2. **A:** ____________ she from?
   B: She's from San Diego.
3. **A:** ____________ her first name?
   B: It's Caroline.
4. **A:** ____________ the two students over there?
   B: Their names are Mason and Ava.
5. **A:** ____________ they from?
   B: They're from Vancouver.
6. **A:** ____________ they ____________?
   B: They're shy, but very friendly.

C **GROUP WORK** Write five questions about your classmates. Then ask and answer the questions.

What's your last name?
Where's Jay from?

6 SNAPSHOT

SCHOOL SUBJECTS

Write the names of the school subjects under the pictures.
What is (or was) your favorite school subject?
What subjects don't (or didn't) you like?

math	literature
history	chemistry
physics	geography
biology	physical education

[CD 1, Track 6]

Wh-questions with be

- Write these questions and answers on the board:

Questions	Answers
Where's your friend?	She's my classmate.
Who's Soo-jin?	It's a very exciting city.
What's Seoul like?	He's in class.
Where are you and Vanessa from?	They're really nice.
	We're from Brazil.
How are your classes?	They're pretty interesting.
What are your classmates like?	

Books closed. Ask Ss to match the questions and answers on the board.

- Books open. Ss check answers with the Grammar Focus box. Answer any questions.
- Play the audio program.
- ***Option:*** Divide the class into two groups. Group A asks the questions and Group B answers. Then change roles.

B

- Ss complete the questions individually. Go over answers with the class.

Answers

1. **Who is/Who's** that?
2. **Where is/Where's** she from?
3. **What is/What's** her first name?
4. **Who are** the two students over there?
5. **Where are** they from?
6. **What are** they **like**?

- Explain the second part of the task. Ss practice the conversations in pairs. Model the task with a strong S and then with another S.
- Ss complete the task in pairs.

C *Group work*

- Explain the task. Read the example questions in the box. Elicit possible Wh-questions from the class.
- ***Option:*** Ss look at the Conversations on pages 2 and 3 for examples of Wh-questions with *be.* (Answers: Where are you from? Who's Soo-jin? Where's she from? What's your last name again? What's Seoul like?)
- Ss write five Wh-questions individually. Go around the class and give help as needed.
- Ss work in small groups. They take turns asking and answering their questions.
- Go around the class and write down any errors. Then write the questions or answers with errors on the board. Ss correct the errors as a class.

End of Cycle 1

See the Supplementary Resources chart at the beginning of this unit for additional teaching materials and student activities related to this Cycle.

Cycle 2, Exercises 6–12

6 SNAPSHOT

Learning Objective: discuss school subjects

- Books closed. Ask Ss what school subjects they study in addition to English. Then ask Ss to name as many school subjects as they can.
- Books open. Focus Ss' attention on the pictures. Then read the list of school subjects in the box. Did the class name all of these subjects? Elicit or explain any unfamiliar subjects.
- Students write the names of the subjects under the pictures individually.
- Go over the answers with the class.

Answers

1. math
2. biology
3. history
4. geography
5. physical education
6. literature
7. chemistry
8. physics

- Discuss the questions with the class. Say the subjects aloud. Have Ss raise their hand when you say their favorite. Then call on individual Ss to name subjects they don't like.
- ***Option:*** Put Ss into small groups based on their favorite subject. Then each group decides on their least favorite subjects and gives reasons. Have groups share their answers with the class.

7 CONVERSATION

Learning Objective: use yes/no questions and short answers with *be* in a conversation about finding out more information about someone

[CD 1, Track 7]

- Introduce the Conversation title. Ask: "How's it going?" Help Ss with responses (e.g., *fine, not bad*).
- Set the scene. A few days after meeting, Arturo sees Soo-jin and starts a conversation.
- Write these questions on the board:

  1. Are Arturo's classes interesting this semester?
  2. Are Arturo and Alexa in the same biology class?
  3. Is Arturo's class in the afternoon?
  4. Does Soo-jin invite Arturo to get coffee?

- Elicit or explain any new vocabulary. A *semester* is a part of the school year, usually about 15–18 weeks.
- Books closed. Play the audio program twice. Elicit answers to the questions on the board. (Answers: 1. yes 2. no 3. no 4. yes)
- Books open. Play the audio program again. Ss look at the picture and read the conversation silently.
- Ss stand up and practice the conversation in pairs.

8 GRAMMAR FOCUS

Learning Objective: ask yes/no questions and give short answers with *be*

[CD 1, Track 8]

Yes/No questions

- Write several statements with *be* about Arturo and Soo-jin or your own Ss on the board. For example:

  Arturo is a student.
  Julia and Elena are sisters.

- Focus Ss' attention on the statements. Point out that statements begin with a subject + verb.

  Arturo (S) is (V) a student.

  Julia and Elena (S) are (V) sisters.

- ***Option:*** If you don't want to teach the terms *subject* and *verb*, use the numbers 1 and 2 instead.
- Explain that yes/no questions begin with a verb + subject. For example:

  Is (V) Arturo (S) a student?

  Are (V) Julia and Elena (S) sisters?

- Ask Ss to change any remaining statements on the board to yes/no questions. Give help as needed.
- Ss study the Grammar Focus box questions.

Short answers with be

- Present the short answers in the Grammar Focus box. Point out that there are two ways of saying "no" for each pronoun, except for *I*.
- Ask yes/no questions with *be* about Ss in the class. Ss respond with short answers.
- Play the audio program. Focus Ss' attention on the stress in short answers (e.g., *Yes, I* ***am***. *No, I'm* ***not***.).

A

- Ss complete the conversations individually. Go over answers with the class.

Answers

1. A: **Is** Mr. Jones from the United States?
   B: Yes, he **is**. **He's** from Baltimore.
2. A: **Is** English class at 2:00?
   B: No, **it isn't**. **It's** at 3:00.
3. A: **Are** you and Giovanna from Italy?
   B: Yes, we **are**. **We're** from Milan.
4. A: **Are** Mr. and Mrs. Flores Brazilian?
   B: No, they **aren't**. **They're** Peruvian.

- Model the first conversation with a strong S and the second conversation with a different S. Then Ss practice the conversations in pairs.

B

- Explain the task. Ss write answers to the questions individually. Then they ask and answer the questions in pairs, giving the correct information for "no" answers.

C *Group work*

- Model the task with the first question. Ss write questions individually. Then they ask their questions.
- ***Option:*** Ss write questions in small groups. Collect the questions and give them to different groups. Ss take turns asking and answering the questions.

7 CONVERSATION How's it going?

Listen and practice.

Arturo: Hi, Soo-jin!

Soo-jin: Hey Arturo. How's it going?

Arturo: Great! How are you?

Soo-jin: I'm fine, thanks. So, are your classes interesting this semester?

Arturo: Yes, they are. I really love biology.

Soo-jin: Biology? Are you and Alexa in the same class?

Arturo: No, we aren't. My class is in the morning. Her class is in the afternoon.

Soo-jin: Oh, OK. Hey, do you have time for coffee?

Arturo: Sure. I'd love some coffee.

8 GRAMMAR FOCUS

Yes/No questions and short answers with *be*

Are you free?	Yes, I **am**.	No, I**'m not**.
Is Arturo from Mexico?	Yes, he **is**.	No, he**'s not**./No, he **isn't**.
Is Alexa's class in the morning?	Yes, it **is**.	No, it**'s not**./No, it **isn't**.
Are you and Alexa in the same class?	Yes, we **are**.	No, we**'re not**./No, we **aren't**.
Are your classes interesting?	Yes, they **are**.	No, they**'re not**./No, they **aren't**.

GRAMMAR PLUS *see page 132*

A Complete the conversations. Then practice with a partner.

1. **A:** __Is__ Mr. Jones from the United States?
   B: Yes, he ________. ________ from Baltimore.
2. **A:** ________ English class at 2:00?
   B: No, it ________. ________ at 3:00.
3. **A:** ________ you and Giovanna from Italy?
   B: Yes, we ________. ________ from Milan.
4. **A:** ________ Mr. and Mrs. Flores Brazilian?
   B: No, they ________. ________ Peruvian.

B Answer these questions. If you answer "no," give the correct information. Then ask your partner the questions.

1. Are you from the United States? ________________
2. Is your teacher from Canada? ________________
3. Is your English class in the morning? ________________
4. Are you free after class? ________________

C **GROUP WORK** Write five questions about your classmates. Then ask and answer the questions.

Are Kate and Phil from Chicago?

9 WORD POWER Hello and good-bye

A Do you know these expressions? Which ones are "hellos" and which ones are "good-byes"? Complete the chart. Add expressions of your own.

✓ Bye.	How are you?
✓ Good morning.	How's it going?
Good night.	See you later.
Have a good day.	See you tomorrow.
Hey.	Talk to you later.
Hi.	What's up?

Hello	Good-bye
Good morning.	*Bye.*

B Match each expression with the best response.

1. Have a good day.	**a.** Oh, not much.
2. Hi. How are you?	**b.** Thank you. You, too.
3. What's up?	**c.** Good morning.
4. Good morning.	**d.** Pretty good, thanks.

C **CLASS ACTIVITY** Practice saying hello. Then practice saying good-bye.

A: Hi, Sakura. How's it going?

B: Pretty good, thanks. How are you?

10 LISTENING Everyone calls me Bill.

Listen to the conversations. Complete the information about each person.

First name	Last name	Where from?	What do they study?
1. *William*			
2.	*Ortiz*		
3. *Min-soo*			

11 INTERCHANGE 1 Getting to know you

Find out about your classmates. Go to Interchange 1 on page 114.

9 WORD POWER

Learning Objective: say *hello* and *good-bye* in various ways

TIP
To show Ss the purpose of an activity, write the learning objective on the board. At the end of the activity, ask Ss to say what they have achieved.

A

- Explain the task. Ss write the expressions they know in the chart.
- Copy the chart headings *Hello* and *Good-bye* on the board. Go over the first two examples with the class.
- Elicit the answers from the class and write them on the chart. Go over each expression as you write it. Then elicit more expressions and have Ss write them in the chart on the board.

Answers

Hello	Good-bye
Good morning.	Bye.
Hey.	Good night.
Hi.	Have a good day.
How are you?	See you later.
How's it going?	See you tomorrow.
What's up?	Talk to you later.
Good afternoon.	*See you.*
Good evening.	*Later.*

(Note: Additional expressions are italicized.)

B

- Model the first greeting and response with a few Ss.
- Ss match the greetings and responses.

Answers

1. b 2. d 3. a 4. c

C *Class activity*

- Model the conversation with a S.
- Ss stand up and go around the room to practice greeting their classmates using expressions from the *Hello* column in part A. Then they practice using expressions from the *Good-bye* column.

10 LISTENING

Learning Objective: listen for detail in conversations of people giving information about themselves

[CD 1, Track 9]

- Explain the task and the information in the chart. Ask the class: "What is William's last name? What else do we need to find out about him?"
- Play the first conversation in the audio program. Ss listen for William's last name, where he's from, and what he studies.
- Play the rest of the audio program. As Ss listen and complete the chart, copy the chart on the board.
- Elicit answers and have Ss write them in the chart on the board. Do not correct wrong answers.
- Play the audio program again. Stop after each conversation and discuss the answers on the board.

Audio script

1.
Man Bill, this is my friend Amber. She studies history, too.
William Hi, Amber. I'm William Davis. But everyone calls me Bill.
Amber Nice to meet you, Bill. What's your last name again?
William It's Davis. D-A-V-I-S.
Amber And where are you from, Bill?
William I'm originally from Chicago. My parents have a house there.
Amber Cool! And do you like studying history?
William Yes, I do. I think it's really exciting.
2.
Clerk OK, Ms. Ortiz. Let me just check this information. Is your first name Josephine?
Josefina Actually, it's Josefina. It's spelled J-O-S-E-F-I-N-A.
Clerk OK. Thanks. And you're from Costa Rica, right?
Josefina Oh, no, I'm not from Costa Rica. I'm from Mexico.
Clerk Oh, sorry. Mexico. But you are studying English.
Josefina Actually, I'm not. I'm a business student.
Clerk Business. OK. Got it.
3.
Man Excuse me. Are you Jun-young Park?
Jun-young Yes, I am.
Man Is your brother Min-soo Park?
Jun-young Yes, he is.
Man Tell me, is Min-soo still here at the university?
Jun-young No, he's not. He's at home in South Korea.
Man Oh, he's in South Korea. Is he in school there?
Jun-young Yeah. He's studying math at Seoul University.

Answers

	First name	Last name	Where from?	What do they study?
1.	William	Davis	Chicago	history
2.	Josefina	Ortiz	Mexico	business
3.	Min-soo	Park	South Korea	math

11 INTERCHANGE 1

See page T-114 for teaching notes.

12 READING

Learning Objective: scan and read for details in an article about names

TIP
Explain that in real life people read in different ways for different purposes. For example, they read manuals or recipes slowly and in detail, but they skim magazines or scan websites more quickly.

A

- Ask: "What names are popular in your country?" Elicit answers.
- Focus Ss' attention on the title of the reading. Elicit or explain the meaning of *trendy*. Ask: "What do you think this article is about?" Elicit ideas.
- Ss scan the text quickly to find the names. Ask: "Are any of these names popular in your country? Can you think of other names like these?" Elicit names from the class.

B

- Explain the task. Read the statements.
- Ss read the article individually.
- Elicit or explain any unfamiliar words from the reading.

Vocabulary
trendy: fashionable, in style at this time
unique: only one of its kind
popular: everybody likes it
space: the area outside of the Earth
star: a small point of light in the sky
moon: the shining round object that moves around the Earth
planet: a large object in space that moves around the Sun

- Then they complete the task. Go over answers with the class.

Answers

1, 4, and 5 should be checked.

- Direct Ss' attention to the question at the end of the text and the name chart. Have Ss cover the answers at the bottom. Read the names with the class and ask Ss to say who made the names popular. Then look at the answers.

C *Group work*

- Explain the task. Read the questions aloud and give your own answers as a model.
- Ss complete the task in small groups.
- Call on students to tell the class about some of the names they discussed.

! For a new way to practice this reading, try ***Running Dictation*** – download it from the website.

End of Cycle 2

See the Supplementary Resources chart at the beginning of this unit for additional teaching materials and student activities related to this Cycle.

12 READING

A Look at the names in the article. Are any of the names popular in your country? What similar names can you think of?

IS YOUR NAME *Trendy?*

Some people have names that are very unusual and unique. Think about the actress Emily Blunt, for example. Her daughters' names are Hazel (an eye color) and Violet (a flower). Alicia Keys has a son named Egypt. How cool is that? Are these names trendy? The answer is . . . maybe.

Many names seem to be trendy for a while, just like clothes. In the United States, some grandmothers and great-grandmothers have names like Mildred and Dorothy. For grandfathers and great-grandfathers, it's old names like Eugene or Larry. These names usually come from Greek and Latin, but they're not very popular now.

Parents sometimes choose names because they like an actor or a famous person. That's how trends usually start. For example, David and Victoria Beckham have a son named Brooklyn and a daughter named Harper. Now, Brooklyn is a popular boy's name and Harper is a popular girl's name. In the United Kingdom, baby boys often get the name George because of Prince George, Prince William and Kate Middleton's first child.

There is also a trend for names that are things or places (like Egypt). Flower names are becoming more popular: Poppy, Daisy, and Lotus, for example. Space names are cool, too. More and more babies have names like Orion (a star), Luna (the moon), or Mars (a planet).

POPULAR NAMES FOR BOYS & GIRLS

Can you guess who helped make these names popular?

BOYS	GIRLS
Bruno	January
Leonardo	Angelina
Liam	Audrey

Bruno Mars, Leonardo di Caprio, Liam Hemsworth, January Jones, Angelina Jolie, Audrey Hepburn

B Read the article. Then check (✓) the sentences that are true.

- ☐ **1.** Baby names like Mildred and Larry aren't so trendy now.
- ☐ **2.** Many babies are named after clothes.
- ☐ **3.** Alicia Keys has a son named Hazel.
- ☐ **4.** There is a famous prince named George.
- ☐ **5.** Some girls' names are the same as flower names.
- ☐ **6.** Babies never have names that are the same as planets or stars.

C **GROUP WORK** What names do you like? Can you think of anyone with an unusual name? Do you know how they got that name? Tell your classmates.

Unit 2 Supplementary Resources Overview

	After the following SB exercises	You can use these materials in class	Your students can use these materials outside the classroom
CYCLE 1	1 **Snapshot**		**DW** Unit 2 Vocabulary 1
	2 **Word Power**		**DW** Unit 2 Vocabulary 2
	3 **Speaking**		
	4 **Conversation**		
	5 **Grammar Focus**	**TR** Unit 2 Vocabulary Worksheet **TR** Unit 2 Listening Worksheet **TR** Unit 2 Extra Worksheet	**SB** Unit 2 Grammar plus, Focus 1 **DW** Unit 2 Grammar 1–4
	6 **Writing**		**WB** Unit 2 exercises 1–6
CYCLE 2	7 **Conversation**		
	8 **Pronunciation**		
	9 **Grammar Focus**	**TR** Unit 2 Grammar Worksheet	**SB** Unit 2 Grammar plus, Focus 2 **DW** Unit 2 Grammar 5–8
	10 **Listening**		
	11 **Interchange 2**	**TR** Unit 2 Writing Worksheet	
	12 **Reading**	**TR** Unit 2 Project Worksheet **VID** Unit 2 **VRB** Unit 2	**DW** Unit 2 Reading 1–2 **DW** Unit 2 Listening 1–2 **DW** Unit 2 Video 1–2 **WB** Unit 2 exercises 7–12

With or instead of the following SB section	You can also use these materials for assessment
Units 1–2 Progress Check	**TESTING PROGRAM** Units 1–2 Oral Quiz **TESTING PROGRAM** Units 1–2 Written Quiz

Key **SB:** Student's Book **DW:** Digital Workbook **TR:** Teacher's Resources
VID: Video (DW/TR) **VRB:** Video Resource Book (TR) **WB:** Print Workbook

My Plan for Unit 2

Use the space below to customize a plan that fits your needs.

With the following SB exercises	I am using these materials in class	My students are using these materials outside the classroom

With or instead of the following SB section	I am using these materials for assessment

2 What do you do?

- Ask and answer questions about jobs
- Describe routines and daily schedules

1 SNAPSHOT

Six Popular Part-time Jobs *in the United States*

Which jobs are easy? difficult? exciting? boring? Why?
Are these good jobs for students? What are some other part-time jobs?

2 WORD POWER Jobs

A Complete the word map with jobs from the list.

✓ accountant
✓ cashier
chef
✓ dancer
✓ flight attendant
musician
pilot
receptionist
server
singer
tour guide
web designer

JOBS

OFFICE WORK
accountant
____

FOOD SERVICE
cashier
____

TRAVEL INDUSTRY
flight attendant
____

ENTERTAINMENT BUSINESS
dancer
____

B Add two more jobs to each category. Then compare with a partner.

2 What do you do?

Cycle 1, Exercises 1–6

In Unit 2, students ask and answer questions about jobs, and describe routines and daily schedules. By the end of Cycle 1, students will be able to ask and answer questions about occupations using the simple present. By the end of Cycle 2, students will be able to describe routines and daily schedules using time expressions.

1 SNAPSHOT

Learning Objective: discuss popular part-time jobs

- Books closed. Introduce the topic of jobs. Ask: "Do you have a job? What is it? Do your parents have jobs? What do they do?"
- List three jobs from the Snapshot on the board. Ss give their opinion on the best job. (Answers will vary.)
- Books open. Ss compare their ideas with the Snapshot.
- Elicit or explain any new vocabulary.

Vocabulary

part-time job: a job for only a few hours or days a week
babysitter: a person who takes care of babies or children when the parents are away
fitness instructor: a person who leads exercise classes
office assistant: a person who provides general support in an office
sales associate: a person who sells things in a retail store
social media assistant: a person who helps create and update content on social media
tutor: a person who teaches private lessons

- Explain the task. Encourage Ss to give reasons for their opinions.
- Ss complete the task in small groups. Go around the class and give help as needed.

2 WORD POWER

Learning Objective: categorize types of jobs

A

- Ask Ss to look through the vocabulary list. Elicit or explain any new words. Model the pronunciation of new words.

TIP
If you don't have enough time to explain new words in class, ask Ss to look them up in a dictionary before class.

- Ss complete the word map individually or in pairs.
- While Ss are working, draw the word map on the board. Ask different Ss to come up and write their answers in the correct category. Go over answers with the class.

TIP
To provide variety, check answers in different ways. For example, write each answer on a separate card. Ss post the cards on the board in the correct category.

B

- Present and model the task. Ss write two more jobs for each category. Then they compare with a partner.
- Ask different Ss to add their ideas to the board. Go over answers with the class.

Answers

Office work	**Food service**
accountant	cashier
receptionist	chef
web designer	server
sales manager	*dishwasher*
secretary	*host/hostess*

Travel industry	**Entertainment business**
flight attendant	dancer
pilot	musician
tour guide	singer
front desk clerk	*actor/actress*
travel agent	*disc jockey*

(Note: Additional examples are italicized.)

To review jobs, play the game ***Simon Says*** – download it from the website. For example, if Simon says, "Be a singer," Ss act out the job.

3 SPEAKING

Learning Objective: describe common occupations and workplaces

Group Work

- Brainstorm workplaces with the class. Write ideas on the board.
- Divide the class into teams and explain the task. Sit in the chair and ask a student to write a job on the board. Then model how to play by asking the example questions with Ss from different teams. Say, "Is this person a server?" to make a guess. Ss should answer *Yes, he or she is./No, he or she isn't.*
- Then teams play the game. Go around the class and give help as needed.
- Make note of any grammar, pronunciation, or intonation problems to review with the class at the end of the game.

4 CONVERSATION

Learning Objective: use simple present Wh-questions and statements in a conversation about jobs

A *[CD 1, Track 10]*

- Set the scene. Derek and Amy are talking about their jobs. Tell Ss to cover the text. Focus their attention on the picture. Ask: "What does Amy do? How does she like her job?" Encourage Ss to guess.

TIP

Give Ss (or ask Ss to bring) small cards to cover the text. That way, they can see the picture but not the text. Ask Ss to keep their cards for future classes.

- Play the audio program. Ss listen to check their guesses.
- Write these focus questions on the board:

  True or false?
  1. Derek has a full-time job.
  2. Derek is always tired after work.
  3. Amy doesn't like her job.
- Books closed (or text covered). Play the audio program again. Then check answers to the focus questions. (Answers: 1. false (He has a part-time job.) 2. true 3. false (She thinks her job is great.))
- Books open (or uncover the text). Play the conversation line by line, giving Ss time to repeat it.
- Ss practice the conversation in pairs.

! For a new way to practice this conversation, try the ***Substitution Dialog*** – download it from the website. Have Ss replace the underlined words:

A: What do you do, Derek?
B: I'm a server. I serve people food. And what do you do, Amy?
A: I'm a dancer. I work with incredible people.

B *[CD 1, Track 11]*

- Read the two focus questions aloud. Then play the second part of the audio program. Elicit answers from the class.

Audio script

Derek	So, where exactly do you work?
Amy	I work at a dance company, but I travel a lot, too.
Derek	Do you always dance with the same group of people?
Amy	Yes and no. I travel with a small group of people from New York. But I also meet new dancers and musicians in every city. Last month I worked in Rome.

Answers

Amy travels with a small group of people from New York. She meets new dancers and musicians in every city.

3 SPEAKING Work and workplaces

GROUP WORK Form teams. One team member sits with his or her back to the board. Choose a job from page 8 or from the box. Write the job on the board. Your team member asks yes/no questions and tries to guess the job.

More jobs	
carpenter	nurse
cook	office manager
dentist	police officer
doctor	reporter
engineer	restaurant host
firefighter	salesperson
front desk clerk	security guard
graphic designer	taxi driver
lawyer	teacher
mechanic	vendor

A: Does the person work in a hospital?
B: No, he or she doesn't.
A: Does he or she work in a restaurant?
C: Yes, that's right!

4 CONVERSATION I'm on my feet all day.

A Listen and practice.

Amy: What do you do, Derek?
Derek: I work part-time as a server.
Amy: Oh, really? What restaurant do you work at?
Derek: I work at Stella's Café downtown.
Amy: That's cool. How do you like it?
Derek: It's OK. I'm on my feet all day, so I'm always tired. What do you do?
Amy: I'm a dancer.
Derek: A dancer! How exciting!
Amy: Yeah, it's great! I work with incredible people.
Derek: That sounds really nice. But is it difficult?
Amy: A little. I'm on my feet all day, too, but I love it.

B Listen to the rest of the conversation. Who does Amy travel with? Who does she meet in other cities?

5 GRAMMAR FOCUS

Simple present Wh-questions and statements

What do you **do**?	I**'m** a student. I **have** a part-time job, too.
Where do you **work**?	I **work** at a restaurant.
Where do you **go** to school?	I **go** to the University of Texas.
What does Amy **do**?	She**'s** a dancer.
Where does she **work**?	She **works** at a dance company. She **travels**, too.
How does she **like** it?	She **loves** it.

I/You	He/She
work	works
take	takes
study	studies
teach	teaches
do	does
go	goes
have	has

GRAMMAR PLUS see page 133

A Complete these conversations. Then practice with a partner.

1. **A:** What ____*do*____ you ____*do*____?
   B: I'm a full-time student. I study the piano.
   A: And ____________ do you ____________ to school?
   B: I ____________ to the Brooklyn School of Music.
   A: Wow! ____________ do you like your classes?
   B: I ____________ them a lot.
2. **A:** What ____________ Tanya do?
   B: She's a teacher. She ____________ an art class at a school in Denver.
   A: And what about Ryan? Where ____________ he work?
   B: He ____________ for a big computer company in San Francisco.
   A: ____________ does he do, exactly?
   B: He's a web designer. He ____________ fantastic websites.
3. **A:** What ____________ Bruce and Ivy do?
   B: They ____________ at an Italian restaurant. It's really good.
   A: That's nice. ____________ is Ivy's job?
   B: Well, she manages the finances and Bruce ____________ in the kitchen.
4. **A:** Where ____________ Ali work?
   B: He ____________ at the university. He ____________ a part-time job.
   A: Really? What ____________ he do?
   B: He ____________ office work.
   A: How ____________ he like it?
   B: Not much, but he ____________ some extra money to spend!

B **PAIR WORK** Ask your partner questions like these about work and school. Take notes to use in Exercise 6.

What do you do?
Do you go to school or do you have a job?
How do you like . . . ?
Do you study another language?
What's your favorite . . . ?
What does your best friend do?

C **CLASS WORK** Tell the class about your partner.

"Regina goes to Chicago University, and she has a part-time job, too. She likes . . ."

5 GRAMMAR FOCUS

Learning Objective: ask and answer simple present Wh-questions

[CD 1, Track 12]

Simple present statements

- Books closed. Write these sentences on the board, allowing space between lines:

  I work part-time as a server.
  I work at Stella's Café downtown.
  I'm on my feet all day, so I'm always tired.

- Books open. Ask: "Who said this?" (Answer: Derek) Ask Ss to describe his job. Write the new version below the original:

  He works part-time as a server.
  He works at Stella's Café downtown.
  He's on his feet all day, so he's always tired.

- Point out that the verbs for *he, she,* and *it* end in *-s.*
- ***Option:*** Repeat the activity with sentences about Amy.

TIP
Write the letter *s* on a card. Every time Ss forget to use the final *-s*, hold up the card. Write the word *does* on a separate card for the same purpose.

- Focus Ss' attention on the last column in the Grammar Focus box. Point out the spelling changes that occur with *he/she.*

Simple present Wh-questions

- Draw a chart with six columns on the board. Number the columns from 1 to 6.
- Focus Ss' attention on the Conversation on page 9. Ask Ss to find questions with the word *do* in part A. Then read the first question about Amy in part B. Write them in the chart:

1	2	3	4	5	6
What	*do*	*you*	*do?*		
What	*restaurant*	*do*	*you*	*work*	*at?*
How	*do*	*you*	*like*	*it?*	
Who	*does*	*Amy*	*travel*	*with?*	

- Focus Ss' attention on the questions in the chart and in the Grammar Focus box. Elicit the rule for forming Wh-questions in the simple present:
  Wh- + *do/does* + subject + verb?
- Ask Ss the questions in the Grammar Focus box. Ss use their own information for the first three questions.
- Play the audio program. Ss listen and repeat.

A

- Ss complete the task individually. Then they compare answers with a partner.

TIP
To build Ss' confidence, have them compare answers in pairs or groups before you check answers as a class.

- Go over answers with the class. Then Ss practice the conversations in pairs.

Answers

1. A: What **do** you **do**?
   B: I'm a full-time student. I study the piano.
   A: And **where** do you **go** to school?
   B: I **go** to the Brooklyn School of Music.
   A: Wow! **How** do you like your classes?
   B: I **like** them a lot.
2. A: What **does** Tanya do?
   B: She's a teacher. She **teaches** an art class at a school in Denver.
   A: And what about Ryan? Where **does** he work?
   B: He **works** for a big computer company in San Francisco.
   A: **What** does he do, exactly?
   B: He's a web designer. He **designs** fantastic websites.
3. A: What **do** Bruce and Ivy do?
   B: They **work** at an Italian restaurant. It's really good.
   A: That's nice. **What** is Ivy's job?
   B: Well, she manages the finances and Bruce **works** in the kitchen.
4. A: Where **does** Ali work?
   B: He **works** at the university. He **has** a part-time job.
   A: Really? What **does** he do?
   B: He **does** office work.
   A: How **does** he like it?
   B: Not much, but he **has/gets** some extra money to spend!

B *Pair work*

- Explain the task. Model asking and answering the questions with a S. Have Ss take notes on their partner's answers so they can use the notes to write about their partner in Exercise 6.
- Ss complete the task in pairs. Go around the class and check for use of the simple present.

C *Class work*

- Model the task. Ask a S to tell the class about their partner.
- Go around the class, giving each S a chance to speak.

6 WRITING

Learning Objective: write a biography

A

- Tell Ss to read the model biography silently. Explain any new vocabulary. Point out that the biography does not have the person's name.
- Ss write their biographies. Go around the class and give help as needed.
- ***Option:*** Ss write the biographies for homework.

B *Class activity*

- Collect the biographies and number them. Then pass them around the class. Ss make a numbered list and write their guesses next to each number.
- Elicit Ss' guesses about each biography.

End of Cycle 1

See the Supplementary Resources chart at the beginning of this unit for additional teaching materials and student activities related to this Cycle.

Cycle 2, Exercises 7–12

7 CONVERSATION

Learning Objective: use time expressions in a conversation about daily routines

A *[CD 1, Track 13]*

- Point out the title and the picture. Ask: "What is this conversation about?" Elicit ideas.
- Books closed (or text covered). Ask: "Where does Kristina work?" Play the audio program. Ss listen for the answer. (Answer: She works at the National Bank.)
- Write these questions on the board:

  1. What time *does* Kristina usually start work?
  2. What time *does* Kristina eat dinner?

- Play the audio program again. Ss listen for the answers. (Answers: 1. at 1:00 in the afternoon 2. at 10:30 P.M.)
- Books open. Play the audio program again. Ss read the conversation silently. Then they practice in pairs.
- ***Option:*** To review the simple present, ask Ss to describe Kristina's daily routine from memory.

B *[CD 1, Track 14]*

- Read the two focus questions.
- Play the audio program. Elicit answers from the class.

Audio script

Kristina	If you go to sleep at 8:00, what time do you wake up?
Taxi Driver	Pretty early. I start work at 4:00 in the morning.
Kristina	Four in the morning! Wow. What's your typical day like?
Taxi Driver	Well, I get up at 3:00 A.M. Then I drive from 4:00 in the morning until 2:00 in the afternoon.
Kristina	That's a long day!
Taxi Driver	Yes, but I like it. I talk to people from all over the world and see many beautiful parts of the city.
Kristina	That's nice. I only see the National Bank.

Answers

The taxi driver starts work at 4:00 in the morning. He finishes at 2:00 in the afternoon.

8 PRONUNCIATION

Learning Objective: use correct syllable stress with two- and three-syllable words

A *[CD 1, Track 15]*

- Explain that some syllables have more stress. Read the examples, clapping on the stressed syllable.
- Play the audio program. Ss clap on stressed syllables.

B *[CD 1, Track 16]*

- Ss complete the chart individually.
- Play the audio program. Ss listen and check their answers. Go over answers with the class.

Answers

●•	dancer, server, tutor
●••	salesperson, carpenter, firefighter
•●•	accountant, musician, reporter

6 WRITING A biography

A Use your notes from Exercise 5 to write a biography of your partner. Don't use your partner's name. Use *he* or *she* instead.

> My partner is a chef. She works in a very nice restaurant near our school. She cooks Italian food and bakes desserts. She likes her English classes a lot. Her favorite activities are speaking and vocabulary practice. She studies another language, too . . .

B **CLASS ACTIVITY** Pass your biographies around the class. Guess who each biography is about.

7 CONVERSATION I work in the afternoon.

A Listen and practice.

KRISTINA I need to go to National Bank downtown, please. I'm late for a meeting.

TAXI DRIVER No problem. What time is your meeting?

KRISTINA In 10 minutes! I don't usually work in the morning.

TAXI DRIVER Really? What time do you usually go to work?

KRISTINA I work in the afternoon. I start at one.

TAXI DRIVER That's pretty late. Do you like to work in the afternoon?

KRISTINA Yes, I do. I work better in the afternoon. I finish at seven or eight, then I go home and eat dinner at around 10:30.

TAXI DRIVER Wow, you have dinner late! I go to bed every night at 8:00.

KRISTINA Really? That seems so early!

B Listen to the rest of the conversation. What time does the taxi driver start work? What time does he finish?

8 PRONUNCIATION Syllable stress

A Listen and practice. Notice which syllable has the main stress.

● •	● • •	• ● •
dancer	salesperson	accountant
________	________	________
________	________	________

B Which stress pattern do these words have? Add them to the columns in part A. Then listen and check.

carpenter musician firefighter reporter server tutor

9 GRAMMAR FOCUS

Time expressions

				Expressing clock time
I get up	**at** 7:00	**in** the morning	**on** weekdays.	7:00
I leave work	**early**	**in** the afternoon	**on** Thursdays.	seven
I go to bed	**around** eleven	**in** the evening	**on** weeknights.	seven o'clock
I get home	**late**	**at** night	**on** weekends.	7:00 A.M. = 7:00 in the morning
I stay up	**until** midnight	**on** Fridays.		7:00 P.M. = 7:00 in the evening
I exercise	**before** noon	**on** Saturdays.		
I wake up	**after** noon	**on** Sundays.		

GRAMMAR PLUS *see page 133*

A Choose the correct word.

1. I get up (at) / **until** six **at** / **on** weekdays.
2. I have lunch **at** / **early** 11:30 **in** / **on** Mondays.
3. I have a snack **in** / **around** 10:00 **in** / **at** night.
4. **In** / **On** Fridays, I leave school **early** / **before**.
5. I stay up **before** / **until** 1:00 A.M. **in** / **on** weekends.
6. I sleep **around** / **until** noon **in** / **on** Sundays.
7. I have dinner **at** / **in** 7:00 **at** / **on** weeknights.
8. I read a book **after** / **before** I go to sleep.
9. **In** / **On** weekends, I go to bed **in** / **at** 1:00 A.M.
10. **In** / **On** Thursdays, I leave work **at** / **in** 9:00 P.M.
11. I work **late** / **until** on Wednesdays.
12. I study **around** / **until** 11:00 **after** / **early** dinner.

B Rewrite the sentences in part A so that they are true for you. Then compare with a partner.

C **PAIR WORK** Take turns asking and answering these questions.

1. Which days do you get up early? late?
2. What's something you do in the morning?
3. What's something you do before English class?
4. What's something you do on Saturday evenings?
5. Which days do you stay up late?
6. Which days do you go to bed early?
7. What do you do after dinner on weeknights?
8. What do you do after lunch on weekends?

10 LISTENING What hours do you work?

A Listen to Aaron, Madison, and Kayla talk about their daily schedules. Complete the chart.

	Aaron	Madison	Kayla
Job	*carpenter*		
Gets up at . . .		*7:00 a.m.*	
Gets home at . . .			
Goes to bed at . . .			

B **CLASS ACTIVITY** Who do you think has the best daily schedule? Why?

11 INTERCHANGE 2 What we have in common

Find out about your classmates' schedules. Go to Interchange 2 on page 115.

9 GRAMMAR FOCUS

Learning Objective: use time expressions with prepositions and adverbs to describe routines and schedules

[CD 1, Track 17]

Prepositions of time: at/in/on + time

- Draw three large circles on the board and label them *at, in,* and *on*.
- Focus Ss' attention on the Grammar Focus box. Ask: "What words follow *at, in,* and *on*?" Different Ss write the words inside the circles on the board.
- Elicit or explain the rules:
  at + times of day; *night*
  in + parts of day (except *night*)
  on + days of the week

For more practice with prepositions of time, play ***Run For It!*** – download it from the website.

Adverbs of time

- Elicit or explain the meanings of *early, around, late, until, before,* and *after*. Then play the audio program.

A

- Ss complete the task individually or in pairs.
- Go around the class and give help as needed. Go over answers with the class.

Answers

1. I get up **at** six **on** weekdays.
2. I have lunch **at** 11:30 **on** Mondays.
3. I have a snack **around** 10:00 **at** night.
4. **On** Fridays, I leave school **early**.
5. I stay up **until** 1:00 A.M. **on** weekends.
6. I sleep **until** noon **on** Sundays.
7. I have dinner **at** 7:00 **on** weeknights.
8. I read a book **before** I go to sleep.
9. **On** weekends, I go to bed **at** 1:00 A.M.
10. **On** Thursdays, I leave work **at** 9:00 P.M.
11. I work **late** on Wednesdays.
12. I study **until** 11:00 **after** dinner.

B

- Model the task. Rewrite one or two sentences on the board so that they are true for you.
- Ss work individually. Then they go over their answers in pairs.

C *Pair work*

- Model the task. First, Ss ask you the questions. Then Ss complete the task in pairs.

10 LISTENING

Learning Objective: listen for specific information in a conversation about routines

A *[CD 1, Track 18]*

- Focus students' attention on the chart. Then play the audio program, stopping after each person talks about his or her schedule. Ss complete the chart individually.
- Play the audio program again.
- Go over answers with the class.

Audio script

Madison What do you do, Aaron?
Aaron I'm a carpenter.
Madison Oh, yeah? So, what hours do you work?
Aaron I work eight hours a day, from Monday to Friday. I get up around 6:00 A.M., and I work from 7:00 A.M. until 3:00 P.M. I get home pretty early, about 4:00 P.M. I go to bed at 10:00. And what do you do, Madison?
Madison Well, I'm an accountant. It's a regular nine-to-five office job, so I get up at 7:00 A.M. and get home around 6:00 P.M. That's OK, though, because I like to go out at night. I go to bed around midnight on weekdays.
Aaron What about you, Kayla?
Kayla Well, my hours are a bit different – I'm a nurse. I start work at 11:00 at night. I work until 7:00 A.M.
Madison Wow! So what time do you get up?
Kayla I get home at 8:00 and go to bed at about 8:30. And I sleep until 4:00 P.M.
Aaron And what do you do in the evenings?
Kayla Oh, you know. I have dinner, watch TV, see friends. It's a great schedule for me.

Answers

	Aaron	Madison	Kayla
Job	carpenter	accountant	nurse
Gets up at . . .	6:00 A.M.	7:00 A.M.	4:00 P.M.
Gets home at . . .	4:00 P.M.	6:00 P.M.	8:00 A.M.
Goes to bed at . . .	10:00 P.M.	midnight	8:30 A.M.

B *Class activity*

- Elicit Ss' responses. Then take a class vote.

11 INTERCHANGE 2

See page T-115 for teaching notes.

12 READING

Learning Objectives: make predictions; read for specific information in an article about jobs

TIP
To help Ss focus on the task, tell them not to worry about words they don't understand. Encourage them to keep reading when they see new words.

A

- Set the scene. Explain that young people have jobs that didn't exist when their parents were young, especially jobs related to computers, the Internet, and smartphones. There are also jobs that weren't popular many years ago. Ask: "What are some jobs that parents don't understand?" Elicit ideas and write them on the board.
- Focus Ss' attention on the pictures. Tell Ss to cover the text. Ask: "Who studies people? Who helps people exercise more?" Encourage Ss to guess.
- Then set a time limit of one minute. Ss skim the article quickly to check their guesses. (Answers: Nico studies people. Lisa helps people exercise more.) Then elicit or explain Danny's and Carla's jobs.
- Have small groups discuss why these jobs, and others, are hard to understand. Have groups share their ideas with the class.

B

- Explain the task. Tell Ss to guess the meanings of any new words.
- Ss read the article and complete the task. Go over answers with the class.

Answers

1. Lisa
2. Nico
3. Carla
4. Danny

- Elicit or explain any new vocabulary.

Vocabulary
posts: online messages, such as blog posts, comments, photos
social media: electronic communication that lets people share information on the Internet
fabrics: cloth, especially that people use to make clothes
sociologist: a person who studies society and relationships between people
behave: to do or say things
apps: short for "applications"; small computer programs that you can use on a smartphone or other device
get fit: to exercise in order to be in good physical condition

C *Pair work*

- Read the focus questions with the class. Elicit ideas from the class for other jobs, hobbies, or school classes that are hard to explain.
- In small groups, Ss discuss the questions.
- Have groups share their ideas with the class.
- ***Option:*** Have small groups look back through the jobs in Exercises 1, 2, and 3 and find the three jobs that are most difficult to explain. Groups determine the reason each job is difficult to understand and then explain it to the class.

End of Cycle 2

See the Supplementary Resources chart at the beginning of this unit for additional teaching materials and student activities related to this Cycle and for assessment tools.

12 READING

A Read the title and skim the blog posts. What are these people's jobs? Why do you think their jobs are hard to understand?

MY PARENTS DON'T UNDERSTAND MY JOB!

DANNY BANGKOK, THAILAND

Do you know what a social media manager is? Right, of course you do, but my mom doesn't. Every week, I try to explain my job to her. I work for a company that makes cars. My job is to tell the world how great our cars are. How do I do that? I get up early and write posts for social media. On weekdays, I go online around 7:00 a.m. and sometimes I work until 9:00 at night. The problem is . . . my mom doesn't use social media.

CARLA BUENOS AIRES, ARGENTINA

It's so funny! I explain my job to my dad, but he just looks very confused. I'm a fashion designer. I always get up early on weekdays because I love my job. I have an office, and most days I draw pictures of cool new clothes, like dresses, jeans, and T-shirts. I also go to stores to look at fabrics to use for my clothes. My dad thinks I'm crazy! He just goes to a store and buys stuff to wear. He doesn't know someone has to design it first.

NICO ATHENS, GREECE

So, I'm a sociologist. I study people. Well, I study how people behave. I also study why they behave the way they do. My mom and dad don't understand why I do that. My mom says, "Nico, people are people! They just do normal things!" I don't agree. There are many reasons why people do the things they do, and I love to learn about that.

LISA LOS ANGELES, UNITED STATES

I'm a software engineer, but my dad doesn't know what that means. I tell him that software is the technology inside his computer, his phone, and his tablet. I make apps for smartphones. One app helps people exercise more. It's very cool because it tracks everything you do during the day. You put your phone in your pocket, and the app does the rest. The app tracks your walk to school, your bike ride on the weekend, and more.

B Read the article. Who does the following things? Check (✓) the correct boxes.

Who does something . . .	Danny	Carla	Nico	Lisa
1. . . . to help people get fit?	☐	☐	☐	☐
2. . . . to understand other people?	☐	☐	☐	☐
3. . . . to make things you can wear?	☐	☐	☐	☐
4. . . . to tell other people about their company?	☐	☐	☐	☐

C **PAIR WORK** Which of the four jobs do you think is the most interesting? the most useful? the hardest to explain? What other things are hard to explain? Think about different jobs, hobbies, or classes at school.

Units 1–2 Progress check

SELF-ASSESSMENT

How well can you do these things? Check (✓) the boxes.

I can . . .	Very well	OK	A little
Make an introduction and use basic greeting expressions (Ex. 1)	☐	☐	☐
Show I didn't understand and ask for repetition (Ex. 1)	☐	☐	☐
Ask and answer questions about myself and other people (Ex. 2)	☐	☐	☐
Ask and answer questions about work (Ex. 3, 4)	☐	☐	☐
Ask and answer questions about habits and routines (Ex. 5)	☐	☐	☐

1 ROLE PLAY Introductions

A **PAIR WORK** You are talking to someone at school. Have a conversation. Then change roles and try the role play again.

A: Hi. How are you?
B: . . .
A: By the way, my name is . . .
B: I'm sorry. What's your name again?
A: . . .
B: I'm . . . . Are you a student here?
A: . . . And how about you?
B: . . .
A: Oh, really? And where are you from?

B **GROUP WORK** Join another pair. Introduce your partner.

2 SPEAKING Interview

Write questions for these answers. Then use the questions to interview a classmate.

1. What's ________________? My name is Midori Oki.
2. ________________? I'm from Kyoto, Japan.
3. ________________? Yes, my classes are very interesting.
4. ________________? My favorite class is English.
5. ________________? No, my teacher isn't American.
6. ________________? My classmates are very nice.
7. ________________? My best friend is Kiara.

Units 1–2

Progress check

SELF-ASSESSMENT

Learning Objectives: reflect on one's learning; identify areas that need improvement

- Ask: "What did you learn in Units 1 and 2?" Elicit Ss' answers.
- Ss complete the Self-assessment. Encourage them to be honest, and point out they will not get a bad grade if they check (✓) *A little*.
- Ss move on to the Progress check exercises. You can have Ss complete them in class or for homework, using one of these techniques:
  1. Ask Ss to complete all the exercises.
  2. Ask Ss: "What do you need to practice?" Then assign exercises based on their answers.
  3. Ask Ss to choose and complete exercises based on their Self-assessment.

1 ROLE PLAY

Learning Objectives: demonstrate one's ability to make an introduction using basic greeting and leave-taking expressions; demonstrate one's ability to ask for repetition or clarification

A *Pair work*

- Read the instructions aloud and focus Ss' attention on the picture. Explain that Ss should pretend they don't know their partners in this role play.
- Model the role play with a S. Explain how to use the conversation cues.
- Ss role-play the conversation in pairs. Encourage Ss to use appropriate body language and gestures, add follow-up questions, and ask for clarification where appropriate.
- ***Option:*** Ss introduce themselves without referring to the example conversation.

B *Group work*

- Each pair joins another pair. Ss introduce their partners to the other pair and ask follow-up questions.

TIP

If you don't have enough class time for the speaking activities, assign each S a speaking partner. Then have Ss complete the activities with their partners for homework.

2 SPEAKING

Learning Objective: demonstrate one's ability to ask and answer questions about oneself and others

- Explain the task and model the first question. Ss should consider if the questions are Wh- or yes/no questions.
- Ss work individually to write the seven questions. Point out that there may be more than one correct question for each answer.
- Go over Ss' questions with the class.

Possible answers

1. What's your name?
2. Where are you from?
3. Are your classes interesting?
4. What's your favorite class?
5. Is your teacher American?
6. What are your classmates like?
7. Who is your best friend?

- Ss work in pairs. They take turns using the questions to interview each other. Encourage Ss to add follow-up questions.
- ***Option:*** Each S uses the questions to interview another S.

3 SPEAKING

Learning Objective: demonstrate one's ability to ask about and describe common jobs

A

- Explain the task. Then elicit things a software engineer does and write them on the board.
- Ss complete the task individually or in pairs.

B *Group work*

- Ss compare their lists in small groups. Encourage Ss to ask Wh-questions about the jobs (e.g., *What does a software engineer do? Where does a software engineer work?*).
- Go around the class and check Ss' use of the simple present.

4 LISTENING

Learning Objective: demonstrate one's ability to understand descriptions of people's occupations and routines

A *[CD 1, Track 19]*

- Set the scene. Austin and Haley are talking about work and school.
- Play the audio program once or twice. Ss listen and complete the chart.

Audio script

Austin Hey, Dylan. How are you?
Dylan I'm great, Austin. Welcome to my house. Oh, Austin, this is my friend Haley.
Austin Hi, Haley. It's nice to meet you.
Haley Nice to meet you, too, Austin.
Dylan Excuse me.
Haley So how do you know Dylan?
Austin Oh, we work in the same office.
Haley Really? What do you do?
Austin I'm a web designer. I'm also in school.
Haley That's exciting! What do you study?
Austin I study art history.
Haley Oh, cool! How do you like it?
Austin It's OK. I'm very busy. I usually finish with work and school at 10:30 and get home at 11:00.
Haley That's late!
Austin Yeah. After work, I usually go to bed right away. What about you? What do you do?
Haley Oh, I'm a student. I study dance.
Austin Wow! Now that's exciting! Where do you study?
Haley At New York Dance.
Austin How do you like your classes?
Haley They're great. I dance all day long. It's hard, but I love it.
Austin What do you do after school?
Haley I have a new part-time job. I work in an office.
Austin Where is the office?
Haley Actually, I work in your office!
Austin You do? Well, stop by and say hello sometime.
Haley OK.

Answers

Austin	**Haley**
web designer	dance student
Dylan's office	New York Dance
OK	loves them
goes to school	works in an office

B *Pair work*

- Explain the task. Ss take turns asking and answering the questions in part A.

5 SPEAKING

Learning Objective: demonstrate one's ability to ask and answer questions about routines

A

- Elicit or explain the meaning of *a perfect day*. Model the task by having a S ask you the questions.
- Ss complete the task individually.

B *Pair work*

- Ss take turns describing their perfect day in pairs. Encourage Ss to ask follow-up questions.

WHAT'S NEXT?

Learning Objective: become more involved in one's learning

- Focus Ss' attention on the Self-assessment again. Ask: "How well can you do these things now?"
- Ask Ss to underline one thing they need to review. Ask: "What did you underline? How can you review it?"
- If needed, plan additional activities or reviews based on Ss' answers.

3 SPEAKING What a great job!

A What do you know about these jobs? List three things each person does.

works on a computer
____
____

____
____
____

____
____
____

____
____
____

B **GROUP WORK** Compare your lists. Take turns asking about the jobs.

4 LISTENING At Dylan's party

A Listen to Austin and Haley talk about work and school. Complete the chart.

	Austin	Haley
What do you do?		
Where do you work/study?		
How do you like your job/classes?		
What do you do after work/school?		

B **PAIR WORK** Practice the questions in part A. Answer with your own information.

5 SPEAKING Survey: My perfect day

A Imagine your perfect day. Read the questions, then add one more. Then write your answers.

What time do you get up? ____________
What do you do after you get up? ____________
Where do you go? ____________
What do you do in the evening? ____________
When do you go to bed? ____________
____________ ____________

B **PAIR WORK** Talk about your perfect day. Answer any questions.

WHAT'S NEXT?

Look at your Self-assessment again. Do you need to review anything?

Unit 3 Supplementary Resources Overview

	After the following SB exercises	You can use these materials in class	Your students can use these materials outside the classroom
CYCLE 1	**1 Snapshot**		**DW** Unit 3 Vocabulary 1
	2 Conversation		
	3 Grammar Focus	**TR** Unit 3 Extra Worksheet	**SB** Unit 3 Grammar plus, Focus 1 **DW** Unit 3 Grammar 1, 3–7
	4 Pronunciation		
	5 Role Play		
	6 Listening		
	7 Interchange 3	**TR** Unit 3 Listening Worksheet	**WB** Unit 3 exercises 1–5
CYCLE 2	**8 Word Power**	**TR** Unit 3 Vocabulary Worksheet	**DW** Unit 3 Vocabulary 2
	9 Conversation		
	10 Grammar Focus	**TR** Unit 3 Grammar Worksheet	**SB** Unit 3 Grammar plus, Focus 2 **DW** Unit 3 Grammar 2, 8
	11 Writing	**TR** Unit 3 Writing Worksheet	
	12 Reading	**TR** Unit 3 Project Worksheet **VID** Unit 3 **VRB** Unit 3	**DW** Unit 3 Reading 1–2 **DW** Unit 3 Listening 1–2 **DW** Unit 3 Video 1–2 **WB** Unit 3 exercises 6–10

Key **SB:** Student's Book **DW:** Digital Workbook **TR:** Teacher's Resources
VID: Video (DW/TR) **VRB:** Video Resource Book (TR) **WB:** Print Workbook

My Plan for Unit 3

Use the space below to customize a plan that fits your needs.

With the following SB exercises	I am using these materials in class	My students are using these materials outside the classroom

With or instead of the following SB section	I am using these materials for assessment

3 How much are these?

- Ask about and describe prices
- Discuss preferences

1 SNAPSHOT

Which words have a positive meaning? Which have a negative meaning?
What meanings do these colors have for you? What colors do you like to wear?

2 CONVERSATION I'll take it!

A Listen and practice.

SALESCLERK Hi! Can I help you?
CUSTOMER Yes, please. I need a birthday present for my sister.
SALESCLERK That's so nice! What does she like?
CUSTOMER She loves anything blue. How much is this sweater?
SALESCLERK The light blue one? It's $150.
CUSTOMER That's pretty expensive. I love my sister, but I need to eat!
SALESCLERK Well, we have that one, too.
CUSTOMER Which one? The green one?
SALESCLERK Yes, and it's on sale for $28.99.
CUSTOMER Well, she also likes green. I'll take it!

B Listen to the rest of the conversation. What else does the customer look at? Does he buy it?

3 How much are these?

In Unit 3, students ask about and describe prices and discuss preferences. By the end of Cycle 1, students will be able to use demonstratives, *one*, and *ones* to ask about and describe prices. By the end of Cycle 2, students will be able to discuss preferences using comparisons with adjectives.

Cycle 1, Exercises 1–7

1 SNAPSHOT

Learning Objective: describe the meaning of colors

- Books closed. Ask several Ss: "What is your favorite color?" Write the colors on the board. Help with vocabulary for colors as needed.
- Ask several Ss to choose between pairs of adjectives for colors. For example, ask: "Is red exciting or sad? Is white jealous or hopeful?"
- Books open. Explain that colors have different meanings in different countries. Discuss the meanings in the Snapshot. Elicit or explain any new vocabulary.

Vocabulary

hopeful: feeling positive about the future
truthful: honest
friendly: nice to other people; sociable
powerful: strong
jealous: unhappy because you want someone's things
confident: believing you can do anything
creative: good at thinking of new, unique ideas

- Focus Ss' attention on the first two questions. Draw this chart on the board:

Positive meanings	Negative meanings
hopeful	sad

- Ask different Ss to add adjectives from the Snapshot to the chart. Does everyone agree on the placement of *exciting*? Of *creative*?
- Ss discuss the remaining questions in pairs. Allow about five minutes. Then discuss the questions as a class.
- ***Option:*** Select three colors. In pairs or groups, Ss make lists of all the things in the room with those colors.

2 CONVERSATION

Learning Objective: use demonstratives, *one*, and *ones* in a conversation about asking about prices while shopping

A *[CD 1, Track 20]*

- To set the scene, focus Ss' attention on the picture. Ask: "Where are they? What are they doing?"
- Write this focus question on the board:

  What color sweater does he buy?
- Books closed (or text covered). Play the audio program. Ss listen for the answer. (Answer: green)
- ***Option:*** Write these focus questions on the board:

  1. *How much is the light blue sweater?*
  2. *Why does he buy the green sweater?*

  Then play the audio again. Ss check answers. (Answers: 1. $150 2. It's on sale./It's not too expensive.)
- Books open (or uncover the text). Play the audio program again. Ss listen and read along silently.
- Elicit or explain any new vocabulary.

Vocabulary

I'll take it!: I'll buy it.

- Ss practice the conversation in pairs.

! For a new way to practice this conversation, try the ***Onion Ring*** technique – download it from the website.

B *[CD 1, Track 21]*

- Read the two focus questions aloud. Then play the audio program. Elicit answers from the class.

Audio script

Salesclerk We also have this beautiful blue watch.
Customer Oh, that's pretty. My sister likes watches.
Salesclerk It's on sale today only.
Customer How much is it?
Salesclerk It's $52.50.
Customer Hmm . . . I don't think so. I'll just take the sweater. Thanks for your help.

Answers

He looks at a watch. He doesn't buy it.

3 GRAMMAR FOCUS

Learning Objective: use demonstratives, *one*, and *ones* to ask about and describe prices

[CD 1, Track 22]

Demonstratives

- Books closed. Point to Ss' things and make statements with *this* and *these* (e.g., "This is Paul's pen. This is Lily's necklace. These are David's glasses.").
- Hold some things close to show how we use *this* or *these* for nearby things. Explain that *this* refers to a singular thing, while *these* refers to plurals.
- ***Option:*** Ss place their things in a bag. Each S takes out something and says whose it is (e.g., "This is Iris's pen.").
- Place something far away to show how we use *that* and *those*. Ss point to things and make statements (e.g., "That is Hector's book. Those are Tony's keys."). Explain that *that* refers to a singular thing, while *those* refers to plural things.
- To check Ss' understanding of demonstratives and review colors, ask about things in the room (e.g., "What color is this pen? What color are those books?").

One/Ones

- Focus Ss' attention on the Conversation on page 16. Ask Ss to find examples of *one* and *ones*.
- For each example, ask: "What noun does *one* replace?" (Answers: the light blue sweater or the green sweater) Elicit the rule: *One* replaces a singular noun. Note that *ones* replaces a plural noun.
- Play the first part of the audio program.

TIP
To raise awareness of both the meaning and form of a new structure, always link the Grammar Focus to the Conversation.

Saying prices

- Play the rest of the audio program. Ss repeat the prices. Present additional examples as needed.

For practice in listening for prices, play ***Bingo*** using prices instead of words – download it from the website.

A

- Model the first line of the first conversation.
- Ss complete the task individually. Go over answers with the class.

Answers

1. A: Excuse me. How much are **those** jeans?
   B: Which **ones**? Do you mean **these**?
   A: No, the light blue **ones**.
   B: Oh, **those** are $59.95.
   A: Wow! That's expensive.
2. A: How much is **that** backpack?
   B: Which **one**?
   A: The orange **one**.
   B: It's $36.99. But **this** green **one** is only $22.25.
   A: That's not bad. Can I see it, please?

- Ss practice the conversations in pairs.
- ***Option:*** Bring in two different pairs of sunglasses, pens, necklaces, or hats. Then Ss practice the conversations again using these things.

B *Pair work*

- Explain the task. Ss work in pairs to choose prices for the boots, baseball caps, and sunglasses.
- Model the example conversation with a S. Point out the useful expressions box. Elicit or explain the meaning of the words *cheap, reasonable, not bad,* and *expensive*. Elicit prices of sneakers to use as examples of each word. Then Ss take turns asking and answering questions about the items. Go around the class to check for the use of demonstratives and *one* or *ones*.
- ***Option:*** If you live in an English-speaking environment, have Ss go to a store to ask the prices of three things in English.
- ***Option:*** Bring in clothing catalogs. Ss use them to practice the conversations.

! For a new way to practice this conversation, try the ***Substitution Dialog*** – download it from the website.

3 GRAMMAR FOCUS

Demonstratives; *one, ones*

How much is	**this** T-shirt?	**that** T-shirt?	Which **one**?	
	this one?	**that one**?	The blue **one**.	**It's** $28.99.
How much are	**these** sneakers?	**those** sneakers	Which **ones**?	
	these?	**those**?	The gray **ones**.	**They're** $40.

saying prices

99¢ = ninety-nine cents

$28 = twenty-eight dollars

$28.99 = twenty-eight ninety-nine

GRAMMAR PLUS *see page 134*

A Complete these conversations. Then practice with a partner.

A: Excuse me. How much are ___those___ jeans?
B: Which ________? Do you mean ________?
A: No, the light blue ________.
B: Oh, ________ are $59.95.
A: Wow! That's expensive!

A: How much is ________ backpack?
B: Which ________?
A: The orange ________.
B: It's $36.99. But ________ green ________ is only $22.25.
A: That's not bad. Can I see it, please?

B **PAIR WORK** Add prices to the items. Then ask and answer questions.

A: How much are these boots?
B: Which ones?
A: The brown ones.
B: They're $95.50.
A: That's expensive!

useful expressions

That's cheap.
That's reasonable.
That's OK/not bad.
That's expensive.

4 PRONUNCIATION Sentence stress

A Listen and practice. Notice that the important words in a sentence have more stress.

● •	• ● •	• • ● •	• • • ●
Let's see . . .	Excuse me.	That's expensive.	Do you mean these?
	I'll take it.	Can I help you?	

B **PAIR WORK** Practice the conversations in Exercise 3, part B again. Pay attention to the sentence stress.

5 ROLE PLAY Can I help you?

A **PAIR WORK** Put items "for sale" on your desk, such as notebooks, watches, phones, or bags.

Student A: You are a salesclerk. Answer the customer's questions.

Student B: You are a customer. Ask the price of each item. Say if you want to buy it.

A: Can I help you?
B: Yes. I like this pen. How much is it?
A: Which one?

B Change roles and try the role play again.

6 LISTENING Wow! It's expensive!

A Listen to two friends shopping. Write the color and price for each item.

	1. tablet	2. headphones	3. sunglasses	4. T-shirt
color				
price				
Do they buy it?	☐ Yes ☐ No	☐ Yes ☐ No	☐ Yes ☐ No	☐ Yes ☐ No

B Listen again. Do they buy the items? Check (✓) Yes or No.

7 INTERCHANGE 3 Flea market

See what kinds of deals you can make as a buyer and a seller. Go to Interchange 3 on pages 116–117.

4 PRONUNCIATION

Learning Objective: sound more natural by using correct sentence stress

A ***[CD 1, Track 23]***

- Remind Ss that in each word, one syllable has more stress. Explain that important words in a sentence also have more stress.
- Read the examples, clapping on the stressed words.
- Play the audio program. Ss clap on each stressed word.
- Play the audio program again. Pause for Ss to repeat the sentences, stressing important words.

B ***Pair work***

- Ss practice the conversations in part A of Exercise 3 again. Correct Ss' use of sentence stress as needed.

5 ROLE PLAY

Learning Objective: ask about prices of items for sale

A ***Pair work***

- Place several items of different colors on your desk. Use things such as notebooks, watches, phones, or bags.
- Model the task with a S.
- Ss work in pairs. Tell Ss to ask about the price of more than one item.

B

- Ss change roles and try the role play again.

6 LISTENING

Learning Objective: listen for details in conversations about shopping

A ***[CD 1, Track 24]***

- Set the scene. Two people are shopping. They want to know the prices of four things.
- Play the audio program. Ss listen and complete the *color* and *price* rows in their books.

Audio script

1.
Woman Look at this! It's really awesome – and it's purple!
Man It's nice. But you have a tablet. How much is it?
Woman Let's see . . . Wow, it's expensive! It's $499. I guess I don't really *need* it. Let's go.
2.
Man Here are some great headphones for you!
Woman Which ones? Those white ones?
Man No, these. The blue ones.
Woman Oh, these are nice. Are they expensive?
Man Not really. They're only $9.95.
Woman That's reasonable. I think I'll get them.
3.
Man What do you think of these sunglasses?
Woman They're . . . interesting. How much are they?
Man They're only $11.50. That's cheap.
Woman Try them on. They look great! Green is a good color on you.
Man OK. I'll get them.
4.
Woman I love these T-shirts! Do you like them?
Man Yeah, I do. Why don't you get one?
Woman Hmm, they're pretty expensive. I only have $20.
Man Hey! These T-shirts aren't bad. They're only $12.
Woman Oh, those are nice, too.
Man So, what color? How about this red and yellow one? Do you like it?
Woman Not really. Hey, *all* these shirts are red and yellow. I think that's why they're on sale.
Man So do you want one?
Woman No, let's go. I'm hungry. It's time for lunch.

Answers

	1. tablet	2. headphones	3. sunglasses	4. T-shirt
color	purple	blue	green	red and yellow
price	$499	$9.95	$11.50	$12
Do they buy it?	No	Yes	Yes	No

B ***[CD 1, Track 25]***

- Play the audio program again. Ss listen to find out if the people buy the things.
- Go over answers with the class.

7 INTERCHANGE 3

See pages T-116 and T-117 for teaching notes.

End of Cycle 1

See the Supplementary Resources chart at the beginning of this unit for additional teaching materials and student activities related to this Cycle.

8 WORD POWER

Learning Objective: identify common clothing items and materials

A

- If possible, bring in one thing made of each material: cotton, rubber, gold, silk, leather, silver, plastic, and wool. Write the names of the materials on cards. Put the items on your desk with the cards next to them.
- Say the word for each material. Ss repeat the word.
- Explain the task. Ss work individually to complete the exercise. Go around the class and give help. Make sure that Ss do not add *-s* to the adjectives (e.g., NOT *wools socks, rubbers boots*).
- Go over answers with the class.

Answers

1. a **silk** tie
2. a **gold** bracelet
3. a **silver** ring
4. a **cotton** shirt
5. a **leather** belt
6. **plastic** earrings
7. **rubber** flip-flops
8. **wool** socks

B *Pair work*

- Write the names of the eight things in part A across the top of the board. Ask the question in the book.
- Ask different Ss to write possible materials below each thing on the board. For example, under *socks* they can write *wool, cotton,* or *silk.*

TIP
Ss usually forget about 80 percent of new words after 24 hours. To help them remember more, recycle or review new vocabulary the next class.

C *Class activity*

- Model the sentence for the class.
- Ss make as many statements as possible. Point out that they can use other patterns (e.g., "I'm wearing . . .").
- ***Option:*** Ss write four sentences about what they have or what they're wearing on a piece of paper. Collect the papers and read the sentences aloud. Then Ss guess who wrote the sentences.
- ***Option:*** Use the materials word cards. Ask Ss to place the cards next to other items in the classroom made of these materials.

For more practice with vocabulary for materials, play ***Change Chairs*** – download it from the website. Give the first command: "Change chairs if you have a leather jacket."

9 CONVERSATION

Learning Objective: use comparisons with adjectives in a conversation about preferences

A *[CD 1, Track 26]*

- Elicit ideas and vocabulary based on the picture.
- Set the scene. Alex and Kristin are shopping. Ask Ss to listen for answers to these focus questions:
  1. *What are they shopping for?*
  2. *Which dress does Alex prefer?*
  3. *Does Alex buy the dress?*
- Books closed. Play the audio program. Then check answers to the focus questions. (Answers: 1. dresses 2. the one with lighter material 3. no)
- Books open. Play the audio program again. Ss listen and read along silently. Elicit or explain any new vocabulary.
- Ss practice the conversation in pairs.

For a new way to teach this Conversation, try ***Say It with Feeling!*** – download it from the website.

B *[CD 1, Track 27]*

- Read the two focus questions aloud. Then play the audio program. Elicit answers from the class.

Audio script

Alex Wow! That dress is really expensive. I don't want to spend that much money.
Kristin Oh, look. There are some things on sale over there.
Alex Oh, you're right. These dresses are really nice. And they're cheap! I like this one. Is it silk?
Kristin Let's see . . . Yes, it is. It's perfect for the wedding.
Alex Great! I'll take it.

Answers

She buys a silk dress. Kristin likes it.

8 WORD POWER Materials

A What are these things made of? Label each one. Use the words from the list.

cotton gold leather plastic rubber silk silver wool

1. a ___silk___ tie

2. a ________ bracelet

3. a ________ ring

4. a ________ shirt

5. a ________ belt

6. ________ earrings

7. ________ flip-flops

8. ________ socks

B **PAIR WORK** What other materials are the things in part A sometimes made of? Make a list.

C **CLASS ACTIVITY** Which materials can you find in your classroom?
"Min-hee has gold earrings, and Ray has a leather jacket."

9 CONVERSATION That's a good point.

A Listen and practice.

Alex: I love these dresses! They are perfect for the wedding on Saturday.

Kristin: Yes! I like this black cotton one.

Alex: The black one? Why?

Kristin: It's more stylish for a wedding.

Alex: That's true, but it's the middle of summer. The material of this one is lighter.

Kristin: That's a good point. The wedding is in the afternoon.

Alex: Hmm . . . there's no price tag. Excuse me. How much is this dress?

Clerk: It's $400. Would you like to try it on?

Alex: Oh, no. That's OK. Thanks anyway.

Clerk: You're welcome.

B Listen to the rest of the conversation. What does Alex buy? What does Kristin think of it?

10 GRAMMAR FOCUS

Preferences; comparisons with adjectives

Which dress do you **prefer**?
I **prefer** the blue one. — It's **nicer than** the black one.
Which one do you **like more**?
I **like** the blue one **more**. — It's **lighter than** the black one.
Which one do you **like better**?
I **like** the black one **better**. — It's **more stylish than** the blue one.

Spelling
cheap ⟶ cheap**er**
nice ⟶ nice**r**
big ⟶ big**ger**
pretty ⟶ prett**ier**

GRAMMAR PLUS *see page 134*

A Complete these conversations. Then practice with a partner.

1. **A:** Which of these jackets do you like more?
   B: I prefer the leather one. The design is __________ (nice), and it looks __________ (expensive) the wool one.

2. **A:** These sweaters are nice. Which one do you prefer?
   B: I like the gray one better. The color is __________ (pretty). It's __________ (attractive) the brown and orange one.

3. **A:** Which rings do you like better?
   B: I like the silver ones more. They're __________ (small) the gold ones. And they're __________ (cheap).

B **PAIR WORK** Compare the things in part A. Give your own opinions.

A: Which jacket do you like more?
B: I like the wool one better. The color is prettier.

useful expressions

The color is prettier.
The design is nicer.
The style is more attractive.
The material is better.

11 WRITING My favorite clothes

A What do you like to wear? Write about your favorite clothes and compare them to clothes you don't like as much.

My favorite clothes are cotton T-shirts and jeans. T-shirts are more comfortable than shirts and ties, and I think jeans are nicer than pants. I know that suits are more stylish, but . . .

B **GROUP WORK** Take turns reading your descriptions. Ask questions to get more information.

10 GRAMMAR FOCUS

Learning Objective: use adjectives to state preferences and make comparisons

[CD 1, Track 28]

Preferences

- Bring some items to class that are similar (e.g., two rings, two hats, two pens, two T-shirts).
- Focus Ss' attention on the Conversation on page 19. Ask: "Which dresses do Alex and Kristin prefer? Why?" Write the answers on the board and underline the words *likes* and *better*:

  Kristin likes the black one better. It looks more stylish.
  Alex likes the other one better. The material is lighter than the black one.

- Point out that *like better* means *prefer*.
- Hold up two similar items (e.g., two hats). Ask two or three Ss: "Which one do you prefer?" Elicit the response: "I prefer . . ." or "I like . . . better." Repeat with other pairs of items.
- ***Option:*** Use two pairs of similar items to review *ones*.

Comparisons with adjectives

- Underline *more stylish* and *lighter* in the sentences on the board. Then draw two columns on the board, like this:

1	2
lighter	more expensive
nicer	more stylish
prettier	more beautiful

TIP
To help Ss see the differences in grammar forms, use different colors on the board.

- Point out that column 1 has two one-syllable adjectives (*light, nice*) and one two-syllable adjective that ends in *-y* (*pretty*). The comparative forms of these adjectives end in *-er*.
- Point out that column 2 has adjectives of two or more syllables (e.g., *expensive*). The comparative forms of these start with *more*.
- Elicit more comparative adjectives for both columns. Ask different Ss to write them on the board.
- Point out the spelling rules in the Grammar Focus box. A final *-y* changes to *-i* when we add *-er* (*pretti**er***), and a single vowel + consonant doubles the consonant (*bi**gger***).
- Present the irregular forms: *good – better* and *bad – worse*. Then play the audio program.
- Hold up two items again. Ask: "Which . . . do you prefer? Why do you prefer it/them?" Elicit answers.
- ***Option:*** Ask Ss to look back over previous units to find more adjectives. (See pages 7 and 16.) Elicit the comparative forms and ask different Ss to write them in column 1 or 2.

A

- Explain the task. Remind Ss to look at the pictures when answering.
- Ss complete the task individually. Then go over answers with the class.

Answers

1. A: Which of these jackets do you like more?
   B: I prefer the leather one. The design is **nicer**, and it looks **more expensive than** the wool one.
2. A: These sweaters are nice. Which one do you prefer?
   B: I like the gray one better. The color is **prettier**. It's **more attractive than** the brown and orange one.
3. A: Which rings do you like better?
   B: I like the silver ones more. They're **smaller than** the gold ones. And they're **cheaper**.

- Ss practice the conversations in pairs.

B *Pair work*

- Focus Ss' attention on the pictures in part A. Model the conversation with a S. Go over the useful expressions.
- Ss work in pairs. They talk about the items, giving their opinions.

For more practice making comparative forms, play ***Tic-Tac-Toe*** – download it from the website.

11 WRITING

Learning Objective: write a paragraph about favorite clothes

A

- Have Ss read the questions and sample paragraph. Allow three minutes.
- Ask: "What are the writer's favorite clothes? What clothes doesn't the writer like so much?" (Answers: cotton T-shirts and jeans; shirts and ties, pants, suits.)
- Have Ss list their favorite clothes and adjectives that describe the clothes or why they like them. Then Ss list the clothes they don't like as much and the reasons.
- Ss work individually. They write a paragraph comparing their favorite clothes and the clothes they don't like.

B

- Ss work in small groups. They read each other's paragraphs and ask questions.

12 READING

Learning Objectives: skim for main ideas; read for specific information in an article about online shopping

TIP
To help Ss understand what reading strategy to use, focus their attention on the purpose of the task. For example: "Today we're going to practice skimming a text to find the main points."

A

- Set the scene. Ask: "How often do you go shopping? Do you shop online? What kind of things do you buy on the Internet?"
- Explain that this article is about unusual things people can buy online.
- ***Option:*** If Ss have access to the Internet, tell them to look at shopping or online auction websites to look for odd and unusual things for sale. If Ss have smartphones, they can look on shopping apps.
- Go over the task. Elicit some reasons from the class. Then they skim the text quickly to check their reasons.
- Elicit or explain any new vocabulary.

Vocabulary
crazy: strange
extraordinary: unusual or out of the ordinary
online: using the Internet
land: the surface of a planet
certificate: an official document
place a bid: compete against other people to buy something by offering a specific amount of money
pet rock: a small rock used as a humorous "pet" in place of living animals or plants in the 1970s

B

- Explain the task. Ss read the article. Ss then answer the questions individually.
- ***Option:*** Ss work in pairs. One S answers questions a and b, while the other S answers questions c and d. Then they share their answers.
- Ss compare answers in pairs or small groups.

Answers

a. sneakers, paragraph 3
b. digital pet rock, paragraph 4
c. someone to stand in line, paragraph 2
d. a piece of land on the moon, paragraph 1

C *Group Work*

- Explain the task. Read the first sentence. Ask the class where they can find information about pet rocks in the article. (Answer: paragraph 4) Read the remaining questions.
- Ss work in small groups to discuss the questions. Go around the class and give help as needed.
- Have groups share their discussions with the class.

End of Cycle 2

See the Supplementary Resources chart at the beginning of this unit for additional teaching materials and student activities related to this Cycle.

12 READING

A Skim the article. Why do you think people shop online?

Home Posts Archives

ONLINE SHOPPING: The Crazy Things People Buy

In this week's blog, we look at some extraordinary things people can buy online.

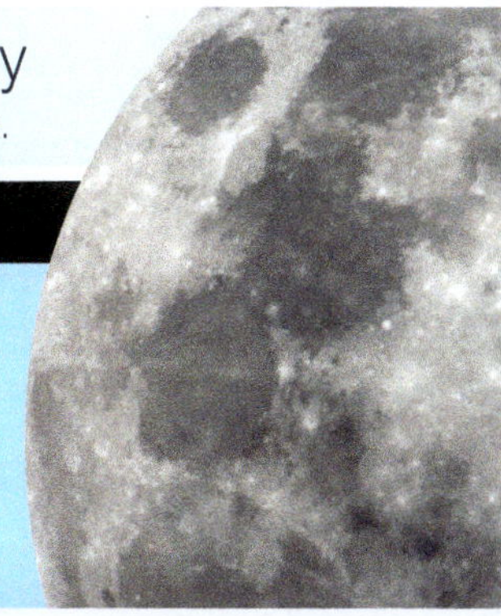

1 A PIECE OF THE MOON: $27.50

It's true. You can own a piece of land on the moon. An acre, or about 4,000 square meters, of moon costs $27.50. That's a lot of space for your stuff. In fact, the price of each acre goes down when you buy more land. Imagine what you could do with all that space . . . if you could travel there! But don't worry, you get a certificate that says the land is yours.

2 SOMEONE TO STAND IN LINE FOR YOU: $25 AN HOUR

No one likes to stand in line, right? Now you don't have to! For $25 an hour, someone waits patiently in line to get the stuff you need. Imagine that! Some people pay for someone to stand in line for movie tickets or for a new video game that's on sale. Make a reservation online in just a few clicks.

3 SOME VERY EXPENSIVE SNEAKERS: $20,000 AND UP

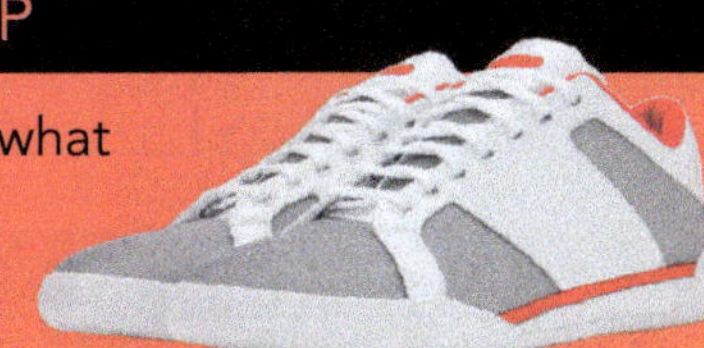

Do you ever think your shoes are boring? Well, our sneakers are just what you need. Just go to our online store, look for a pair of sneakers you like, and place a bid. Maybe you'll win! Some of the sneakers are from famous basketball players.

4 NO TIME FOR A REAL PET: $12

Many people like dogs and cats, but they just don't have the time to take care of them. If that sounds like you, here's the answer to your problem: a digital pet rock. It's clean, it's quiet, and it doesn't need food. It comes in a box. We think it's just about the perfect pet. You plug it into your laptop, and it's always with you!

B Read the blog. Find the item and write its name. Then write the number of the paragraph where you find the answers.

Find something . . .

a. . . . that you can wear. ______

b. . . . that you use with your laptop. ______

c. . . . that saves you a lot of time. ______

d. . . . that is huge. ______

C **GROUP WORK** The person who invented the first pet rock, Gary Dahl, became a millionaire. Why do you think people bought pet rocks? Do you think Mr. Dahl was a smart man? Would you buy a pet rock? Would you buy any of the other things? How much would you spend? Tell your classmates.

Unit 4 Supplementary Resources Overview

	After the following SB exercises	You can use these materials in class	Your students can use these materials outside the classroom
CYCLE 1	**1 Snapshot**		
	2 Word Power	**TR** Unit 4 Extra Worksheet	**DW** Unit 4 Vocabulary 1–2
	3 Conversation		
	4 Grammar Focus		**SB** Unit 4 Grammar plus, Focus 1 **DW** Unit 4 Grammar 1, 3–5
	5 Pronunciation		
	6 Speaking	**TR** Unit 4 Vocabulary Worksheet **TR** Unit 4 Writing Worksheet	
	7 Listening		**WB** Unit 4 exercises 1–6
CYCLE 2	**8 Conversation**	**TR** Unit 4 Listening Worksheet	
	9 Grammar Focus	**TR** Unit 4 Grammar Worksheet	**SB** Unit 4 Grammar plus, Focus 2 **DW** Unit 4 Grammar 2, 6–8
	10 Writing		
	11 Interchange 4		
	12 Reading	**TR** Unit 4 Project Worksheet **VID** Unit 4 **VRB** Unit 4	**DW** Unit 4 Reading 1–2 **DW** Unit 4 Listening 1–2 **DW** Unit 4 Video 1–2 **WB** Unit 4 exercises 7–12

With or instead of the following SB section	You can also use these materials for assessment
Units 3–4 Progress Check	**TESTING PROGRAM** Units 3–4 Oral Quiz **TESTING PROGRAM** Units 3–4 Written Quiz

Key **SB:** Student's Book **DW:** Digital Workbook **TR:** Teacher's Resources
VID: Video (DW/TR) **VRB:** Video Resource Book (TR) **WB:** Print Workbook

My Plan for Unit 4

Use the space below to customize a plan that fits your needs.

With the following SB exercises	I am using these materials in class	My students are using these materials outside the classroom

With or instead of the following SB section	I am using these materials for assessment

4 Do you play the guitar?

- Discuss entertainment likes and dislikes
- Make, accept, and decline invitations

1 SNAPSHOT

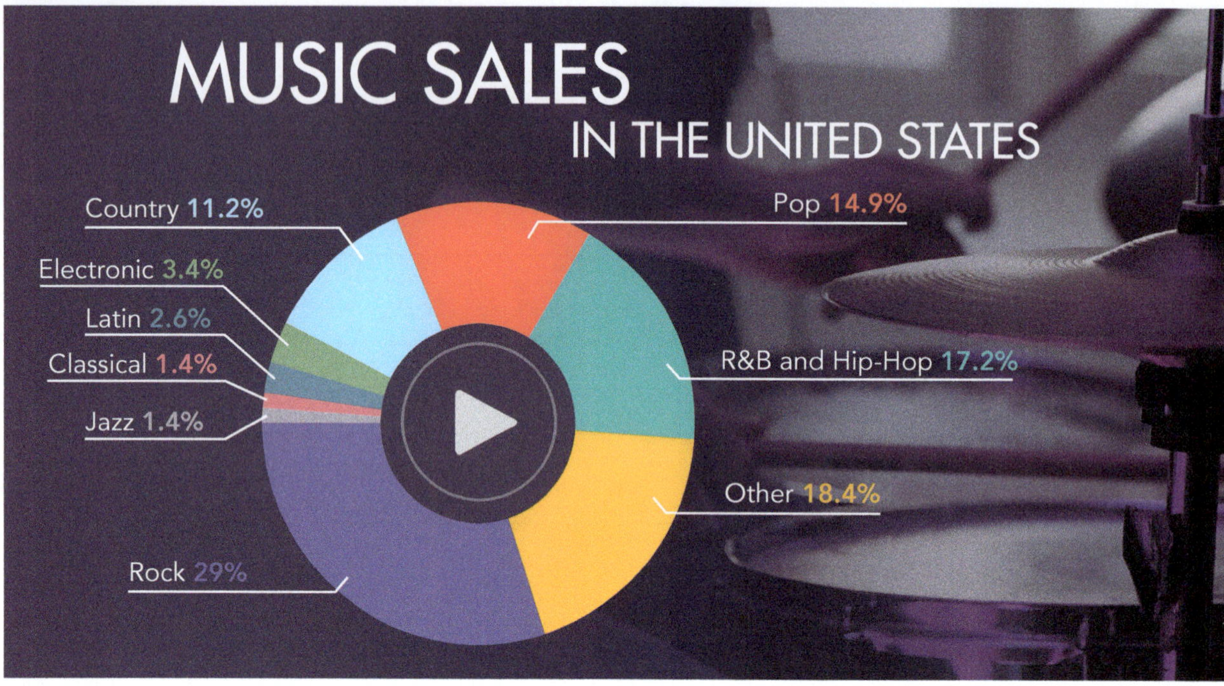

What styles of music do you like? What styles do you dislike?
What styles of music are popular in your country?

2 WORD POWER That's entertainment!

A Complete the word map with words from the list. Some words can go in more than one category.

action	reality show
electronic	reggae
game show	salsa
horror	science fiction
musical	soap opera
rap	talk show

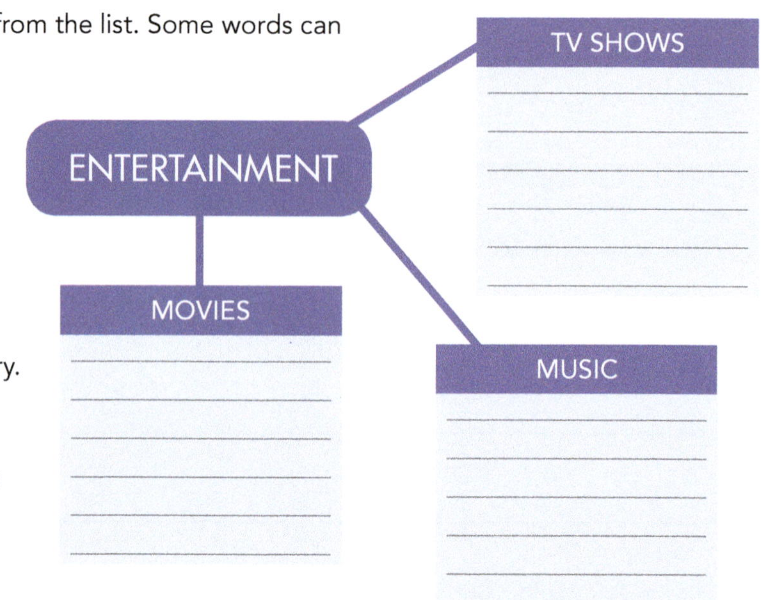

B Add two more words to each category. Then compare with a partner.

C **GROUP WORK** Number the items in each list from 1 (you like it the most) to 6 (you like it the least). Then compare your ideas.

4 Do you play the guitar?

Cycle 1, Exercises 1–7

In Unit 4, students discuss entertainment likes and dislikes and make, accept, and decline invitations. By the end of Cycle 1, students will be able to discuss entertainment likes and dislikes using yes/no and Wh-questions with *do*. By the end of Cycle 2, students will be able to make, accept, and decline invitations using *would* and verb + *to* + verb.

1 SNAPSHOT

Learning Objective: discuss popular types of music

- Books closed. Ask: "What kind of music is popular in your country?" Help with vocabulary as needed. Write answers on the board.
- Books open. Point out the percentage signs. Ask: "What is this symbol called? What does this chart show?" (Answers: percent; music sales in the U.S.)
- Read out the names of the music styles. Ask: "What kind of music is popular in the U.S.? What music is unpopular? Does anything surprise you about the information?" Elicit answers.
- Elicit or explain any new vocabulary.

Vocabulary

R&B: rhythm and blues
hip-hop: music of African American origin, with rhyming words and a strong beat
country: music from the southern and western U.S.
electronic: music created by electric instruments and computers
Latin: music from any Spanish-speaking area (e.g., Latin America and Spain)
jazz: music of African American origin, with a strong rhythm

- Brainstorm with Ss what the "other" category might include (e.g., *reggae, salsa*).
- Go over the discussion questions. Ss discuss them in small groups. Then elicit answers from the class.
- ***Option:*** What kind of music does the class like best? Take a poll.

2 WORD POWER

Learning Objective: categorize types of movies, TV shows, and music

A

- Explain the task. Ss work in pairs or small groups. Allow them to use dictionaries. Remind Ss that some words can go in more than one category.
- Draw the word map on the board. Ask different Ss to write the answers on the board. Model the pronunciation of the words as you check answers.

B

- Ss add two more words to each category. Then they compare answers in pairs.
- Ask different Ss to write their new words on the board. Go over their answers and model the pronunciation.

Answers

TV shows	Movies	Music
game show	action	electronic
reality show	horror	rap
soap opera	musical	reggae
talk show	science fiction	salsa
cartoon	*adventure*	*classical*
documentary	*animation*	*hip-hop*
news	*comedy*	*jazz*
sitcom	*drama*	*opera*
sports event	*western*	*pop*

(Note: *Additional examples are italicized.*)

- ***Option:*** To help Ss remember the words in the categories, add names of popular TV shows, movies, and songs or musicians.

C *Group work*

- Explain the task. Ss work individually to rank their items from 1 to 6.
- ***Option:*** Review language for preferences from Unit 3.
- Ss compare their ideas in small groups.

3 CONVERSATION

Learning Objective: use yes/no and Wh-questions with *do* in a conversation about entertainment likes and dislikes

A ***[CD 1, Track 29]***

- Set the scene. Seth and Leanne are talking about music. Ask: "Who do you see in the pictures?" (Answers: Taylor Swift, Drake)
- Books closed. Write these statements on the board:

  1. I can't wait for the Taylor Swift concert this Friday!
  2. I guess I don't listen to pop music a lot.
  3. I really like hip-hop.
  4. Drake is my favorite musician.

- Ask: "Who says these things – Seth or Leanne?" Play the audio program and Ss listen for the answers. Then elicit the answers. (Answers: 1. Leanne 2. Seth 3. Seth 4. Seth)
- Point out the expressions *I guess I don't listen to . . .*, *I really like . . .*, and *. . . is my favorite*. Ask: "What do you think of Taylor Swift? Drake?"
- Books open. Play the audio program again. Ss listen and read silently.
- Ask these comprehension questions: "What kind of music does Seth like? What does he think of pop music?" Elicit Ss' answers. (Answers: Hip-hop. He doesn't listen to it.)
- Ss practice the conversation in pairs. Go around the class and give help as needed.

! For a new way to practice this conversation, try ***Say It with Feeling!*** – download it from the website.

B ***[CD 1, Track 30]***

- Read the focus questions aloud. Play the audio program once or twice.
- Ss compare answers in small groups. Go over answers with the class.

Audio script

Leanne	What about bands, Seth? Who do you like?
Seth	Well, they're not new, but my favorite band of all time is Maroon 5.
Leanne	Maroon 5? Really?
Seth	Why? Don't you like them? They're classic!
Leanne	No, I don't. I guess they have some good songs, but they're very . . . noisy.

Answers

His favorite band is Maroon 5. No, because she thinks their music is very noisy.

4 GRAMMAR FOCUS

Learning Objective: ask and answer yes/no and Wh-questions with *do* to discuss entertainment likes and dislikes

[CD 1, Track 31]

Yes/No and Wh-questions with do

- Ask Ss to find three questions with *do* or *does* in the Conversation in Exercise 3. Write the questions on the board, in columns:

1	2	3	4	5
	Does	she	play	the violin?
What kind of . . .	do	you	like?	
	Doesn't	Drake	play	the guitar?

- Focus Ss' attention on the questions on the board. Elicit the rule for forming questions with *do*:

  Wh-question + *do/does* + subject + verb?

- Elicit new questions from Ss and write them in the columns on the board.
- Point out the language in the Grammar Focus box. Play the audio program for the first and second columns.

Object pronouns

- Go over the object pronouns in the Grammar Focus box. Play the audio program for the third column.
- Ask Ss to find and circle the example of an object pronoun in the Conversation in Exercise 3. (Answer: her) Ask: "What does *her* refer to?" (Answer: Taylor Swift)
- Explain the task. Model the first answer.
- Ss complete the task individually. Then Ss compare answers with a partner. Go over the answers with the class.

Answers

1. A: I like Alabama Shakes a lot. **Do** you know **them**?
   B: Yes, I **do**, and I love this song. Let's download **it**.
2. A: **Do** you like science fiction movies?
   B: Yes, I **do**. I like **them** very much.
3. A: **Do** Vinnie and Midori like soap operas?
   B: Vinnie **does**, but Midori **doesn't**. She hates **them**.
4. A: What kind of music **does** Maya like?
   B: Classical music. She loves Yo-Yo Ma.
   A: Yeah, he's amazing. I like **him** a lot.

- Ss practice the conversations in pairs.

3 CONVERSATION What kind of music do you like?

A Listen and practice.

LEANNE I can't wait for the Taylor Swift concert this Friday!

SETH I think I know her. Does she play the violin?

LEANNE No. She's a pop star.

SETH Of course! I guess I don't listen to pop music a lot.

LEANNE Oh, really? What kind of music do you like?

SETH I really like hip-hop. Drake is my favorite musician.

LEANNE Doesn't Drake play the guitar?

SETH No, Leanne. He sings and raps.

LEANNE OK. Well, I think we need to teach each other about music!

B Listen to the rest of the conversation. Who is Seth's favorite band? Does Leanne like them?

4 GRAMMAR FOCUS

Simple present questions; short answers

Do you **like** country music?
Yes, I **do**. I love it.
No, I **don't**. I don't like it very much.

Does she **play** the piano?
Yes, she **does**. She plays very well.
No, she **doesn't**. She doesn't play an instrument.

Do they **like** Imagine Dragons?
Yes, they **do**. They like them a lot.
No, they **don't**. They don't like them at all.

What kind of music **do** you **like**?
I really like rap.

What does she **play**?
She plays the guitar.

Who do they **like**?
They like Maroon 5.

Object pronouns
me
you
him
her
it
us
them

GRAMMAR PLUS see page 135

Complete these conversations. Then practice with a partner.

1. **A:** I like Alabama Shakes a lot. __________ you know __________?
   B: Yes, I __________, and I love this song. Let's download __________.
2. **A:** __________ you like science fiction movies?
   B: Yes, I __________. I like __________ very much.
3. **A:** ______________ Vinnie and Midori like soap operas?
   B: Vinnie __________, but Midori __________. She hates __________.
4. **A:** What kind of music __________ Maya like?
   B: Classical music. She loves Yo-Yo Ma.
   A: Yeah, he's amazing. I like __________ a lot.

Alabama Shakes

5 PRONUNCIATION Intonation in questions

A Listen and practice. Yes/No questions usually have rising intonation. Wh-questions usually have falling intonation.

Do you like pop music? What kind of music do you like?

B **PAIR WORK** Practice these questions.

Do you like TV?	What shows do you like?
Do you like video games?	What games do you like?
Do you play a musical instrument?	What instrument do you play?

6 SPEAKING Entertainment survey

A **GROUP WORK** Write five questions about entertainment and entertainers. Then ask and answer your questions in groups.

What kinds of . . . do you like?
(music, TV shows, video games)
Do you like . . . ?
(reggae, game shows, action movies)
Who's your favorite . . . ?
(singer, actor, athlete)

B **GROUP WORK** Complete this information about your group. Ask any additional questions.

Our group FAVORITES

What's your favorite kind of . . . ?

music ______
movie ______
TV show ______

What's your favorite . . . ?

song ______
movie ______
video game ______

Who's your favorite . . . ?

singer ______
actor ______
athlete ______

Adele

Steph Curry

Star Wars: The Force Awakens

Top Chef

C **CLASS ACTIVITY** Read your group's list to the class. Find out the class favorites.

5 PRONUNCIATION

Learning Objective: sound more natural by using intonation when asking questions

A *[CD 1, Track 32]*

- Books closed. Use your voice and gestures to demonstrate intonation. Explain that intonation is the rise and fall of the voice.
- Play the audio program. After each question, ask: "Is the voice going up or down?"
- Elicit or explain the rule: Yes/no questions have rising intonation, and Wh-questions have falling intonation.
- Books open. Play the audio program again. Ss repeat the questions. Ask different Ss to read the questions and check their intonation.

TIP
If Ss repeat things as a group, it's hard to hear if they're using correct pronunciation or intonation. Therefore, check some individual Ss' pronunciation.

B ***Pair work***

- Explain the task. Model the questions using correct intonation.
- Ss work in pairs. Go around the class and check individual Ss' use of intonation.
- ***Option:*** Ss look back at the Conversation in Exercise 3 on page 23 and mark (with arrows) rising or falling intonation above the questions. Ss then practice the conversation again in pairs, paying special attention to intonation.

6 SPEAKING

Learning Objective: discuss entertainment likes and dislikes

A ***Group work***

- Write two example questions on the board, e.g.:

  Do you like TV?
  What kind of TV shows do you like?
- Ask different Ss to answer the questions.
- Explain the task. Ss work individually to write five questions. Go around the class and give help as needed.
- Ss take turns asking their questions in small groups. Set a time limit of five to seven minutes. Remind students to pay attention to intonation.
- Go around the class and listen to Ss' responses.
- ***Option:*** Encourage Ss to give longer responses (e.g., *No, I don't, but I love . . . , I'm a big fan of . . . , I prefer . . .*).

B ***Group work***

- Ss work in small groups. One S leads the discussion to make sure everybody speaks (e.g., *What's your favorite . . . ? What about you, . . . ? What do you think, . . . ? It's your turn to ask a question.*). Another S records the answers.
- The S who recorded the answers reads the responses, and the group decides the favorites. Then the Ss complete their charts.

TIP
Assigning each S in the group a role (e.g., *note-taker, leader, English monitor, reporter*) encourages all Ss to participate.

C ***Class activity***

- Write these expressions on the board:

  Our favorite . . . is . . .
  We all like . . .
  We don't agree on . . .
- Explain that Ss can use these expressions to report their group's favorites.
- One S from each group reports the results to the class. Another S from each group writes the results on the board.
- Discuss the favorites as a class.

! For more practice with yes/no questions, play ***Twenty Questions*** – download it from the website.

7 LISTENING

Learning Objective: listen for details about people's likes and dislikes

A *[CD 1, Track 33]*

- Set the scene. Alexis is on a game show. She is going to interview three men. The audience will choose one for a date.
- Play the audio program. Ss complete the chart.

TIP
If an audio program is long and contains many details, break it into parts. Pause the audio program after each part.

- Ss compare answers in pairs.

Audio script

Host [*applause*] Welcome to *The Perfect Date*, the show where we help people find their perfect date! Today, we're going to help Alexis. I'm going to introduce her to Jacob in Miami, Tyler in Chicago, and Andrew in Los Angeles. They're all waiting for her right now on video chat. Right, guys?
Jacob, Tyler, and Andrew Right!
Host So, Alexis, are *you* ready?
Alexis Yes, I'm ready.
Host Then go ahead!
Alexis OK. My first question is about music. Jacob, what kind of music do you like?
Jacob Oh, classical music.
Alexis Classical. OK. And how about you, Tyler?
Tyler Well, I like jazz.
Alexis And you, Andrew?
Andrew My favorite music is rock.
Host How about you, Alexis?
Alexis Well, I like pop music. I don't like jazz or classical music very much.
Host Hmm. The guys aren't doing very well, yet. Try another question, Alexis.
Alexis OK. Next I'll ask about movies. Jacob, what kind of movies do you like?
Jacob I like action movies.
Alexis And how about you, Tyler?
Tyler Oh, I like musicals.
Alexis And how about you, Andrew?
Andrew I love horror movies.
Host And what about you, Alexis?
Alexis I really like horror movies, too. [*applause*]
Host That's better! We have time for another question. Go ahead!
Alexis OK. Jacob, what kind of TV shows do you like?
Jacob Well, I like to watch reality shows.
Alexis Tyler?
Tyler Uh, well, you know, I really like talk shows.
Alexis And, Andrew, how about you?
Andrew I like game shows a lot.
Host So, Alexis, what do you like?
Alexis Well, I like talk shows and game shows.
Host OK! Time is up! Now, who's the perfect date for Alexis? Go to perfectdate.cambridge.org to choose, or text us at the number on your screen.

Answers

	Jacob	Tyler	Andrew	Alexis
Music	classical	jazz	rock	pop
Movies	action	musicals	horror	horror
TV shows	reality shows	talk shows	game shows	talk and game shows

B ***Class activity***

- Ss discuss the best date for Alexis as a class and give reasons for their opinions.

Possible answers

Andrew is the best date because he and Alexis like horror movies and game shows. They all disagree about music.

End of Cycle 1

See the Supplementary Resources chart at the beginning of this unit for additional teaching materials and student activities related to this Cycle.

Cycle 2, Exercises 8–12

8 CONVERSATION

Learning Objective: use *would* and verb + *to* + verb in a conversation about making, accepting, and declining invitations

A *[CD 1, Track 34]*

- Play the audio program. Ss look at the picture and read the conversation silently. Then Ss practice the conversation in pairs.

B *[CD 1, Track 35]*

- Read the focus questions aloud. Then play the audio program. Elicit answers from the class.

Audio script

Connor So, do you like the concert?
Camila Well, the Purple Lips are a little noisy. But I like The Arcades a lot. Where is your brother? I don't see him.
Connor Um . . . he's at home.
Camila What? Why?
Connor He's in bed with the flu. See, here's his text.
Camila Oh, that's too bad!
Connor I know. Would you like to go to his concert next month?

Answers

She thinks it is OK. No, he didn't play because he is in bed with the flu.

7 LISTENING The perfect date

A Listen to a host and four people on a TV game show. Three men want to invite Alexis on a date. What kinds of things do they like? Complete the chart.

	Jacob	Tyler	Andrew	Alexis
Music				
Movies				
TV shows				

B **CLASS ACTIVITY** Who do you think is the best date for Alexis? Why?

8 CONVERSATION What time does it start?

A Listen and practice.

CONNOR I have tickets to my brother's concert on Friday night. Would you like to go?

CAMILA Thanks, I'd love to. What time does it start?

CONNOR At 8:00.

CAMILA Do you want to have dinner before? Maybe at 6:00?

CONNOR Well, I'd like to, but I have to work late. Let's just meet before the concert, around 7:30.

CAMILA No problem. We can have dinner another day. Let's meet at your office and go together.

CONNOR Sounds good! See you on Friday.

B Listen to Connor and Camila talking at the concert. Does Camila like the concert? Does Connor's brother play well?

9 GRAMMAR FOCUS

Would; verb + _to_ + verb

Would you **like to go** out on Friday?
Yes, I **would**.
Yes, I'**d love to**. Thanks.

Would you **like to go** to a concert?
I'**d like to**, but I **have to work** late.
I'**d like to**, but I **need to save** money.
I'**d like to**, but I **want to visit** my parents.

Contractions
I'**d** = I would

GRAMMAR PLUS *see page 135*

A Respond to three invitations. Then write three invitations for the given responses.

1. **A:** I have tickets to the soccer game on Sunday. Would you like to go?
   B: ________________
2. **A:** Would you like to come over for dinner tomorrow night?
   B: ________________
3. **A:** Would you like to go to a hip-hop dance class with me this weekend?
   B: ________________
4. **A:** ________________
   B: Yes, I'd love to. Thank you!
5. **A:** ________________
   B: Well, I'd like to, but I have to study.
6. **A:** ________________
   B: Yes, I would. I really like electronic music.

B **PAIR WORK** Ask and answer the questions in part A. Give your own responses.

C **PAIR WORK** Think of three things you would like to do. Then invite a partner to do them with you. Your partner responds and asks follow-up questions like these:

When is it? Where is it? What time does it start? When does it end?

10 WRITING Text messages

A What do these text messages say?

text message abbreviations

u = you	afaik = as far as I know
r = are	lol = laugh out loud
2 = to / too	idk = I don't know
pls = please	msg = message
thx = thanks	nm = never mind
imo = in my opinion	brb = be right back
tbh = to be honest	ttyl = talk to you later

B **GROUP WORK** Write a "text message" to each person in your group. Then exchange messages. Write a response to each message.

11 INTERCHANGE 4 Are you free this weekend?

Make weekend plans with your classmates. Go to Interchange 4 on page 118.

9 GRAMMAR FOCUS

Learning Objective: use *would* and verb + *to* + verb to make, accept, and decline invitations

[CD 1, Track 36]

Would

- Refer Ss to the Conversation on page 25. Ask: "How does Connor invite Camila?" Write his question on the board: *Would you like to go?*
- Explain that we use *Would you like to . . . ?* for polite invitations. It is more polite than *Do you want to . . . ?*
- Ask Ss to find Camila's response. Ask: "What does she say?" Write it on the board:

  Thanks, I'd love to.
- Point out that *I'd* = *I would*. Explain that there are different ways to accept an invitation. Camila uses one. Add two more to the board:

  Yes, I would.
  Yes, I'd love to (go).
- Play the audio program for the first column in the Grammar Focus box. Ss read silently.

Verb + to + verb

- Refer Ss again to the Conversation on page 25. Camila invites Connor to have dinner at 6:00, but he doesn't accept. Ask: "What were his words?" Write them on the board:
  Well, I'd like to, but I have to work late.
- Explain that we often use the structure verb + *to* + verb when making excuses. Focus Ss' attention on the Grammar Focus box. Elicit examples.
- Play the audio program for the second and third columns.

A

- Explain the task. Questions 1–3 require an acceptance or a refusal. Questions 4–6 require an invitation.
- Ss work individually. Go around the class and check their answers. If you notice common problems, stop and go over them with the class.

B *Pair work*

- Explain the task. Ss work in pairs. They take turns asking and answering the questions.

C *Pair work*

- Explain the task. With Ss, brainstorm three things to do. Model inviting a S to do one of those things. Your S partner uses some of the follow-up questions.
- Have Ss first think of three real or imaginary things they would like to do. Then they practice inviting each other. Remind Ss to use *Would you like to . . . ?* and to include follow-up questions.

10 WRITING

Learning Objective: write and respond to text messages

A

- Point out that Ss practiced oral invitations. Now they will make text message invitations.
- Focus Ss' attention on the text message. Ask Ss to guess its meaning. (Answer: Are you busy Saturday? Do you want to go to the beach? I don't know. I have to ask my parents. I'll be right back.)
- Discuss abbreviations. Explain that people use abbreviations because there is very little space on smartphone screens. Elicit the words the text message abbreviations stand for. (Answers: R = are, u = you, 2 = to, IDK = I don't know, BRB = be right back)
- Ask the class: "Who do you write text messages to? What do you write about? Which abbreviations do you use?"

B *Group work*

- Ss work in groups of three. Ss work individually to write a message to the other two Ss in their group.
- Ss exchange messages with the other Ss in the group. They read each message and write a response (e.g., *Would u like 2 study English 2morrow? / Yes pls.*). Then they return the responses. (Note: If Ss can't think of an invitation, encourage them to look at the Grammar Focus or at the Conversation on page 25 for ideas.)
- ***Option:*** In Ss' responses, they write questions asking for more information. They continue to exchange and return responses, answering questions and asking for more information until they accept or refuse the invitations.
- ***Option:*** If Ss have smartphones, they can practice sending text messages in class or for homework.

11 INTERCHANGE 4

See page T-118 for teaching notes.

12 READING

Learning Objectives: scan a time line for details; read a biography of an entertainer; develop skills in sequencing events

- Books closed. Draw these diagrams on the board:

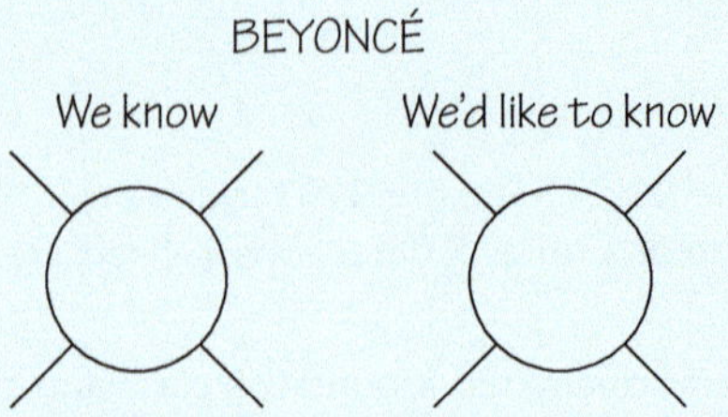

- Ss brainstorm ideas in pairs. If they have difficulty, suggest possible topics (e.g., *hit songs, age, full/real name, nationality*). Then Ss come to the board and write things they know or would like to know in the correct diagram. Don't correct Ss if they are wrong. Just correct their language.

A

- Books open. Point out that the time line shows the history of Beyoncé's life.
- Focus Ss' attention on the pictures. Ask Ss to talk about who and what they see.
- Allow Ss two minutes to scan the article quickly and find the dates for the pictures. (Answers: 2008 and 2013) Remind Ss not to read the whole article but to look quickly for key words (e.g., *Jay-Z, president*).

! For a new way to introduce this Reading, try ***Cloud Prediction*** – download it from the website.

B

- Explain the task. Focus Ss' attention on the first event on the time line. Tell Ss to find the sentence in part B that matches this event. (Answer: b)
- Elicit or explain any new vocabulary.

Vocabulary

performer: a person who sings or acts
go platinum: to sell more than a million (1,000,000) albums/records/CDs
chill out: relax
fans: people who love a celebrity
recording contract: a legal agreement between a musical performer and a recording company to sell the performer's albums
album: a collection of songs on a CD or record
Grammy Awards: a set of prizes given to people who work in the music industry
hurricane victims: people who have been in a violent storm (e.g., Hurricane Katrina in New Orleans, U.S., in 2005)
inauguration: a ceremony to celebrate a new start, such as a new job or a new building

- Ss complete the task individually. Go around the class and give help as needed.
- Ss compare answers in pairs. Then go over answers with the class.

Answers

8. a. She performs at a president's inauguration.
1. b. She is born in Texas.
3. c. She acts in a movie.
5. d. She wins five Grammys.
4. e. She releases her first solo album.
7. f. She has a baby.
2. g. Her group gets its first recording contract.
6. h. She helps hurricane victims.

TIP

If your Ss speak languages that have similar vocabulary to English, encourage them to look for cognates, or words with similar forms and meanings (e.g., *solo, president*).

- Focus Ss' attention on the diagrams on the board. Ask: "What did you learn? What do you still want to know? Where can you find this information?"
- ***Option:*** Books closed. Ask: "How much can you remember about Beyoncé?" Ss work in pairs to list facts.

C *Pair work*

- Read the questions aloud. Ss discuss their favorite musicians in pairs. Then ask Ss to share information with the class.

To review vocabulary from this reading, play ***Picture It!*** – download it from the website.

End of Cycle 2

See the Supplementary Resources chart at the beginning of this unit for additional teaching materials and student activities related to this Cycle and for assessment tools.

12 READING

A Scan the article and look at the pictures. In what year did each event take place?

The World's Most Powerful FEMALE MUSICIAN

Beyoncé Knowles-Carter is a singer, songwriter, performer, actress, clothing designer, and Grammy Award–winning superstar. Many people call her one of the most powerful female musicians in history. Beyoncé works really hard for her success. As she says, "I wanted to sell a million records, and I sold a million records. I wanted to go platinum; I went platinum. I've been working nonstop since I was 15. I don't even know how to chill out." Many people talk about Beyoncé's energy on stage. She's an amazing entertainer. Millions of fans love her singing and dancing. Beyoncé uses many different styles of music, including funk, soul, and pop. In her career so far, Beyoncé has sold over 100 million records as a solo artist and another 60 million records with her group Destiny's Child.

Beyoncé marries Jay-Z.

Beyoncé performs at the U.S. president's inauguration.

BEYONCÉ FAST FACTS

1981	Beyoncé is born in Houston, Texas.
1996	Her girl group, Destiny's Child, gets its first recording contract.
2001	Beyoncé experiences her first time acting. She stars in *Carmen: A Hip Hopera* on MTV.
2003	She releases her first solo album, *Dangerously in Love*.
2004	She wins five Grammys at the Grammy Awards.
2005	Beyoncé starts an organization to help hurricane victims.
2008	She marries rapper Jay-Z.
2010	She wins six Grammys at the Grammy Awards for her album *I Am . . . Sasha Fierce*.
2012	Beyoncé has a daughter and names her Blue Ivy.
2013	Beyoncé performs at the U.S. president's inauguration.
2013	She releases a secret album online named *Beyoncé*.
2016	Beyoncé performs her song "Formation" at a huge sporting event.

B Read the article. Then number these sentences from 1 (first event) to 8 (last event).

_____ **a.** She performs at a president's inauguration.
_____ **b.** She is born in Texas.
_____ **c.** She acts in a movie.
_____ **d.** She wins five Grammys.
_____ **e.** She releases her first solo album.
_____ **f.** She has a baby.
_____ **g.** Her group gets its first recording contract.
_____ **h.** She helps hurricane victims.

C **PAIR WORK** Who is your favorite musician? What do you know about his or her life?

Units 3–4 Progress check

SELF-ASSESSMENT

How well can you do these things? Check (✓) the boxes.

I can . . .	Very well	OK	A little
Give and understand information about prices (Ex. 1)	☐	☐	☐
Say what I like and dislike (Ex. 1, 2, 3)	☐	☐	☐
Explain why I like or dislike something (Ex. 2)	☐	☐	☐
Describe and compare objects and possessions (Ex. 2)	☐	☐	☐
Make and respond to invitiations (Ex. 4)	☐	☐	☐

1 LISTENING Price Cut City

A Listen to a commercial for Price Cut City. Choose the correct prices.

B **PAIR WORK** What do you think of the items in part A? At what stores or websites can you find items like these at low prices? Give your own ideas and opinions.

2 ROLE PLAY Shopping trip

Student A: Choose things from Exercise 1 for your family. Ask for Student B's opinion.
Student B: Help Student A choose presents for his or her family.

A: I want to buy a laptop for my parents. Which one do you like better?
B: Well, I like . . . better. It's nicer, and . . .

Change roles and try the role play again.

Units 3–4

Progress check

SELF-ASSESSMENT

Learning Objectives: reflect on one's learning; identify areas that need improvement

- Ask: "What did you learn in Units 3 and 4?" Elicit Ss' answers.
- Ss complete the Self-assessment. Encourage them to be honest, and point out they will not get a bad grade if they check (✓) *A little*.
- Ss move on to the Progress check exercises. You can have Ss complete them in class or for homework, using one of these techniques:
  1. Ask Ss to complete all the exercises.
  2. Ask Ss: "What do you need to practice?" Then assign exercises based on their answers.
  3. Ask Ss to choose and complete exercises based on their Self-assessment.

1 LISTENING

Learning Objectives: demonstrate one's ability to listen for prices; demonstrate one's ability to discuss likes and dislikes

A *[CD 1, Track 37]*

- Set the scene. Price Cut City is having a sale today. Ss will hear the prices of six items.
- Play the audio program once or twice. Ss listen and circle the correct price of each item. Then check the answers.

Audio script

Announcer Come in to Price Cut City today! Everything is on sale – for one day only. Here are some of our terrific sale prices. First, in the clothing department, we have great sales on both men's and women's jackets. We have leather jackets for only $70. That's right! All our stylish leather jackets are only $70. And wool jackets are on sale for $50. Just $50 for a wool jacket. Amazing! But that's not all. Every style and color of shirt is on sale. Designer silk shirts are now only $40. Again, that's $40 for a silk shirt. And cotton shirts are on sale for just $18. Unbelievable! Finally, in the electronics department, we have a great selection of computers. We have laptops for only $319. And we have desktop computers for $460. A complete computer system for only $460. What a deal! Remember, these prices are for today only, so come in and save at our one-day sale. Get everything you need . . . at Price Cut City!

Answers

leather jacket: $70
wool jacket: $50
silk shirt: $40
cotton shirt: $18
laptop: $319
desktop computer: $460

B *Pair work*

- Explain the task. Ss talk about the items in part A and give their own opinions about them in pairs. Are the things expensive, reasonable, or cheap? Where would they buy these items?

2 ROLE PLAY

Learning Objective: demonstrate one's ability to state preferences and make comparisons while shopping

- Focus Ss' attention on the pictures in Exercise 1 and explain the task. Ss work in pairs. Student A wants to buy presents for his or her family at Price Cut City. Student B is helping Student A choose presents.
- Model the example conversation with a S. Elicit other expressions and comparisons to use in the role plays.
- Ss practice the role play in pairs. Then they change roles. Go around the class and give help as needed.
- ***Option:*** Have Ss give the items different prices and try the role play again.

3 SPEAKING

Learning Objective: demonstrate one's ability to ask and answer questions about entertainment using the simple present

A

- Explain the task. Ss work individually. They write one more question in the first column. Then they write answers to the questions in the *Me* column.

B *Class activity*

- Explain and model the task. Say: "I usually watch TV at (7:00). When do you usually watch TV?" Ask different Ss until someone gives the same answer.
- Explain that you will write that person's name in the *My classmate* column. Point out that Ss should write a classmate's name only once.
- Ss go around the class and ask questions to complete the activity. Note any grammar, vocabulary, or pronunciation errors.
- ***Option:*** Go over any grammar, vocabulary, or pronunciation errors after Ss complete the activity.

4 SPEAKING

Learning Objective: demonstrate one's ability to make, accept, and decline invitations using *would* and verb + *to* + verb

A

- Explain the task. Then ask a S to read the example invitation in the book.
- Elicit suggestions for other interesting activities and write them on the board.
- Hand out three index cards to each S. Explain the task. Ss write three different invitations individually (one per card). Point out that they should not put their names on the cards.
- Ss complete the task. Go around the class and give help as needed.

B

- Ask different Ss to read the three response cards. Elicit other ways of accepting or refusing an invitation. Encourage Ss to suggest silly or unusual excuses for refusals.
- Hand out three index cards to each S. Explain the task. Ss write one acceptance and two refusals. The acceptance cards should include a question about where or when to meet. Point out that they should not put their names on the cards.
- Ss complete the task. Go around the class and give help as needed.

C *Group work*

- Ss work in small groups. One S collects all the invitation cards, shuffles them, and puts them in a pile.
- A different S collects all the response cards, shuffles them, and puts them in a different pile.
- Explain the task. Each S takes three invitation cards and three response cards. Then they read them silently.
- Model the task. Read an invitation card aloud. Ss accept or refuse the invitation by reading a response card.
- Ss take turns completing the task.

WHAT'S NEXT?

Learning Objective: become more involved in one's learning

- Focus Ss' attention on the Self-assessment again. Ask: "How well can you do these things now?"
- Ask Ss to underline one thing they need to review. Ask: "What did you underline? How can you review it?"
- If needed, plan additional activities or reviews based on Ss' answers.

3 SPEAKING Survey: Likes and dislikes

A Add one more question to the chart. Write your answers to these questions.

	Me	My classmate
When do you usually watch TV?		
What kinds of TV shows do you like?		
Do you like game shows?		
Do you read the news online?		
Who is your favorite singer?		
What do you think of hip-hop?		
What is your favorite movie?		
Do you like musicals?		
What kinds of movies do you dislike?		
______________________		

B **CLASS ACTIVITY** Go around the class. Find someone who has the same answers as you. Write a classmate's name only once!

4 SPEAKING What an excuse!

A Make up three invitations to interesting activities. Write them on cards.

My friends and I are going to the amusement park on Sunday at 2 p.m. Would you like to come?

B Write three response cards. One is an acceptance card, and two are refusals. Think of silly or unusual excuses.

That sounds great! What time do you want to meet?

I'd like to, but I have to wash my cat tomorrow.

I'd love to, but I want to take my bird to a singing contest.

C **GROUP WORK** Shuffle the invitation cards together and the response cards together. Take three cards from each pile. Then invite people to do the things on your invitation cards. Use the response cards to accept or refuse.

WHAT'S NEXT?

Look at your Self-assessment again. Do you need to review anything?

Unit 5 Supplementary Resources Overview

	After the following SB exercises	You can use these materials in class	Your students can use these materials outside the classroom
CYCLE 1	**1 Word Power**	**TR** Unit 5 Vocabulary Worksheet	**DW** Unit 5 Vocabulary 1–2
	2 Listening		
	3 Conversation	**TR** Unit 5 Listening Worksheet	
	4 Pronunciation		
	5 Grammar Focus	**TR** Unit 5 Extra Worksheet	**SB** Unit 5 Grammar plus, Focus 1 **DW** Unit 5 Grammar 1–5
	6 Discussion		
	7 Interchange 5		**WB** Unit 5 exercises 1–6
CYCLE 2	**8 Snapshot**		
	9 Conversation		
	10 Grammar Focus	**TR** Unit 5 Grammar Worksheet **TR** Unit 5 Writing Worksheet	**SB** Unit 5 Grammar plus, Focus 2 **DW** Unit 5 Grammar 6–8
	11 Writing		
	12 Reading	**TR** Unit 5 Project Worksheet **VID** Unit 5 **VRB** Unit 5	**DW** Unit 5 Reading 1–2 **DW** Unit 5 Listening 1–2 **DW** Unit 5 Video 1–2 **WB** Unit 5 exercises 7–11

Key **SB:** Student's Book **DW:** Digital Workbook **TR:** Teacher's Resources
VID: Video (DW/TR) **VRB:** Video Resource Book (TR) **WB:** Print Workbook

My Plan for Unit 5

Use the space below to customize a plan that fits your needs.

With the following SB exercises	I am using these materials in class	My students are using these materials outside the classroom

With or instead of the following SB section	I am using these materials for assessment

5 What an interesting family!

- Describe families
- Talk about habitual and current activities

1 WORD POWER Family

A Look at Joseph's family tree. How are these people related to him? Add the words to the family tree.

cousin	niece
daughter	sister-in-law
father	uncle
grandmother	wife

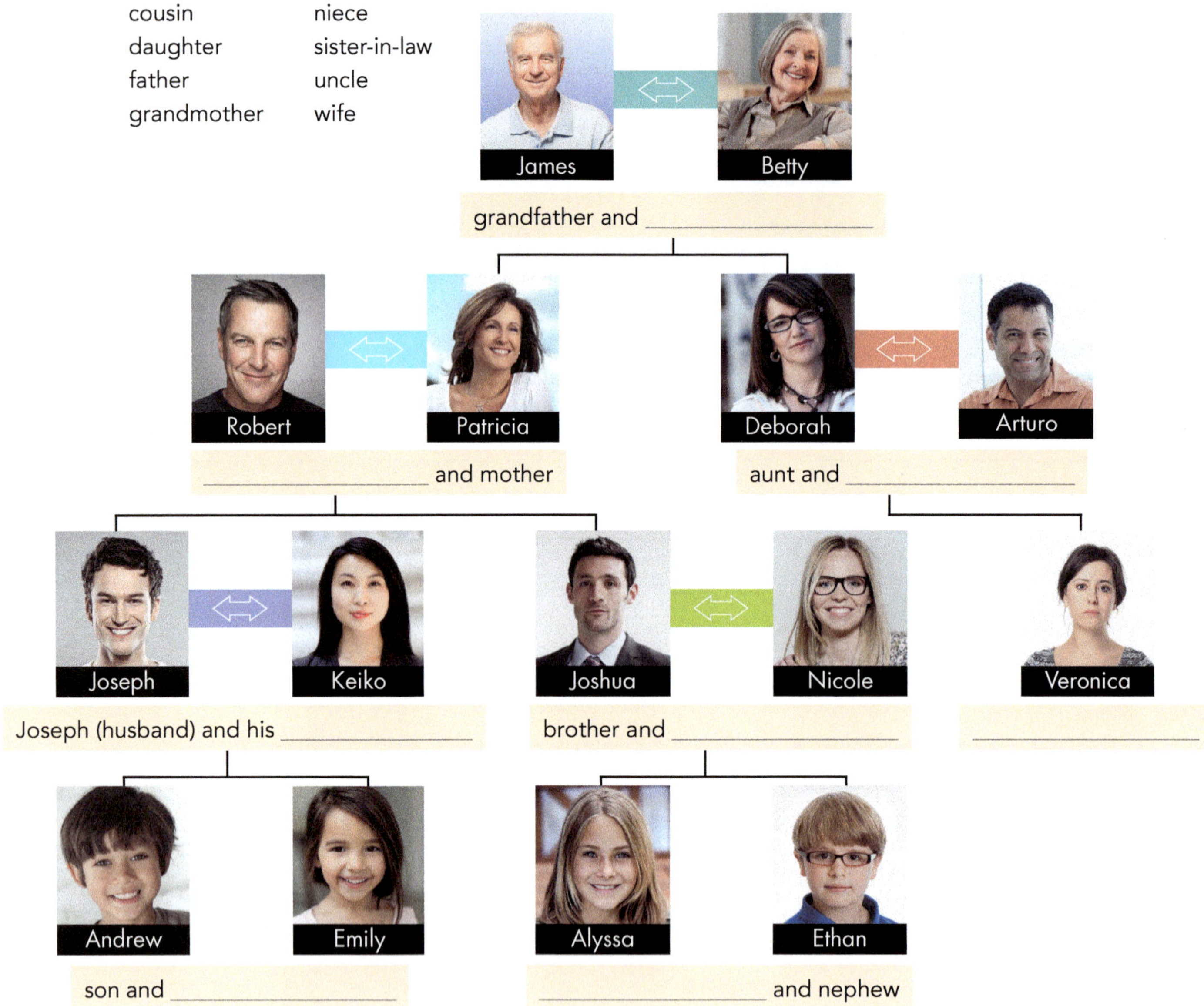

B Draw your family tree (or a friend's family tree). Then take turns talking about your families. Ask follow-up questions to get more information.

A: There are six people in my family. I have one brother and two sisters.
B: How old is your brother?

5 What an interesting family!

Cycle 1, Exercises 1–7

In Unit 5, students describe families and talk about habitual and current activities. By the end of Cycle 1, students will be able to describe families and ask and answer questions using the present continuous. By the end of Cycle 2, students will be able to use quantifiers to describe families.

1 WORD POWER

Learning Objective: identify and discuss family relationships

A

- Write the word *family* in a circle on the board. Then write the words *mother* and *father* around the circle.
- In pairs, Ss brainstorm words for family members and make a list. Then they compare lists with another pair. Go around the class and note the words on their lists.

TIP
To avoid teaching words Ss already know, start by asking Ss the words they know. Then teach any remaining vocabulary.

- Ask Ss to find Joseph and circle his picture. Then ask: "Who is Keiko?" (Answer: his wife) Ask Ss to write *wife* under Keiko's picture and check (✓) *wife* in the vocabulary list.
- Ss complete the exercise in pairs. Go over the answers with the class and check pronunciation.

Answers

grandfather and **grandmother** (Betty)
father (Robert) and mother
aunt and **uncle** (Arturo)
Joseph (husband) and his **wife** (Keiko)
brother and **sister-in-law** (Nicole)
cousin (Veronica)
son and **daughter** (Emily)
niece (Alyssa) and nephew

- As needed, teach other family words (e.g., *great-grandfather, great-grandmother, grandson, granddaughter, son, stepbrother, stepsister, only child, twins, parents, ex-wife, ex-husband*). Use pictures to present additional vocabulary.
- ***Option:*** For more practice, ask questions about another person in the family tree (e.g., *Deborah*). Possible questions include: *Who is Deborah's husband? Who is her sister-in-law?*

B

- Explain the task. Ss draw their family trees individually. Point out that single Ss can include their grandparents, parents, brothers, and sisters, while married Ss can include their husband or wife, children, and grandchildren.
- Draw your family tree on the board while Ss complete the task.
- Model the task by describing your own family. Then encourage Ss to ask you questions. If needed, present or review words such as *married, single, divorced, widowed*, or *deceased*.
- Ss complete the task in pairs or small groups. Go around the room and encourage Ss to ask follow-up questions (e.g., *How old is he? What does he do?*).
- Elicit interesting things Ss learned about their partners.
- ***Option:*** Ask Ss to bring in pictures of their family. Ss show each other family photos in small groups. Encourage them to add two pieces of information for each photo (e.g., *This is my brother. He's 27, and he's a lawyer.*).

TIP
To personalize the class and make the language more meaningful, encourage Ss to bring their own materials to class.

! To review the vocabulary of family, try ***Picture Dictation*** – download it from the website. Ask Ss to draw a family tree while you say: "Amanda has one brother and one sister. Her brother, Edward, is married to Jean. They have three children. Amanda's sister, Mary, is married to Mike. They have one daughter. Amanda has a husband. His name is Charlie."

For more practice matching words for family members with their meanings, play ***Concentration*** – download it from the website.

2 LISTENING

Learning Objective: listen for specific information on how people are related

[CD 1, Track 38]

- Focus Ss' attention on the pictures. Ask: "How are the people related?" Encourage Ss to make guesses.
- Play the audio program. Ss listen and complete the task.

Audio script

1.
Woman Who's that guy?
Ryan That's Quincy Jones. He's famous for his work in the music business, and he's a great musician himself.
Woman That's strange. I don't think I've seen him before.
Ryan Well, I know you've seen his daughter.
Woman Is her last name Jones, too?
Ryan Yes, it is. Her name's Rashida Jones.
Woman Rashida Jones? Oh, I love her! She was in my favorite TV show!
2.
Man What are you reading, Brianna?
Brianna An article about Ashton Kutcher. He's in a new TV show.
Man That's good news! I really liked his last show.
Brianna Do you know who he married in 2015?
Man Hmm . . . Demi Moore?
Brianna No. Mila Kunis.
Man I didn't know that! What a cool couple!
3.
Mom What are you watching, Samantha?
Samantha Oh, hi, Mom. I'm watching a new movie with Emma Roberts.
Mom Oh, yes, Emma Roberts. I thought her aunt was great in *Notting Hill*.
Samantha Who's her aunt?
Mom Julia Roberts. She's such a great actress.
Samantha I've never heard of her. What's *Notting Hill*?
Mom It's a movie from the nineties. You should watch it. It's great.
Samantha The nineties? That's kind of old. But I'll watch it – if I can find it.
4.
Man What website is that?
Woman It's called Star Watcher. It has all kinds of news about famous people. Look at this picture.
Man Oh, cool! That's Cameron Diaz. I love her. But who's that with her?
Woman That's Nicole Richie, the fashion designer.
Man Oh, yeah, I know her. But I didn't know they were friends.
Woman Actually, they're more than just friends. Cameron married the musician Benji Madden, and Nicole married Joel Madden, Benji's brother.
Man So they're sisters-in-law! I didn't know that. I need to follow celebrity news more often.

- Go over answers with the class.

Answers

1. daughter 2. wife 3. aunt 4. sister-in-law

3 CONVERSATION

Learning Objective: use the present continuous in a conversation about families

A ***[CD 1, Track 39]***

- Set the scene. Max is asking about Tina's family. Focus Ss' attention on the pictures. Ask: "How do you think they're related to Tina?" Elicit ideas.
- Play the audio program. Ss listen and read silently.
- Ss practice the conversation in pairs.

B ***[CD 1, Track 40]***

- Read the two focus questions aloud. Play the audio program once or twice.
- Go over answers with the class.

Audio script

Tina So, what about your parents, Max? Where do they live?
Max They live in California.
Tina Oh, where in California?
Max In Sausalito. It's a small city, but it's very nice.
Tina Are they still working?
Max Oh, yes. My mother is teaching at a university in San Francisco, and my father has a bookstore.

Answers

They live in Sausalito, California. Max's mother teaches at a university in San Francisco, and his father has a bookstore.

4 PRONUNCIATION

Learning Objective: sound more natural when using intonation in statements

A ***[CD 1, Track 41]***

- Play the audio program. Point out the falling intonation. Ss repeat the statements. Ask different Ss to say the statements to check their intonation.

B ***Pair work***

- Explain the task. Ss work in pairs. Go around the class and check Ss' intonation.

2 LISTENING Famous relatives

Listen to four conversations about famous people. How is the second person related to the first person?

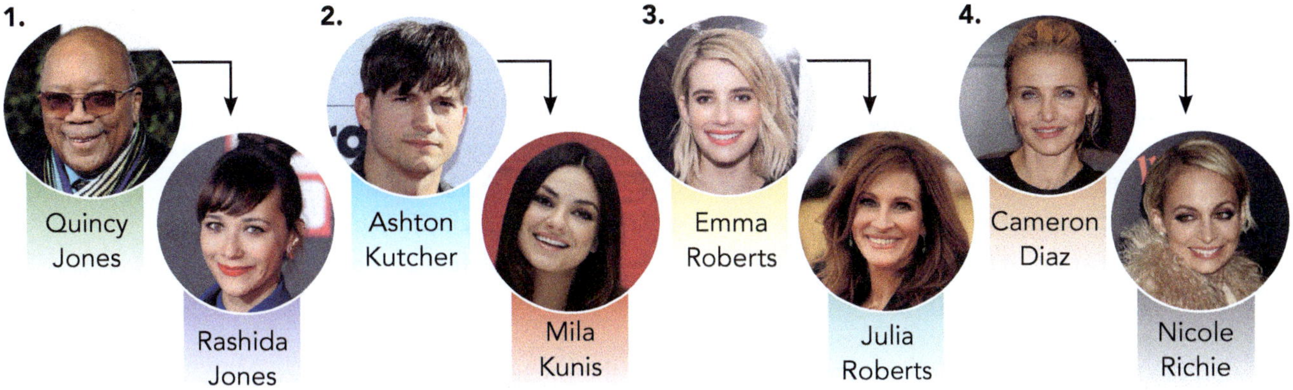

________ ________ ________ ________

3 CONVERSATION He's traveling in Thailand.

A Listen and practice.

MAX Do you have brothers and sisters, Tina?

TINA Yes, I have a brother and a sister.

MAX Oh, what does your sister do?

TINA She's a surgeon. She works for a medical aid organization.

MAX Wow! And what about your brother?

TINA He's a writer. He travels and writes about his experiences for a magazine.

MAX What an interesting family! Can I meet them?

TINA Sure, but my sister's not here right now. She's treating patients in Cameroon.

MAX And your brother?

TINA He's traveling in Thailand, and then he wants to visit my sister. I miss them!

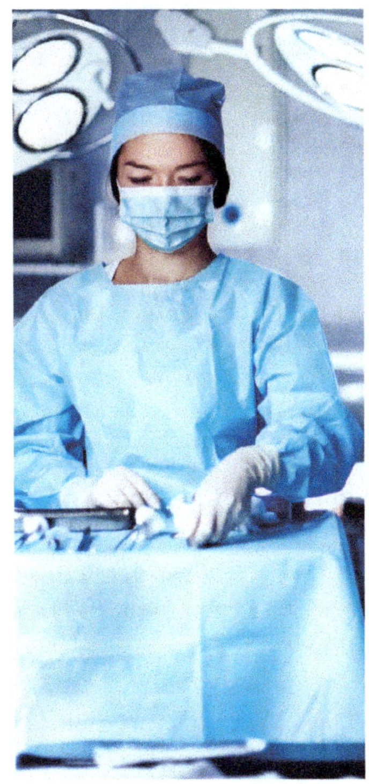

B Listen to the rest of the conversation. Where do Max's parents live? What do his parents do?

4 PRONUNCIATION Intonation in statements

A Listen and practice. Notice that statements usually have falling intonation.

She's working in Cameroon. He's traveling in Thailand.

B **PAIR WORK** Practice the conversation in Exercise 3 again.

5 GRAMMAR FOCUS

Present continuous

Are you **living** at home now?	Yes, I **am**.	No, I**'m not**.
Is your sister **working** in another city?	Yes, she **is**.	No, she**'s not**./No, she **isn't**.
Are your parents **studying** English this year?	Yes, they **are**.	No, they**'re not**./No, they **aren't**.

Where **are** you **working** now?	I**'m not working**. I need a job.
What **is** your brother **doing**?	He**'s traveling** in Thailand.
What **are** your friends **doing** these days?	They**'re studying** for their exams.

GRAMMAR PLUS *see page 136*

A Complete these phone conversations using the present continuous.

1

A: Hi, Brittany. What ______________ you ______________ (do)?
B: Hey, Zach. I ______________ (eat) a sandwich at O'Connor's.
A: Mmm! Is it good?
B: Yeah. It's delicious. Wait, they ______________ (bring) my dessert now. It's chocolate cake with ice cream. Call you later! Bye!

2

A: So, Madison, how ______________ you and your sister ______________ (do) in college?
B: We ______________ (have) a lot of fun, Mom!
A: Fun? OK, but ______________ your sister ______________ (go) to class every morning?
B: Yeah, Mom. She ______________ (work) hard and I am, too. I'm serious!

B **PAIR WORK** Write a short dialogue using the present continuous, then practice it.

C **CLASS WORK** Read your dialogue to the class.

6 DISCUSSION What are you doing these days?

GROUP WORK Ask and answer questions about what you are doing. Use the topics in the box and your own ideas. Ask follow-up questions to get more information.

A: So, what are you doing these days?
B: I'm playing basketball in college.
A: That's nice. And are you enjoying it?

topics to talk about

traveling	going to high school or college
playing a sport	learning a musical instrument
living alone	working or studying

5 GRAMMAR FOCUS

Learning Objective: ask and answer questions using the present continuous

[CD 1, Track 42]

Simple present vs. present continuous

- Draw this chart on the board:

	Usually	Right now
Tina's sister		
Tina's brother		

- Focus Ss' attention on the Conversation on page 31. Ask: "What does Tina's sister do? What is she doing right now?" (Answers: She works for a medical aid organization. She's treating patients in Cameroon.) Complete the chart. Repeat the procedure for Tina's brother. (Answers: He's a writer. He's traveling in Thailand.)
- Elicit or explain the difference between the two tenses (simple present = habitual actions; present continuous = actions that are happening right now).
- Compare the formation of the two tenses:
  She works. (subject + verb)
  She is working. (subject + *be* + verb + *-ing*)

Present continuous questions and statements

- Focus Ss' attention on the Conversation on page 31. Ask: "Why can't Max meet Tina's family?" Elicit the answers, and write them on the board:

  Tina's sister is not working in the U.S. right now.
  Tina's brother is traveling in Thailand.

- Focus Ss' attention on the Grammar Focus box. Elicit the rule for forming yes/no and Wh-questions in the present continuous:
  Be + subject + verb + *-ing*?
  (Wh-question) + *be* + subject + verb + *-ing*?
- Ask Ss to underline the time expressions in the Grammar Focus box that show the action is temporary or current: *this year, now, these days.*
- Play the audio program.

A

- Explain the task and model the first question.
- Ss complete the task individually. Encourage Ss to use contractions in statements. Review contractions as needed.
- Ss go over their answers in pairs. Then go over answers with the class.

Answers

1. A: Hi, Brittany. What **are** you **doing**?
   B: Hey, Zach. I**'m eating** a sandwich at O'Connor's.
   A: Mmm! Is it good?
   B: Yeah. It's delicious. Wait, they**'re bringing** my dessert now. It's chocolate cake with ice cream. Call you later! Bye!
2. A: So, Madison, how **are** you and your sister **doing** in college?
   B: We**'re having** a lot of fun, Mom!
   A: Fun? OK, but **is** your sister **going** to class every morning?
   B: Yeah, Mom. She**'s working** hard and I am, too. I'm serious!

B *Pair work*

- Explain the task. Elicit some examples of opening questions that use the present continuous.
- Ss complete the task in pairs. Encourage Ss to use contractions in statements. Go around the class and help as needed.
- Ss practice their dialogues in pairs.
- ***Option:*** Ss practice the conversations sitting back-to back or with their cell phones.

C *Class work*

- Pairs read their dialogue to the class.
- ***Option:*** Collect all of the written dialogues and distribute them randomly to new pairs. Each pair reads a new dialogue aloud.

6 DISCUSSION

Learning Objective: ask and answer questions about current activities using the present continuous

Group work

- Explain the task and go over the topics in the box. Explain any new vocabulary and elicit other possible discussion topics.
- Model the conversation with one or two Ss. Encourage Ss to add follow-up questions and introduce new topics.
- Give Ss a few minutes to prepare things to say about what they are doing these days.
- Ss complete the task in small groups. Go around the class and note any common errors. Then go over them with the class.

TIP
To help you decide if additional controlled grammar practice is necessary, watch the Ss' performance during the speaking activities.

7 INTERCHANGE 5

See page T-119 for teaching notes.

End of Cycle 1

See the Supplementary Resources chart at the beginning of this unit for additional teaching materials and student activities related to this Cycle.

Cycle 2, Exercises 8–12

8 SNAPSHOT

Learning Objective: discuss facts about different countries

- Books closed. Write these statements on the board:
  1. In Argentina, 80% of the population lives in rural areas.
  2. In Russia, 99.7% of the population can read and write.
- Review percentages if needed. Ask Ss to guess if these facts are true or false. Then elicit their guesses.
- Books open. Tell Ss the answers. (Answers: 1. False (around 10% live in rural areas) 2. True) Ask: "Who was right? Do these facts surprise you? Why?"
- Go over the other facts about the countries. Explain any unfamiliar vocabulary. Then Ss mark each fact as *True* or *False*.
- Go over the answers with the class. Elicit a few examples of facts that surprised the Ss.
- Ss then discuss which facts surprised them and why in small groups. Ss discuss how they think their country compares to the facts in the quiz and then share other interesting facts they know.
- Have groups share their discussion with the class.

9 CONVERSATION

Learning Objective: use quantifiers in a conversation about families

A *[CD 1, Track 43]*

- Ask the class: "How many brothers do you have? How many sisters?" Elicit answers.
- Draw this chart on the board:

	Where from?	Number of brothers/sisters?	Typical?
1. Vicky			
2. Luis			

- Books closed. Set the scene. Luis and Vicky are talking about their families.
- Play the audio program. Ss listen for the answers. Ask Ss to complete the chart on the board if they know the answers. Play the audio program again as needed and ask Ss to add to or change the information in the chart. (Answers: 1. China, no brothers or sisters, yes 2. Peru, two brothers and four sisters, no)
- Books open. Play the audio program again. Ss look at the picture and read the conversation silently.
- Ss practice the conversation in pairs.

! For a new way to practice this conversation, try the ***Disappearing Dialog*** – download it from the website.

B *[CD 1, Track 44]*

- Ask: "Why does Luis like having a big family?" (Answer: Because he gets lots of birthday presents.)
- Read the focus question aloud. Ask Ss to make predictions and write them on the board.
- Play the audio program. Ss listen to find out if any prediction on the board is correct.

Audio script

Luis So, do you like being an only child?
Vicky Of course. I get all my parents' attention.
Luis Yeah, I share my parents' attention with six other people.
Vicky Well, you probably never feel lonely!
Luis Do you ever feel lonely?
Vicky Sure. But it's OK. I have a lot of friends.

Answer

She gets all her parents' attention.

7 INTERCHANGE 5 Is that true?

Find out about your classmates' families. Go to Interchange 5 on page 119.

8 SNAPSHOT

Countries of the World Quiz

True or false? Take the quiz, then check your answers.

1. In Argentina, 80% of the population lives in rural areas.
2. In Russia, 99.7% of the population can read and write.
3. In South Korea, more than 85% of high school students go on to college.
4. In Denmark, 70% of the women have jobs.
5. In Mexico, 20% of the population is 65 years old or more.
6. Brazil occupies 60% of the area of South America.
7. In Chile, more than 90% of the population lives with family.
8. Japan imports about 25% of Jamaica's total coffee production.
9. In India, more than 25% of the population goes to the movies regularly.

Answers: 1. False – around 10% live in rural areas 2. True 3. True 4. True 5. False – 6% 6. False – 47.3% 7. True 8. False – 80% 9. False – less than 4%

Which facts surprise you? Why?
What interesting facts do you know about your country?

9 CONVERSATION I didn't know that.

A Listen and practice.

LUIS What a great picture! Are those your parents?

VICKY Thanks! Yes, it's my favorite picture of us.

LUIS It's really nice. So, do you have any brothers or sisters?

VICKY No, I'm an only child. Actually, a lot of families in China have only one child.

LUIS Oh, really? I didn't know that.

VICKY What about you, Luis?

LUIS I come from a big family. I have two brothers and four sisters.

VICKY Wow! Is that typical in Peru?

LUIS I'm not sure. Many families are smaller these days. But big families are great because you get a lot of birthday presents!

B Listen to the rest of the conversation. What does Vicky like about being an only child?

10 GRAMMAR FOCUS

Quantifiers

100%	**All**	
	Nearly all	families have only one child.
	Most	
	Many	
	A lot of	families are smaller these days.
	Some	
	Not many	couples have more than one child.
	Few	
0%	**No one**	gets married before the age of 18.

GRAMMAR PLUS *see page 136*

A Rewrite these sentences using quantifiers. Then compare with a partner.

1. In the U.S., 69% of high school students go to college.
2. Seven percent of the people in Brazil are age 65 or older.
3. In India, 0% of the people vote before the age of 18.
4. Forty percent of the people in Sweden live alone.
5. In Canada, 22% of the people speak French at home.

B PAIR WORK Rewrite the sentences in part A so that they are true about your country.

In the U.S., most high school students go to college.

11 WRITING An email to an online friend

A You have an online friend in another country. Write an email to your friend about your family.

100%

Email

New email — Reply — Forward

Dear Jessie,

Thanks for your email. You have a very nice family! Now let me tell you about my family. My parents are teachers in our local school. Most families here are large. I have three brothers, but I don't have a sister. I'm the only daughter. My brothers' names are . . .

B GROUP WORK Take turns reading your emails. Ask questions to get more information.

10 GRAMMAR FOCUS

Learning Objective: use quantifiers to state facts

[CD 1, Track 45]

- Explain that when people don't know the exact percentage of something, they use words like *most* or *some*. Point out the quantifiers in the Grammar Focus box.
- Explain that all these quantifiers come before plural nouns except one. Ask Ss which one does not. (Answer: no one)
- Play the audio program.
- Ask Ss to find two sentences with quantifiers in the Conversation on page 33. (Answers: a lot of families in China . . . , Many families . . .)
- Ask: "Who is from a big family? Raise your hand." Then elicit a statement about the class that starts with a quantifier (e.g., *Most students in the class are from big families.*). Ask more questions and elicit more statements with quantifiers (e.g., *Are you single? Do you live at home? Are you an only child?*).

A

- Explain the task. Model the first answer.
- Ss rewrite the sentences individually. Point out that more than one quantifier may be possible. Then Ss go over their answers in pairs.
- Go over answers with the class.

Possible answers

1. In the U.S., most high school students go to college.
2. Few people in Brazil are age 65 or older.
3. In India, no one votes before the age of 18.
4. Some people in Sweden live alone.
5. In Canada, not many people speak French at home.

B *Pair work*

- Explain the task and elicit the first answer. Write it on the board.
- Ss complete the task in pairs. Go around the class and give help as needed. Then each pair joins another pair to compare answers.
- ***Option:*** Ss make statements about the true versions of the facts in the Snapshot on page 33 using quantifiers instead of percentages.

For more practice with quantifiers, play ***Tic-Tac-Toe*** – download it from the website.

11 WRITING

Learning Objective: write an email describing one's family

A

- Ss read the example email silently.
- Elicit information Ss can include in a description of their family (e.g., names, ages, jobs, where they live). Write all ideas on the board.

For a new way to prepare for this Writing, try ***Mind Mapping*** – download it from the website.

- Ss write emails about their family. Encourage them to use quantifiers.

B *Group work*

- Ss read each other's emails in small groups and ask each other for more information.

12 READING

Learning Objectives: make predictions; read an article for main ideas and details about families

- Books closed. Ask: "Does your family spend a lot of time together?" Elicit answers from Ss.

A

- Books open. Read the title and go over the task.
- Explain that the first sentence of a paragraph usually gives you its main idea. This is called a "topic sentence."
- Ss read the topic sentences of the paragraphs. Ask: "Do families spend a lot of time together?" (Answer: Some families do, some families don't.)

B

- Go over the six questions. Then Ss read the article silently and answer the questions.
- Elicit or explain any new vocabulary.

Vocabulary

fresh air: air outside buildings that is clean and cool
barbecue: cooking food over a fire outdoors
housework: work people do to take care of the home, such as cleaning
make an effort: try to do something

- Ss compare their answers in groups. Go around the class and give help as needed.
- Go over answers with the class.

Answers

1. Billy
2. Carla
3. Jane
4. Nick
5. Billy
6. Nick

C *Group work*

- Read the four questions. Then Ss discuss the questions in small groups.
- Go over the answers with the class.

End of Cycle 2

See the Supplementary Resources chart at the beginning of this unit for additional teaching materials and student activities related to this Cycle.

12 READING

A A journalist interviewed four people. Read the title of the article. What do you think the answer will be? Check (✓) the answer.

☐ Yes, most families do. ☐ No, most families don't. ☐ Some families do, some families don't.

DO FAMILIES SPEND A LOT OF TIME TOGETHER?

We spend a lot of time together on the weekends. My husband and I always take our son, Oliver, and daughter, Samantha, out to do something fun. Some weeks we go for a long bike ride and get a lot of fresh air! We go to the beach in the summer, of course. In the evenings, we have a barbecue together. During the week, it's more difficult to spend time together because of work and school.
– Jane Chambers

It's a little sad, but most of the time we spend as a family is watching TV. We don't talk much. My mom and dad both work, and they're often tired when they get home. My sister just plays games on her tablet all evening. It's kind of boring. Maybe we spend about an hour a day together. It's never more than that.
– Billy Foster

I'm a stay-at-home dad, and I'm having a great time with my family! When the kids are in school, I do housework. When they come home, I help them with their homework. After that, we all have fun together. We play a lot of sports and read books. I love all the time I get with my two boys.
– Nick Ramos

We're always really busy, but we make an effort to spend time together. My grandparents come over to our house twice a week for dinner. I think family is very important. I often help my mom or dad cook the meals. Sometimes we all go to the movies. I like that a lot.
– Carla Costantini

B Read the interviews. Then check the correct names.

Who . . . ?	**Jane**	**Billy**	**Nick**	**Carla**
1. watches a lot of TV	☐	☐	☐	☐
2. sees their grandparents twice a week	☐	☐	☐	☐
3. spends time outdoors	☐	☐	☐	☐
4. stays at home with the kids	☐	☐	☐	☐
5. doesn't spend much time with family	☐	☐	☐	☐
6. does housework during the day	☐	☐	☐	☐

C **GROUP WORK** What do families look like in your country? Do dads stay at home with their children? Do you think that's a good thing or a bad thing? Is it important to you to spend time with your family?

Unit 6 Supplementary Resources Overview

	After the following SB exercises	You can use these materials in class	Your students can use these materials outside the classroom
CYCLE 1	**1 Snapshot**		**DW** Unit 6 Vocabulary 1
	2 Word Power	**TR** Unit 6 Vocabulary Worksheet	**DW** Unit 6 Vocabulary 2
	3 Conversation		
	4 Grammar Focus	**TR** Unit 6 Listening Worksheet	**SB** Unit 6 Grammar plus, Focus 1 **DW** Unit 6 Grammar 1, 3–4, 7–8
	5 Pronunciation		
	6 Speaking		
	7 Listening		
	8 Discussion	**TR** Unit 6 Extra Worksheet	
	9 Writing	**TR** Unit 6 Writing Worksheet	**WB** Unit 6 exercises 1–6
CYCLE 2	**10 Conversation**		
	11 Grammar Focus	**TR** Unit 6 Grammar Worksheet	**SB** Unit 6 Grammar plus, Focus 2 **DW** Unit 6 Grammar 2, 5–6
	12 Listening		
	13 Interchange 6		
	14 Reading	**TR** Unit 6 Project Worksheet **VID** Unit 6 **VRB** Unit 6	**DW** Unit 6 Reading 1–2 **DW** Unit 6 Listening 1–2 **DW** Unit 6 Video 1–2 **WB** Unit 6 exercises 7–11

With or instead of the following SB section	You can also use these materials for assessment
Units 5–6 Progress Check	**TESTING PROGRAM** Units 5–6 Oral Quiz **TESTING PROGRAM** Units 5–6 Written Quiz

Key **SB:** Student's Book **DW:** Digital Workbook **TR:** Teacher's Resources
VID: Video (DW/TR) **VRB:** Video Resource Book (TR) **WB:** Print Workbook

My Plan for Unit 6

Use the space below to customize a plan that fits your needs.

With the following SB exercises	I am using these materials in class	My students are using these materials outside the classroom

With or instead of the following SB section	I am using these materials for assessment

6 How often do you run?

- ▸ Discuss sports and exercise habits
- ▸ Ask and answer questions about frequency of free-time activities

1 SNAPSHOT

Top Sports and Fitness Activities in the United States

Sports
- ☐ football
- ☐ baseball
- ☐ soccer
- ☐ ice hockey
- ☐ basketball

Fitness Activities
- ☐ treadmill
- ☐ running/jogging
- ☐ walking
- ☐ bowling
- ☐ weight training

Do people in your country enjoy any of these sports or activities?
Check (✓) the sports or fitness activities you enjoy.
Make a list of other activities you do. Then compare with the class.

2 WORD POWER Sports and fitness

A Which of these activities are popular with the following age groups in your country? Check (✓) the activities. Then compare with a partner.

	Children	Teens	Young adults	Middle-aged people	Older people
bike riding	☐	☐	☐	☐	☐
golf	☐	☐	☐	☐	☐
jogging	☐	☐	☐	☐	☐
martial arts	☐	☐	☐	☐	☐
Pilates	☐	☐	☐	☐	☐
soccer	☐	☐	☐	☐	☐
swimming	☐	☐	☐	☐	☐
volleyball	☐	☐	☐	☐	☐
yoga	☐	☐	☐	☐	☐

B **PAIR WORK** Which activities in part A are used with *do*, *go*, or *play*?

do martial arts	*go bike riding*	*play golf*

6 How often do you run?

Cycle 1, Exercises 1–9

In Unit 6, students discuss sports and exercise habits, and ask and answer questions about frequency of free-time activities. By the end of Cycle 1, students will be able to discuss sports and exercise habits. By the end of Cycle 2, students will be able to ask and answer questions about frequency of free-time activities.

1 SNAPSHOT

Learning Objective: identify and discuss common sports and fitness activities

- Books closed. Introduce the topics of sports and fitness. Ss brainstorm sports and fitness activities. Write Ss' ideas in two columns on the board:

Sports	Fitness activities
football	walking
baseball	jogging
basketball	weight training

TIP
To make new vocabulary easy for your Ss to copy, make a vocabulary list on one side of the board. Add new words to the list throughout the class.

- Ask Ss to guess the sports and fitness activities people from the U.S. like best.
- Books open. Ss look at the Snapshot. Tell Ss the answers. (Answers: football, walking) Ask: "Who guessed right?"
- Elicit or explain any new vocabulary. Help Ss with the pronunciation of difficult words (e.g., *weight*, *treadmill*). If needed, explain that American football is different from international football. Players use their hands, throw and run with the ball, and wear safety equipment. In the U.S., international football is called *soccer*.

Vocabulary
ice hockey: a game played on ice between two teams who use a curved stick to try to get a puck into the other team's goal
treadmill: a machine for walking or running
bowling: a game where you roll a heavy ball down a long wooden lane to try to knock down ten wooden "pins" that are arranged in a triangle
weight training: lifting weights to become stronger

- Go over the discussion questions and tasks.
- Ss complete the tasks individually. Go around the class and give help as needed. Then elicit Ss' answers.

2 WORD POWER

Learning Objective: describe sports and fitness activities using collocations with *do, go,* and *play*

A

- Go over the activities in the chart. In pairs, Ss match the activities to the pictures. Elicit or explain any unfamiliar vocabulary. *Martial arts* are traditional methods of fighting and self-defense, and include karate, judo, and taekwondo. *Pilates* is a fitness activity done on a machine or a mat that strengthens the body's core.
- Explain and model the task. Ask: "What age groups like bike riding?" Point out that there is no single correct answer.
- While Ss complete the task individually, write this conversation on the board:

  A: What age groups like (bike riding)?
  B: I think it's popular with (young adults).
  A: I agree OR I don't really agree. I think it's popular with (children).
- Model the conversation with one or two Ss. Then Ss use the model conversation to compare answers in pairs.

B *Pair work*

- Present the rules for these collocations:
  go + activities ending in *-ing*, except *weight training*
  play + games, such as sports played with a ball
  do + fitness activities and individual exercises
- Ss complete the task in pairs. To check answers, write the verbs *do*, *go*, and *play* on the board. Ask different Ss to write the answers. Give help as needed.

Answers

do	go	play
do martial arts	go bike riding	play golf
do Pilates	go jogging	play soccer
do yoga	go swimming	play volleyball

- ***Option:*** Ss circle the activities and sports they enjoy. Then they compare with a partner.

For more practice with sports and exercise vocabulary, play ***Sculptures*** – download it from the website.

3 CONVERSATION

Learning Objective: use adverbs of frequency in a conversation about exercise

A *[CD 2, Track 1]*

- Use the pictures to set the scene. Ask: "Where are Riley and Aaron? What are they doing? What do you think they like to do in their free time?"
- Books closed. Write these sentences on the board:

  1. *Riley does yoga often.*
  2. *Aaron exercises every day.*

  Ask: "Are these sentences true or false?" Play the audio program and elicit the answers. (Answers: 1. false 2. false) Elicit the correct answers. (Answers: 1. Riley runs on the treadmill/lifts weights often. 2. Aaron hardly ever exercises.)
- Elicit or explain any new vocabulary.

Vocabulary
Seriously?: Really?
couch potato: a person who watches a lot of TV and is not very active

- Books open. Play the audio program again. Ss listen and read silently. Ask: "Are you more like Riley or Aaron?" Elicit Ss' answers.
- Ss practice the conversation in pairs.

! For a new way to practice this conversation, try the ***Moving Dialog*** – download it from the website.

B *[CD 2, Track 2]*

- Read the focus question aloud. Ask Ss to make guesses. Write their ideas on the board.
- Play the audio program. Then elicit the answer.

Audio script

Aaron What else do you like to do, Riley?
Riley Well, I like to play the drums a lot. I play every day. It drives my mom crazy!
Aaron Hey, I play the guitar!
Riley Well, listen, we could start our own band! Why don't we play after class today?
Aaron Cool!

Answer

She plays the drums.

4 GRAMMAR FOCUS

Learning Objective: ask and answer questions about how frequently one engages in various free-time activities

[CD 2, Track 3]

Adverbs of frequency

- Write these sentences on the board:

  I ________ exercise.
  I ________ just watch TV.
- Ask Ss to find the missing words in the Conversation in Exercise 3 and write them on the board. (Answers: hardly ever, usually) Explain that these are adverbs of frequency. Point out that they go before most verbs. Focus Ss' attention on the second column of the Grammar Focus box.
- On the board, write: *I'm always late.* Point out that adverbs of frequency go after the verb *be*.
- Point out the third column. Explain that the percentages show how often something happens.
- Now focus Ss' attention on the first column. Ask: "Where do these adverbs go?" (Answer: at the end of a statement or question)
- Play the audio program.

A

- Explain the task. Model the first example. Ss complete the task individually.
- Check the answers with the class. Then Ss practice the conversations in pairs.

Answers

1. A: Do you **ever** play sports?
   B: Sure. I play soccer **twice a week**.
2. A: What do you **usually** do on Saturday mornings?
   B: Nothing much. I **almost always** sleep until noon.
3. A: Do you **often** lift weights at the gym?
   B: No, I **hardly ever** lift weights.
4. A: Do you **always** exercise on Sundays?
   B: No, I **never** exercise on Sundays.
5. A: What do you **usually** do after class?
   B: I go out with my classmates **about three times a week**.
6. A: Do you **often** go to the movies?
   B: Yes, I go to the movies **once a week.**
7. A: Do you **ever** go bike riding?
   B: No, I **hardly ever** ride a bike.
8. A: Do you **sometimes** walk to school?
   B: Sure. I walk to school **five days a week**.

B *Pair work*

- Explain the task. Ss ask and answer the questions in part A in pairs, using their own information.

For more practice with adverbs of frequency, play ***Tic-Tac-Toe*** – download it from the website. Write different adverbs of frequency in the nine boxes.

3 CONVERSATION I run every day.

A Listen and practice.

Aaron: You have a lot of energy, Riley. Do you exercise a lot?
Riley: Well, I get up early and run on the treadmill for an hour every day.
Aaron: Seriously?
Riley: Sure. And I do weight lifting.
Aaron: Wow! How often do you lift weights?
Riley: I usually do it about three times a week. What about you?
Aaron: Oh, I hardly ever exercise. I usually just watch TV or listen to music in my free time. I guess I'm a real couch potato!

B Listen to the rest of the conversation. What else does Riley do in her free time?

4 GRAMMAR FOCUS

Adverbs of frequency

How often do you exercise?
I run on the treadmill **every day**.
I go jogging **once a week**.
I play soccer **twice a month**.
I swim about **three times a year**.
I don't exercise very **often/much**.
Usually I exercise before class.*

Do you **ever** watch TV in the evening?
Yes, I **often** watch TV after dinner.
I **sometimes** watch TV before bed.
Sometimes I watch TV before bed.*
I **hardly ever** watch TV.
No, I **never** watch TV.

**Usually and sometimes can begin a sentence.*

100%	**always**
	almost always
	usually
	often
	sometimes
	hardly ever
	almost never
0%	**never**

GRAMMAR PLUS see page 137

A Put the adverbs in the correct place. Sometimes there is more than one correct answer. Then practice with a partner.

1. **A:** Do you play sports? (ever)
   B: Sure. I play soccer. (twice a week)
2. **A:** What do you do on Saturday mornings? (usually)
   B: Nothing much. I sleep until noon. (almost always)
3. **A:** Do you lift weights at the gym? (often)
   B: No, I lift weights. (hardly ever)
4. **A:** Do you exercise on Sundays? (always)
   B: No, I exercise on Sundays. (never)
5. **A:** What do you do after class? (usually)
   B: I go out with my classmates. (about three times a week)
6. **A:** Do you go to the movies? (often)
   B: Yes, I go to the movies. (once a week)
7. **A:** Do you go bike riding? (ever)
   B: No, I ride a bike. (hardly ever)
8. **A:** Do you walk to school? (sometimes)
   B: Sure. I walk to school. (five days a week)

B **PAIR WORK** Take turns asking the questions in part A. Give your own information when answering.

5 PRONUNCIATION Intonation with direct address

A Listen and practice. Notice these statements with direct address. There is usually falling intonation and a pause before the name.

You have a lot of energy, Riley. You look tired, Aaron. I feel great, Dr. Yun.

B **PAIR WORK** Write four statements using direct address. Then practice them.

6 SPEAKING Fitness programs

A **GROUP WORK** Take a poll in your group. Take turns asking each person these questions. Each person gets two points for each *Yes* answer and one point for each *No* answer.

1
Do you have a regular fitness program?
YES ☐ NO ☐
How often do you exercise?

2
Do you ever go to a gym?
YES ☐ NO ☐
How often do you go? What do you do there?

3
Do you play any sports?
YES ☐ NO ☐
Which ones? How often do you play them?

4
Do you ever take long walks?
YES ☐ NO ☐
How often? Where do you go?

5
Do you do anything else to keep fit?
YES ☐ NO ☐
What do you do?

B **GROUP WORK** Add up your points and study the results of the poll. Who in your group got at least six points?

C **CLASS WORK** Tell the class about one of the people in your group.

"Cynthia does Pilates twice a week, and sometimes she goes jogging. She doesn't . . ."

7 LISTENING I swim twice a week.

A Listen to three people discuss what they like to do in the evening. Complete the chart.

	Activity	How often?
Joseph		
Victoria		
Carlos		

B Listen again. Who is most similar to you – Joseph, Victoria, or Carlos?

5 PRONUNCIATION

Learning Objective: sound more natural when using direct address

A *[CD 2, Track 4]*

- Play the audio program. Use gestures to demonstrate falling intonation. Elicit or explain that direct address statements end with falling intonation.
- Play the audio program again. Ss repeat the statements individually.

B *Pair work*

- Explain the task and model it by writing an example statement.
- Ss write four statements in pairs. Then they practice them. Go around the class and check Ss' intonation.

6 SPEAKING

Learning Objective: ask and answer questions about how frequently one exercises

A *Group work*

- Focus Ss' attention on the directions. Explain that a poll has two parts. First everyone answers the same questions. Then you compare and summarize the answers.
- In small groups, Ss take turns asking each other questions. One S takes notes. Go around the class and give help as needed.

B *Group work*

- Ss add up their points and compare the results of their poll to see who got at least six points. Then one S in each group reports the information to the class.

C *Class work*

- Explain the task. Model the example. Give groups a few minutes to decide who to tell about. One S in each group reports on another person from their group.

7 LISTENING

Learning Objective: listen for key words and specific information in a conversation about exercise

A *[CD 2, Track 5]*

- Set the scene. Three people are talking about their favorite evening activities. Have Ss brainstorm things people do in the evening.
- Explain the task. Ss listen only for favorite activities and complete the first column in the chart. Write the chart on the board.
- Play the audio program. Ss complete the task individually and compare their answers in pairs. Ask different Ss to write the answers on the board.
- Explain the task. Ss listen only for how often Joseph, Victoria, and Carlos do the activities. Ss complete the second column.
- Play the audio program again. Ss complete the task individually and compare their answers in pairs. Ask different Ss to write the answers on the board.

TIP

If Ss have difficulty understanding the audio program, try to find out where they have difficulty. Replay that part of the program and ask what they hear.

Audio script

Victoria So, what do you usually do in the evening, Joseph?
Joseph Well, I exercise a lot. I like to go swimming after work.
Victoria Oh yeah? How often do you go swimming?
Joseph I swim twice a week – on Tuesdays and Thursdays.
Victoria Well, you are in great shape.
Joseph Thanks!
Carlos You're in great shape, too, Victoria.
Victoria Oh, thanks, Carlos. I usually exercise in the evenings. I love it! My friends and I take a yoga class at a gym downtown.
Joseph How often do you go?
Victoria Three times a week. And what about you, Carlos? Do you ever go to the gym in the evenings?
Carlos Actually, I don't exercise very much. I play tennis about twice a month, but I'm not very good.

Answers

	Activity	How often?
Joseph	swimming	twice a week
Victoria	yoga	three times a week
Carlos	tennis	twice a month

B *[CD 2, Track 6]*

- Play the audio program again. Ss listen to find out who is most similar to them. Then they discuss their answers in pairs or small groups.

8 DISCUSSION

Learning Objective: discuss Olympic sports and athletes

Group work

- Focus Ss' attention on the picture. Ask: "What are the Olympics?" Elicit or explain that the Olympics are a series of sports contests that take place every four years in winter and in summer. See if Ss can name when and where any of the recent Olympics have taken place (e.g., Winter: 2014 Sochi, Russia; 2010 Vancouver, Canada; 2006, Turin, Italy; Summer: 2016 Rio de Janeiro, Brazil; 2012 London, U.K.; 2008 Beijing, China)
- Explain that you want Ss to discuss the questions for ten minutes. Point out that it's important to speak fluently, so it's OK to make errors.
- Ss take turns asking and answering the questions in small groups. Go around the class and ask follow-up questions.
- ***Option:*** If the groups want to discuss the questions in more depth, allow them to look up answers to the questions and additional information on their smartphones.

9 WRITING

Learning Objective: write about weekly activities

A

- Explain the task. Point out that Ss can write about any weekly activities, not just sports. Ss read the example paragraph silently.
- Ss make notes about their weekly activities individually.
- Ss write a paragraph based on their notes. Remind Ss to include their favorite activity, but not to reveal which one it is.

! For a new way to teach this Writing, try ***Pass the Paper*** – download it from the website.

B *Group work*

- Explain the task and read the example question. In small groups, Ss read their own descriptions and group members guess which activity is the writer's favorite.

End of Cycle 1

See the Supplementary Resources chart at the beginning of this unit for additional teaching materials and student activities related to this Cycle.

Cycle 2, Exercises 10–14

10 CONVERSATION

Learning Objective: ask and answer questions with *how* in a conversation about exercise

A *[CD 2, Track 7]*

- Ss cover the text and look at the picture. Elicit ideas and vocabulary.
- Write this focus question on the board:

  Do Steph and Mick usually play tennis together?
- Then play the audio program and elicit the answer. (Answer: no)
- Write these focus questions on the board:
  1. *How often does Mick play tennis?*
  2. *How well does Mick play tennis?*
  3. *How good is Steph at tennis?*
- Play the audio program again and elicit the answers. (Answers: 1. three times a week 2. pretty well 3. not very good)
- ***Option:*** Have Ss close their eyes as they listen to the audio program.
- Ss read the conversation silently. Then they practice the conversation in pairs.

B *[CD 2, Track 8]*

- Read the focus question and ask Ss to guess who wins. Then play the audio program. Ss listen to find the answer.

Audio script

Steph Good game, Mick.
Mick Thanks. You, too. And congratulations on the win. You play pretty well.
Steph Oh, no, not really.
Mick How often do you play?
Steph Once or twice a year. I'm just lucky today, I guess. Want to play another game?
Mick Um . . . sure. Just let me take a five-minute break.

Answer

Steph is the winner.

8 DISCUSSION Olympic sports and athletes

GROUP WORK Take turns asking and answering these questions.

Can you remember the names of five Olympic sports? What are they?
Do you ever watch Olympic sports on TV? Which ones?
Would you like to see Olympic sports live? Why? Why not?
Do you prefer the summer or winter Olympics? Why?
What's your favorite Olympic sport? Why?
What's an Olympic sport that you really don't like? Why not?
Who's a famous male athlete in your country? What sport does he play?
Who's a famous female athlete? What sport does she play?

9 WRITING Your weekly activities

A Write about your weekly activities. Include your favorite activity, but don't say which one is your favorite.

> *I usually exercise four or five times a week. I always do yoga on Mondays and Wednesdays. I often go jogging in the morning on Tuesdays and Thursdays. I sometimes go to the beach and play volleyball with my friends on weekends. I . . .*

B **GROUP WORK** Take turns reading your descriptions. Can you guess your partners' favorite activities?

"Your favorite activity is volleyball, right?"

10 CONVERSATION You're in great shape.

A Listen and practice.

STEPH You're in great shape, Mick.
MICK Thanks. I guess I'm a real fitness freak.
STEPH How often do you work out?
MICK Well, I go swimming and lift weights every day. And I play tennis three times a week.
STEPH Tennis? That sounds like a lot of fun.
MICK Oh, do you want to play sometime?
STEPH Uh . . . how well do you play?
MICK Pretty well, I guess.
STEPH Well, all right. But I'm not very good.
MICK No problem. I'll give you a few tips.

B Listen to Mick and Steph after their tennis match. Who's the winner?

11 GRAMMAR FOCUS

Questions with *how*; short answers

How often do you work out?	**How well** do you play tennis?
Every day.	**Pretty well.**
Twice a week.	**About average.**
Not very often.	**Not very well.**
How long do you spend at the gym?	**How good** are you at sports?
Thirty minutes a day.	**Pretty good.**
Two hours a week.	**OK.**
About an hour on weekends.	**Not so good.**

GRAMMAR PLUS *see page 137*

A Complete these questions. Then practice with a partner.

1. **A:** ______________ at sports?
   B: I guess I'm pretty good. I play a lot of different sports.
2. **A:** ______________ spend online?
   B: About an hour after dinner. I like to chat with my friends.
3. **A:** ______________ go to the beach?
   B: Once or twice a month. It's a good way to relax.
4. **A:** ______________ swim?
   B: Not very well. I need to take swimming lessons.

B **GROUP WORK** Take turns asking the questions in part A. Give your own information when answering. Then ask more questions with *how often*, *how long*, *how well*, and *how good*.

12 LISTENING You're in great shape!

Listen to Rachel, Nicholas, Zack, and Jennifer discuss sports and exercise. Who is a couch potato? a fitness freak? a sports nut? a gym rat?

a couch potato

a fitness freak

a sports nut

a gym rat

1. ______________ 2. ______________ 3. ______________ 4. ______________

13 INTERCHANGE 6 What's your talent?

Find out how well your classmates do different activities. Go to Interchange 6 on page 120.

11 GRAMMAR FOCUS

Learning Objective: ask and answer questions with *how*

[CD 2, Track 9]

Questions with how

- Books closed. Write these questions and answers on the board in two columns:

A	B
How often do you work out?	*Pretty well.*
How long do you spend at the gym?	*Twice a week.*
	Not so good.
How well do you play tennis?	*Two hours a week.*
How good are you at sports?	

- Ss match the questions in A with the answers in B.
- Books open. Ss check their answers in the Grammar Focus box.
- Focus Ss' attention on the first column of the Grammar Focus box. Elicit or explain the difference between *how often* and *how long* (*how often* = with what frequency, *how long* = in how much time).
- Focus Ss' attention on the second column. Ask: "How are *how well* and *how good* different?" (They have the same meaning, but *good* is an adjective and *well* is an adverb. Use *how good* with *be* and *how well* with other verbs.)

Short answers

- Point out that answering in complete sentences sounds unnatural. Therefore, people use short answers.
- Play the audio program.

A

- Explain the task. Ss work individually to complete the questions. Check Ss' work as they finish. Ask Ss with correct questions to write them on the board.
- Ss check answers against the board. Then they practice the conversations in pairs.

Answers

1. A: **How good are you** at sports?
2. A: **How long do you** spend online?
3. A: **How often do you** go to the beach?
4. A: **How well can you** swim?

B *Group work*

- Explain the task. Ss take turns asking and answering the questions in small groups. Tell Ss to ask follow-up questions using *how often, how long, how well*, and *how good*.

12 LISTENING

Learning Objective: listen for details in a conversation about exercise

[CD 2, Track 10]

- Books closed. Set the scene. Four friends (Rachel, Nicholas, Zack, and Jennifer) are talking about sports and exercise.
- Play the audio program.
- Books open. Focus Ss' attention on the pictures and read the captions aloud. Ask: "What do you think each type of person is like?"
- Play the audio program again. Have Ss identify the four people.
- Go over answers with the class.

Audio script

Rachel How good are you at sports, Nicholas?
Nicholas Are you kidding? I'm terrible! But I love to watch sports. I go to basketball games all the time. I really love college basketball. I like to read sports news, too. I check a few websites every day.
Rachel Awesome!
Zack Do you like sports, Rachel?
Rachel Oh, yeah. I like to exercise. But I don't watch sports very much, and I never follow sports news.
Zack How much time do you spend exercising?
Rachel Well, I guess I exercise about two or three hours a day. I do aerobics at home three times a week, and the other days I go swimming. Oh, and sometimes I ride my bike.
Zack That's great, Rachel. Hey, Jennifer, you're in great shape, too!
Jennifer Thanks. I go to the gym six days a week.
Rachel Six days a week? Wow!
Jennifer I love the gym. I run on the treadmill and then lift weights for about an hour.
Nicholas And what about you, Zack?
Zack Oh, I'm too lazy to play sports – I really hate exercising. And I almost never go to any sporting events. In my free time, I like to sit with my feet up and watch my favorite TV shows.

Answers

1. Zack 2. Rachel 3. Nicholas 4. Jennifer

13 INTERCHANGE 6

See page T-120 for teaching notes.

14 READING

Learning Objective: skim and make inferences about items in a health and fitness quiz

A

- Read the title. Ask: "What is this? How is it different from a quiz in class?" Elicit ideas.
- Tell Ss to look over the quiz. Ask: "Where can you find this kind of quiz? What is the quiz about?" (Answers: in a magazine or newspaper; health and fitness)
- Go over the task. Then Ss skim the questions in the quiz. Ask Ss to write down the score they think they're going to get.

B

- Explain the task. Read the first question and ask Ss to choose the answer that is true for them.
- Ss read the quiz individually and mark their answers.
- ***Option:*** Ss work in pairs and take turns asking each other the questions. They complete the quiz for each other.
- Go around the class and elicit or explain any new vocabulary.

Vocabulary
servings: portions of food
junk food: food that is not good for you

- Ss add up their points. Then they read the *Rate yourself!* section.
- Ask: "Are the points the same as you guessed? More than you guessed? Fewer than you guessed? Do you agree with your score? Why or why not?"
- ***Option:*** Ss give the quiz to friends or family members for homework. Then they share the results in class.

C *Group work*

- Ss compare their scores in small groups. Ask Ss to list five things they can do to improve their health and fitness. Point out that they can use ideas from the quiz.
- Each group joins another group and shares ideas. Then elicit ideas from the groups.

End of Cycle 2

See the Supplementary Resources chart at the beginning of this unit for additional teaching materials and student activities related to this Cycle and for assessment tools.

14 READING

A How healthy and fit do you think you are? Skim the questions. Then guess your health and fitness score from 0 (very unhealthy) to 50 (very healthy).

FIT AND HEALTHY?

Take the quiz!

1. How many servings of fruits or vegetables do you eat each day?

Five or more.	5
Between one and four.	3
I don't eat fruits or vegetables.	0

2. How much sugar do you use in food and drinks?

I hardly ever use sugar in my food and drink.	5
A little, but I'm careful.	3
A lot. I love sugar!	0

3. How often do you eat junk food?

Never.	5
Maybe once a week.	3
As often as possible.	0

4. How many glasses of water do you drink each day?

Eight or more.	5
Between one and three.	3
I almost always drink soda.	0

5. Do you eat oily fish (for example, sardines, salmon)?

Yes, I love fish!	5
Yes, about twice a month.	3
No, I really don't like fish.	0

6. How often do you exercise?

I usually exercise every day.	5
Two or three times a week.	3
What's exercise?	0

7. Do you walk or bike to work or school?

Yes, whenever I can.	5
I do when I have time.	3
No, never.	0

8. Is fitness important to you?

Yes, it's extremely important.	5
I think it's pretty important.	3
No, it's not important at all.	0

9. What do you do on weekends?

I play as many kinds of sports as I can!	5
I sometimes go for walks or bike rides.	3
I watch TV all day long.	0

10. When you're at work or school, how active are you?

Very active. I walk around a lot.	5
A little active. I go for a walk at lunchtime.	3
I sit at my desk and order lunch.	0

RATE YOURSELF!

42 to 50: Good job! You're doing all the right things for a healthy life.

28 to 41: You're on the right track. With a little more work, you'll be great.

15 to 27: Keep trying! You can be very fit and healthy, so don't give up!

14 or below: It's time to improve your health and fitness. You can do it!

B Take the quiz and add up your score. Is your score similar to your original guess? Do you agree with your score? Why or why not?

C **GROUP WORK** Compare your scores. Who is healthy and fit? What can your classmates do to improve their health and fitness?

Units 5–6 Progress check

SELF-ASSESSMENT

How well can you do these things? Check (✓) the boxes.

I can . . .	Very well	OK	A little
Ask about and describe present activities (Ex. 1, 2, 3)	☐	☐	☐
Describe family life (Ex. 3)	☐	☐	☐
Ask for and give personal information (Ex. 3)	☐	☐	☐
Give information about quantities (Ex. 3)	☐	☐	☐
Ask and answer questions about free time (Ex. 4)	☐	☐	☐
Ask and answer questions about routines and abilities (Ex. 4)	☐	☐	☐

1 LISTENING What are they doing?

A Listen to people do different things. What are they doing? Complete the chart.

What are they doing?

1. ____________________
2. ____________________
3. ____________________
4. ____________________

B **PAIR WORK** Compare your answers.

A: In number one, someone is watching TV.
B: I don't think so. I think someone is . . .

2 SPEAKING Memory game

GROUP WORK Choose a person in the room, but don't say who! Other students ask yes/no questions to guess the person.

A: I'm thinking of someone in the classroom.
B: Is it a man?
A: Yes, it is.
C: Is he sitting in the front of the room?
A: No, he isn't.
D: Is he sitting in the back?
A: Yes, he is.
E: Is he wearing a black T-shirt?
A: No, he isn't.
B: Is it . . . ?

The student with the correct guess has the next turn.

Units 5–6

Progress check

SELF-ASSESSMENT

Learning Objectives: reflect on one's learning; identify areas that need improvement

- Ask: "What did you learn in Units 5 and 6?" Elicit Ss' answers.
- Ss complete the Self-assessment. Encourage them to be honest, and point out they will not get a bad grade if they check (✓) *A little*.
- Ss move on to the Progress check exercises. You can have Ss complete them in class or for homework, using one of these techniques:
  1. Ask Ss to complete all the exercises.
  2. Ask Ss: "What do you need to practice?" Then assign exercises based on their answers.
  3. Ask Ss to choose and complete exercises based on their Self-assessment.

1 LISTENING

Learning Objective: demonstrate one's ability to listen and infer what people are doing

A *[CD 2, Track 11]*

- Explain the task. Ss will hear four sounds of people doing different things. Ss guess what the person is doing and write sentences using the present continuous.
- Model the task. Ask Ss to close their eyes. Then do something that makes a distinctive sound (e.g., write on the board, sharpen your pencil). Ask: "What am I doing?" Ss answer in the present continuous (e.g., *You're writing on the board.*).
- Play the audio program once or twice. Ss listen and complete the chart. Help with vocabulary as needed.

Answers

1. Someone is using/running on a treadmill.
2. Someone is weight training/lifting weights.
3. Someone is bowling.
4. Someone is playing a computer game.

B *Pair work*

- Explain the task. Model the example conversation with a S. Elicit different ways of agreeing and disagreeing.
- Ss compare answers in pairs. Go around the class and check Ss' use of the present continuous.

2 SPEAKING

Learning Objective: demonstrate one's ability to ask and answer questions about present activities

Group work

- Explain the task. Ss work in small groups. One S chooses a person in the room. The other Ss take turns asking present continuous yes/no questions until they guess the person's identity. The S who guesses correctly has the next turn.
- Model the example conversation. Take the role of Student A and ask other Ss to take the roles of Students B, C, D, and E.
- Ss play the game in small groups.

3 SPEAKING

Learning Objective: demonstrate one's ability to ask and answer questions about oneself, one's routines, and one's family

A *Group work*

- Explain the task and read the instructions aloud.
- Ss read the questions in small groups. Then, as a group, they add two more yes/no questions about family life. Encourage Ss to use both the simple present and the present continuous.
- Explain the task. Ss take turns asking and answering the questions. They write the number of *yes* and *no* answers in the correct columns. Remind Ss to include their own answers.

B *Group work*

- Explain the task. For each question, Ss add up the number of yes/no responses in their group. Then they write a sentence to describe the group's responses using determiners (e.g., *most, some, a few, all*).
- Ss complete the task in groups. Then they read their sentences to the class.
- ***Option:*** Complete the activity as a class.

4 DISCUSSION

Learning Objective: demonstrate one's ability to ask and answer questions about free-time activities, routines, and abilities

Group work

- Explain the task. Ss choose three questions and check (✓) them individually. Then they ask each other the questions in small groups. When someone answers "yes," the S must add at least one follow-up question, including *how* questions (e.g., *how well, how often, how good*).
- ***Option:*** Ss think of their own questions beginning with *Do you ever . . . ?*
- Ask three Ss to read the example conversation. Elicit other possible follow-up questions.
- Ss complete the task. Go around the class and check for use of follow-up questions.

WHAT'S NEXT?

Learning Objective: become more involved in one's learning

- Focus Ss' attention on the Self-assessment again. Ask: "How well can you do these things now?"
- Ask Ss to underline one thing they need to review. Ask: "What did you underline? How can you review it?"
- If needed, plan additional activities or reviews based on Ss' answers.

3 SPEAKING Family life survey

A GROUP WORK Add two more yes/no questions about family life to the chart. Then ask and answer the questions in groups. Write down the number of "yes" and "no" answers. (Remember to include yourself.)

	Number of "yes" answers	Number of "no" answers
1. Are you living with your family?		
2. Do your parents both work?		
3. Do you eat dinner with your family?		
4. Are you exercising these days?		
5. Are you studying something these days?		
6. Do you have brothers or sisters?		
7. ______________		
8. ______________		

B GROUP WORK Write up the results of the survey. Then tell the class.

1. In our group, most people are living with their families.
2. Nearly all of our mothers and fathers work.

Quantifiers

All	100%
Nearly all	
Most	
Many	
A lot of	
Some	
Not many	
Few	
No one	0%

4 DISCUSSION Routines and abilities

GROUP WORK Choose three questions. Then ask your questions in groups. When someone answers "yes," think of more questions to ask.

Do you ever . . . ?

- ☐ cook for friends
- ☐ do yoga
- ☐ go jogging
- ☐ listen to English songs
- ☐ play video games
- ☐ play volleyball
- ☐ sing in the shower
- ☐ tell jokes
- ☐ write emails in English

A: Do you ever cook for friends?
B: Yes, I often do.
C: What do you cook?
B: I usually cook fish or pasta.
A: When do you cook?
B: On weekends.
C: How often do you cook?
B: Once a month.
A: How well do you cook?
B: About average. But they always ask for more!

WHAT'S NEXT?

Look at your Self-assessment again. Do you need to review anything?

Unit 7 Supplementary Resources Overview

	After the following SB exercises	You can use these materials in class	Your students can use these materials outside the classroom
CYCLE 1	**1 Snapshot**		**DW** Unit 7 Vocabulary 1
	2 Conversation		
	3 Grammar Focus		**SB** Unit 7 Grammar plus, Focus 1 **DW** Unit 7 Grammar 1–4
	4 Pronunciation		
	5 Word Power	**TR** Unit 7 Vocabulary Worksheet	**DW** Unit 7 Vocabulary 2
	6 Discussion		
	7 Listening		
	8 Interchange 7		**WB** Unit 7 exercises 1–6
CYCLE 2	**9 Conversation**		
	10 Grammar Focus	**TR** Unit 7 Grammar Worksheet **TR** Unit 7 Listening Worksheet **TR** Unit 7 Extra Worksheet	**SB** Unit 7 Grammar plus, Focus 2 **DW** Unit 7 Grammar 5–7
	11 Discussion		
	12 Writing	**TR** Unit 7 Writing Worksheet	
	13 Listening		
	14 Reading	**TR** Unit 7 Project Worksheet **VID** Unit 7 **VRB** Unit 7	**DW** Unit 7 Reading 1–2 **DW** Unit 7 Listening 1–2 **DW** Unit 7 Video 1–2 **WB** Unit 7 exercises 7–11

Key **SB:** Student's Book **DW:** Digital Workbook **TR:** Teacher's Resources
VID: Video (DW/TR) **VRB:** Video Resource Book (TR) **WB:** Print Workbook

My Plan for Unit 7

Use the space below to customize a plan that fits your needs.

With the following SB exercises	I am using these materials in class	My students are using these materials outside the classroom

With or instead of the following SB section	I am using these materials for assessment

7 We went dancing!

- Describe past daily and free-time activities
- Describe past vacations

1 SNAPSHOT

Free-time Activities

☐ check social media

☐ go dancing

☐ listen to music

☐ play video games

☐ read

☐ relax

☐ spend time with friends and family

☐ watch TV

Check (✓) the activities you do in your free time. List three other activities you do in your free time.
What are your favorite free-time activities? Are there activities you don't like? Which ones?

2 CONVERSATION What did you do last weekend?

A Listen and practice.

NEIL So, what did you do last weekend, Cara?

CARA Oh, I had a great time. My friends and I had pizza on Saturday and then we all went dancing.

NEIL How fun! Did you go to The Treadmill?

CARA No, we didn't. We went to that new place downtown. How about you? Did you go anywhere?

NEIL No, I didn't go anywhere all weekend. I just stayed home and studied for today's Spanish test.

CARA Our test is today? I forgot about that!

NEIL Don't worry. You always get an A.

B Listen to the rest of the conversation. What does Cara do on Sunday afternoons?

7 We went dancing!

Cycle 1, Exercises 1–8

In Unit 7, students describe past daily and free-time activities, and describe past vacations. By the end of Cycle 1, students will be able to discuss daily and free-time activities using the simple past with regular and irregular verbs. By the end of Cycle 2, students will be able to discuss vacations using the past tense of *be*.

1 SNAPSHOT

Learning Objective: discuss free-time activities

- Books closed. Ask: "What do you do in your free time?" Help with vocabulary as needed. Write Ss' responses on the board.
- ***Option:*** Ask Ss to guess eight free-time activities. Later, Ss compare their ideas with the Snapshot.
- Books open. Ask different Ss to read the leisure activities aloud. Elicit or explain any new vocabulary.
- Ask: "Do you think these are popular free-time activities? Why or why not?" Elicit Ss' answers.
- Read and explain the four tasks. Point out that, for the third task, Ss should list the activities starting with their favorite. For the last task, Ss should list the activities they don't like.
- Ss complete the tasks individually. Go around the class and give help as needed.
- Elicit Ss' responses.
- ***Option:*** Use Ss' responses to make a list of the top five activities for the class.

! For a new way to practice the Snapshot vocabulary, try ***Vocabulary Steps*** – download it from the website.

2 CONVERSATION

Learning Objective: use the simple past in a conversation about past events

A *[CD 2, Track 12]*

- Set the scene. Neil and Cara are talking about their weekends. Ask Ss to use the pictures to predict what each person did. Elicit or explain vocabulary in the pictures.
- ***Option:*** Ss list all the words they can see in the pictures. Find out who has the most words.
- Books closed. Write these focus questions on the board:

  1. *What did Cara do on Saturday?*
  2. *What did Neil do?*
- Play the audio program. Ss listen for the answers. Then elicit the answers. (Answers: 1. She had pizza and then went dancing with some friends. 2. He stayed home all weekend and studied for the Spanish test.)
- Books open. Play the audio program again. Ss listen and read silently.
- Ss practice the conversation in pairs. Go around the class and give help as needed.

! For a new way to practice this conversation, try the ***Disappearing Dialog*** – download it from the website.

B *[CD 2, Track 13]*

- Read the focus question aloud. Ask Ss to guess. Write some of their ideas on the board.
- Play the audio program. Ss work individually. Then go over the answer with the class.

Audio script

Neil So, Cara, what did you do on Sunday?
Cara I stayed home in the morning. I just watched TV and read.
Neil How about in the afternoon?
Cara Oh, I worked. I have a part-time job at the university bookstore.
Neil I didn't know you had a job.
Cara Yeah, I'm a cashier there. I work every Sunday from 1:00 to 6:00.

Answer

She works on Sunday afternoons.

For more practice talking about last weekend's activities, play the ***Chain Game*** – download it from the website.

TIP
To help Ss who are weak at listening, write the answers on the board. That way, they can *see* the answers.

3 GRAMMAR FOCUS

Learning Objectives: ask and answer simple past questions; use simple past regular and irregular verbs

[CD 2, Track 14]

Simple past questions with did

- Focus Ss' attention on the Conversation on page 44. Ask Ss to find three questions with *did*. Then write them on the board. (Answers: What did you do last weekend? Did you go to the Treadmill? Did you go anywhere?)

TIP
Use a different color for target features (e.g., *did* + verb). This helps Ss visualize the grammar pattern.

- Point out the questions in the Grammar Focus box. Elicit the rules for forming yes/no and Wh-questions in the simple past:
  Did + subject + verb?
  Wh-question + *did* + subject + verb?
- Elicit more examples and write them on the board.
- Play the audio program. Have Ss repeat the questions and responses.

Regular and irregular verbs

- Point out the regular and irregular verbs to the right of part A. Then draw this chart on the board:

Regular verbs	Irregular verbs
work – worked	do – did
invite – invited	drive – drove

- Focus Ss' attention on the Conversation on page 44 again. Ask Ss to find the simple past forms of *stay* and *study*. (Answers: stayed, studied) Ask a S to write them on the board in the *Regular* column. Then ask Ss to find and circle the simple past of *go* and *forget*. (Answers: went, forgot) Ask a different S to write them in the *Irregular* column.
- Have Ss turn to the appendix at the back of the book. Tell them to use this list as needed.
- ***Option:*** Ask Ss to look for patterns in the list of irregular verbs (e.g., *i → a: sit → sat, swim → swam, drink → drank*).

TIP
Some Ss like to repeat things aloud. Others prefer to mouth words or sentences silently. Help Ss find learning styles they prefer.

A

- Explain the task. Model the first conversation with a strong S. Then model it with a different S.
- Ss complete the task individually. Go over answers with the class.

Answers

1. A: **Did** you **stay** home on Sunday?
   B: No, I **called** my friend Anna. We **drove** to a nice little restaurant for lunch.
2. A: How **did** you **spend** your last birthday?
   B: I **had** a party. Everyone **enjoyed** it, but the neighbors next door **didn't like** the noise.
3. A: What **did** you **do** last night?
   B: I **saw** a sci-fi movie at the Cineplex. I **loved** it! Amazing special effects!
4. A: **Did** you **do** anything special over the weekend?
   B: Yes, I **did**. I **went** shopping. Unfortunately, I **spent** all my money. Now I'm broke!
5. A: **Did** you **go** out on Friday night?
   B: No, I **didn't**. I **invited** friends over, and I **cooked** spaghetti for them.

- Ss practice the conversations in pairs.

B *Pair work*

- Explain the task. Then model it by asking different Ss to ask you the questions in part A. Give your own responses.
- Point out that Ss can avoid answering a question by saying *I'd rather not say*. They can also make up answers.
- Ss complete the task in pairs.

For more practice with regular and irregular verbs, play ***Bingo*** – download it from the website.

4 PRONUNCIATION

Learning Objective: use the reduction of *did you* to sound more natural when asking past-tense questions

A *[CD 2, Track 15]*

- Play the audio program. Ss listen for the reduction of *did you*.
- Play the audio program again. Ss practice saying the questions with reductions.
- Tell different Ss to ask the questions. Check their use of reduced forms.

B *Pair work*

- Explain and model the task. Ss complete the task in pairs. Go around the class and check Ss' use of reductions.

3 GRAMMAR FOCUS

Simple past

Did you **work** on Saturday?
Yes, I **did**. I **worked** all day.
No, I **didn't**. I **didn't work** at all.

Did you **go** anywhere last weekend?
Yes, I **did**. I **went** to the movies.
No, I **didn't**. I **didn't go** anywhere.

What **did** Neil **do** on Saturday?
He **stayed** home and **studied** for a test.

How **did** Cara **spend** her weekend?
She **went** to a club and **danced** with some friends.

GRAMMAR PLUS *see page 138*

A Complete these conversations. Then practice with a partner.

1. **A:** ______ you ______ (stay) home on Sunday?
   B: No, I ______ (call) my friend Anna. We ______ (drive) to a nice little restaurant for lunch.
2. **A:** How ______ you ______ (spend) your last birthday?
   B: I ______ (have) a party. Everyone ______ (enjoy) it, but the neighbors next door ______ (not, like) the noise.
3. **A:** What ______ you ______ (do) last night?
   B: I ______ (see) a sci-fi movie at the Cineplex. I ______ (love) it! Amazing special effects!
4. **A:** ______ you ______ (do) anything special over the weekend?
   B: Yes, I ______. I ______ (go) shopping. Unfortunately, I ______ (spend) all my money. Now I'm broke!
5. **A:** ______ you ______ (go) out on Friday night?
   B: No, I ______. I ______ (invite) friends over, and I ______ (cook) spaghetti for them.

regular verbs

work ⟶ work**ed**
invite ⟶ invit**ed**
study ⟶ stud**ied**
stop ⟶ stop**ped**

irregular verbs

buy ⟶ **bought**
do ⟶ **did**
drive ⟶ **drove**
have ⟶ **had**
go ⟶ **went**
sing ⟶ **sang**
see ⟶ **saw**
spend ⟶ **spent**

B **PAIR WORK** Take turns asking the questions in part A. Give your own information when answering.

A: Did you stay home on Sunday?
B: No, I didn't. I went dancing with some friends.

4 PRONUNCIATION Reduction of *did you*

A Listen and practice. Notice how **did you** is reduced in the following questions.

[dɪdʒə]
Did you have a good time?

[wədɪdʒə]
What did you do last night?

[haʊdɪdʒə]
How did you like the movie?

B **PAIR WORK** Practice the questions in Exercise 3, part A again. Pay attention to the pronunciation of **did you**.

5 WORD POWER Chores and activities

A **PAIR WORK** Find two other words or phrases from the list that usually go with each verb. Then add one more word or phrase to each verb.

a lot of fun	dancing	a good time	shopping	a bike ride
the bed	chores	the laundry	a trip	a video

do	*my homework*			
go	*online*			
have	*a party*			
make	*a phone call*			
take	*a day off*			

B **GROUP WORK** Choose the things you did last weekend. Then compare with your partners.

A: I went shopping with my friends. We had a good time. What about you?
B: I didn't have a very good time. I did chores.
C: I did chores, too. But I went dancing in the evening, and . . .

6 DISCUSSION Ask some questions!

GROUP WORK Take turns. One student makes a statement about the weekend. Other students ask questions. Each student answers at least three questions.

A: I went shopping on Saturday afternoon.
B: **Where** did you go?
A: To the Mayfair Center.
C: **Who** did you go with?
A: I went with my friends and my sister.
D: **What time** did you go?
A: We went around 3:00.

7 LISTENING Did you have a good holiday?

A Listen to Andrew tell Elizabeth what he did yesterday. Check (✓) the things Andrew did.

Activities	Reasons
☐ went to the gym	
☐ played soccer	
☐ saw a movie	
☐ watched TV	
☐ went to a baseball game	
☐ spent time with family	

B Listen again. Look at the activities Andrew didn't do. Why didn't he do them? Write the reason.

5 WORD POWER

Learning Objective: discuss daily chores and activities using *do, go, have, make,* and *take*

A *Pair work*

- Copy the chart onto the board. Explain the task.
- Ss complete the task in pairs. Go around the class and give help with new vocabulary.
- ***Option:*** Allow Ss to use dictionaries.
- Ask different Ss to write their answers on the board. Give help with any collocations they don't know.

Answers

do	my homework	chores	the laundry
go	online	dancing	shopping
have	a party	a lot of fun	a good time
make	a phone call	the bed	a video
take	a day off	a bike ride	a trip

B *Group work*

- Explain the task. Model the conversation with two Ss. Then Ss complete the task and compare with a partner.

6 DISCUSSION

Learning Objective: discuss past activities and ask follow-up questions

Group work

- Model the example discussion with three Ss.
- Point out that a good listener shows interest in a conversation by asking follow-up questions.
- Ss complete the activity in groups. Remind Ss to use reduced forms of *did you*.
- ***Option:*** The Ss get one point for each follow-up question they ask. The Ss with the most points in each group win.

7 LISTENING

Learning Objective: listen for details about past activities

A *[CD 2, Track 16]*

- Set the scene. Explain that Andrew is telling Elizabeth what he did, but things didn't go according to plan.
- Explain the task. Play the audio program and Ss complete the chart.
- Ss compare answers in pairs. Then go over answers with the class.

Audio script

Elizabeth So, did you have a good holiday yesterday?
Andrew Yes. It was nice to have the day off.
Elizabeth Did you go to the gym?
Andrew No, I couldn't. It was closed. They were repairing the machines. Instead, a friend and I played soccer.
Elizabeth That's nice. At least you were able to get some exercise. Did you do anything else interesting?
Andrew Well, I wanted to see the new Matt Damon movie. I went to the movie theater, and it wasn't playing.
Elizabeth I hate when that happens.
Andrew I know. So, I went back to my house and watched TV for a while.
Elizabeth Did you do anything fun in the evening?
Andrew I had tickets for last night's baseball game, but it was canceled because of the rain. So, I went to my parents' house and spent the evening with them instead. My mother baked an awesome chocolate cake.
Elizabeth Oh, I love chocolate cake.
Andrew I know. That's why I brought you a piece. Here, enjoy!
Elizabeth Thanks, Andrew!

Answers

Andrew played soccer, watched TV, and spent time with family.

B *[CD 2, Track 17]*

- Explain the task. Read the questions aloud.
- Play the audio program.
- Go over the answers with the class.

Answers

Activities Andrew didn't do:

went to the gym	Reason: It was closed.
saw a movie	Reason: The movie wasn't playing.
went to a baseball game	Reason: The game was canceled because of the rain.

8 INTERCHANGE 7

See page T-121 for teaching notes.

End of Cycle 1

See the Supplementary Resources chart at the beginning of this unit for additional teaching materials and student activities related to this Cycle.

Cycle 2, Exercises 9–14

9 CONVERSATION

Learning Objective: use the simple past of *be* in a conversation about vacations

A *[CD 2, Track 18]*

- Books closed. Set the scene. Leah and Cody are talking about Cody's vacation. Write these focus questions on the board:

  1. *Did Cody enjoy his vacation?*
  2. *Where did he go?*
  3. *How long was he there?*

- Play the audio program. Elicit Ss' answers to the focus questions. (Answers: 1. yes 2. California 3. about a week) Go over any expressions Ss don't understand.
- Books open. Play the audio program again. Ss listen and read the conversation silently.
- Ss practice the conversation in pairs.

B *[CD 2, Track 19]*

- Ask Ss to predict what happened. Write their ideas on the board.
- Play the audio program. Ss listen to find out if any prediction was correct.

Audio script

Leah So, tell me! What happened?
Cody Well, like I said, I went surfing every day. One day, I entered a contest and I won. I got first prize!
Leah Wow! Congratulations!
Cody But that's not all. Someone made a video of me surfing and posted it online. Do you want to see it?
Leah Sure!

Answers

Cody went surfing. He won a contest. Someone made a video of him surfing and posted it online.

10 GRAMMAR FOCUS

Learning Objective: use the past of *be* in questions and short answers

[CD 2, Track 20]

Past of be questions

- Write these questions from the Conversation in Exercise 9 on the board, with *was* or *were* underlined:

  1. *<u>Was</u> the weather OK?*
  2. *What <u>was</u> the best thing about the trip?*
  3. *How <u>was</u> your vacation?*
  4. *How long <u>were</u> you there?*

- Focus Ss' attention on the underlined words on the board and elicit the rules for yes/no and Wh-questions:
  Was/Were + subject + verb?
  Wh-question + *was/were* + subject + verb?

Was/Were and contractions

- Elicit when to use *was* and *were*. Focus Ss' attention on the Grammar Focus box if they aren't sure.
- Use the audio program to present the questions, short answers, and contractions.
- Explain the task. Model the first conversation with a S.
- Ss complete the task individually. Then Ss practice the conversations in pairs.

Answers

1. A: **Were** you in New York last weekend?
   B: No, I **wasn't**. I **was** in Chicago.
   A: How **was** it?
   B: It **was** great! But it **was** cold and windy as usual.
2. A: How long **were** your parents in Chile?
   B: They **were** there for two weeks.
   A: **Were** they in Santiago the whole time?
   B: No, they **weren't**. They also went to Valparaiso.
3. A: **Were** you away last week?
   B: Yes, I **was** in Madrid.
   A: Really? How long **were** you there?
   B: For almost a week. I **was** there on business.

8 INTERCHANGE 7 Memories

Play a board game. Go to Interchange 7 on page 121.

9 CONVERSATION Lucky you!

A Listen and practice.

Leah: Hi, Cody. How was your vacation?
Cody: It was excellent! I went to California with my cousin. We had a great time.
Leah: Lucky you! How long were you there?
Cody: About a week.
Leah: Cool! Was the weather OK?
Cody: Not really. It was pretty cloudy. But we went surfing every day. The waves were amazing.
Leah: So, what was the best thing about the trip?
Cody: Well, something incredible happened. . . .

B Listen to the rest of the conversation. What happened?

10 GRAMMAR FOCUS

Past of *be*

		Contractions
Were you in California?	Yes, I **was**.	wasn**'t** = was **not**
Was the weather OK?	No, it **wasn't**.	weren**'t** = were **not**
Were you and your cousin on vacation?	Yes, we **were**.	
Were your parents there?	No, they **weren't**.	
How long **were** you away?	I **was** away for a week.	
How **was** your vacation?	It **was** excellent!	

GRAMMAR PLUS *see page 138*

Complete these conversations. Then practice with a partner.

1. **A:** ______ you in New York last weekend?
   B: No, I ______ . I ______ in Chicago.
   A: How ______ it?
   B: It ______ great! But it ______ cold and windy as usual.
2. **A:** How long ______ your parents in Chile?
   B: They ______ there for two weeks.
   A: ______ they in Santiago the whole time?
   B: No, they ______ . They also went to Valparaiso.
3. **A:** ______ you away last week?
   B: Yes, I ______ in Madrid.
   A: Really? How long ______ you there?
   B: For almost a week. I ______ there on business.

11 DISCUSSION Past and future vacations

A **GROUP WORK** Ask your classmates about their last vacations.
Ask these questions or use your own ideas.

Where did you spend your last vacation?
How long was your vacation?
Who were you with?
What did you do?
How was the weather?
What would you like to do on your next vacation?

B **CLASS ACTIVITY** Who had an interesting vacation?
Tell the class who and why.

12 WRITING A blog post

A Read the blog post.

TRAVEL BLOG   Home   About   Posts   Subscribe

Greetings from sunny Puerto Vallarta, Mexico! I'm having a great time. Yesterday, I took a tour of the old town. The buildings and monuments were amazing! This morning, I went swimming and snorkeling. Then I went shopping at one of the town's open markets. I bought a very beautiful handmade ceramic vase and tried the famous fish on a stick. Delicious!

I'm having a really great vacation!

Casey

B **PAIR WORK** Write a blog post to your partner about your last vacation. Then exchange posts. Do you have any questions about your partner's vacation?

13 LISTENING I was on vacation.

A Listen to Daniel and Amanda talk about their vacations.
Did they have a good time? Check (✓) Yes or No.

	Yes	No
Daniel	☐	☐
Amanda	☐	☐

B Listen again. Complete the chart with information about their vacations.

Daniel's vacation		Amanda's vacation	
Place		Place	
Who with		Who with	
Activities		Activities	

11 DISCUSSION

Learning Objective: discuss past vacations and retell a story using the simple past

A *Group work*

- Books closed. Ss work in small groups. Assign different groups the topics *transportation, weather,* and *food.* Groups brainstorm words related to the topics.
- Ask a S from each group to write their words on the board. For example:

Transportation	Weather	Food
car, bus	rainy, sunny	good, bad

- Books open. Explain the task and read the example questions. Ask Ss to think of more questions related to vacations. Write their questions on the board.
- Model the task by describing a vacation you took.
- Ss take turns talking about their vacations in small groups. Go around the class and note any errors.
- Write any errors you noted on the board. Ss try to correct them as a class.

TIP
It's best not to interrupt Ss during a discussion or fluency activity. Instead, listen and note any errors you hear. Go over the most common ones after the activity.

B *Class activity*

- Ss in each group vote for the most interesting vacation. Then one S from each group tells the class about it. Encourage other Ss to ask questions.

12 WRITING

Learning Objective: write a post about a past vacation

A

- Ss read the blog post silently. Elicit or explain any new vocabulary. *Snorkeling* is swimming while using a curved pipe called a *snorkel* to breathe. *Ceramic* means made from clay.

B *Pair Work*

- Explain the task. Tell Ss to use the questions in Exercise 11 for ideas about the topic.
- Ss write blog posts individually. Go around the class and check Ss' work.
- Ss exchange posts with a partner. Partners read each other's posts and ask questions about each other's vacations.
- ***Option:*** Ss find vacation posts from social media or travel websites and share them with the class.

! For a new way to teach this Writing, try ***Pass the Paper*** – download it from the website.

13 LISTENING

Learning Objective: listen for main ideas and details about vacations discussed using the simple past of *be*

A *[CD 2, Track 21]*

- Set the scene. Two friends, Daniel and Amanda, are talking about their vacations.
- Play the audio program. Ask Ss to listen to find out if they enjoyed their vacations. They check *yes* or *no* in the chart.

Audio script

Amanda Daniel! Hi! Welcome back. You were away last week, right?
Daniel Yeah, I was on vacation.
Amanda Where did you go?
Daniel I went to San Francisco.
Amanda Nice! How was it?
Daniel Oh, I loved it! It's a really pretty city.
Amanda So . . . why San Francisco?
Daniel Oh, my sister lives there. I stayed with her. I went sightseeing, and she loves to shop, so we went shopping every day. Look, I got this sweater.
Amanda Nice! I didn't go anywhere on my last vacation. I didn't have enough money to go anywhere.
Daniel Oh, that's too bad.
Amanda Oh, not really. I actually enjoyed my vacation a lot. A friend from college stayed with me for a week. We just talked and watched a lot of old movies.
Daniel That sounds fun, too.

Answers

Daniel: Yes Amanda: Yes

B *[CD 2, Track 22]*

- Play the audio program again. Ss complete the chart with information about Daniel's and Amanda's vacations. Pause the audio for Ss to write as needed.
- Go over answers with the class.

Answers

Daniel's vacation
Place: San Francisco Who with: sister
Activities: went sightseeing, went shopping
Amanda's vacation
Place: home Who with: a friend from college
Activities: talked, watched movies

14 READING

Learning Objective: read for main ideas and details in online posts about past vacations

- ***Option:*** Ask Ss to bring in recent vacation photos. In pairs or small groups, Ss talk about the places.

A

- Ask Ss to cover the writing of the online posts and look at the pictures. Ask: "Where did each person go on his or her vacation? What do you think he or she did there?" Elicit ideas. Help with vocabulary as needed (e.g., *China, mountains, desert, Egypt, lake, Bolivia*).
- ***Option:*** Bring in a world map and help Ss find the Tianzi Mountains, Hunan Province, China; the Sahara Desert, Hurghada, Egypt; and Salar de Uyuni, Uyuni, Bolivia. Elicit Ss' knowledge about these places.

B

- Explain the task. Remind Ss to try to guess the meanings of any words they don't know.
- Ss read the three posts silently and complete the task individually. Then they compare answers in pairs or small groups.
- ***Option:*** Ask pairs or groups to find the place in each post where the sentences fit best.
- Elicit or explain any new vocabulary.

Vocabulary

cable car: a vehicle that hangs from cables and carries people up mountains
man-made: made by people, not natural
desert: a large, hot dry area of land with little water and few plants
land art: art that uses the natural materials of the earth in the landscape
satellite: a piece of equipment that travels in space and sends signals to Earth
prehistoric: of a time in the past before there were written records

- Go over answers with the class.

Answers

1. 3 2. 1 3. 2

C *Pair work*

- Ss discuss the questions in pairs. Go around the class and give help as needed.
- To check answers, have pairs share their responses with the class.

Answers

1. Marco took a cable car.
2. Letitia saw a piece of land art.
3. Kelly had a very active vacation.
4. Answers will vary.

! For a new way to teach this Reading, try ***Jigsaw Learning*** – download it from the website.

End of Cycle 2

See the Supplementary Resources chart at the beginning of this unit for additional teaching materials and student activities related to this Cycle.

14 READING

A Look at the pictures. What do you think each person did on his or her vacation?

Profile Photos Share Friends

Awesome Vacations

1

Marco Tianzi Mountains

I came to this awesome place three days ago. These are the Tianzi Mountains, in Hunan Province, China. The mountains cover 67 square kilometers (or over 16,000 acres), and they are named for a famous farmer who lived in the area. I took a cable car up to the mountains. The ride was about six minutes long. The views are breathtaking! The mountains look almost like they are man-made. Sadly, my trip is almost over and I have to go home. But I want to come back soon!

2

Letitia Desert Breath

Guys, look at this! This is in the desert near Hurghada, Egypt. I was just there with my friend Carla. Desert Breath is a piece of land art made by three people in the nineties – an artist, an architect, and an engineer. It's made of sand, and it covers a large area of the Sahara Desert – 100,000 square meters (or about 25 acres). Every year, some of the art disappears. The wind moves the sand away. For now, it's so large that satellites in space take photos of it. How cool is that?

3

Kelly Giant Salt Lake

I flew from La Paz to Uyuni to see this spectacular place. I took so many pictures. It's called Salar de Uyuni, and it's in beautiful Bolivia. It was part of a giant salt lake in prehistoric times. I went there in a group with a guide. You have to walk a lot, so you need to be in pretty good shape. We walked for a whole day! Sometimes you feel like you're walking on clouds. When I saw the lake, it looked like a giant mirror. I'll never forget it!

B Read the online posts. Then write the number of the post where each sentence could go.

_____ It was pretty tiring, but I enjoyed every minute of it.
_____ The ride was scary because we were so high up.
_____ I hope to meet the people who made it.

C **PAIR WORK** Answer these questions.

1. Which person used an unusual form of transportation?
2. Who saw a piece of art?
3. Who had a very active vacation?
4. Which place do you think is the most interesting? Why?

Unit 8 Supplementary Resources Overview

	After the following SB exercises	You can use these materials in class	Your students can use these materials outside the classroom
CYCLE 1	**1 Word Power**	**TR** Unit 8 Extra Worksheet	**DW** Unit 8 Vocabulary 1–2
	2 Conversation		
	3 Grammar Focus	**TR** Unit 8 Vocabulary Worksheet	**SB** Unit 8 Grammar plus, Focus 1 **DW** Unit 8 Grammar 1–4
	4 Pronunciation		
	5 Speaking		
	6 Listening		**WB** Unit 8 exercises 1–5
CYCLE 2	**7 Snapshot**		
	8 Conversation		
	9 Grammar Focus	**TR** Unit 8 Grammar Worksheet **TR** Unit 8 Listening Worksheet	**SB** Unit 8 Grammar plus, Focus 2 **DW** Unit 8 Grammar 5–7
	10 Interchange 8		
	11 Writing	**TR** Unit 8 Writing Worksheet	
	12 Reading	**TR** Unit 8 Project Worksheet **VID** Unit 8 **VRB** Unit 8	**DW** Unit 8 Reading 1–2 **DW** Unit 8 Listening 1–2 **DW** Unit 8 Video 1–2 **WB** Unit 8 exercises 6–9

With or instead of the following SB section	You can also use these materials for assessment
Units 7–8 Progress Check	**TESTING PROGRAM** Units 7–8 Oral Quiz **TESTING PROGRAM** Units 7–8 Written Quiz **TESTING PROGRAM** Units 1–8 Test

Key **SB:** Student's Book **DW:** Digital Workbook **TR:** Teacher's Resources
VID: Video (DW/TR) **VRB:** Video Resource Book (TR) **WB:** Print Workbook

My Plan for Unit 8

Use the space below to customize a plan that fits your needs.

With the following SB exercises	I am using these materials in class	My students are using these materials outside the classroom

With or instead of the following SB section	I am using these materials for assessment

8 How's the neighborhood?

- Ask about and describe places
- Describe a neighborhood

1 WORD POWER Places and activities

A Match the places and the definitions. Then ask and answer the questions with a partner.

What's a . . . ?	*It's a place where you . . .*
1. clothing store ______	**a.** get food and small items for the home
2. grocery store ______	**b.** can connect to the Internet
3. hair salon ______	**c.** get a haircut
4. laundromat ______	**d.** buy newspapers and magazines
5. newsstand ______	**e.** see a game or a concert
6. stadium ______	**f.** find new fashions
7. Wi-Fi hot spot ______	**g.** wash and dry your clothes

B **PAIR WORK** Write definitions for these places.

coffee shop **drugstore** **gas station** **library** **post office**

It's a place where you drink coffee and tea and eat small meals. (coffee shop)

C **GROUP WORK** Read your definitions. Can your classmates guess the places?

2 CONVERSATION I just moved in.

Listen and practice.

Greg: Excuse me! Hi, I'm your new neighbor, Greg. I just moved in.

Mrs. Cook: Oh. Yes?

Greg: I'm looking for a grocery store. Are there any around here?

Mrs. Cook: Yes, there are some on Pine Street.

Greg: Oh, good. And is there a laundromat near here?

Mrs. Cook: Well, I think there's one across from the shopping center.

Greg: Thank you.

Mrs. Cook: By the way, there's a hair salon in the shopping center.

Greg: A hair salon?

8 How's the neighborhood?

Cycle 1, Exercises 1–6

In Unit 8, students ask about and describe places, and describe a neighborhood. By the end of Cycle 1, students will be able to ask about and describe places using *there is/there are* and prepositions of place. By the end of Cycle 2, students will be able to describe features of a neighborhood using quantifiers.

1 WORD POWER

Learning Objective: describe what you do at places in a neighborhood

A

- Introduce the topic of neighborhoods. Ask: "What places do you need to find in a neighborhood?" Elicit Ss' answers and write them on the board.
- Focus Ss' attention on the picture. Elicit the names of places that might be in the picture (e.g., *clothing store, gift shop*).
- Model the task. Ask: "What's a clothing store?" Tell Ss to say "stop" when you read the correct definition. Read out possible answers (e.g., *It's a place where you get food and small items for the home. It's a place where you can connect to the Internet.*) until the Ss say "stop."
- Ss match the words and definitions individually. Then go over answers with the class.

Answers

1. f 2. a 3. c 4. g 5. d 6. e 7. b

- Ss take turns asking and answering the questions in pairs. Go around the class and give help as needed.
- Go over any errors you noticed, including pronunciation errors.

B *Pair work*

- Present the example definition for *coffee shop*. Then elicit more possible definitions from the class (e.g., *It's a place where you meet friends after class.*) and write them on the board.
- Ss write definitions for each place in pairs. Go around the class and give help as needed.

Possible answers

Place	It's a place where you . . .
coffee shop	drink coffee and eat small meals
drugstore	buy medicine and toiletries
gas station	get gas for your vehicle
library	read and borrow books
post office	mail letters, cards, and packages

C *Group work*

- Model the task. Each pair from part B joins another pair. Pairs take turns giving definitions and guessing places.

2 CONVERSATION

Learning Objective: use *there is/there are* and *one/any/some* in a conversation about places in a neighborhood

[CD 2, Track 23]

- Books closed. Write this question on the board:

  When you move to a new neighborhood, what do you need to find?
- Elicit answers from the class and write them on the board.
- Set the scene. Greg just moved into a new neighborhood, and he is looking for two things. What are they? Play the audio program.
- Go over answers with the class. (Answer: He's looking for a grocery store and a laundromat.)
- Books open. Elicit information about the picture. Ask: "What other place does Mrs. Cook suggest? Why?" Then play the audio program again. Ss listen and find the answers. (Answer: She suggests a hair salon because Greg needs a haircut.)
- Play the audio program again. Ss listen and read the conversation silently.
- Ss practice the conversation in pairs.

3 GRAMMAR FOCUS

Learning Objectives: ask and answer questions with *there is/there are*; answer questions with *one/any/some/* prepositions of place

[CD 2, Track 24]

Is there/Are there?

- Before class, write these words on nine large cards:

is	There	a laundromat
one	are	grocery stores
any	some	near/around here

TIP
Cards are useful for helping Ss visualize grammar in an active way. They work well with grammar topics such as word order and substitution.

- Focus Ss' attention on the Conversation on page 50. Ask: "What question does Greg ask beginning with *is there?*" Elicit the question. Then ask four Ss to come to the front of the class. Have them stand in line holding up these cards:

  S1: is　　S2: there
  S3: a laundromat　　S4: near/around here

- Ask: "What question does Greg ask beginning with *are there?*" Elicit the question. Then ask five Ss to stand in line holding up these cards:

  S1: are　　S2: there　　S3: any
  S4: grocery stores　　S5: near/around here

- Focus Ss' attention on the two questions in the Grammar Focus box. Elicit the rule for forming questions with *is there* and *are there*.
  Is there + *a/an* + singular noun + *near/around here?*
  Are there + *any* + plural noun + *near/around here?*

One *and* some

- Ask four Ss to hold up these cards:

  S1: there　　S2: is
  S3: a laundromat　　S4: near/around here

- Point out that a singular noun and its article such as *a laundromat* can be replaced by *one*. Ask another S to take the card *one* and replace S3.
- Repeat the activity with plural nouns. This time, replace *grocery stores* with *some*.
- Play the audio program.

Prepositions

- Elicit or explain the meaning of the prepositions. Use the map. Ask: "What places are *on* Elm Street?" (Answer: Star Plaza Hotel, Bing's Café, Clifford Hotel) Ask Ss about other places using prepositions.
- ***Option:*** For more practice visualizing the prepositions in an active way, ask Ss to stand *across from* each other, *next to* the wall, *near* the board, etc.

A

- Explain the task and read the example questions. Ss write questions individually. Point out that there should be a preposition in each question.
- Ss compare their questions in small groups. They read out their questions and check for grammatical accuracy.
- Go around the class and give help as needed. Ask three or four Ss with correct questions to write them on the board.

Possible answers

All questions should follow these patterns:
Is there + a singular noun + a preposition + a place?
(e.g., *Is there a bank across from the hotel?*)
Are there any + plural noun + a preposition + a place?
(e.g., *Are there any hotels on Elm Street?*)

B *Pair work*

- Model the task two or three times using the map and the questions on the board:

  T: Is there a bank across from the hotel?
  S1: Yes, there is. There's one next to the grocery store.
  T: Are there any gas stations on Pine Street?
  S2: No, there aren't. But there's one on Main Street.

TIP
To make sure that Ss understand instructions, always model the task at least twice. If possible, model it with different Ss each time.

- Ss take turns asking and answering their questions in pairs. Go around the class and give help as needed.

! For a new way to teach this Grammar Focus, try ***Picture Dictation*** – download it from the website. Describe a town or city center to your Ss. Include streets and places.

3 GRAMMAR FOCUS

There is, there are; one, any, some

Is there a laundromat near here?
Yes, **there is**. There's **one** across from the shopping center.
No, **there isn't**, but there's **one** next to the library.

Are there any grocery stores around here?
Yes, **there are**. There are **some** nice stores on Pine Street.
No, **there aren't**, but there are **some** on Third Avenue.
No, **there aren't any** around here.

Prepositions
in
on
next to
near/close to
across from/opposite
in front of
in back of/behind
between
on the corner of

GRAMMAR PLUS *see page 139*

A Look at the map below. Write questions about these places.

| an ATM | coffee shops | a department store | an electronics store | Wi-Fi hot spots |
| gas stations | grocery stores | a gym | hotels | a post office |

Is there a gym around here?
Are there any restaurants on Main Street?

B **PAIR WORK** Ask and answer the questions you wrote in part A.

A: Is there a gym around here?
B: Yes, there is. There's one on Main Street next to the post office.

4 PRONUNCIATION Reduction of *there is/there are*

A Listen and practice. Notice how *there is* and *there are* are reduced in conversation, except for short answers.

Is there a bank near here?
Yes, **there is**. **There's** one on First Avenue.

Are there any coffee shops around here?
Yes, **there are**. **There are** some on Pine Street.

B Practice the questions and answers in Exercise 3, part B again.

5 SPEAKING A nice neighborhood

A **PAIR WORK** Choose a neighborhood in your city or town. Fill in the chart with information about the neighborhood. Write three examples for each category. Go to Exercises 1 and 3 for ideas and use your own ideas, too.

There is a/an . . . (where?)	There are some . . . (where?)
There isn't a/an . . . (where?)	**There aren't any . . . (where?)**

B **GROUP WORK** Take turns asking and answering questions with another pair about the neighborhoods. If you don't know about a place your new partners ask about, answer, "Sorry, I don't know." Who gets more "Yes" answers?

A: Is there a gym in your neighborhood?
B: Yes, there's one across from the park.
C: Are there any coffee shops?
D: No, there aren't any in our neighborhood.
B: Is there a bookstore in your neighborhood?
A: Sorry, I don't know.

6 LISTENING We need some directions.

A Listen to hotel guests ask about places to visit. Complete the chart.

Place	Location	Interesting? Yes	Interesting? No
Flavors of Hollywood		☐	☐
Museum of Modern Art		☐	☐
City Zoo		☐	☐

B **PAIR WORK** Which place sounds the most interesting to you? Why?

4 PRONUNCIATION

Learning Objective: sound more natural by reducing *there is/there are* in long answers

A *[CD 2, Track 25]*

- Play the audio program. Point out the reduced forms. Ask Ss to practice the short conversations using the reductions. Point out that *there is* is often contracted to *there's* in writing, but *there are* is not.

B

- Go over the instructions and model the task.
- Go around the class and give individual feedback on Ss' use of reductions.

TIP
It's more important to recognize reductions than to produce them. Don't force Ss to produce reductions if they are not ready.

5 SPEAKING

Learning Objective: ask and answer questions with *there is/there are* and *one/any/some/*prepositions of place

A *Pair work*

- Model the task. Tell the class the name of a neighborhood that they are familiar with. Then model some examples, such as, "In the village center, there's a bank on Green Street. There aren't any restaurants on Tenth Avenue."
- Focus Ss' attention on the chart. Explain the task. Elicit what Ss will write to explain *where*. (Answer: a preposition and a place) Encourage Ss to look at Exercises 1 and 3 and to use their own ideas.
- Ss complete the task in pairs. Go around the class and help where needed.

B *Group work*

- Explain the task. Model the conversation with three Ss. Point out that Ss should say, "Sorry, I don't know," if they don't know about a place.
- In groups, pairs take turns asking and answering about places. Go around and listen for Ss' use of *there is/there are*. Note any errors, but don't correct them.
- Have groups report who got the most "yes" answers. Then go over any errors on the board with the class.

6 LISTENING

Learning Objective: listen for details about places

A *[CD 2, Track 26]*

- Read out the instructions to set the scene. Then play the audio program. Ss listen and complete the *Location* column in the chart.
- Play the audio program again. Ss listen, decide if the hotel clerk thinks the places are interesting, and check (✓) *Yes* or *No*.
- Go over answers with the class.

Audio script

Clerk Good morning. Can I help you?
Guest 1 Yes, please. We need some directions.
Clerk Sure. What are you looking for?
Guest 1 Well, first of all, we're looking for the Flavors of Hollywood restaurant. How far is it from here?
Clerk Oh, it's just a few minutes from here – right across from the post office.
Guest 2 The post office on Western Avenue?
Clerk Yes, that's the one.
Guest 2 Is Flavors of Hollywood a nice place?
Clerk Well, I think so. The food is good, and there are some interesting things to look at in the restaurant from movies like *Rocky*, *The Terminator*, and *Titanic*.
Guest 2 Great! And where is the Museum of Modern Art?
Clerk Well, that's near the City Concert Hall.
Guest 1 Near the City Concert Hall. OK, I know where that is. And what's the museum like?
Clerk Actually, it's small, and it doesn't have any famous art, so some people think it's not very interesting.
Guest 1 Oh, then maybe we won't go there.
Guest 2 Hmm, one last question – is there a zoo in the city?
Clerk Yes, there's a very good one. The City Zoo is only about six blocks from here. It's in the park next to the train station.
Guest 2 Oh, good! That's not very far from here.
Clerk No, it isn't. Definitely visit the zoo.
Guest 1 OK! Thanks a lot.
Clerk You're welcome. Have a good day.

Answers

Place	Location	Interesting?
Flavors of Hollywood	across from the post office on Western Avenue	Yes
Museum of Modern Art	near the City Concert Hall	No
City Zoo	in the park next to the train station	Yes

B *Pair work*

- Ss discuss the questions in pairs.

End of Cycle 1

See the Supplementary Resources chart at the beginning of this unit for additional teaching materials and student activities related to this Cycle.

7 SNAPSHOT

Learning Objective: describe different neighborhoods

- Focus Ss' attention on the pictures. Elicit information about the pictures. Elicit or explain new vocabulary.

Vocabulary
suburb: an area outside of a city where people live
district: a part of a city that has a lot of one kind of business
campus: the land and buildings that belong to a college or university
industrial: connected with industry; having a lot of factories

- Ask pairs of Ss to brainstorm businesses and things that you might find in one of the neighborhoods. Elicit ideas from the class and write them on the board.
- Ss answer the questions in small groups. Go around the groups and give help as needed.

8 CONVERSATION

Learning Objective: ask and answer questions and use quantifiers in a conversation about a neighborhood

[CD 2, Track 27]

- Elicit information about the picture. Ask: "What is the woman doing? What floor do you think she lives on? What does the neighborhood look like?"
- Books closed. Write these focus questions on the board:
  1. What are Barry and Alana talking about?
  2. What does Alana invite Barry to do at the end of the conversation?
- Play the audio program. Ask Ss to listen for the answers to the focus questions. Then go over the answers. (Answers: 1. Alana's new apartment and neighborhood 2. She invites him to have dinner at the Italian restaurant downstairs.)

TIP
To reduce anxiety, point out that Ss will hear the audio program several times. Remind them that they aren't expected to understand every word.

- Write these additional focus questions on the board:
  1. Where is Alana's new apartment?
  2. Is Alana's new neighborhood safe?
  3. When does it get noisy in Alana's apartment?
- Play the audio program again. Elicit Ss' answers. (Answers: 1. downtown 2. yes, there isn't much crime 3. on the weekends) Then elicit or explain any new vocabulary.

Vocabulary
downtown: the business center of a city
convenient: easy to get to or find things
traffic: the amount of cars and trucks using a road
crime: illegal activities
safe: not dangerous; without crime

- Books open. Play the audio program again. Ss listen and read the conversation silently.
- Ss practice the conversation in pairs.
- ***Option:*** Ss practice the conversation in pairs again but change the details, such as the amounts of traffic, noise, and crime, and the restaurant type.

! For a new way to practice this conversation, try the ***Onion Ring*** technique – download it from the website.

7 SNAPSHOT

NEIGHBORHOODS

What types of businesses are or aren't found in these neighborhoods?
Which areas do you visit often? Which areas do you hardly ever visit? Why?

8 CONVERSATION It's very convenient.

Listen and practice.

BARRY How do you like your new apartment, Alana?

ALANA I love it. It's downtown, so it's very convenient.

BARRY Downtown? Is there much traffic?

ALANA Yeah, there's a lot. But I don't drive, so it's OK.

BARRY Oh, that's right. Is there much crime in the area?

ALANA No, it's pretty safe. The difference is the noise.

BARRY Really? Is there a lot of noise?

ALANA There's a lot on the weekend from the Italian restaurant downstairs.

BARRY Oh, that's too bad. But is the food at the restaurant good?

ALANA It's incredible! Hey, would you like to have dinner there on Saturday?

BARRY Yes! I love Italian food.

9 GRAMMAR FOCUS

Quantifiers; *how many* and *how much*

Count nouns

Are there **many restaurants**?

Yes, there are **a lot**.

There are **a few**.

No, there are**n't many**.

No, there are**n't any**.

No, there are **none**.

How many restaurants are there?

There are 10 or 12.

Noncount nouns

Is there **much crime**?

Yes, there's **a lot**.

There's **a little**.

No, there is**n't much**.

No, there is**n't any**.

No, there's **none**.

How much crime is there?

There's a lot of crime.

GRAMMAR PLUS *see page 139*

A Write answers to these questions about your neighborhood. Then practice with a partner.

1. Is there much parking?
2. Are there many apartment buildings?
3. How much traffic is there?
4. How many drugstores are there?
5. Is there much noise?
6. Are there many shopping malls?
7. Is there much pollution?
8. How many fast-food restaurants are there?

B **GROUP WORK** Write questions like those in part A about these topics. Then ask and answer the questions.

cafés crime parks trash public transportation schools traffic lights

10 INTERCHANGE 8 Where are we?

Play a guessing game. Go to Interchange 8 on page 122.

11 WRITING My neighborhood

A Read this paragraph Kate wrote about her neighborhood.

B Now write a paragraph about your neighborhood. Describe what type of neighborhood it is and what places are or aren't in your area.

C **PAIR WORK** Read your partner's paragraph. Ask follow-up questions to get more information.

I live in a very nice neighborhood near my office, so I walk or ride my bike to work every morning. It's a very green area with many trees and a small but beautiful park. It's also very convenient. There is a shopping mall behind my building. In the mall, there are two drugstores, a bank, and a grocery store. And there is a café with great food and good prices. I get coffee there every morning. But there isn't a library, and most books at the bookstore are expensive. Oh well, nothing is perfect!

9 GRAMMAR FOCUS

Learning Objective: ask and answer questions with count and noncount nouns and quantifiers

[CD 2, Track 28]

Count and noncount nouns

- Write this chart on the board:

Count nouns	Noncount nouns
restaurant	traffic
café	crime

- Ask: "Which nouns take a plural *-s* ending?" (Answer: restaurant and café) "Which nouns usually don't take a plural *-s* ending?" (Answer: traffic and crime) Explain that *restaurant* and *café* are count nouns because we can count them (e.g., *one restaurant, two restaurants*). However, we don't count *traffic* or *crime*.

For more practice with count and noncount nouns, play ***Tic-Tac-Toe*** – download it from the website.

How many *and* how much

- Focus Ss' attention on the Conversation on page 53. Have Ss underline questions with *is there* and *are there* (e.g., *Is there much traffic? Is there much crime in that area? Is there a lot of noise?*).
- Elicit or explain the rules:
  Is there + *much* + noncount noun?
  How many + count noun + *are there*?

Quantifiers

- Focus Ss' attention on the Grammar Focus box. Point out that quantifiers are used to describe different amounts of things (e.g., *a lot, a few, any, many, much, none*).
- Ask Ss to look at the Grammar Focus box. Ask "How are *a lot, any,* and *none* similar?" (Answer: They can be used with both count or noncount nouns.)
- Play the audio program.

A

- Model the first question. Ss complete the exercise individually. Then Ss compare their answers in pairs.
- Go over the answers as a class.

Possible answers

1. Yes, there's a lot. There's a little. No, there isn't much/any. No, there's none.
2. Yes, there are a lot/many. There are a few. No, there aren't any. No, there are none.
3. There's a lot/a little/none. There isn't much/any.
4. There are a lot/many. There are a few. There aren't any. There are none.
5. Yes, there's a lot. There's a little. No, there isn't much/any. No, there's none.
6. Yes, there are a lot/many. There are a few. No, there aren't any. No, there are none.
7. There is a lot/a little/none. There isn't much/any.
8. There are a lot/many. There are a few. There aren't any. There are none.

- Ss ask and answer the questions in pairs.
- ***Option:*** Ss repeat the task with a new partner.

B *Group work*

- Explain and model the task.
- Ss write questions individually. Then they take turns asking and answering the questions in pairs.

10 INTERCHANGE 8

See page T-122 for teaching notes.

11 WRITING

Learning Objective: write a paragraph about one's neighborhood

A

- Ss read the example paragraph silently. Elicit or explain any new vocabulary.
- Point out that Kate wrote about what she likes and doesn't like about her neighborhood, the places in it, and what she does every day.

B

- Explain the task. Ss write their paragraphs individually. Go around the class and give help as needed.

C *Pair work*

- Explain the task. While Ss are asking questions, check for correct use of count and noncount nouns.

12 READING

Learning Objective: scan and read for details in an article about three neighborhoods

A

- Ss cover the text and look at the pictures. Ask: "What do you think this neighborhood in Tokyo is like?" Elicit ideas from the class.
- Go over the task. Point out that Ss should scan quickly to look for the word *nightlife*. Set a time limit.

TIP
When Ss scan an article, set a time limit. This encourages them to read quickly, focusing only on the task.

- Ss silently scan the article and check (✓) the neighborhood that is famous for nightlife. (Answer: Pigneto, Rome) Elicit answers from the class.

B

- Model the task. Ask Ss to read the first paragraph. Then elicit the main idea.
- Ss read the article in detail. Elicit or explain any new vocabulary.

Vocabulary
hip: very fashionable at the moment
indie: not controlled by anyone else
live music venue: a place where musicians perform music for an audience
festival: a series of special events or performances
boutique: a small shop that carries specially selected items
locally made: something that is created very close to where it is sold

- Ss write the paragraph letters next to the items.
- Go over answers with the class.

Answers

1. C 2. A 3. B 4. A
5. C 6. B 7. A 8. B

C *Pair work*

- Read the questions aloud. Model an example of your favorite neighborhood.
- Ss discuss the questions in pairs. Have some pairs share their answers with the class.

End of Cycle 2

See the Supplementary Resources chart at the beginning of this unit for additional teaching materials and student activities related to this Cycle and for assessment tools.

12 READING

A Scan the article. Check (✓) the neighborhood that is famous for nightlife.

☐ Roma Norte ☐ Shimokitazawa ☐ Pigneto

Locations Reservations Shop Sign in Register

HIP NEIGHBORHOODS OF THE WORLD

Ⓐ Shimokitazawa, Tokyo

This is the place to be for fans of indie music! Head over to this creative neighborhood and discover record stores, concert halls, and theaters in the narrow streets. Shimokitazawa (or Shimokita, for short) is a relaxed place full of young people who visit the cafés and live music venues. Every year, there is a theater festival here. It's a very popular place for students.

Ⓑ Pigneto, Rome

La Sapienza, a famous college in Rome, is near this neighborhood. It's an extremely cool place to hang out. Pigneto has a huge choice of restaurants, cafés, and ice cream stores. Pigneto is famous for its nightlife. As you walk around, you hear electronic music coming from different clubs. People also come here for the Nuovo Cinema Aquila, the best place to see indie movies from around the world.

Ⓒ Roma Norte, Mexico City

This place is popular with artists, students, tourists, and musicians. Feeling hungry? Go to a huge food market, Mercado Roma, to taste delicious ceviche, squid torta, and other Mexican specialties. Next, check out the trendy restaurants for dinner, or shop for beautiful fashion items in the boutiques. There are hip T-shirts and sneakers for sale everywhere. There's locally made jewelry you can buy, too!

B Read the article. Then write the letter of the paragraph where these things are mentioned.

1. ______ local jewelry
2. ______ festivals
3. ______ indie movies
4. ______ record stores
5. ______ food specialties
6. ______ a college
7. ______ theaters
8. ______ ice cream

C **PAIR WORK** What's your favorite neighborhood in your city or country? What is interesting about it? What do you like to do there?

Units 7–8 Progress check

SELF-ASSESSMENT

How well can you do these things? Check (✓) the boxes.

I can . . .	Very well	OK	A little
Understand descriptions of past events (Ex. 1)	☐	☐	☐
Describe events in the past (Ex. 1)	☐	☐	☐
Ask and answer questions about past activities (Ex. 2)	☐	☐	☐
Give and understand simple directions (Ex. 3)	☐	☐	☐
Talk about my neighborhood (Ex. 4)	☐	☐	☐

1 LISTENING Jimmy's weekend

A A thief robbed a house on Saturday. A detective is questioning Jimmy. The pictures show what Jimmy really did on Saturday. Listen to their conversation. Are Jimmy's answers true (**T**) or false (**F**)?

1:00 P.M. T F 3:00 P.M. T F 5:00 P.M. T F 6:00 P.M. T F 8:00 P.M. T F 10:30 P.M. T F

B **PAIR WORK** What did Jimmy really do? Use the pictures to retell the story.

2 DISCUSSION How good is your memory?

A Do you remember what you did yesterday? Check (✓) the things you did. Then add two other things you did.

☐ got up early	☐ went to class	☐ did the laundry	☐ went to bed late
☐ exercised	☐ ate at a restaurant	☐ did the dishes	☐ ________
☐ texted a friend	☐ went shopping	☐ went online	☐ ________

B **GROUP WORK** Ask questions about each thing in part A.

A: Did you get up early yesterday?
B: No, I didn't. I got up at 10:00. I was very tired.

Units 7–8

Progress check

SELF-ASSESSMENT

Learning Objectives: reflect on one's learning; identify areas that need improvement

- Ask: "What did you learn in Units 7 and 8?" Elicit Ss' answers.
- Ss complete the Self-assessment. Encourage them to be honest, and point out they will not get a bad grade if they check (✓) *A little*.
- Ss move on to the Progress check exercises. You can have Ss complete them in class or for homework, using one of these techniques:
  1. Ask Ss to complete all the exercises.
  2. Ask Ss: "What do you need to practice?" Then assign exercises based on their answers.
  3. Ask Ss to choose and complete exercises based on their Self-assessment.

1 LISTENING

Learning Objective: demonstrate one's ability to understand descriptions of and describe past events

A *[CD 2, Track 29]*

- Explain the task. Elicit or explain that a *thief* is someone who commits the crime of *stealing*, which is taking something that doesn't belong to him. When the thief enters a house illegally and steals, it is called *robbing*. A *detective* is a member of the police who tries to find out what happened.
- Play the audio program. Ss complete the task. Then go over answers with the class.

Audio script

Detective Hello, Jimmy. I'm Detective Roberts. Can I ask you a few questions about your weekend?
Jimmy Hi, Detective. Um, sure. What do you want to know about my weekend?
Detective Now just tell the truth. Where were you at 1:00 P.M. on Saturday?
Jimmy Ah . . . 1:00 P.M. . . . on Saturday? Well, oh, I remember! I was at home. I watched the baseball game on TV. Yeah, the White Hats won, four to nothing. It was a great game.
Detective OK . . . OK. Where were you at 3:00 P.M.?
Jimmy Ah . . . at 3:00? Oh yeah, I went to my martial arts class like I always do, every Saturday at 3:00.
Detective Martial arts, huh? Well . . . OK. And what did you do after that? At 5:00 P.M.?
Jimmy Uh . . . oh, well, after class, I visited some old friends of mine – Jordan and Stephanie Smith, on Lake Street.
Detective Yeah? Jordan and Stephanie Smith. We'll talk to them. Now, Jimmy, 6:00. Where were you at 6:00?
Jimmy Hmm . . . at 6:00? Well, I went home at 6:00 . . . yeah . . . to . . . uh . . . clean the house.
Detective Yeah, yeah, so you cleaned the house. Now, listen carefully, Jimmy. Where were you at 8:00 on Saturday night?
Jimmy Uh . . . at 8:00? Uh . . . oh, yeah . . . I remember now. I was at home. I watched a terrific movie online. Yeah . . . it was great!
Detective Oh, you watched a movie? And what movie did you watch? What was the name of the movie, Jimmy?
Jimmy The movie? The name of the movie? Uh, let me think a minute. It was a fantastic movie.
Detective Really?
Jimmy No, wait! I remember, it was, uh . . . uh . . . well, it was exciting.
Detective OK, Jimmy . . .
Jimmy . . . and I clearly remember that I went to bed at 10:30, uh, exactly . . . Yeah. I watched the movie, and I went to bed right after . . . uh . . . the movie. Yeah, boy, I was tired – a long day, like I said.
Detective Interesting. Very interesting, Jimmy. Come on, Jimmy. Let's go down to the police station.
Jimmy The police station? Me? Why me? I was at home on Saturday night!
Detective Sure, Jimmy, sure.

Answers

T, T, F, T, F, F

B *Pair work*

- Ss retell the story in pairs.

2 DISCUSSION

Learning Objective: demonstrate one's ability to ask and answer questions about past activities

A

- Ss check (✓) the things they did individually yesterday. Then they add two more things.

B *Group work*

- Model the conversation with a S. Then Ss ask and answer questions about the things in part A in small groups.

3 SPEAKING

Learning Objective: demonstrate one's ability to give and follow simple directions

A

- Explain the task. Ss create a neighborhood. They choose five places from the list and add them to *My map*.
- For plurals, tell Ss to be sure to draw two places on their maps.
- Ss complete the task individually.
- Go around the class and give help as needed.

B *Pair work*

- Read the instructions aloud. Ask two Ss to model the example conversation. Explain that Student A draws one gas station on the corner of Center Street and First Avenue and another gas station on Center Street across from the park on *My partner's map*. Point out that Ss cannot look at their partners' maps.
- Ss take turns asking and answering questions in pairs.
- Tell Ss to ask any additional questions to find the exact location of each place (e.g., *Is it next to the grocery store?*).
- Ss then compare maps. Ask: "Did you draw the places in the correct locations?"

4 ROLE PLAY

Learning Objective: demonstrate one's ability to describe a neighborhood

- Explain the task. Ss work in pairs. Student A is a visitor in Student B's neighborhood. Student A asks questions and Student B answers them.
- Model the example conversation with a S.
- Go over the topics in the box. Explain or elicit any new vocabulary.
- Ss practice the role play in pairs. Then they change roles and practice again.
- Go around the class and check Ss' use of *how many, how much*, and quantifiers.

WHAT'S NEXT?

Learning Objective: become more involved in one's learning

- Focus Ss' attention on the Self-assessment again. Ask: "How well can you do these things now?"
- Ask Ss to underline one thing they need to review. Ask: "What did you underline? How can you review it?"
- If needed, plan additional activities or reviews based on Ss' answers.

3 SPEAKING What's your neighborhood like?

A Create a neighborhood. Add five places to "My map." Choose from this list. Add plural words two or more times.

a bank **a bookstore** **cafés** **drugstores** **gas stations** **a gym** **a theater**

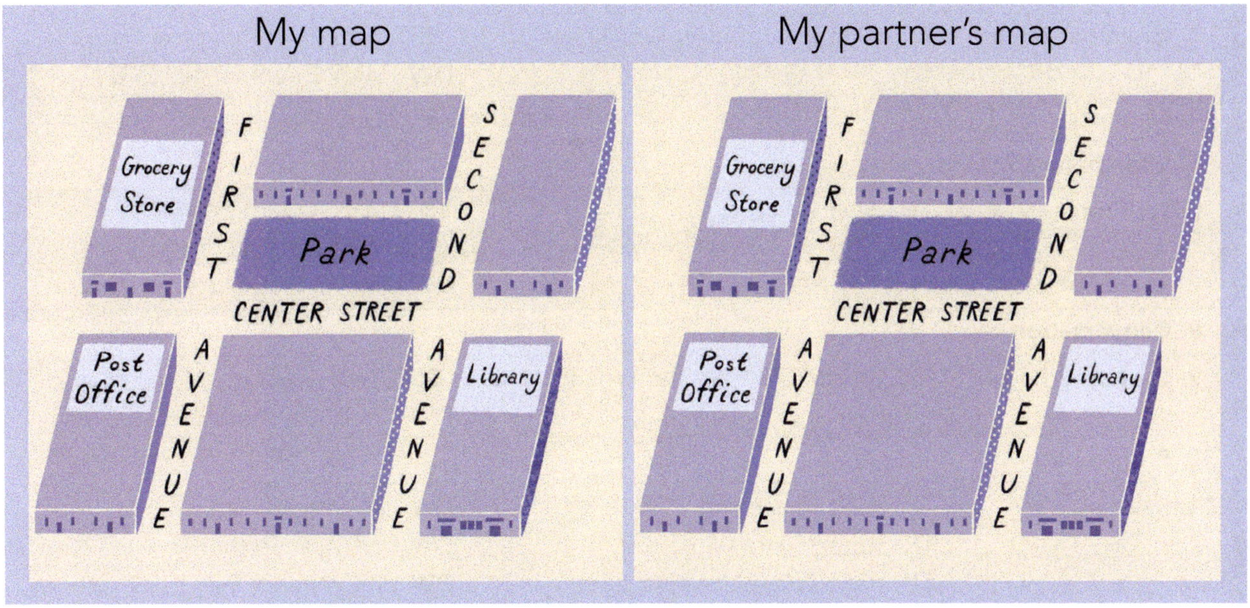

B **PAIR WORK** Ask questions about your partner's map. (But don't look!) Draw the places on "My partner's map." Then compare your maps.

A: Are there any gas stations in the neighborhood?
B: Yes, there are two. There's one on the corner of Center Street and First Avenue and one on Center Street across from the park.

4 ROLE PLAY Tell me about your neighborhood.

Student A: Imagine you are a visitor in Student B's neighborhood. Ask questions about it.

Student B: Imagine a visitor wants to find out about your neighborhood. Answer the visitor's questions.

A: Is there much crime?
B: There isn't much. It's a very safe neighborhood.
A: Is there much noise?
B: Well, yes, it's a shopping district, so . . .

Change roles and try the role play again.

topics to ask about

buildings
crime
noise
parking
parks
places to shop
pollution
public transportation
schools
traffic

WHAT'S NEXT?

Look at your Self-assessment again. Do you need to review anything?

Unit 9 Supplementary Resources Overview

	After the following SB exercises	You can use these materials in class	Your students can use these materials outside the classroom
CYCLE 1	**1 Word Power**		**DW** Unit 9 Vocabulary 1
	2 Conversation		
	3 Grammar Focus	**TR** Unit 9 Vocabulary Worksheet	**SB** Unit 9 Grammar plus, Focus 1 **DW** Unit 9 Grammar 1–2, 7–8
	4 Listening		
	5 Interchange 9		
	6 Writing	**TR** Unit 9 Writing Worksheet	**WB** Unit 9 exercises 1–5
CYCLE 2	**7 Snapshot**		**DW** Unit 9 Vocabulary 2
	8 Conversation		
	9 Grammar Focus	**TR** Unit 9 Grammar Worksheet	**SB** Unit 9 Grammar plus, Focus 2 **DW** Unit 9 Grammar 3–6
	10 Pronunciation		
	11 Reading	**TR** Unit 9 Listening Worksheet **TR** Unit 9 Extra Worksheet **TR** Unit 9 Project Worksheet **VID** Unit 9 **VRB** Unit 9	**DW** Unit 9 Reading 1–2 **DW** Unit 9 Listening 1–2 **DW** Unit 9 Video 1–2 **WB** Unit 9 exercises 6–11

Key **SB:** Student's Book **DW:** Digital Workbook **TR:** Teacher's Resources
VID: Video (DW/TR) **VRB:** Video Resource Book (TR) **WB:** Print Workbook

My Plan for Unit 9

Use the space below to customize a plan that fits your needs.

With the following SB exercises	I am using these materials in class	My students are using these materials outside the classroom

With or instead of the following SB section	I am using these materials for assessment

9 What does she look like?

- Describe people's physical appearance
- Identify people by describing how they look and what they're doing

1 WORD POWER Physical appearance

A Look at these expressions. What are three more words or expressions to describe people? Write them in the box below.

HAIR

long brown hair | short blond hair | straight black hair | curly red hair | bald | a mustache and a beard

AGE

young | middle-aged | elderly

LOOKS

handsome | good-looking | pretty

HEIGHT

short | fairly short | medium height | pretty tall | very tall

Other words or expressions

______

______

______

B **PAIR WORK** Choose at least four expressions to describe yourself and your partner. Then compare. Do you agree?

A: You have long blond hair. You're pretty tall.

B: I don't think so. My hair isn't very long.

Me	My partner

9 What does she look like?

In Unit 9, students describe people's physical appearance and identify people by describing how they look and what they're doing. By the end of Cycle 1, students will be able to describe people's physical appearance. By the end of Cycle 2, students will be able to identify people using modifiers with participles and prepositions to describe how they look, what they are wearing, what they're doing, and where they are.

Cycle 1, Exercises 1–6

1 WORD POWER

Learning Objective: describe people's physical characteristics

A

- Books closed. Explain that Ss will learn ways to describe what people look like. Ask questions about different Ss: "Is he tall or short? Does she have straight or curly hair?"
- ***Option:*** Ask Ss to bring pictures of friends or family members to class. Alternatively, bring magazine pictures of people to class.
- Books open. Focus Ss' attention on the expressions and pictures. Ask them to circle any words they don't know.
- Ask different Ss to read the expressions. Give help with pronunciation as needed. Point out that *handsome* usually refers to men and *pretty* to women, but *good-looking* describes both men and women. Also point out that adverbs such as *fairly* and *pretty* can modify the strength of different descriptions (e.g., *fairly short, pretty tall*).
- Write these headings across the top of the board:

  Hair Age Looks Height Other
- Ss work in groups. Ask Ss to brainstorm at least three more expressions to describe people. Then ask a S from each group to write their expressions under the correct headings on the board.

Possible answers

Hair: light brown hair, dark brown hair, gray hair, medium length hair, wavy hair, a ponytail
Age: ten, in his or her teens/twenties/thirties, old
Looks: thin, heavy, cute, beautiful, gorgeous
Height: rather short, quite tall
Other: blue eyes, green eyes, dark eyes, brown eyes

TIP
Don't give your Ss too much new vocabulary. If they already know the presented vocabulary, add more. If not, add just a few extra words they want to know.

- Explain or elicit the rules for using the new words:
  be + adjective
  have + noun

  Then ask Ss to write *have* or *be* next to the expressions on the board. Stress that we use *be* with age.
- ***Option:*** Ss write sentences about famous people using expressions from the boxes (e.g., *Chris Hemsworth is handsome.*). Then they read their sentences to their classmates, who agree or disagree.

B *Pair work*

- Ss choose at least four expressions to describe themselves and their partners. They complete the chart individually. Go around the class and give help as needed.
- Ask two Ss to read the example conversation. Elicit other expressions for agreeing or disagreeing (e.g., *That's true. No way!*). Write them on the board.
- Ss compare charts in pairs. Go around the class and give help as needed.
- ***Option:*** Ss work with different partners. This time, they sit back-to-back and describe each other from memory.

! For a new way to review, categorize, or expand on the vocabulary in this Word Power, try ***Mind Mapping*** – download it from the website.

2 CONVERSATION

Learning Objective: ask and answer questions to describe a person in a conversation

A [CD 2, Track 30]

- Ss cover the text. Ask Ss to describe the people in the picture.
- Write these focus questions on the board:

  1. *Who are Justin and Lauren talking about?*
  2. *How does Justin describe her?*
  3. *How old is she?*

- Play the audio program and elicit the answers. (Answers: 1. Justin's new girlfriend 2. She's really smart and pretty. She's tall and has beautiful brown hair. 3. Justin doesn't know.)
- Ss uncover the text. Play the audio program again. Ss listen and read silently.
- Elicit or explain any new vocabulary.

Vocabulary
5 foot 10: 178 centimeters
rude: not polite

- Ss practice the conversation in pairs. Go around the class and give help as needed.
- ***Option:*** Ss cover the conversation and look only at the picture. Then they practice the conversation again using their own words.

B [CD 2, Track 31]

- Read the focus question aloud. Ask Ss to make predictions. Write their predictions on the board.
- Play the audio program. Ss listen for the answer to the focus question.
- Ss compare answers in small groups. Then go over answers with the class. Was anyone's prediction correct?

Audio script

Lauren So you don't know her age?
Justin No. But I don't really care.
Lauren OK. Well, how old do you think she is?
Justin Who knows? I think she's in her thirties.
Lauren And how old are you?
Justin I'm 29.
Lauren Oh, cool, so she's older than you.

Possible answer

TIffany is probably in her thirties. Tiffany is older than Justin.

3 GRAMMAR FOCUS

Learning Objective: ask and answer questions about physical appearance and age

[CD 2, Track 32]

- Books closed. Write these questions and statements on the board:

1. *What does she look like?*	a. *It's pretty short.*
2. *How old is she?*	b. *She's pretty.*
3. *How tall is she?*	c. *She's about 32.*
4. *How long is her hair?*	d. *She's 5 foot 10.*

- Ask Ss to match the questions with the answers. (Answers: 1. b, 2. c, 3. d, 4. a)
- Books open. Tell Ss to look at the Grammar Focus box to check their answers. Play the audio program.

A

- Explain the task. Read the first answer and elicit the question.
- Ss complete the task individually. Then they compare answers in pairs.
- Write the numbers 1 to 7 on the board. Ask different Ss to write the questions on the board. Then go over them as a class.

Answers

1. How old is your father?
2. How tall are you?
3. What color is your cousin's hair?/What color hair does your cousin have?
4. Does he wear glasses?
5. What does he look like?
6. How long is your sister's hair?
7. What color are your eyes?/What color eyes do you have?

B Pair work

- Explain the task and model the example conversation with a S.
- Ss complete the task in pairs. Go around the class and check Ss' grammar.

For more practice asking questions about appearance, play ***Twenty Questions*** – download it from the website.

2 CONVERSATION She's so pretty!

A Listen and practice.

Lauren: I hear you have a new girlfriend, Justin.

Justin: Yes. Her name's Tiffany. She's really smart, and she's so pretty!

Lauren: Really? What does she look like?

Justin: Well, she's very tall.

Lauren: How tall?

Justin: About 5 foot 10, I suppose.

Lauren: Yeah, that *is* pretty tall. What color is her hair?

Justin: She has beautiful brown hair.

Lauren: And how old is she?

Justin: I don't know. I think it's a little rude to ask.

B Listen to the rest of the conversation. What else do you learn about Tiffany?

3 GRAMMAR FOCUS

Describing people

General appearance	Height	Hair	Age
What does she look like?	How tall is she?	How long is her hair?	How old is she?
She's tall, with brown hair.	She's 1 meter 78.	It's pretty short.	She's about 32.
She's pretty.	She's 5 foot 10.		She's in her thirties.
Does he wear glasses?	How tall is he?	What color is his hair?	How old is he?
No, he wears contacts.	He's medium height.	It's dark/light brown.	He's in his twenties.

Saying heights

	U.S.	Metric
	five (foot) ten.	one meter seventy-eight tall.
Tiffany is	five foot ten inches (tall).	1 meter 78.
	5'10".	178 cm.

GRAMMAR PLUS *see page 140*

A Write questions to match these statements. Then compare with a partner.

1. ______________________? My father is 52.
2. ______________________? I'm 167 cm (5 foot 6).
3. ______________________? My cousin has red hair.
4. ______________________? No, he wears contact lenses.
5. ______________________? He's tall and very good-looking.
6. ______________________? My sister's hair is medium length.
7. ______________________? I have dark brown eyes.

B **PAIR WORK** Choose a person in your class. Don't tell your partner who it is. Your partner will ask questions to guess the person's name.

A: Is it a man or a woman?
B: It's a man.

A: What color is his hair?
B: . . .

4 LISTENING Which one is Justin?

A Listen to descriptions of six people. Number them from 1 to 6.

B Listen again. How old is each person?

5 INTERCHANGE 9 Find the differences

Compare two pictures of a party. Student A go to Interchange 9A on page 123. Student B go to Interchange 9B on page 124.

6 WRITING Describing physical appearance

A You are helping to organize a special event at your school with sports, arts, and a surprise celebrity guest. Write an email to a friend inviting him or her to the event, and describe the celebrity. Don't give the celebrity's name.

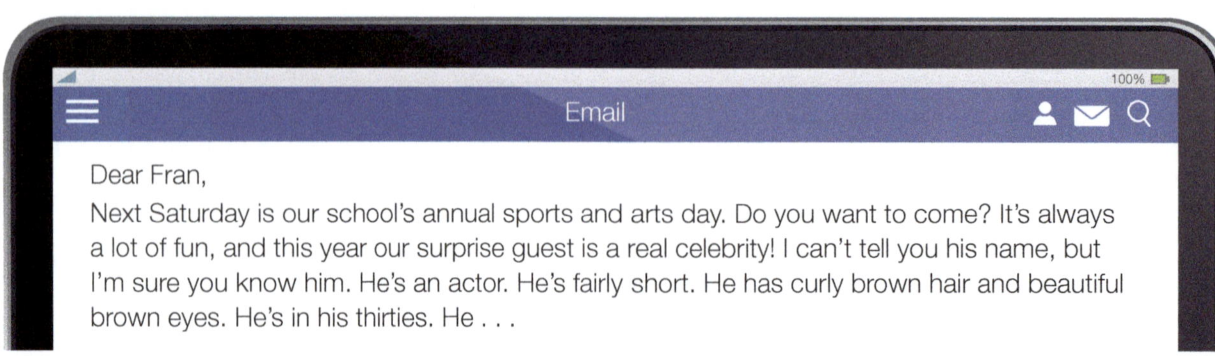

B **GROUP WORK** Read your email to the group. Can they guess the celebrity you are describing?

4 LISTENING

Learning Objective: listen for details about people's physical appearance and age

A ***[CD 2, Track 33]***

- Focus Ss' attention on the picture. In pairs Ss brainstorm words or expressions to describe each person. Point out that they should describe the people, not their clothes.
- Each pair joins another pair and compares ideas. Go around the class and give help as needed.
- Explain the task. Tell Ss to listen for key words (e.g., *short, glasses*) and not worry about understanding every word.
- Play the audio program. Ss complete the task individually.
- Go over answers with the class.

Audio script

1. I think Chris is good-looking. He's pretty tall, with dark brown hair, and he has a beard. I think he's about 30.
2. Courtney's 18. She has blond hair – shoulder length and straight – and she always wears interesting hats, just for fun.
3. Victoria is pretty tall for her age. She has curly red hair and always wears a baseball cap. She just turned 10.
4. Justin's in his twenties. He's fairly short and wears glasses. His hair isn't very long.
5. Mark is middle-aged. He's going bald and has a mustache. He likes to wear sunglasses. And he always wears a leather jacket.
6. Hannah is very tall, and she has long black hair. She's around 25. Oh, and she's very slim. I don't think she wears glasses, but I'm not sure.

Answers

3, 5, 2, 6, 1, 4

B ***[CD 2, Track 34]***

- Ask a S to read the focus question aloud. Then play the audio program. Ss listen for the answers.
- Ss compare answers in pairs. Elicit their answers. Play the audio program again if needed.

Answers

1. Chris is 30.
2. Courtney is 18.
3. Victoria is 10.
4. Justin is in his twenties.
5. Mark is middle-aged.
6. Hannah is around 25.

5 INTERCHANGE 9

See pages T-123 and T-124 for teaching notes.

6 WRITING

Learning Objective: write an email describing someone

A

- Set the scene. Say: "Imagine you're organizing a special event at your school and a *celebrity* – a famous person like a singer, actor, or sports star – will be the surprise guest. You will write an email to a friend describing the celebrity without naming him or her. How will you describe the celebrity?"
- Ask a S to read the model email. Elicit or explain any new words or expressions.
- Explain the task. Each S writes an email describing a celebrity. Point out that Ss should not write the name of the celebrity.
- ***Option:*** Ss write the email for homework.

B ***Group work***

- Explain the task and read the question.
- Ss take turns reading their descriptions in small groups. Their classmates guess which celebrity they are describing.

End of Cycle 1

See the Supplementary Resources chart at the beginning of this unit for additional teaching materials and student activities related to this Cycle.

Cycle 2, Exercises 7–11

7 SNAPSHOT

Learning Objective: discuss clothing styles

- Books closed. Ask: "What kind of clothing is in fashion now?" Help Ss with vocabulary as needed.
- Write these clothing styles on the board: *boho, classic prep, hipster,* and *streetwear*. Elicit or explain their meanings.

Vocabulary
boho: short for "bohemian"; an informal style
flowy: moves in a floating manner
floral print: a pattern made from flowers
classic: always fashionable
prep: short for "preparatory school"; a traditional style
pastel: pale, soft colors
hipster: someone who is influenced by the latest ideas
hip: short form of "hipster"; fashionable
logo: a company's symbol or design

- Ss brainstorm examples of clothing for each style.
- Books open. Ss compare their ideas with the Snapshot.
- Ask different Ss to read the questions.
- Ss complete the task individually. Then they compare answers in pairs or small groups. Elicit Ss' answers.
- ***Option:*** Bring fashion magazines to class. Ss discuss which styles are boho, classic prep, hipster, or streetwear.
- ***Option:*** Assign classes of younger Ss to make their own Snapshots. Ss cut pictures of clothing from fashion magazines, put them on cards, and label the items and styles. Then display the Ss' work. Or Ss can create online picture boards and share them with the class.

8 CONVERSATION

Learning Objective: use modifiers, prepositions, and participles in a conversation about identifying people

A *[CD 2, Track 35]*

- Write these questions on the board:
  1. *Where are these people?*
  2. *What are they doing?*
  3. *What are they wearing?*
  4. *What do they look like?*
- Focus Ss' attention on the picture. Have Ss ask each other the questions about the people in the picture. Then elicit possible answers.
- Set the scene. Diego comes to a party alone. He meets his friend Brooke. She tells him about some people at the party.
- Write these focus questions on the board:
  1. *Where's Cora?*
  2. *Where's Paula?*
  3. *Does Paula know anyone at the party?*
- Play the audio program once or twice. Elicit Ss' answers to the focus questions. (Answers: 1. She's at a concert. 2. She's standing near the window. 3. No, she doesn't.)
- Play the audio program again. Ss look at the picture and read the conversation silently.
- Elicit or explain any new vocabulary.

Vocabulary
couldn't make it: wasn't able to come

- Ss practice the conversation in pairs.

! For a new way to teach this Conversation, try the ***Musical Dialog*** – download it from the website.

B *[CD 2, Track 36]*

- Explain the task.
- Play the audio program. Ss listen and label the people in the picture individually.
- Ss compare answers in pairs. Then go over answers with the class. Play the audio program again if needed.

Audio script

Brooke	Let's see. Who else is here? Do you know Liam? He's really nice.
Diego	No, I don't. Which one is he?
Brooke	He's over there. He's the one wearing gray pants, a white shirt, and . . .
Diego	. . . and a light blue sweater?
Brooke	That's right. And then there's Hina Sasaki. She works with me at the office.
Diego	Oh? Which one is Hina?
Brooke	She's the woman in a long dress. She's wearing glasses.
Diego	Yeah, I see her. She's the one talking to Liam, right?
Brooke	Yep.
Diego	And who are those two people dancing?
Brooke	Oh, that's my best friend. Her name is Sierra. She's really nice.
Diego	That's a pretty red dress. And who's that guy dancing with her?
Brooke	That's Matt Segal, her new boyfriend.
Diego	Oh, that's her boyfriend?
Brooke	Yeah. Hey, didn't you want to meet Paula?
Diego	Sorry, but which one is Paula again?

Answers

(from left to right) Sierra, Liam, Hina, Matt

7 SNAPSHOT

New York *Street Fashion*

Boho (Bohemian)

The boho girl wears comfortable clothes – long skirts and flowy dresses in colorful floral prints.

Classic Prep

The preppy guy wears shirts and sweaters in pastel colors, khaki pants, and leather belts.

Hipster

The hipster wears hip hats, jewelry, and large glasses. Black is a popular color. The men often have unique hairstyles and long beards.

Streetwear

The streetwear fan wears casual and trendy clothes: jeans, basketball jerseys, baseball caps, T-shirts with logos, and cool sneakers.

Do you see your style(s)? Which one(s)?
Which style(s) do you like? Which do you dislike? Why?
Do you see any of these styles on the streets in your town or city? Which one(s)?

8 CONVERSATION Which one is she?

A Listen and practice.

Brooke: Hi, Diego! Good to see you! Is Cora here, too?

Diego: Oh, she couldn't make it. She went to a concert with Alanna.

Brooke: Oh! Let's go talk to my friend Paula. She doesn't know anyone here.

Diego: Paula? Which one is she? Is she the woman wearing a long skirt over there?

Brooke: No, she's the tall one in jeans and a scarf. She's standing near the window.

Diego: OK. I'd like to meet her.

B Listen to the rest of the conversation. Label Liam, Hina, Sierra, and Matt in the picture.

9 GRAMMAR FOCUS

Modifiers with present participles and prepositions

		Participles
Who's Diego?	He's **the man**	**wearing** a blue shirt.
Which one is Diego?	He's **the one**	**talking** to Brooke.
		Prepositions
Who's Brooke?	She's **the woman**	**with** long black hair.
Which one is Paula?	She's **the tall one**	**in** jeans.
Who are the Harrisons?	They're **the people**	**next to** the window.
Which ones are the Harrisons?	They're **the ones**	**on** the couch.

GRAMMAR PLUS *see page 140*

A Rewrite these statements using modifiers with participles or prepositions.

1. Kyle is the tall guy. He's wearing a yellow shirt and brown pants.
   Kyle is the tall guy wearing a yellow shirt and brown pants.
2. Mark and Eve are the middle-aged couple. They're talking to Michael.
   ____
3. Alexis is the young girl. She's in a white T-shirt and blue jeans.
   ____
4. Britney is the woman in the green dress. She's sitting to the left of Javier.
   ____
5. J.P. is the serious-looking boy. He's playing a video game.
   ____

B **PAIR WORK** Complete these questions using your classmates' names and information. Then take turns asking and answering the questions.

1. Who's the guy (man) sitting next to ______________________?
2. Who's the girl (woman) wearing ______________________?
3. Who is ______________________?
4. Which one is ______________________?
5. Who are the people ______________________?
6. Who are the ones ______________________?

10 PRONUNCIATION Contrastive stress in responses

A Listen and practice. Notice how the stress changes to emphasize a contrast.

A: Is Rob the one wearing the red shirt?
B: No, he's the one wearing the **black** shirt.

A: Is Rachel the woman on the couch?
B: No, **Jen** is the woman on the couch.

B Mark the stress changes in these conversations. Listen and check. Then practice the conversations.

A: Is Sophie the one sitting next to Judy?
B: No, she's the one standing next to Judy.

A: Is David the one on the couch?
B: No, he's the one behind the couch.

9 GRAMMAR FOCUS

Learning Objective: use modifiers with participles and prepositions to describe people

[CD 2, Track 37]

Modifiers with participles and prepositions

- Write these five sentences on the board:
  1. He's the man dancing in the living room.
  2. She's the one wearing a red dress.
  3. She's the one with glasses.
  4. He's the one in gray pants.
  5. She's the tall person next to the window.
- Focus Ss' attention on the Conversation on page 61. Ss identify each person in pairs.
- Go over the answers as a class. (Answers: 1. Matt 2. Sierra 3. Hina 4. Liam 5. Paula)
- Explain the form of a present participle (verb + *-ing*). Then elicit the participles in the sentences on the board (*dancing* and *wearing*) and underline them.
- Elicit the prepositions in the sentences on the board (*with, in,* and *next to*) and circle them.
- Focus Ss' attention on the Grammar Focus box. Point out that *one* replaces *man* or *woman* and *ones* refers to more than one person.
- Play the audio program. Answer any remaining questions.

A

- Explain the task and ask two Ss to read the example statement and rewritten statement.
- Ss complete the task individually. Then they compare answers in pairs.
- Ask different Ss to write the answers on the board. Then go over them with the class.

Answers

1. Kyle is the tall guy wearing a yellow shirt and brown pants.
2. Mark and Eve are the middle-aged couple talking to Michael.
3. Alexis is the young girl in a white T-shirt and blue jeans.
4. Britney is the woman in the green dress sitting to the left of Javier.
5. J.P. is the serious-looking boy playing a video game.

B *Pair work*

- Explain the task. Ss complete the task using the names of classmates.
- Ss complete the task individually. Go around the class and give help as needed.
- Ss take turns asking and answering their questions in pairs. Go around the class and note any grammar errors.
- ***Option:*** For more practice, Ss change partners and complete the task again.

10 PRONUNCIATION

Learning Objective: sound more natural by using contrastive stress

A *[CD 2, Track 38]*

- Play the audio program. Ss listen for the stressed words.
- Focus Ss' attention on the conversations. Point out that people use more stress when they correct information. Ask: "What words does Student B stress?" (Answers: black, Jen)
- Play the audio program again. Ss listen and clap when they hear the stressed words.

B *[CD 2, Track 39]*

- Focus Ss' attention on the conversations. Ask them to mark the words they think Student B will stress.
- Play the audio program. Ss check and correct their guesses.
- Check answers as a class. Then Ss practice the conversations in pairs.

Answers

(Contrastive stress is in boldface.)
1. A: Is Sophie the one sitting next to Judy?
   B: No, she's the one **standing** next to Judy.
2. A: Is David the one on the couch?
   B: No, he's the one **behind** the couch.

- ***Option:*** Ask Ss to write questions about classmates or classroom objects with incorrect information (e.g., *Is the teacher the one sitting in the back? Is your backpack the one on the floor?*). Then Ss ask each other the questions in pairs. Go around the class and check their use of contrastive stress.

! For a new way to teach this Pronunciation, try ***Walking Stress*** – download it from the website.

11 READING

Learning Objective: read for main ideas and details in a reading about selfies

A

- Books closed. Write *The Age of Selfies* on the board. Ask Ss to write down words related to this topic in pairs. If Ss don't know anything about the topic, ask them to write questions they have about it. Elicit Ss' answers and questions.
- Books open. Go over the task. Read the descriptions with the class.
- Ss match the descriptions with the pictures individually. Then check the answers.

Answers

This picture is out of this world!: B
My life in fashion.: D
An old idea meets the twenty-first century.: A
The real me or the "perfect" me?: C

B

- Ss read the blog silently. Ask Ss to guess the meanings of any words they don't know.

TIP
Encourage Ss to guess the meaning of a new word by looking at the part of speech, its position in the sentence, and the context.

- Explain the task and model the first question as an example. Ss should read the questions and answers first. Then Ss find the name *Poppy Dinsey* in the blog. They scan that section of the blog to find one of the answers.
- Ss complete the task individually. Then they compare their answers in pairs.
- Go over answers with the class.

Answers

1. e 2. a 3. d 4. f 5. c 6. b

- Elicit or explain any remaining vocabulary.

Vocabulary
selfie: a photo taken of oneself, by oneself
astronaut: a person who travels in space
International Space Station: a space station that orbits the Earth; astronauts live on it
orbit (v): to make a circular path around a planet that has gravity
psychologist: someone who studies human behavior
control: to decide how something will happen
flattering: making someone appear attractive

- Ask Ss what they learned or found interesting in the blog.
- ***Option:*** Ask Ss to find these details in each paragraph. Write these questions on the board:
  1. When was the first selfie taken?
  2. What do people use to look "perfect"?
  3. What two things appeared with astronaut Aki Hoshide in his selfie?
  4. What kind of dress did Poppy wear?

  (Answers: 1. 1839, 2. apps, 3. the sun and deep space, 4. a hip dress)

C *Pair work*

- Ss discuss the questions in pairs. Then elicit their ideas.
- ***Option:*** In small groups, Ss share and discuss their own selfies.
- ***Option:*** Take a class selfie.

End of Cycle 2

See the Supplementary Resources chart at the beginning of this unit for additional teaching materials and student activities related to this Cycle.

11 READING

A Match the descriptions with the pictures. Write the letter.

This picture is out of this world! ____
My life in fashion. ____
An old idea meets the twenty-first century. ____
The real me or the "perfect" me? ____

THE AGE OF SELFIES

A

THE BIRTH OF THE SELFIE

Most of us take selfies now and then. Presidents, rock stars, actors, and sports stars all take them. It's very easy to take selfies on a smartphone. But the selfie isn't really a new idea. Back in 1839, a man named Robert Cornelius took the very first selfie. Cornelius was a photographer from Philadelphia, in the U.S. He took the picture of himself by setting up his camera and then running to stand in front of it. On the back of the picture, Cornelius wrote: "The first light picture ever taken. 1839."

B

WORLD'S BEST SELFIE?

Astronaut Aki Hoshide is the third Japanese astronaut to walk in space. But that's not the only reason he's famous. Hoshide created an amazing image! The astronaut took this picture while he was at the International Space Station. The photo shows him, the sun, and deep space in the same shot. He named it "Orbiting Astronaut Self-Portrait."

C

THE PSYCHOLOGY OF SELFIES

Why do people want to take pictures of themselves? Psychologists say that it's a way of understanding who we are. It's also a way of controlling how other people see us. When we take selfies, we can choose the flattering ones – the ones that make us look really good – and share them with our friends on social media or over text. Some people take their selfies very seriously. There are even apps people can use to make their faces look "perfect."

D

THE DAILY SELFIE

Several years ago, Poppy Dinsey started a fashion blog. She had a simple but great idea. Every day for a year she posted a selfie of herself wearing a different outfit. So one day, she's wearing jeans. Another day, she's wearing skinny pants and a baggy sweater. The next day, she's wearing a hip dress. People loved Poppy's blog. Many people started their own fashion blogs because they liked her so much.

B Read the blog. Match each question with the correct answer.

1. What is Poppy Dinsey famous for? ____
2. Where did Aki Hoshide take a selfie? ____
3. Who says selfies are a way of understanding ourselves? ____
4. Who took the first selfie? ____
5. Where do many people post selfies? ____
6. What is Hoshide's job? ____

a. at the International Space Station
b. astronaut
c. on social media
d. psychologists
e. a fashion blog
f. a man from Philadelphia

C **PAIR WORK** What do you think of selfies? When and where do you take selfies? What's the main reason you take selfies?

Unit 10 Supplementary Resources Overview

	After the following SB exercises	You can use these materials in class	Your students can use these materials outside the classroom
CYCLE 1	**1 Snapshot**		**DW** Unit 10 Vocabulary 2
	2 Conversation		
	3 Grammar Focus		**SB** Unit 10 Grammar plus, Focus 1 **DW** Unit 10 Grammar 1, 3–5, 7 **WB** Unit 10 exercises 1–3
CYCLE 2	**4 Conversation**		
	5 Grammar Focus	**TR** Unit 10 Extra Worksheet **TR** Unit 10 Grammar Worksheet	**SB** Unit 10 Grammar plus, Focus 2 **DW** Unit 10 Grammar 2, 6, 8
	6 Pronunciation		
	7 Listening		
	8 Word Power	**TR** Unit 10 Vocabulary Worksheet	**DW** Unit 10 Vocabulary 1
	9 Speaking	**TR** Unit 10 Listening Worksheet	
	10 Writing	**TR** Unit 10 Writing Worksheet	
	11 Interchange 10		
	12 Reading	**TR** Unit 10 Project Worksheet **VID** Unit 10 **VRB** Unit 10	**DW** Unit 10 Reading 1–2 **DW** Unit 10 Listening 1–2 **DW** Unit 10 Video 1–2 **WB** Unit 10 exercises 4–10

With or instead of the following SB section	You can also use these materials for assessment
Units 9–10 Progress Check	**TESTING PROGRAM** Units 9–10 Oral Quiz **TESTING PROGRAM** Units 9–10 Written Quiz

Key **SB:** Student's Book **DW:** Digital Workbook **TR:** Teacher's Resources
VID: Video (DW/TR) **VRB:** Video Resource Book (TR) **WB:** Print Workbook

My Plan for Unit 10

Use the space below to customize a plan that fits your needs.

With the following SB exercises	I am using these materials in class	My students are using these materials outside the classroom

With or instead of the following SB section	I am using these materials for assessment

10 Have you ever been there?

- Describe recent activities
- Describe experiences from the recent and distant past

1 SNAPSHOT

Fun for everyone around Orlando!

Which activities have you done?
Check (✓) the activities you would like to try.
Where can you do these or similar activities in your country?

2 CONVERSATION My feet are killing me!

A Listen and practice.

Erin: It's great to see you again, Carlos! Have you been in Orlando long?

Carlos: You too, Erin! I've been here for about a week.

Erin: I can't wait to show you the city. Have you been to the theme parks yet?

Carlos: Yeah, I've already been to three. The lines were so long!

Erin: OK. Well, how about shopping? I know a great store. . .

Carlos: Well, I've already been to so many stores. I can't buy any more clothes.

Erin: I know what! I bet you haven't visited the Kennedy Space Center. It's an hour away.

Carlos: Actually, I've already been to the Space Center and met an astronaut!

Erin: Wow! You've done a lot! Well, is there anything you want to do?

Carlos: You know, I really just want to take it easy today. My feet are killing me!

B Listen to the rest of the conversation. What do they plan to do tomorrow?

10 Have you ever been there?

Cycle 1, Exercises 1–3

In Unit 10, students describe recent activities and experiences from the recent and distant past. By the end of Cycle 1, students will be able to describe recent activities using the present perfect, *already*, and *yet*. By the end of Cycle 2, students will be able to describe experiences from the recent and distant past using the present perfect, simple past, *for*, and *since*.

1 SNAPSHOT

Learning Objective: discuss activities one has done or would like to try

- Books closed. Explain that this unit is about fun and unusual activities. Elicit fun or unusual activities Ss like to do and write them on the board.
- Books open. Ss look at the Snapshot and compare their ideas. Elicit or explain any new vocabulary.

Vocabulary
theme park: a park with rides, entertainment, and restaurants, usually about one subject (such as cartoon characters or superheroes)
space center: a center for human spaceflight

- Point out that this information is from an online travel guide, a website that lists things to do. Explain the task and read the questions.
- Ss do the task individually. Go around the class to give help as needed. Then elicit the answers from the class.

2 CONVERSATION

Learning Objective: use the present perfect in a conversation about recent activities

A *[CD 2, Track 40]*

- Books closed. Ask: "Where is Orlando? What famous theme parks are there? What space center is there?" (Answers: Florida, Disney World and Universal Studios, NASA's Kennedy Space Center)
- Books open. Set the scene. Carlos is visiting Orlando. His friend Erin wants to show him the city.
- Draw this chart on the board:

Activities	Yes	No
1. Go to a theme park		
2. Go shopping		
3. Visit the space center		
4. Relax		

  Ask Ss to copy the chart.
- Explain the task. Ss listen to the audio program and check (✓) *Yes* if Carlos has done the activities and *No* if he hasn't.
- Play the audio program and Ss complete the task. Then elicit their answers. (Answers: 1. yes 2. yes 3. yes 4. no)
- Play the audio program again. Ss listen and read along silently.
- Ask these comprehension questions: "When did Carlos arrive in Orlando? Who has he met?" Elicit Ss' answers. (Answers: about a week ago, an astronaut)
- Elicit or explain any new vocabulary.

Vocabulary
I can't wait to: I'm excited about; I'm looking forward to
take it easy: relax
My feet are killing me!: My feet really hurt!

- Ss practice the conversation in pairs.

B *[CD 2, Track 41]*

- Explain the task and read the focus question.
- Play the audio program. Ss listen for the answer individually. Then elicit the answer.

Audio script

Carlos Thanks, Erin. We can plan something for tomorrow.
Erin Great! Have you been to a Cuban restaurant yet?
Carlos No, I haven't. But I've heard Cuban food is delicious. Let's have lunch at a Cuban restaurant tomorrow.
Erin Good idea. I know a great little place on Orange Blossom Trail.
Carlos Cool! Maybe in the evening we can go listen to some jazz. Do you know a good club?
Erin Sure, I've been to several. We can go to Casey's on Central. I've been there a couple of times. It's really good.
Carlos OK! Sounds like a plan!

Answers

They plan to have lunch at a Cuban restaurant and listen to jazz in the evening.

3 GRAMMAR FOCUS

Learning Objectives: ask and answer questions using the present perfect with regular and irregular past participles; use *already* and *yet* with the present perfect in responses

[CD 2, Track 42]

Present perfect

- Focus Ss' attention on the Conversation on page 64. Ask: "What has Carlos done in Orlando?" Elicit Ss' answers and write them on the board:

been to three theme parks.
He has been to many stores.
been to the Kennedy Space Center.

- Ask: "When did he do these things?" (Answer: sometime in the past week)
- Explain that these sentences are in the present perfect. We use this tense with past actions when the exact time is not important.
- Draw this time line on the board:

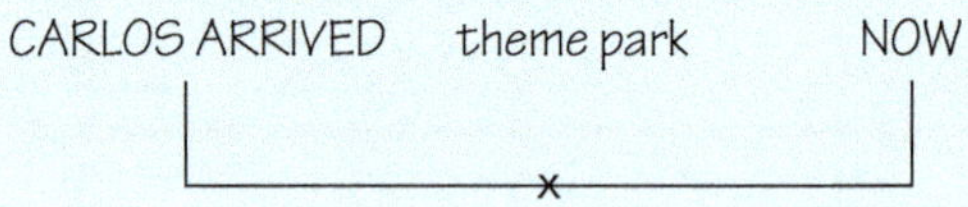

Explain that Carlos has been to a theme park sometime in the past week. We don't know the exact time, and it's not important.

- Say: "Carlos said he's been to three theme parks this week." Draw two more X's on the time line and say: "Carlos has been to a theme park three times this week."
- Focus Ss' attention on the Grammar Focus box. Elicit or explain the rules for forming present perfect statements and yes/no questions:

Subject + *has/have* + past participle.

Has/Have + subject + past participle?

- Point out the placement of *yet* and *already* and explain the meaning. *Yet* goes at the end of present perfect questions and at the end of negative statements. *Already* goes before the past participle and means "earlier than expected."
- Play the audio program and answer any questions.

A

- Explain the task and read the examples. Elicit adverbs of frequency such as *once*, *twice*, and *a couple of times*. Then ask different Ss and elicit their answers.
- Call on Ss to read the regular and irregular past participles. Then point out the list of irregular past participles in the appendix.
- Ss complete the task individually and compare answers in pairs. Then ask different Ss to write their answers on the board.

Possible answers

1. I've cooked dinner every day/four times this week. I haven't cooked dinner this week.
2. I've washed the dishes once/five times this week. I haven't washed the dishes this week.
3. I've listened to music every day/three times this week. I haven't listened to music this week.
4. I've done laundry once/twice this week. I haven't done laundry this week.
5. I've gone to a restaurant once/twice this week. I haven't gone to a restaurant this week.
6. I've cleaned the house once/twice this week. I haven't cleaned the house this week.

B

- Explain the task and model the first conversation with a S.
- Ss complete the task individually. Encourage Ss to use contractions in their answers. Go around the class and give help as needed. Then elicit Ss' answers.

Answers

1. A: **Have** you **done** much exercise this week?
   B: Yes, I**'ve** already **been** to Pilates class four times.
2. A: **Have** you **played** any sports this month?
   B: No, I **haven't had** the time.
3. A: How many movies **have** you **been** to this month?
   B: Actually, I **haven't seen** any yet.
4. A: **Have** you **been** to any interesting parties recently?
   B: No, I **haven't gone** to any parties for quite a while.
5. A: **Have** you **cooked** any food this week?
   B: Yes, I**'ve** already **made** dinner twice.
6. A: How many times **have** you **gone** out to eat this week?
   B: I**'ve eaten** at fast-food restaurants a couple of times.

C *Pair work*

- Ss take turns asking and answering the questions in part B in pairs.

For more practice with present perfect questions, play ***Hot Potato*** – download it from the website.

End of Cycle 1

See the Supplementary Resources chart at the beginning of this unit for additional teaching materials and student activities related to this Cycle.

3 GRAMMAR FOCUS

Present perfect; *already, yet*

The present perfect is formed with the verb *have* + the past participle.

Have you **been** to a jazz club?
Yes, I**'ve been** to several. No, I **haven't been** to one.
Has Carlos **visited** the theme parks?
Yes, he**'s visited** three or four. No, he **hasn't visited** any parks.
Have they **eaten** dinner yet?
Yes, they**'ve** already **eaten**. No, they **haven't eaten** yet.

Contractions

I**'ve**	=	I have
you**'ve**	=	you have
he**'s**	=	he has
she**'s**	=	she has
it**'s**	=	it has
we**'ve**	=	we have
they**'ve**	=	they have
has**n't**	=	has not
have**n't**	=	have not

GRAMMAR PLUS *see page 141*

A How many times have you done these things in the past week? Write your answers. Then compare with a partner.

1. cook dinner
2. wash the dishes
3. listen to music
4. do the laundry
5. go to a restaurant
6. clean the house

I've cooked dinner twice this week.
OR
I haven't cooked dinner this week.

B Complete these conversations using the present perfect. Then practice with a partner.

1. **A:** ___*Have*___ you ___*done*___ much exercise this week? (do)
   B: Yes, I ________ already ________ to Pilates class four times. (be)
2. **A:** ________ you ________ any sports this month? (play)
   B: No, I ________ the time. (not have)
3. **A:** How many movies ________ you ________ to this month? (be)
   B: Actually, I ________ any yet. (not see)
4. **A:** ________ you ________ to any interesting parties recently? (be)
   B: No, I ________ to any parties for quite a while. (not go)
5. **A:** ________ you ________ any food this week? (cook)
   B: Yes, I ________ already ________ dinner twice. (make)
6. **A:** How many times ________ you ________ out to eat this week? (go)
   B: I ________ at fast-food restaurants a couple of times. (eat)

C **PAIR WORK** Take turns asking the questions in part B. Give your own information when answering.

regular past participles

visit	→	visited
like	→	liked
stop	→	stopped
try	→	tried

irregular past participles

be	→	been
do	→	done
eat	→	eaten
go	→	gone
have	→	had
hear	→	heard
make	→	made
ride	→	ridden
see	→	seen

4 CONVERSATION Have you ever had a Cuban sandwich?

A Listen and practice.

Erin: I'm sorry I'm late. Have you been here long?

Carlos: No, only for a few minutes. So, have you chosen a restaurant yet?

Erin: I can't decide. We can go to a big restaurant or a have a sandwich at a café. Have you ever had a Cuban sandwich?

Carlos: No, I haven't. Are they good?

Erin: They're delicious. I've had them many times.

Carlos: You really like Cuban food! Have you ever been to Cuba?

Erin: No, but I went to college in Miami. I ate empanadas and rice and beans all the time!

B Listen to the rest of the conversation. Where do they decide to go after lunch?

5 GRAMMAR FOCUS

Present perfect vs. simple past

	Use the present perfect for an indefinite time in the past.	Use the simple past for a specific event in the past.
Have you ever **eaten** Cuban food?	Yes, I **have**. I'**ve had** it many times. No, I **haven't**. I **haven't tried** it yet.	I **ate** a lot of Cuban food when I **lived** in Miami. No, I never **tried** it when I **lived** in Miami.
Have you ever **seen** an alligator?	Yes, I **have**. I'**ve seen** a few alligators in my life. No, I **haven't**. I'**ve** never **seen** one.	I **saw** a big alligator at the new park last week. I **didn't go** to the alligator park last week, so I **didn't see** any.

GRAMMAR PLUS *see page 141*

A Complete these conversations. Use the present perfect and simple past of the verbs given and short answers.

1. **A:** ____________ you ever ____________ in public? (sing)
   B: Yes, I ____________. I ____________ at a friend's birthday party.
2. **A:** ____________ you ever ____________ something valuable? (lose)
   B: No, I ____________. But my brother ____________ his cell phone on a trip once.
3. **A:** ____________ you ever ____________ a traffic ticket? (get)
   B: Yes, I ____________. Once I ____________ a ticket and had to pay $50.
4. **A:** ____________ you ever ____________ a live concert? (see)
   B: Yes, I ____________. I ____________ Adele at the stadium last year.
5. **A:** ____________ you ever ____________ late for an important event? (be)
   B: No, I ____________. But my sister ____________ two hours late for her wedding!

B **PAIR WORK** Take turns asking the questions in part A. Give your own information when answering.

Cycle 2, Exercises 4–12

4 CONVERSATION

Learning Objective: use the present perfect and simple past in a conversation about past experiences

A *[CD 2, Track 43]*

- Set the scene. Carlos and Erin are discussing where to eat dinner. Elicit ideas and vocabulary from the picture.
- Write this focus question on the board:

  What does Carlos learn about Erin?
- Books closed. Play the audio program and Ss listen for the answer. (Answer: She went to college in Miami.)
- Books open. Play the audio program again. Ss read the conversation silently.
- Ss practice the conversation in pairs.

! For a new way to practice this Conversation, try the ***Moving Dialog*** – download it from the website.

B *[CD 2, Track 44]*

- Explain the task and read the focus question. Encourage Ss to make predictions.
- Play the audio program. Ss listen for the answer. Then elicit the answer from the class.

Audio script

Carlos	So, what would you like to do this afternoon?
Erin	Let's see . . . Have you ever been close to an alligator?
Carlos	What? No, I haven't! Why?
Erin	There's a new alligator park that I haven't been to yet. I've heard it's very exciting! You can see alligators up close and take pictures with them.
Carlos	OK. Just let me finish my sandwich. Maybe this will be my last meal. . . .
Erin	Haha! Wow. I've never seen you this scared before.

Answer

They decide to go to an alligator park.

5 GRAMMAR FOCUS

Learning Objectives: ask present perfect questions about experiences and answer in the present perfect and simple past; use the present perfect with *for* and *since* to describe past experiences

[CD 2, Track 45]

Present perfect

- Write these questions on the board:

  1. *Has Carlos ever had a Cuban sandwich?*
  2. *Has Erin ever eaten rice and beans?*
- Focus Ss' attention on the Conversation in Exercise 4 and elicit the answers. (Answers: 1. No, he hasn't. 2. Yes, she has.)
- Ask a few *Have you ever* questions around the class (e.g., "Have you ever eaten a Cuban sandwich? Have you ever eaten rice and beans?"). Elicit Ss' answers.
- Write this on the board:

  Have you ever eaten a Cuban sandwich?
  (No,) I've never eaten a Cuban sandwich.
- Point out that *ever* means "at any time in your life." We use it in present perfect questions, but not in answers. *Never* means "not ever," and we use it in present perfect statements.

Simple past

- Ask: "When did Erin eat rice and beans?" Then elicit possible answers (e.g., She ate it several years ago/as a college student.).
- Focus Ss' attention on the Grammar Focus box. Point out that we use the simple past to talk about a specific event in the past.
- Play the audio program.

A

- Explain the task and model the first conversation with a S.
- Ss complete the task individually. Go around and encourage Ss to use contractions in short answers.
- Elicit the answers. Then Ss practice with a partner.

Answers

1. A: **Have** you ever **sung** in public?
   B: Yes, I **have**. I **sang** at a friend's birthday party.
2. A: **Have** you ever **lost** something valuable?
   B: No, I **haven't**. But my brother **lost** his cell phone on a trip once.
3. A: **Have** you ever **gotten** a traffic ticket?
   B: Yes, I **have**. Once I **got** a ticket and had to pay $50.
4. A: **Have** you ever **seen** a live concert?
   B: Yes, I **have**. I **saw** Adele at the stadium last year.
5. A: **Have** you ever **been** late for an important event?
   B: No, I **haven't**. But my sister **was** two hours late for her wedding!

B ***Pair work***

- Explain the task. Then Ss complete it in pairs.

[CD 2, Track 46]

For *and* since

- Write this on the board:

  I lived in Miami for four years.
  I've lived in Miami for four years.
- Elicit or explain the difference. The first sentence is in the simple past. It means "I lived in Miami in the past, but I don't live in Miami now." The second sentence is in the present perfect. It means "I moved to Miami four years ago, and I still live in Miami now."
- Focus Ss' attention on the two expression boxes. Ask: "When do we use *for*? When do we use *since*?"
- Elicit or explain that we use *for* with periods of time and *since* with points in time. Elicit other expressions that go with *for* (e.g., *a day/a week/a year*), and *since* (*yesterday/last week/2 P.M.*).
- Play the audio program.

C

- Explain the task and model the first sentence. Then Ss complete the task individually. Go over answers with the class.

Answers

1. for	3. since	5. for	7. for
2. for	4. for	6. since	8. since

For more practice with *for* and *since*, play ***Run For It!*** – download it from the website.

D *Pair work*

- Explain the task and ask the first question. Elicit different answers with *for* and *since*.
- Ss complete the task in pairs. Go around the class and note any errors. Then write the errors on the board and correct them with the class.

6 PRONUNCIATION

Learning Objective: sound more natural by linking final /t/ and /d/ sounds in verbs with the vowels that follow

A *[CD 2, Track 47]*

- Explain the task. Focus Ss' attention on the linked sounds in the example conversations. Then play the audio program.

B *Pair work*

- Explain and model the task. Elicit the linked sounds in the answers (i.e., *cut it, tasted it, tried it, lost it, looked at it*). Ask Ss to repeat the linked sounds.
- Ss work in pairs. They ask and answer the questions. Go around the class and check their use of linked sounds.

7 LISTENING

Learning Objective: listen for details about recent events

[CD 2, Track 48]

- Ask: "What's the most interesting thing you've done recently?" Elicit Ss' answers.
- Set the scene and explain the task. Ss listen to find out where Nicole went, what she did there, and whether Tyler had been there before.
- Play the audio program. Ss complete the first column of the chart individually. While they listen, draw the chart on the board. Then elicit the answers and ask Ss to write the answers on the board.
- Play the audio program again. Ss complete the second and third columns of the chart individually. Then elicit the answers.

Audio script

Tyler Hi, Nicole! Great to see you! What have you been up to lately?
Nicole Hey, Tyler. Well, let's see . . . I went shopping at a discount store last week. It's called The Sports Discount Center. Have you ever shopped there?
Tyler No, I haven't. What's it like?
Nicole It's awesome! The prices are always very low, but when something's on sale, it's so cheap you can't believe it.
Tyler What was on sale?
Nicole Skateboards. I got a really nice one. It has a picture of the city on it.
Tyler Nice! Will you show it to me sometime? I love skateboard art.
Nicole Of course I will. And speaking of art, I went to the City Museum last week.
Tyler Oh, nice. I went there once when I was a kid.
Nicole Oh, cool. It's such a beautiful building.
Tyler Yeah! What kind of art did you see?
Nicole They had an exhibit of modern Mexican art. It was wonderful.
Tyler Oh, I love modern art. I definitely want to see that.
Nicole Well, don't wait too long! The exhibit ends next week.

Answers

Places Nicole went	What she did there	Has Tyler been there before?
1. The Sports Discount Center	bought a skateboard	No
2. the City Museum	saw modern Mexican art	Yes

For and since

How long **did** you **live** in Miami?	I **lived** there **for** four years. It was a great experience.
How long **have** you **lived** in Orlando?	I'**ve lived** here **for** three years. I'm very happy here. I'**ve worked** at the hotel **since** last year. I love it there.

GRAMMAR PLUS *see page 141*

C Complete these sentences with *for* or *since*. Then compare with a partner.

1. Maura was in Central America ____________ a month last year.
2. I've been a college student ____________ almost four years.
3. Hiroshi has been at work ____________ 6:00 A.M.
4. I haven't gone to a party ____________ a long time.
5. Sean lived in Bolivia ____________ two years as a kid.
6. My parents have been on vacation ____________ Monday.
7. Jennifer was engaged to Theo ____________ six months.
8. Alex and Brianna have been best friends ____________ high school.

expressions with *for*

two weeks
a few months
several years
a long time

expressions with *since*

6:45
last weekend
2009
elementary school

D **PAIR WORK** Ask and answer these questions.

How long have you had your current hairstyle?
How long have you studied at this school?
How long have you known your best friend?
How long have you been awake today?

6 PRONUNCIATION Linked sounds

A Listen and practice. Notice how final /t/ and /d/ sounds in verbs are linked to the vowels that follow them.

A: Have you cooked lunch yet?
B: Yes, I've already cooke*d i*t. (/t/)

A: Have you ever tried Key Lime Pie?
B: Yes, I trie*d i*t once in Miami. (/d/)

B **PAIR WORK** Ask and answer these questions. Use *it* in your responses. Pay attention to the linked sounds.

Have you ever cut your own hair?
Have you ever tasted blue cheese?
Have you ever tried Vietnamese food?
Have you ever lost your ID?
Have you looked at Unit 11 yet?

7 LISTENING Great to see you!

Listen to Nicole tell Tyler about some interesting things she's done recently. Complete the chart.

Places Nicole went	What she did there	Has Tyler been there before?
1.		☐ Yes ☐ No
2.		☐ Yes ☐ No

8 WORD POWER Life experiences

A Find two phrases to go with each verb. Write them in the chart.

a bike	your English books	a costume	a truck	your phone	a motorcycle
sushi	chocolate soda	iced coffee	octopus	a sports car	a uniform

eat			
drink			
drive			
lose			
ride			
wear			

B Add another phrase for each verb in part A.

9 SPEAKING Have you ever . . . ?

A **GROUP WORK** Ask your classmates questions about the activities in Exercise 8 or your own ideas.

A: Have you ever worn a costume?
B: Yes, I have.
C: Really? Where were you?

B **CLASS ACTIVITY** Tell the class one interesting thing you learned about a classmate.

10 WRITING An email to an old friend

A Write an email to someone you haven't seen for a long time. Include three things you've done since you last saw that person.

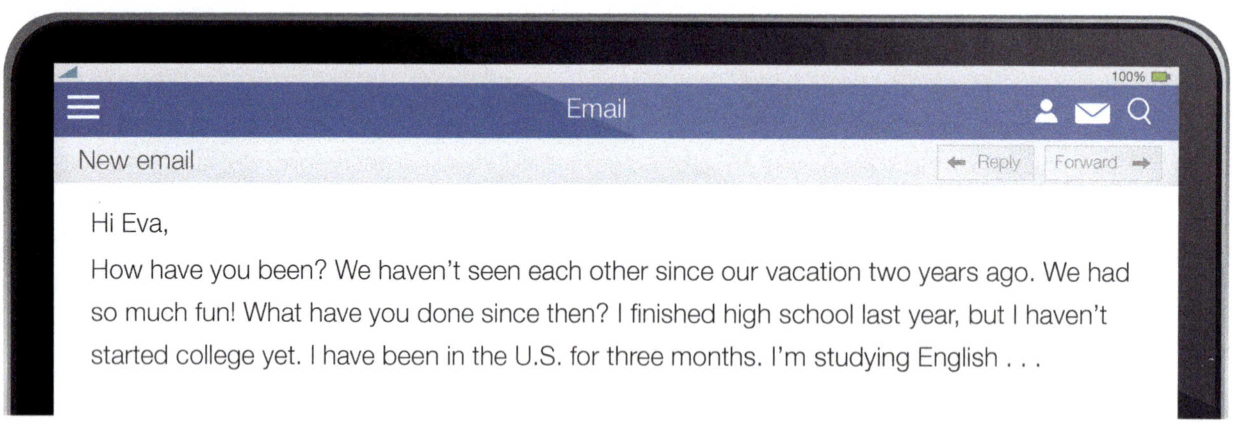

B **PAIR WORK** Exchange emails with a partner. Write a response about the three things your partner has done.

11 INTERCHANGE 10 Fun survey

How much fun do you have? Go to Interchange 10 on page 125.

8 WORD POWER

Learning Objective: discuss activities using common collocations

A

- Explain the task. Ss find two phrases in the list that go with each verb. Model the first example (*eat* + *sushi*). Then elicit other words or phrases that go with *eat* (e.g., *octopus*).
- Elicit or explain any new vocabulary.
- Ss complete the task in pairs. While they work, draw the chart on the board. Then go around the class and give help as needed.
- ***Option:*** Allow Ss to use their dictionaries.
- Elicit Ss' answers. Ask different Ss to write their answers on the board.

Answers

eat sushi/octopus/*lobster/cake*
drink iced coffee/chocolate soda/*iced tea/ginger ale*
drive a truck/a sports car/*an electric car/a new car*
lose your phone/your English books/*your keys/your ID*
ride a bike/a motorcycle/*the train/a skateboard*
wear a costume/a uniform/*a swimsuit/a hat*

(Note: Possible answers are italicized.)

- Elicit the past participle forms of the verbs. (Answers: *eaten, drunk, driven, lost, ridden, worn*)

For more practice with these collocations, play ***Concentration*** – download it from the website. Ss match each verb and a phrase to make collocations.

B

- Explain the task.
- Ss complete the task individually or in pairs.
- Elicit Ss' answers.

9 SPEAKING

Learning Objective: ask and answer questions about past experiences

A *Group work*

- Write these expressions on the board:

  Really? Wow! I'm impressed! You're kidding!

  Point out that we use these expressions to show interest or surprise. Model how to say them. Ss repeat.
- ***Option:*** Ss find more examples of responses in previous conversations. Practice them as a class.
- Explain the activity and model the example conversation with two Ss. Focus Ss' attention on the picture and ask: "Where was she?" Encourage Ss to make guesses.
- Elicit other follow-up questions and write them on the board.
- Ss complete the activity in small groups. Go around the class and encourage Ss to ask follow-up questions.
- ***Option:*** Ss get one point for each follow-up question they ask. The S in each group with the most points wins.

B *Class activity*

- Ss share things they learned about their classmates with the class.

10 WRITING

Learning Objective: write an email to someone one hasn't seen recently

A

- Ask the class: "Who haven't you seen in a long time?" Elicit Ss' answers.
- Explain the task. Then Ss read the example email silently.
- Ss write their emails individually. Remind Ss to check their use of present perfect and simple past.

B *Pair work*

- Ss exchange emails in pairs. They imagine they are the "old friend" and write a response.

11 INTERCHANGE 10

See page T-125 for teaching notes.

12 READING

Learning Objective: skim and read blog posts for specific information

A

- Books closed. Write *Unique Experiences* on the board. Elicit or explain that *unique* means "very unusual" or "one of a kind."
- Ss brainstorm unique experiences in small groups. Then ask different Ss to write them on the board.

TIP
To prepare Ss for a Reading, ask Ss to brainstorm things they already know about the topic.

- Books open. Go over the task. Elicit ideas from the pictures.
- Ss skim the blog posts and complete the task.

Answers

Jennifer Aniston set off the burglar alarm in her house by sleepwalking. Mervyn Kincaid crossed the Irish Sea in a bathtub with an engine.

B

- Elicit, explain, or ask Ss to look up new vocabulary.

Vocabulary
underground: below the ground
Guinness Book of Records: a collection of interesting records covering a wide variety of topics, e.g., most expensive pizza, world's tallest man, or most hot dogs eaten in a minute
burglar alarm: a system to alert the people in a house that someone (like a burglar) is moving around inside
sail: to travel in a boat
engine: a motor that powers a vehicle like a boat or a car
raise (v): to collect money from people
charity: a group or organization that helps people who need help
donation: money or goods that are given to help people

TIP
To avoid confusing Ss, only pre-teach the words they need to complete the task. They can look up the other words later.

- Explain the task. Ss read the blog posts and answer the questions. Then go over the answers with the class.

Answers

1. F 2. T 3. T 4. F 5. F 6. T 7. T 8. F

C *Group work*

- Explain the task and read the discussion questions. Ss discuss the questions in pairs.

End of Cycle 2

See the Supplementary Resources chart at the beginning of this unit for additional teaching materials and student activities related to this Cycle and for assessment tools.

12 READING

A Look at the photos. Skim the blog posts. What did Jennifer Aniston do in her sleep? How did Mervyn Kincaid cross the Irish Sea?

UNIQUE EXPERIENCES

How much is that pizza?!

Do you like pizza? Do you *really* like pizza? Do you like pizza enough to spend over $100 on one? Some people do! And here's the reason why. Truffles are similar to mushrooms, but they grow underground. They're extremely expensive. They can cost hundreds of dollars each. Pizza usually only costs a few dollars, but some people have paid as much as $178 to eat pizza with fresh white truffles on it. Celebrity TV chef Gordon Ramsay has won a place in the Guinness Book of Records for inventing this expensive dish.

Do you sleepwalk?

Did you know that some people walk in their sleep? Well, you probably do because it's a surprisingly common problem. In fact, almost a third of the U.S. population has sleepwalked at some point in their lives. The actress Jennifer Aniston is one of them. Jennifer has set off the burglar alarm in her own house by walking around while she was asleep.

Set sail in a bathtub!

Have you ever dreamed of going on a really big adventure? One man has crossed the Irish Sea . . . in a bathtub! Yes, you heard that right. Mervyn Kincaid has sailed from Ireland to Scotland in a bathtub with a small engine attached. Even better, Mervyn has raised a lot of money for charity. His friends and family have all made donations.

Oh no! I hit "send"!

Have you ever pushed "send" on a text message and then realized you've just sent a text to the wrong person? Hopefully not! But Burt Brown has. This 30-year-old software engineer has just sent 30 cute pictures of his baby to his boss instead of his mom! Luckily, his boss is a good guy and understood the mistake.

B Read the blog posts. Check (✓) True or False.

	True	False
1. Pizza is very expensive in the U.S.	☐	☐
2. Truffles grow underground.	☐	☐
3. Mervyn Kincaid didn't use a boat for his journey.	☐	☐
4. Mervyn Kincaid crossed the Irish Sea to pay for his bathtub.	☐	☐
5. Sleepwalking is extremely rare.	☐	☐
6. There was a lot of noise when Jennifer Aniston walked in her sleep.	☐	☐
7. Burt Brown sent photos to his boss.	☐	☐
8. Burt's boss was very angry about the baby pictures.	☐	☐

C **GROUP WORK** What unique experiences have you had in your life? Were they fun? Were they embarrassing? Tell your classmates.

Units 9–10 Progress check

SELF-ASSESSMENT

How well can you do these things? Check (✓) the boxes.

I can . . .	Very well	OK	A little
Ask about and describe people's appearance (Ex. 1)	☐	☐	☐
Identify people by describing what they're doing, what they're wearing, and where they are (Ex. 2)	☐	☐	☐
Find out whether or not things have been done (Ex. 3)	☐	☐	☐
Understand descriptions of experiences (Ex. 4)	☐	☐	☐
Ask and answer questions about experiences (Ex. 4)	☐	☐	☐
Find out how long people have done things (Ex. 5)	☐	☐	☐

1 ROLE PLAY Missing person

Student A: One of your classmates is lost. You are talking to a police officer. Answer the officer's questions and describe your classmate.

Student B: You are a police officer. Someone is describing a lost classmate. Ask questions to complete the form. Can you identify the classmate?

Change roles and try the role play again.

MISSING PERSON REPORT

NAME ______________________

HEIGHT: ________ WEIGHT: ________ AGE: ________

EYE COLOR:		HAIR COLOR:	
☐ BLUE	☐ BROWN	☐ BLOND	☐ BROWN
☐ GREEN	☐ HAZEL	☐ RED	☐ BLACK
		☐ GRAY	☐ BALD

CLOTHING: ______________________

GLASSES, ETC: ______________________

2 SPEAKING Which one is . . . ?

A Look at this picture. How many sentences can you write to identify the people?

Mia and Derek are the people in sunglasses.
They're the ones looking at the tablet.

B PAIR WORK Try to memorize the people in the picture. Then close your books. Take turns asking about the people.

A: Which one is Allen?
B: I think Allen is the guy eating . . .

Units 9–10

Progress check

SELF-ASSESSMENT

Learning Objectives: reflect on one's learning; identify areas that need improvement

- Ask: "What did you learn in Units 9 and 10?" Elicit Ss' answers.
- Ss complete the Self-assessment. Encourage them to be honest, and point out they will not get a bad grade if they check (✓) *A little*.
- Ss move on to the Progress check exercises. You can have Ss complete them in class or for homework, using one of these techniques:
  1. Ask Ss to complete all the exercises.
  2. Ask Ss: "What do you need to practice?" Then assign exercises based on their answers.
  3. Ask Ss to choose and complete exercises based on their Self-assessment.

1 ROLE PLAY

Learning Objective: demonstrate one's ability to ask about and describe a person's appearance

- Read the instructions aloud and explain the task. Student A makes a report about a lost classmate and Student B completes the *Missing person report*. Point out that Student A should not give the name of the classmate. Then Student B guesses the identity of the lost classmate.
- Go over the information in the report. Elicit different things Ss can write in the report.
- Write this example conversation on the board:

  A: Excuse me, Officer. Can you help me? One of my classmates is lost.
  B: Sure. Um, is the person a man or a woman?
  A: A woman.
  B: OK. I need to know her age. How old is she?
  A: I think she's 19 or 20.
  B: All right. And how tall is she?

  Model the conversation with a S. The S is person A and you are person B. Whenever the S gives additional information, pretend to write it in the report.
- Ss complete the task in pairs. Then Student B looks around the room and identifies the lost classmate.
- Set a time limit of about three minutes. Then Ss change roles. Go around the class and give help as needed.

TIP
If you don't have enough class time for the speaking activities, assign each S a speaking partner. Then have Ss complete the activities with their partners for homework.

2 SPEAKING

Learning Objective: demonstrate one's ability to identify people by describing what they're wearing, what they're doing, or where they are

A

- Focus Ss' attention on the picture. Ask a S to read the example sentences.
- Ss write sentences about each person individually.
- ***Option:*** Go around the class and check Ss' work.

Possible answers

Demi is the woman/one with a scarf/in jeans/wearing a hat.
Adele is the woman/one with blond hair/in the long dress.
Allen is the man/one eating popcorn/in jeans and a T-shirt.
Mia and Derek are the people/ones in sunglasses/looking at the tablet/sitting in chairs.

B *Pair work*

- Write the names Demi, Adele, Allen, and Mia and Derek on the board.
- Books closed. Explain the task. Ss ask questions about the people on the board in pairs (e.g., *Which one is Allen?*). They answer using their memory of the picture. If they have difficulty, they can look at their sentences.
- Model the example conversation with a few Ss. Elicit different ways Ss can answer.
- Ss complete the task.

3 SPEAKING

Learning Objective: demonstrate one's ability to use the present perfect to ask and answer questions about whether things have been done

A

- Explain the task. Ss imagine they are preparing for three situations. Read the situations and the example.
- Ss list four things they need to do for each situation.

B *Pair work*

- Explain the task. Ss exchange lists. Student A asks Student B what he or she has done in each situation. Student B gives responses using *already* or *yet*.
- Ss complete the task in pairs.

4 LISTENING

Learning Objectives: demonstrate one's ability to understand descriptions of experiences; demonstrate one's ability to ask and answer questions about one's experiences

A *[CD 2, Track 49]*

- Set the scene. Alyssa has just met a friend in San Diego and is talking about things she has done.
- Go over the chart and explain any new vocabulary. Then play the audio program. Ss complete the task.

Audio script

Matthew Alyssa? What are you doing here in San Diego?
Alyssa Matthew! What a surprise meeting you here! Actually, I'm here because I won a contest, and the prize was one week at the Seaside Resort Hotel, right on the beach.
Matthew Wow, that's fantastic! Just one night in that hotel costs over $400. Did the contest pay for your flight to San Diego?
Alyssa Actually, I'm afraid of flying. I've never flown on a plane. But I didn't need to pay for the train fare from Los Angeles to San Diego and back.
Matthew That's great.
Alyssa Yeah, it is. Oh, and I think I saw Mario Lopez here yesterday. You know, the actor.
Matthew Maybe you did. He was born here, you know.
Alyssa Really? Wow. I'd love to meet him. I've never met a famous person.
Matthew Well, keep your eyes open and maybe you will. Famous people sometimes stay at the Seaside Resort Hotel. I've heard that it's very beautiful and that there are lots of cool things to do there.
Alyssa Oh, yeah. The hotel activities are lots of fun. I even tried windsurfing.
Matthew Oh, awesome!
Alyssa Yeah, it was. But I did something stupid. I took my wallet with me and almost lost it. I'm always very careful with my wallet, and I have never lost it. It almost fell into the ocean. Luckily, I caught it.
Matthew That was lucky! Well, it sounds like you've really enjoyed your trip.
Alyssa For the most part. I mean, I got sunburned – as you can see – but I'll remember this trip forever. I've even been posting on a blog. I'll email you the address.
Matthew Nice! I look forward to reading it. Well, enjoy the rest of the week.
Alyssa Thanks. I will.

Answers

won a contest, stayed in an expensive hotel, gone windsurfing, gotten sunburned, posted on a blog

B *Group work*

- Ss take turns asking about the events in part A in small groups.

5 SURVEY

Learning Objective: demonstrate one's ability to use the present perfect, *for*, and *since* to describe one's experiences

A

- Ss complete the *My answers* column individually. Point out that they should use *for* or *since*.

B *Class activity*

- Model the task. Ask several Ss the first question until one gives the same answer. Explain that you will write that S's name in the *Classmate's name* column.
- Ss go around the room and complete the task.

WHAT'S NEXT?

Learning Objective: become more involved in one's learning

- Focus Ss' attention on the Self-assessment again. Ask: "How well can you do these things now?"
- Ask Ss to underline one thing they need to review. Ask: "What did you underline? How can you review it?"
- If needed, plan additional activities or reviews based on Ss' answers.

3 SPEAKING "To do" lists

A Imagine you are preparing for these situations. Make a list of four things you need to do for each situation.

You are going to go to the beach this weekend.
Your first day of school is in a week.
You are going to move to a new apartment.

"To do" list: trip to the beach
1. buy a swimsuit

B **PAIR WORK** Exchange lists. Take turns asking about what has been done. When answering, decide what you have or haven't done.

A: Have you bought a swimsuit yet?
B: Yes, I've already gotten one.

4 LISTENING I won a contest!

A Alyssa has just met a friend in San Diego. Listen to her talk about things she has done. Check (✓) the correct things.

Alyssa has . . .	
☐ won a contest.	☐ gone windsurfing.
☐ flown in a plane.	☐ lost her wallet.
☐ stayed in an expensive hotel.	☐ gotten sunburned.
☐ met a famous person.	☐ posted on a blog.

B **GROUP WORK** Have you ever done the things in part A? Take turns asking about each thing.

5 SURVEY How long have you . . .?

A Add one more question to the chart. Write answers to these questions using *for* and *since*.

How long have you . . . ?	My answers	Classmate's name
owned this book		
studied English		
known your teacher		
lived in this town or city		
been a student		

B **CLASS ACTIVITY** Go around the class. Find someone who has the same answers. Write a classmate's name only once.

WHAT'S NEXT?

Look at your Self-assessment again. Do you need to review anything?

Unit 11 Supplementary Resources Overview

	After the following SB exercises	You can use these materials in class	Your students can use these materials outside the classroom
CYCLE 1	**1 Word Power**		**DW** Unit 11 Vocabulary 1–2
	2 Conversation		
	3 Grammar Focus	**TR** Unit 11 Vocabulary Worksheet	**SB** Unit 11 Grammar plus, Focus 1 **DW** Unit 11 Grammar 1, 3, 7–8
	4 Listening		
	5 Writing		**WB** Unit 11 exercises 1–5
CYCLE 2	**6 Snapshot**		
	7 Conversation		
	8 Grammar Focus	**TR** Unit 11 Extra Worksheet **TR** Unit 11 Grammar Worksheet	**SB** Unit 11 Grammar plus, Focus 2 **DW** Unit 11 Grammar 2, 4–6
	9 Pronunciation		
	10 Listening		
	11 Speaking	**TR** Unit 11 Listening Worksheet **TR** Unit 11 Writing Worksheet	
	12 Interchange 11		
	13 Reading	**TR** Unit 11 Project Worksheet **VID** Unit 11 **VRB** Unit 11	**DW** Unit 11 Reading 1–2 **DW** Unit 11 Listening 1–2 **DW** Unit 11 Video 1–2 **WB** Unit 11 exercises 6–10

Key **SB:** Student's Book **DW:** Digital Workbook **TR:** Teacher's Resources
VID: Video (DW/TR) **VRB:** Video Resource Book (TR) **WB:** Print Workbook

My Plan for Unit 11

Use the space below to customize a plan that fits your needs.

With the following SB exercises	I am using these materials in class	My students are using these materials outside the classroom

With or instead of the following SB section	I am using these materials for assessment

11 It's a really nice city.

- Describe hometowns, cities, and countries
- Make recommendations about places to visit

1 WORD POWER Adjectives to describe places

A **PAIR WORK** Match each word in column A with its opposite in column B. Then add two more pairs of adjectives to the list.

A	B
1. beautiful	**a.** boring
2. cheap	**b.** crowded
3. clean	**c.** dangerous
4. interesting	**d.** expensive
5. quiet	**e.** noisy
6. relaxing	**f.** polluted
7. safe	**g.** stressful
8. spacious	**h.** ugly
9. ________	**i.** ________
10. ________	**j.** ________

beautiful

ugly

B **PAIR WORK** Choose two places you know. Describe them to your partner using the words in part A.

2 CONVERSATION It looks so relaxing.

A Listen and practice.

Ron: That photo is really cool! Where is that?

Camila: That's a beach near my house in Punta Cana, in the Dominican Republic.

Ron: It looks so relaxing. I've heard the area is really beautiful.

Camila: Yeah, it is. The weather is great, and there are some fantastic beaches. The water is really clear, too.

Ron: Is it expensive there?

Camila: Well, it's not cheap. But prices for tourists can be pretty reasonable.

Ron: Hmm . . . and how far is it from Santo Domingo?

Camila: It's not *too* far from the capital. About 200 kilometers . . . a little over 120 miles.

Ron: It sounds very interesting. I should plan a trip there sometime.

Punta Cana, Dominican Republic

B Listen to the rest of the conversation. What does Camila say about entertainment in Punta Cana?

11 It's a really nice city.

In Unit 11, students describe hometowns, cities, and countries, and make recommendations about places to visit. By the end of Cycle 1, students will be able to describe their hometowns using adjectives, adverbs, and conjunctions, and make suggestions about places using *can* and *should*. By the end of Cycle 2, students will be able to make suggestions about places using *can* and *should*.

Cycle 1, Exercises 1–5

1 WORD POWER

Learning Objective: describe places using adjectives

A *Pair work*

- Books closed. Elicit adjectives that describe places (e.g., *beautiful*, *ugly*) and write them on the board.
- Books open. Ss check (✓) the adjectives they listed. Then they read the other words silently.
- Elicit words Ss don't understand or know how to pronounce. Explain or pronounce these words.
- Explain the task and elicit the first example. Pairs complete the matching task.
- Go over answers with the class.

Answers

1. h 2. d 3. f 4. a 5. e 6. g 7. c 8. b

- Then pairs add two more sets of opposites. Ss may use their dictionaries if they wish. Go over possible answers.

Possible answers

modern/traditional, large/small, hot/cold

- Ask Ss to write the new adjectives in their notebooks and check (✓) the ones that describe their city or town.

For more practice matching opposite adjectives, play ***Concentration*** – download it from the website.

B *Pair work*

- Ss choose two cities or towns that they know and describe them in pairs. Encourage them to use the adjectives in part A.

2 CONVERSATION

Learning Objectives: use adjectives, adverbs, and conjunctions in a conversation about a city

A *[CD 3, Track 1]*

- Books closed. Set the scene. Ron is asking Camila about her hometown of Punta Cana, Dominican Republic.
- Ask: "What do you know about the Dominican Republic? Where is it? What's it like?"
- Write this on the board:

  1. Weather: OK or great?
  2. Beaches: polluted or fantastic?
  3. Prices: reasonable or expensive?

- Play the audio program. Ss listen to the audio program to find the answers. Then they compare answers with a partner.
- Go over the answers with the class. (Answers: 1. great 2. fantastic 3. reasonable)
- Books open. Play the audio program again.
- Ss listen and read silently. Then they practice the conversation in pairs. Go around the class and give help as needed.

! For a new way to teach this Conversation, try the ***Disappearing Dialog*** – download it from the website.

B *[CD 3, Track 2]*

- Explain the task and read the focus question.
- Play the audio program. Ss listen for the answer. Then they compare answers in small groups. Go over the answer with the class.

Audio script

Ron	So what kinds of things are there to do in Punta Cana?
Camila	Oh, there's so much to do! There are beautiful beaches, of course. You can go scuba diving, see dolphins, ride a horse on the beach . . .
Ron	Really? I've never ridden a horse on the beach. It sounds fun! Anything else?
Camila	Yes! There are a lot of nightclubs. Dominicans love to dance!
Ron	That's great. I love to dance, too!

Possible answer

There are beautiful beaches and a lot of nightclubs.

- ***Option:*** Ask Ss: "Would you like to visit Punta Cana? Why or why not?"

3 GRAMMAR FOCUS

Learning Objective: use adjectives, adverbs, and conjunctions to describe cities

[CD 3, Track 3]

Adverbs before adjectives

- Focus Ss' attention on the Conversation on page 72. Ask: "What has Ron heard about Punta Cana?" (Answer: *It's really beautiful.*) Then ask: "How far is it from Santo Domingo?" (Answer: *It's not too far.*)
- Explain that sometimes we use adverbs like *too, really,* and *pretty* to modify adjectives.
- Ask Ss to find more examples of adverbs that modify adjectives in the Conversation and underline them (e.g., *really cool, really clear, pretty reasonable, very interesting*). Elicit other adverbs.
- Focus Ss' attention on the adverbs box. Point out that they are organized from the most to the least.
- Focus Ss' attention on the Grammar Focus box. Point out the position of the adverb and elicit the rule:
  X *is* adverb + adjective.
  X *is a/an* adverb + adjective + noun.
- Explain that *too* means "more than you want," so we usually use it with negative adjectives (e.g., *too bad,* NOT *too nice*). Also, we cannot use *too* with an adverb + adjective + noun (e.g., *too expensive,* NOT *a too expensive city*).
- Play the audio program.
- ***Option:*** Focus Ss' attention on part B of the Word Power on page 72. Ss describe a place again, using adverbs + adjectives.

A

- Explain the task. Ss match the questions with the answers.
- Go over answers with the class. Then Ss practice the conversations in pairs.

Answers

1. e 2. d 3. a 4. b 5. c

For practice asking questions about cities, play ***Twenty Questions*** – download it from the website.

[CD 3, Track 4]

Conjunctions

- Focus Ss' attention on the first sentence in the second Grammar Focus box. Ask: "Are *big* and *nice* positive or negative?" (Answer: Both are positive.)
- Point out that we use *and* to connect two positive or two negative ideas. Elicit a sentence with two negative ideas (e.g., *The city is ugly, and the weather is terrible.*). Ask: "What punctuation comes before *and*?" (Answer: a comma)
- Focus Ss' attention on the other three sentences. Ask: "Are they positive + positive, negative + negative, or positive + negative?" (Answer: positive + negative) Explain that we use *but, though,* and *however* to connect a positive idea with a negative idea.
- Tell Ss to look at the position of *but, though,* and *however.* Ask: "How are *though* and *however* different from *but*?" (Answer: *But* is in the middle of the sentence. *Though* and *however* are at the end.)
- Ask: "What punctuation comes before each conjunction?" (Answer: a comma) Point out that *and* and *but* connect two complete sentences.
- Play the audio program.

B

- Explain the task and model the first answer. Ss complete the task individually. Go around the class and check Ss' use of punctuation.
- Ask different Ss to write their answers on the board. Go over answers with the class.

Answers

1. Kyoto is very nice, and everyone is extremely friendly.
2. The streets are crowded during the day. They're very quiet at night, though.
3. The weather is nice. Summers get pretty hot, however.
4. You can rent a bicycle, but it's expensive.
5. It's an amazing city, and I love to go there.

C *Group work*

- Write these topics on the board:

People	Food	Shopping
Weather	Crime	Things to do

- Explain the task and ask two Ss to read the example conversation. Point out that Ss can discuss the topics on the board.
- Ss complete the task. Ask Ss to name the negative statement in each description.
- Go around the class and note any errors. Then write them on the board and ask Ss to correct them.

TIP
To check if Ss have understood the grammar, write their errors on the board. Then ask Ss to correct them.

3 GRAMMAR FOCUS

Adverbs before adjectives

Punta Cana is **really** nice. It's a **really** nice place.
It's **fairly** expensive. It's a **fairly** expensive destination.
It's not **very** big. It's not a **very** big city.

New York is **too** noisy, and it's **too** crowded for me.

GRAMMAR PLUS *see page 142*

adverbs

too
extremely
very/really
pretty
fairly/somewhat

A Match the questions with the answers. Then practice the conversations with a partner.

1. What's Seoul like? Is it an interesting place? ______
2. Do you like your hometown? Why or why not? ______
3. What's Sydney like? I've never been there. ______
4. Have you ever been to São Paulo? ______
5. What's the weather like in Chicago? ______

a. Oh, really? It's beautiful and very clean. It has a great harbor and beautiful beaches.
b. Yes, I have. It's an extremely large and crowded place, but I love it. It has excellent restaurants.
c. It's really nice in the summer, but it's too cold for me in the winter.
d. Not really. It's too small, and it's really boring. That's why I moved away.
e. Yes. It has amazing shopping, and the people are pretty friendly.

Conjunctions

Los Angeles is a big city, **and** the weather is nice.
Boston is a big city, **but** it's not too big.
It's a big city. It's not too big, **though**.
It's a big city. It's not too big, **however**.

GRAMMAR PLUS *see page 142*

B Choose the correct conjunctions and rewrite the sentences.

1. Kyoto is very nice. Everyone is extremely friendly. (and / but)
   ____
2. The streets are crowded during the day. They're very quiet at night. (and / though)
   ____
3. The weather is nice. Summers get pretty hot. (and / however)
   ____
4. You can rent a bicycle. It's expensive. (and / but)
   ____
5. It's an amazing city. I love to go there. (and / however)
   ____

Kyoto, Japan

C **GROUP WORK** Describe three cities or towns in your country. State two positive features and one negative feature for each.

A: Singapore is very exciting and there are a lot of things to do, but it's too expensive.
B: The weather in Bogotá is . . .

4 LISTENING Describing hometowns

A Listen to Abby and Christopher talk about their hometowns. What do they say about them? Choose the correct words.

Abby's hometown	Christopher's hometown
a fairly / not very large town	a really / fairly stressful place
somewhat / extremely beautiful	pretty / too crowded
pretty / very cheap	not very / extremely clean
____________ quiet	____________ expensive

B Listen again. Write another adverb you hear them use to describe their hometowns.

5 WRITING A great place to live

A Write about interesting places for tourists to visit in your hometown.

Otavalo is a very interesting town in Ecuador. It's to the north of Quito. It has a fantastic market, and a lot of tourists go there to buy handmade art and crafts. The scenery around Otavalo is very pretty and . . .

B **PAIR WORK** Exchange papers and read each other's articles. What did you learn about your partner's hometown?

6 SNAPSHOT

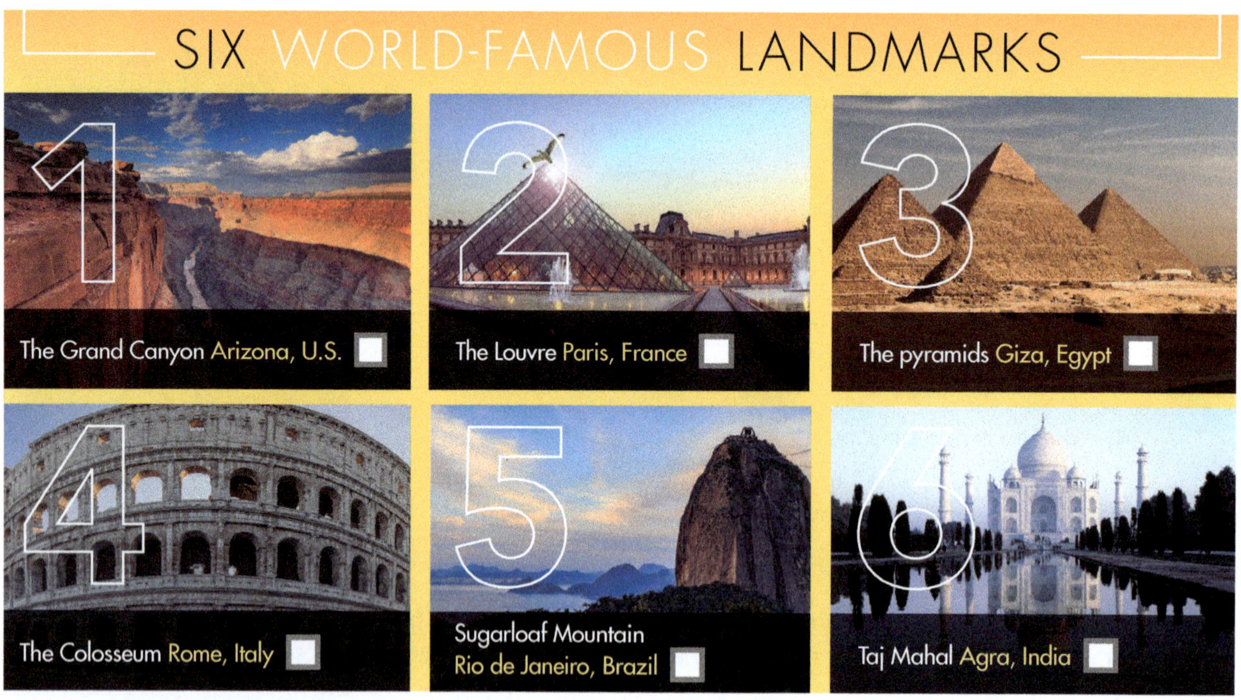

Which places would you like to visit? Why?
Put the places you would like to visit in order from most interesting (1) to least interesting (6).
Which interesting places around your country or the world have you already visited?
What three other places around the world would you like to visit? Why?

4 LISTENING

Learning Objective: listen for details about people's hometowns

A *[CD 3, Track 5]*

- Books closed. Set the scene. Abby and Christopher are talking about their hometowns.
- Books open. Explain the task. Play the audio program and Ss circle the correct words.
- Ss compare answers in pairs. Then go over answers.

Audio script

1.

Man	So tell me about your hometown, Abby.
Abby	Well, not many people live there, but it's actually a fairly large town. It has some large farms, a river, two lakes, and even a mountain.
Man	Do you like those kinds of things?
Abby	Oh, yes. I love nature. I think it's extremely beautiful. And the fresh food from the farms is delicious.
Man	Is it an expensive town?
Abby	No, it's very cheap.
Man	It sounds like a great place.
Abby	It was OK growing up, but I couldn't live there now.
Man	Really? Why?
Abby	It's too quiet for me. I've lived in the city for a long time now. I like to hear the sounds of cars and people and things around me.

2.

Woman	Where did you grow up, Christopher?
Christopher	I grew up in a city. So I guess you could say my hometown isn't really a *town* – it's a city. For me, it's a really stressful place, though.
Woman	Why do you say that?
Christopher	Well, for one thing, it's too crowded. The streets and the subways are full of people day and night.
Woman	Really? Is it a polluted place?
Christopher	I wouldn't say that. But it's not very clean.
Woman	Like many cities, I guess.
Christopher	Right. And like many cities, it's somewhat expensive. My parents still live there, and they always talk about the high prices.

Answers

Abby's hometown	Christopher's hometown
a **fairly** large town	a **really** stressful place
extremely beautiful	**too** crowded
very cheap	**not very** clean

B *[CD 3, Track 6]*

- Explain the task. Play the audio again.
- Ss write another adverb they hear in the chart. Check the answers.

Answers

Abby's hometown	Christopher's hometown
too quiet	**somewhat** expensive

5 WRITING

Learning Objective: write an article about interesting places to visit in one's hometown

A

- Explain the task. Then Ss read the example silently.
- Ss write their article in class or for homework.

B *Pair work*

- Explain the task. Ss complete the task in pairs.

End of Cycle 1

See the Supplementary Resources chart at the beginning of this unit for additional teaching materials and student activities related to this Cycle.

Cycle 2, Exercises 6–13

6 SNAPSHOT

Learning Objective: discuss popular places to visit

- Books closed. Write the six countries from the Snapshot on the board. Ask: "Which country would you like to visit? Why?"
- Books open. Ss read the Snapshot. Elicit or explain any new vocabulary.

Vocabulary

The Grand Canyon: a steep canyon created by a river in the western U.S.
The Louvre: the world's largest museum
The pyramids at Giza: a wonder of the ancient world
The Colosseum: a famous stadium of ancient Rome
Sugarloaf Mountain: a famous mountain with panoramic views
Taj Mahal: a famous building built to contain an emperor's wife's tomb

- Explain the tasks. Ss complete the tasks individually. Then they discuss their answers in small groups.

7 CONVERSATION

Learning Objective: use *can* and *should* in a conversation about sightseeing suggestions

A ***[CD 3, Track 7]***

- Books closed. Set the scene. Two friends are talking about a city. Ask: "What city is it?" Play the first part of the audio program and Ss listen for the answer. (Answer: Mexico City)
- Write these focus questions on the board:

  1. What's the Museum of Anthropology like?
  2. What are the Diego Rivera murals like?
  3. How many kinds of street food does Claudia recommend?

- Play the rest of the audio program. Then elicit Ss' answers to the questions on the board. (Answers: 1. amazing 2. incredible 3. three)
- Books open. Play the audio program again and Ss read the conversation silently. Elicit or explain any new vocabulary.
- Ss practice the conversation in pairs.

Vocabulary

Anything else?: Is there anything more?
you shouldn't miss: you should see

B ***[CD 3, Track 8]***

- Explain the task and read the focus questions. Play the audio program. Elicit Ss' answers.

Audio script

Claudia	Where are you from again, Jason?
Jason	I'm from Montreal, Canada.
Claudia	Oh! I've always wanted to go there. What's it like? What can you do there?
Jason	Well, there's a lot to do. Visitors should definitely plan to spend a day visiting museums. At Space for Life, you can learn a lot about nature and the world.

Answers

He's from Montreal, Canada. You should definitely visit Space for Life.

8 GRAMMAR FOCUS

Learning Objective: ask for recommendations and make suggestions about places using *can* and *should*

[CD 3, Track 9]

Can *and* should

- Focus Ss' attention on the Conversation in Exercise 7. Ask: "How does Jason ask for advice about Mexico City?" Write his question on the board:

  Can you tell me a little about Mexico City?

- Ask: "How does Claudia suggest what to see?" Elicit the answers and write them on the board:

  You should definitely visit . . .
  You shouldn't miss the . . .
  You can . . .

- Point out that *can* and *should* are modals. They show a speaker's attitude or "mood." People use *can* and *should* to ask for and give advice.
- Elicit or explain the rule for using *can* and *should* in Wh-questions and statements:

  Wh-question + modal + subject + verb?

  Subject + modal (+ *not*) + verb.

  Point out that modals do not take a final *-s*.

- Focus Ss' attention on the Grammar Focus box and play the audio program.

A

- Explain the task and model the first conversation with a S. Ss complete the task individually.
- Go over answers with the class. Then Ss practice the conversations in pairs.

Answers

1. A: I **can't** decide where to go on my vacation.
   B: You **should** go to Morocco. It's my favorite place to visit.
2. A: I'm planning to go to Puerto Rico next year. When do you think I **should** go?
   B: You **can** go anytime. The weather is nice almost all year.
3. A: **Should** I rent a car when I arrive in New York? What do you recommend?
   B: No, you **should** definitely use the subway. It's fast and not too expensive.
4. A: Where **can** I get some nice jewelry in Istanbul?
   B: You **shouldn't** miss the Grand Bazaar. It's the best place for bargains.
5. A: What **can** I see from the Eiffel Tower?
   B: You **can** see all of Paris, but in bad weather you **can't** see anything.

B

- Explain the task and read the questions. Ss complete the task individually. Then they compare answers in pairs.
- Elicit answers from the class.

7 CONVERSATION What should I do there?

A Listen and practice.

JASON Can you tell me a little about Mexico City?

CLAUDIA Sure. What would you like to know?

JASON Well, I'm going to be there for a few days next month. What should I do there?

CLAUDIA Oh! You should definitely visit the National Museum of Anthropology. It's amazing.

JASON OK. It's on my list now! Anything else?

CLAUDIA You shouldn't miss the Diego Rivera murals. They're incredible. Oh, and you can walk around the historic center.

JASON That sounds perfect. And what about the food? What should I eat?

CLAUDIA You can't miss the street food. The tacos, barbecue, fruit . . . it's all delicious.

National Museum of Anthropology

Diego Rivera murals

B Listen to the rest of the conversation. Where is Jason from? What should you do there?

8 GRAMMAR FOCUS

Modal verbs *can* and *should*

What **can** I do in Mexico City?	What **should** I see there?
You **can** walk around the historic center.	You **should** visit the National Museum of Anthropology.
You **can't** miss the street food.	You **shouldn't** miss the Diego Rivera murals.

GRAMMAR PLUS *see page 142*

A Complete these conversations using *can*, *can't*, *should*, or *shouldn't*. Then practice with a partner.

1. **A:** I ______________ decide where to go on my vacation.
   B: You ______________ go to Morocco. It's my favorite place to visit.
2. **A:** I'm planning to go to Puerto Rico next year. When do you think I ______________ go?
   B: You ______________ go anytime. The weather is nice almost all year.
3. **A:** ______________ I rent a car when I arrive in New York? What do you recommend?
   B: No, you ______________ definitely use the subway. It's fast and not too expensive.
4. **A:** Where ______________ I get some nice jewelry in Istanbul?
   B: You ______________ miss the Grand Bazaar. It's the best place for bargains.
5. **A:** What ______________ I see from the Eiffel Tower?
   B: You ______________ see all of Paris, but in bad weather, you ______________ see anything.

B Write answers to these questions about your country. Then compare with a partner.

What time of year should you go there?
What are three things you can do there?
What can you do for free?
What shouldn't a visitor miss?

9 PRONUNCIATION *Can't and shouldn't*

A Listen and practice these statements. Notice how the *t* in **can't** and **shouldn't** is not strongly pronounced.

You can get a taxi easily.
You can'**t** get a taxi easily.
You should visit in the summer.
You shouldn'**t** visit in the summer.

Las Vegas, United States

B Listen to four sentences. Choose the modal verb you hear.

1. can / can't
2. should / shouldn't
3. can / can't
4. should / shouldn't

10 LISTENING Where should you go?

A Listen to speakers talk about three countries. Complete the chart.

Country	Largest city	What visitors should see or do
1. Japan		
2.		
3.		

B Listen again. What else do the speakers say about the countries?

11 SPEAKING What can visitors do there?

GROUP WORK Has anyone visited an interesting place in your country or in another country? Find out more about it. Start like this and ask questions like the ones below.

A: I visited Jeju Island once.
B: Really? What's the best time of year to visit?
A: Springtime is very nice. I went in May.
C: What's the weather like then?

What's the best time of year to visit?
What's the weather like then?
What should tourists see and do there?
What special foods can you eat?
What's the shopping like?
What things should people buy?
What else can visitors do there?

Jeju Island, South Korea

12 INTERCHANGE 11 Welcome to our city!

Make a guide to fun places in your city. Go to Interchange 11 on page 126.

9 PRONUNCIATION

Learning Objective: sound more natural when pronouncing *can't* and *shouldn't*

A ***[CD 3, Track 10]***

- Books closed. Play the audio program. Ask: "What do you notice about the pronunciation of *t* in *can't* and *shouldn't*?" (Answer: It is not strongly pronounced.)
- Books open. Play the audio program again. Ss listen and repeat. Go around the class and check their pronunciation of *can't* and *shouldn't*.

B ***[CD 3, Track 11]***

- Explain the task. Play the audio program, and Ss circle the modal verb. Then elicit the correct answers.

Answers

1. can't 2. should 3. can 4. shouldn't

10 LISTENING

Learning Objective: listen for details about suggested things to do in major world cities

A ***[CD 3, Track 12]***

- Books closed. Write *Japan* on the board. Ask: "What do you know about this country?" Elicit Ss' answers.
- Books open. Explain the task. Ss listen for the names of three countries. Play the audio program, pausing after each country. Ss write the names of the countries in the chart individually. Elicit Ss' answers.
- Explain the task. Play the audio program again. Ss complete the chart individually. Then they compare answers in pairs. Elicit answers from the class.

Audio script

1. Japan has several big islands and many smaller islands. The largest city is Tokyo. There are many beautiful Buddhist temples in Japan. Visitors should try Japanese food, especially sashimi, which is raw fish. And here's a fun fact: the highest mountain in Japan is Mount Fuji.
2. Argentina is a large country in South America. The largest city is Buenos Aires. People visiting Buenos Aires shouldn't miss the downtown area. Many interesting people gather in this area. Argentina is also a good place to buy leather. And by the way, the people there all speak Spanish.
3. The capital of Turkey is Ankara, but its largest city is Istanbul. There are many colorful markets in Istanbul where visitors should definitely buy some souvenirs. Then they should try the delicious Turkish street food. They should also try Turkish coffee. It's thick, dark, and delicious. Most of Turkey is in Asia, but a small part is in Europe.

Answers

Country	Largest city	What visitors should see or do
1. Japan	Tokyo	go to temples; eat Japanese food, especially sashimi
2. Argentina	Buenos Aires	see the downtown area; buy leather
3. Turkey	Istanbul	go to markets and buy souvenirs; try Turkish street food and coffee

B ***[CD 3, Track 13]***

- Explain the task and read the focus question. Play the audio program, and Ss listen for the answers.

Answers

1. Japan's highest mountain is Mount Fuji.
2. Argentineans speak Spanish.
3. Most of Turkey is in Asia.

11 SPEAKING

Learning Objective: describe a place using *can* and *should*

Group work

- Explain the task and ask three Ss to read the example conversation. Go over the discussion questions.
- ***Option:*** Brainstorm additional discussion questions with the class. Write them on the board.
- Ss complete the activity in small groups.

12 INTERCHANGE 11

See page T-126 for teaching notes.

13 READING

Learning Objective: scan and read for specific information about places

A

- Books closed. Write these questions on the board:

  1. *When on vacation, do you ever write to people?*
  2. *Do you send emails, texts, or postcards?*
  3. *Who do you write to?*
  4. *What do you write about?*

  Ss discuss the questions in pairs. Then elicit their answers.
- Books open. Write *Barcelona, Cartagena,* and *Bangkok* on the board. Then go over the task. Ss complete the task individually.
- Ss skim the emails to check their guesses.

Answers

famous for small plates of food: Barcelona
a good place to ride your bike at night: Bangkok

- Ask Ss to underline any new vocabulary and look it up before class. Elicit or explain any words Ss cannot find.

Vocabulary

church: a place where people go to practice their religion
tapas: small plates of Spanish food
district: a specific area of a country or town
salsa steps: the movements of the South American dance called *salsa*
mangrove: a tropical tree found near water
bike path: a special part of the road for people riding bikes

! For a new way to teach the vocabulary in this Reading, try ***Vocabulary Mingle*** – download it from the website.

B

- Explain the task and go over the activities in the chart. Tell Ss to only check (✓) the cities first. Model the first example. Tell Ss to look quickly through the emails for words related to *swim with sharks*. Ss complete the task individually.
- Tell Ss to look through the emails in detail for specific examples. Ss complete the task individually. Then they go over answers in pairs.
- Ask different Ss to write their answers on the board, using sentences with *can* (e.g., *You can swim with sharks in Bangkok.*).

Answers

1. Bangkok: surf or swim with sharks
2. Barcelona: La Sagrada Familia
3. Bangkok: pad thai – a spicy noodle dish
4. Cartagena: old dance club
5. Cartagena: canoe tour of a mangrove forest
6. Barcelona: tapas

C *Pair work*

- Read the discussion questions. Ss discuss them in pairs.

! For a new way to practice reading for specific information, try the ***Reading Race*** – download it from the website.

End of Cycle 2

See the Supplementary Resources chart at the beginning of this unit for additional teaching materials and student activities related to this Cycle.

READING

A Skim the emails. What city is famous for small plates of food? Where is a good place to ride your bike at night?

A big "Hello!" from . . .

New mail — **Barcelona, Spain** — Reply | Forward | ×

Barcelona is simply awesome! The city is famous for the architect Antoni Gaudí. I've seen a different Gaudí building every day. Gaudí designed some amazing places like the church *La Sagrada Familia*. Workers started building the church in 1882, but it isn't finished yet. Some people say it might be finished by 2030. I've also visited *Las Ramblas*, a street with great cafés. I've eaten delicious tapas every day. A *tapa* is a small plate of food. My friends and I usually order several tapas and share them. The weather is great! I think I came here at just the right time of the year.

Kathy

New mail — **Cartagena, Colombia** — Reply | Forward | ×

I've discovered that Cartagena has two different personalities. One is a lively city with fancy restaurants and crowded old plazas. And the other is a quiet and relaxing place with sandy beaches. If you come here, you should stay in the historic district – a walled area with great shopping, nightclubs, and restaurants. It has some wonderful old Spanish buildings. Last night I learned some salsa steps at an old dance club. Today, I went on a canoe tour of *La Ciénaga* mangrove forest.

Mike

New mail — **Bangkok, Thailand** — Reply | Forward | ×

Bangkok is the most exciting place I've ever visited. There's something for everyone. You can surf or swim with sharks. Or why not try out some extreme cycling at Peppermint Bike Park? The park has two great bike paths. You can ride your bike there until 10:00 at night. I ate the most delicious food in Bangkok, including the famous pad thai – a spicy noodle dish. At night, there are clubs, restaurants, cafés, and movie theaters to visit. It's impossible to be bored. I love it!

Jasmin

B Read the emails. Check (✓) the cities where you can do these things. Then complete the chart with examples from the emails.

Activity	Barcelona	Cartagena	Bangkok	Examples
1. swim with sharks	☐	☐	☐	
2. see a famous church	☐	☐	☐	
3. eat spicy food	☐	☐	☐	
4. go dancing	☐	☐	☐	
5. take a boat tour	☐	☐	☐	
6. eat small plates of local food	☐	☐	☐	

C **PAIR WORK** Which city is the most interesting to you? Why? Which other city or cities in the world would you like to visit? Why?

Unit 12 Supplementary Resources Overview

	After the following SB exercises	You can use these materials in class	Your students can use these materials outside the classroom
CYCLE 1	1 Snapshot		DW Unit 12 Vocabulary 1
	2 Conversation		
	3 Grammar Focus		SB Unit 12 Grammar plus, Focus 1 DW Unit 12 Grammar 1, 3–4
	4 Pronunciation		
	5 Interchange 12		
	6 Discussion		WB Unit 12 exercises 1–4
CYCLE 2	7 Word Power	TR Unit 12 Extra Worksheet TR Unit 12 Vocabulary Worksheet	DW Unit 12 Vocabulary 2
	8 Conversation		SS Unit 12 Speaking 2
	9 Grammar Focus	TR Unit 12 Grammar Worksheet	SB Unit 12 Grammar plus, Focus 2 DW Unit 12 Grammar 2, 5–7
	10 Listening	TR Unit 12 Listening Worksheet	
	11 Role Play		
	12 Writing	TR Unit 12 Writing Worksheet	
	13 Reading	TR Unit 12 Project Worksheet VID Unit 12 VRB Unit 12	DW Unit 12 Reading 1–2 DW Unit 12 Listening 1–2 DW Unit 12 Video 1–2 WB Unit 12 exercises 5–8

With or instead of the following SB section	You can also use these materials for assessment
Units 11–12 Progress Check	**TESTING PROGRAM** Units 11–12 Oral Quiz **TESTING PROGRAM** Units 11–12 Written Quiz

Key **SB:** Student's Book **DW:** Digital Workbook **TR:** Teacher's Resources
VID: Video (DW/TR) **VRB:** Video Resource Book (TR) **WB:** Print Workbook

My Plan for Unit 12

Use the space below to customize a plan that fits your needs.

With the following SB exercises	I am using these materials in class	My students are using these materials outside the classroom

With or instead of the following SB section	I am using these materials for assessment

12 It's important to get rest.

- State health problems and give advice
- Ask for advice and give suggestions about health products

1 SNAPSHOT

Common Health Problems

- ☐ a headache
- ☐ a cough
- ☐ a cold
- ☐ the flu
- ☐ a stomachache
- ☐ a backache
- ☐ sore muscles
- ☐ insomnia

How many times have you been sick in the past year?
Check (✓) the health problems you have had recently.
What do you do for the health problems you checked?

2 CONVERSATION It really works!

A Listen and practice.

Mila: Are you all right, Keith?
Keith: Not really. I don't feel so well. I have a terrible cold.
Mila: Oh, that's too bad. You shouldn't be at the gym, then.
Keith: Yeah, I know. But I need to run for an hour every day.
Mila: Not today, Keith! It's really important to get some rest.
Keith: Yeah, you're right. I should be in bed.
Mila: Well, yeah! And have you taken anything for your cold?
Keith: No, I haven't. What should I take?
Mila: Well, you know, pain medicine, lots of water. Sometimes it's helpful to drink garlic tea. Just chop up some garlic and boil it for a few minutes, then add lemon and honey. Try it! It really works!
Keith: Yuck! That sounds awful!

B Listen to advice from Keith's next-door neighbors. What do they suggest?

12 It's important to get rest.

Cycle 1, Exercises 1–6

In Unit 12, students state health problems and give advice, and ask for advice and give suggestions about health products. By the end of Cycle 1, students will be able to state health problems and give advice using adjective + infinitive and noun + infinitive. By the end of Cycle 2, students will be able to ask for advice and give suggestions about health care products using *can*, *could*, and *may*.

1 SNAPSHOT

Learning Objective: identify and discuss common health problems

- Books closed. Elicit common health problems from the class and write them on the board.
- Books open. Ss compare their ideas with the Snapshot. Explain any new vocabulary, using gestures if needed.
- Explain the tasks. Ss complete the tasks in small groups. Go around the class and give help as needed.
- Ask the class: "How many of you have had a headache recently? Raise your hands." Ask about each health problem. Count the number of Ss who have had each one.

! For a new way to practice the vocabulary in this Snapshot, try ***Vocabulary Steps*** – download it from the website. Ss rank the health problems according to most/least serious or most/least common.

2 CONVERSATION

Learning Objective: use adjective + infinitive and noun + infinitive in a conversation about advice for a health problem

A *[CD 3, Track 14]*

- Ss cover the text and look at the picture. Elicit or explain vocabulary. Ask: "What health problem do you think Keith has? How do you know?"
- Play the first part of the audio program. Ss listen to check the answer. (Answer: a cold)
- Write this focus question on the board:

  What does Mila suggest for Keith's cold?
- Play the audio program and ask Ss to listen for the answer. Elicit the answer. (Answer: garlic tea)
- Elicit or explain any new vocabulary.

Vocabulary

get some rest: relax or sleep
Have you taken anything for your cold?: Have you taken any medicine?
chop up: cut into small pieces
Yuck!: an expression of dislike, especially about food

- Play the audio program again. Ss listen and read silently.
- Ss practice the conversation in pairs. Go around the class and give help as needed.

TIP

To encourage Ss to look at each other while practicing Conversations, ask them to stand up and face each other. This also makes the conversation more active and natural.

B *[CD 3, Track 15]*

- Read the task and focus question. Ask Ss to make predictions. Write their ideas on the board.
- Play the audio program. Ss listen for the answers individually. Then elicit answers from the class.

Audio script

1.
Keith [*coughs*]
Woman That cold sounds pretty bad, Keith!
Keith Yeah, it is, Mrs. Gray. Don't get too close.
Woman Well, you know, it's important to drink a lot of liquids. Can I get you some orange juice? I have some in the refrigerator.
Keith Oh, OK. That sounds good. Thanks a lot.

2.
Man How's that cold, Keith?
Keith Not so good. [*sneezes*] I've still got it.
Man Oh, too bad. Well, listen, it's a good idea to take some cold medicine. And you should take a long, hot bath.
Keith You're right. Maybe I should. Thanks for the advice.

Answers

The woman suggests orange juice. The man suggests cold medicine. He also says Keith should take a long, hot bath.

3 GRAMMAR FOCUS

Learning Objective: ask for and give advice using adjective + infinitive and noun + infinitive

[CD 3, Track 16]

- Books closed. Write these sentences on the board:

  You should get some rest.
  You should drink garlic tea.

- Point out that these sentences give suggestions with *should*. We can also give suggestions using an adjective or a noun followed by an infinitive. Cross out the words *You should* and replace them with *It's important to* and *It's helpful to*.
- Books open. Focus Ss' attention on the Grammar Focus box. Elicit the rule for forming adjective or noun + infinitive structures:
  It's important/helpful/a good idea to + verb.
- Focus Ss' attention on the Conversation on page 78. Ask Ss to underline the two examples of adjective or noun + infinitive structures.
- Play the audio program.
- ***Option:*** Present additional positive adjective or noun + infinitive structures (e.g., *It's useful to . . . , It's best to . . . , It's essential to . . .*) and also negative infinitives (e.g., *It's important* ***not*** *to . . . , It's best* ***not*** *to . . .*).

A

- Explain the task. Ss read the problems and advice silently. Use the picture or gestures to explain new vocabulary (e.g., *a sore throat, a fever, a toothache, a burn*).
- Read the first problem. Elicit different pieces of advice.
- Ss complete the task individually. Then go over answers with the class.

Possible answers

1. c, e, f, h
2. a, c, i
3. d, f, h
4. a, b, h
5. a, c, h, i
6. a, c, h, i, j
7. a, b, c, h, i, j
8. g, i

B *Group work*

- Explain the task. Then model the example conversation with two Ss.
- Ss take turns giving advice in small groups. Go around the class and check their use of adjective or noun + infinitive structures.

TIP
Use your fingers to help Ss self-correct their errors. For example, if the error is in the fourth word in a sentence, show four fingers and point to the fourth finger.

C

- Explain the task and elicit endings for the first example. Write them on the board.
- Ss complete the task individually. Go around the class and give help as needed.

! For a new way to practice the vocabulary in this Grammar Focus, try ***Mime*** – download it from the website.

4 PRONUNCIATION

Learning Objective: sound more natural by reducing *to* in conversation

A *[CD 3, Track 17]*

- Model the reduction of *to*. Then play the audio program. Ss listen for the reduction of *to*.
- Play the audio program again. Ss take turns practicing the conversation in pairs.

TIP
If you are concerned about your pronunciation and intonation, always use the audio program to present material.

B *Pair work*

- Explain the task. Ss work in pairs. They ask for and give advice using their sentences from part C of Exercise 3. Ask a few pairs of Ss to model the task.
- Ss complete the task in pairs. Go around the class and check their reduction of *to*. Then elicit the most popular advice for each problem.

3 GRAMMAR FOCUS

Adjective + infinitive; noun + infinitive

What should you do for a cold?	It's **important**	**to get** some rest.
	It's sometimes **helpful**	**to drink** garlic tea.
	It's **a good idea**	**to take** some vitamin C.

GRAMMAR PLUS *see page 143*

A Look at these health problems. Choose several pieces of good advice for each problem.

Problems	**Advice**
1. a backache ______	**a.** drink lots of liquids
2. a bad headache ______	**b.** get some medicine
3. a burn ______	**c.** go to bed and rest
4. a cough ______	**d.** put it under cold water
5. a fever ______	**e.** put a heating pad on it
6. the flu ______	**f.** put some cream on it
7. a sore throat ______	**g.** see a dentist
8. a toothache ______	**h.** see a doctor
	i. take some pain medicine
	j. take some vitamin C

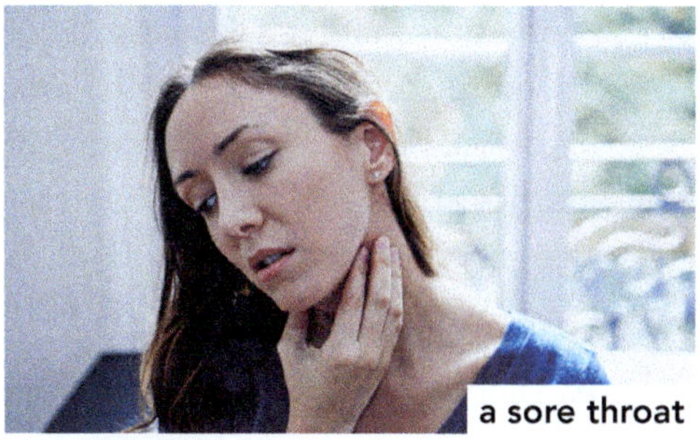
a sore throat

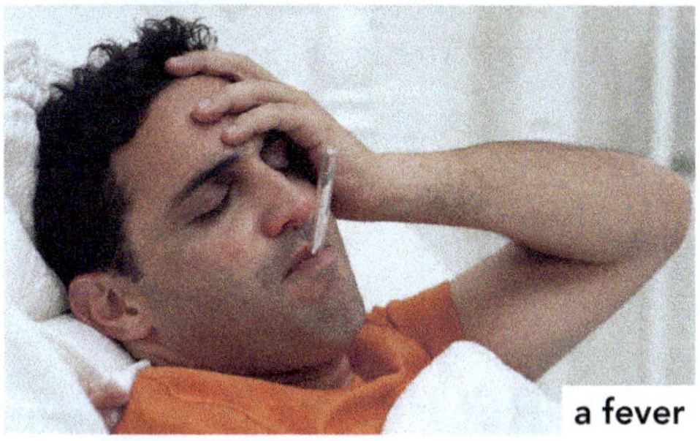
a fever

a toothache

a burn

B **GROUP WORK** Talk about the problems in part A and give advice. What other advice do you have?

A: What should you do for a backache?
B: It's a good idea to put a heating pad on it.
C: It's also important to see a doctor and . . .

C Write advice for these problems. (You will use this advice in Exercise 4.)

an earache **a cold** **a sunburn** **sore muscles**

For an earache, it's a good idea to . . .

4 PRONUNCIATION Reduction of *to*

A Listen and practice. In conversation, **to** is often reduced to /tə/.

A: What should you do for a toothache?
B: It's sometimes helpful **to** take some pain medicine. And it's important **to** see a dentist.

B **PAIR WORK** Look back at Exercise 3, part C. Ask for and give advice about each health problem. Pay attention to the pronunciation of **to**.

5 INTERCHANGE 12 What should I do?

Play a board game. Go to Interchange 12 on page 127.

6 DISCUSSION Good advice

A GROUP WORK Imagine these situations are true for you. Get three suggestions for each one from your partners.

I sometimes feel really stressed.
I need to study, but I can't concentrate.
I feel sick before every exam.
I forget about half the new words I learn.
I get nervous when I speak English to foreigners.
I get really hungry before I go to bed.

A: I sometimes feel really stressed. What should I do?
B: It's a good idea to take a hot bath.
C: It's sometimes helpful to go for a walk.

B CLASS ACTIVITY Have any of the above situations happened to you recently? Share what you did with the class.

7 WORD POWER Containers

A Use the words in the list to complete these expressions. Then compare with a partner. Sometimes more than one answer is correct.

bag	jar
bottle	pack
box	stick
can	tube

1. a _______________ of pain medicine
2. a _______________ of bandages
3. a _______________ of cough drops
4. a _______________ of deodorant
5. a _______________ of face cream
6. a _______________ of shaving cream
7. a _______________ of tissues
8. a _______________ of toothpaste

B PAIR WORK What is one more thing you can buy in each of the containers above?

"You can buy a bag of breath mints."

C PAIR WORK What are the five most useful items in your medicine cabinet?

5 INTERCHANGE 12

See page T-127 for teaching notes.

6 DISCUSSION

Learning Objective: ask for and give advice using adjective + infinitive and noun + infinitive

A *Group work*

- Books closed. Ask: "What should you do when you forget someone's name?" Elicit Ss' answers, encouraging them to use *should,* adjective + infinitive, or noun + infinitive.
- Books open. Explain the task and ask different Ss to read the example situations. Elicit or explain any new vocabulary. Then ask three Ss to read the example conversation.
- Ss discuss the situations in small groups. Go around the class and write down any errors you hear.
- Write the most common errors on the board. Ask Ss to correct them in pairs.

! For a new way to practice this Discussion, try the ***Onion Ring*** technique – download it from the website.

B *Class activity*

- Read the question to the class. Elicit Ss' answers. Encourage Ss to ask follow-up questions.

End of Cycle 1

See the Supplementary Resources chart at the beginning of this unit for additional teaching materials and student activities related to this Cycle.

Cycle 2, Exercises 7–13

7 WORD POWER

Learning Objective: match types of containers to health care products

A

- Books closed. Write the names of the various products from the Word Power on the board. Ask Ss which ones they use. Elicit or explain any new vocabulary.
- ***Option:*** Bring some of the products to class (e.g., toothpaste, deodorant). Elicit the vocabulary.

TIP
To teach the vocabulary for small everyday objects, bring the actual objects to class.

- Books open. Focus Ss' attention on the picture. Elicit or present the words for containers.
- Ss complete the task individually.
- Go over answers with the class. Point out that we don't stress the word *of.*

Answers

1. a **bottle** of pain medicine
2. a **box/pack** of bandages
3. a **bag** of cough drops
4. a **stick** of deodorant
5. a **jar** of face cream
6. a **can** of shaving cream
7. a **box/pack** of tissues
8. a **tube** of toothpaste

B *Pair work*

- Explain the task and ask a S to read the model sentence. Point out that Ss can include any items (e.g., foods).
- Ss work in pairs. Then Ss write their ideas on the board.

Possible answers

1. a bottle of vitamins/shampoo/juice
2. a box of herbal tea/cereal/candy
3. a bag of breath mints/potato chips/rice
4. a stick of gum/butter
5. a jar of coffee/mayonnaise/jam
6. a can of hair spray/foot spray/soda
7. a pack of lozenges/gum/mints
8. a tube of ointment/hand cream/hair gel

C *Pair work*

- Read the question. Ss complete the task in pairs.

8 CONVERSATION

Learning Objective: use *can, could,* and *may* for requests and suggestions in a conversation about suggestions for health problems

A [CD 3, Track 18]

- Books closed. Ask: "Where do you think the speakers are?" Play the audio program and Ss listen for the answer. Elicit the answer. (Answer: a pharmacy)
- Books open. Ss cover the text and look at the picture. Then ask: "What problems do you think the man has?" Encourage Ss to guess. Then play the audio program and elicit the answers. (Answers: a backache, sore muscles, a bad cough (his wife), insomnia)
- Ask: "What four things does the pharmacist suggest?" Play the audio program again. Ss listen for the answers. Elicit the answers. (Answers: a heating pad, cream, cough drops, chamomile tea)
- ***Option:*** Ss work in two groups. Group A listens for the problems the man talks about. Group B listens for the things the pharmacist suggests. Then they share information.
- Ss uncover the text. Then they read the conversation silently.
- Ss stand and practice the conversation in pairs. Encourage them to role-play the conversation, as if they are in a pharmacy.

! For a new way to practice this Conversation, try ***Say It with Feeling!*** – download it from the website.

B [CD 3, Track 19]

- Write these phrases on the board:

  tired eyes *a headache* *insomnia*
- Ask: "What problem does the customer have?" Play the audio program. Ss listen to find the answer. (Answer: a headache)
- Explain the task and read the focus question. Then play the audio program again. Elicit the answer.

Audio script

Customer	Excuse me.
Pharmacist	Yes? How can I help you?
Customer	What do you suggest for a headache?
Pharmacist	Well, you should take some pain medication. And it's important to see a doctor if it doesn't go away.
Customer	Oh, and where is the pain medication?
Pharmacist	Right over there, near the door.
Customer	Thanks a lot.

Answer

She wants some pain medication.

9 GRAMMAR FOCUS

Learning Objective: ask for advice and give suggestions using *can, could,* and *may*

[CD 3, Track 20]

- Explain that it's impolite to say *Give me* or *I want* when asking for things in a store. People usually use modal verbs such as *can, could,* and *may.*
- Focus Ss' attention on the Conversation in Exercise 8. Ask: "How did Mr. Peters ask for things?" Ask Ss to underline the examples. (Answers: *Could I have . . . ? Can you suggest . . . ? May I have . . . ? . . . what do you suggest?*)
- Focus Ss' attention on the example questions in the first column of the Grammar Focus box. Point out that the first question (*Can/May I help you?*) is an offer of help. The other three questions are requests for help. Explain that people can use *can, could,* and *may* to make a request, but *may* is the most formal.
- Elicit the rule for questions with modals: Modal + subject + verb?
- Focus Ss' attention on the three ways to make suggestions in the second column. Ask Ss to find similar examples in the Conversation in Exercise 8 and underline them twice.
- Play the audio program.
- Explain the task and model the first conversation with a S.
- Ss circle the correct modal verbs individually. Then they compare answers in pairs.

Answers

1. A: **Can** I help you?
   B: What do you **suggest** for dry skin?
   A: Why don't you **try** this lotion? It's excellent.
   B: OK. I'll take it.
2. A: **May** I have something for itchy eyes?
   B: Sure. You **could** try a bottle of eyedrops.
3. A: Could I **have** a box of bandages, please?
   B: Here you are.
   A: And what do you **suggest** for insomnia?
   B: You **should** try this herbal tea. It's very relaxing.
   A: OK. Thanks.

- Ss practice the conversations in pairs.

! For a new way to practice the conversations in this Grammar Focus, try the ***Substitution Dialog*** – download it from the website. Ss replace the health problems and suggestions with ideas of their own.

8 CONVERSATION Can you suggest anything?

A Listen and practice.

Pharmacist: Hi. May I help you?

Mr. Peters: Yes, please. Could I have something for a backache? My muscles are really sore.

Pharmacist: Well, it's a good idea to use a heating pad. And why don't you try this cream? It works really well.

Mr. Peters: OK, I'll take one tube. Also, my wife has a bad cough. Can you suggest anything?

Pharmacist: She should try these cough drops.

Mr. Peters: Thanks! May I have a large bag? And what do you suggest for insomnia?

Pharmacist: Well, you could get a box of chamomile tea. Is it for you?

Mr. Peters: Yes, I can't sleep.

Pharmacist: A sore back and your wife's bad cough? I think I know why you can't sleep!

B Listen to the pharmacist talk to the next customer. What does the customer want?

9 GRAMMAR FOCUS

Modal verbs *can, could,* and *may* for requests; suggestions

Can/May I help you?	What do you suggest/have for a backache?
Can I have a bag of cough drops?	You could try this new cream.
Could I have something for a cough?	You should get a heating pad.
May I have a bottle of pain medicine?	Why don't you try these pills?

GRAMMAR PLUS *see page 143*

Choose the correct words. Then compare and practice with a partner.

1. **A:** **Can** / **Could** I help you?
   B: What do you **suggest** / **try** for dry skin?
   A: Why don't you **suggest** / **try** this lotion? It's excellent.
   B: OK. I'll take it.
2. **A:** **May** / **Do** I have something for itchy eyes?
   B: Sure. You **could** / **may** try a bottle of eyedrops.
3. **A:** Could I **suggest** / **have** a box of bandages, please?
   B: Here you are.
   A: And what do you **suggest** / **try** for insomnia?
   B: You **should** / **may** try this herbal tea.
   It's very relaxing.
   A: OK. Thanks.

10 LISTENING What's wrong?

Listen to four people talking about problems and giving advice. Write the problem and the advice.

	Problem	Advice
1. John		
2. Ashley		
3. Brandon		
4. Rachel		

11 ROLE PLAY Can I help you?

Student A: You are a customer in a drugstore. You need:

something for a backache
something for dry skin
something for the flu
something for low energy
something for sore feet
something for an upset stomach

Ask for some suggestions.

Student B: You are a pharmacist in a drugstore.
A customer needs some things.
Make some suggestions.

Change roles and try the role play again.

12 WRITING Reacting to a blog post

A Read this health and fitness blog post on how to avoid stress.

Home About Healthy living

Suggestions for a Relaxing Life

Tuesday, March 29

healthyandhappy

Can we avoid stress in our lives? What should we do to have a relaxing life? Everyone wants the answers to these questions. Well, we have a few suggestions:

- We should not work long hours or work on our days off.
- We should try to exercise three or four times a week.
- It's a good idea to buy only the things we really need.
- It's really important to have fun. Fun is the perfect remedy for stress!

B Now imagine you have your own blog. Write a post with your ideas on how to reduce stress and have a relaxing life. Think of an interesting name for your blog.

C **GROUP WORK** Exchange blog posts. Read your partners' blogs and write a suggestion at the bottom of each post. Then share the most interesting blog and suggestions with the class.

10 LISTENING

Learning Objective: listen for specific information about health problems and health care products

[CD 3, Track 21]

- Explain that four people are going to talk about their problems and someone will offer advice. Draw Ss' attention to the chart. Then play the audio program. Ss listen for the problems and write them in the chart.
- Play the audio again and have Ss write the advice in the correct column.

Audio script

1.
John Oh! I just know I'm going to fail!
Samantha What's bothering you, John?
John Oh, sorry, Samantha. I'm really stressed. I have my final exam in math tomorrow.
Samantha Don't worry, John. You'll do fine on the test. For now, I think you should take a break. Let's go get some ice cream. I'll buy it.

2.
Ashley Those cookies smell so good!
Man I know, they do. But they're not ready yet.
Ashley Not ready? I'm so hungry! And now the whole apartment smells like delicious cookies. Ooh! My stomach hurts!
Man I'm sorry, Ashley. I made a nice salad, too. It's in the refrigerator. You should have some.

3.
Brandon I'm really happy about my report. It's really good.
Woman I'm sure it is, Brandon. Hey, do you know your eyes are all red?
Brandon Are they? Sometimes they get red when I spend a lot of time on the computer.
Woman Don't you use eyedrops? You should. I think I have some in my bag.

4.
Don Rachel? Rachel?
Rachel Huh? Oh, sorry, Don. I was thinking about my vacation. I leave tomorrow for Gramado in Brazil, you know.
Don Oh, right, that's a beautiful town. I'm sure you're excited.
Rachel I really am. I'm so excited, it's difficult to work.
Don Well, it's already 3:00. You should go home now and start getting ready.
Rachel Really? Thanks, Don!

- Ss go over their answers in pairs. Then go over answers with the class.

Answers

	Problem	Advice
1. John	He is stressed about his final exam.	He should take a break.
2. Ashley	She is hungry and the cookies aren't ready.	She should have some salad.
3. Brandon	His eyes are red from spending time on the computer.	He should use eyedrops.
4. Rachel	She is excited about her trip and can't work.	She should go home.

11 ROLE PLAY

Learning Objective: use *can, could,* and *may* for requests and suggestions in a conversation about a health problem

- Set the scene and explain the task. Ss work in pairs. Student A is a customer in a drugstore, and Student B is a pharmacist. The customer asks for six things and the pharmacist makes suggestions.
- ***Option:*** If Ss need help getting started, refer them to the first few lines of the Conversation on page 81.
- Ss complete the role play in pairs.
- Ss change roles. Go around the class and take notes on their grammar, pronunciation, fluency, and ideas.

! For a new way to teach this Role Play, try ***Time Out!*** – download it from the website.

12 WRITING

Learning Objectives: write a blog post giving health advice; respond to a blog post

A

- Ask: "Do you ever feel stressed? What can you do to help relax?" Elicit ideas from the class.
- Ss read the blog post suggestions silently. Elicit or explain any new vocabulary.

B

- Explain the task. Ss complete the task individually in class or for homework.

C *Group work*

- Explain the task. Then Ss complete the task in small groups. Groups share their most interesting suggestions with the class.

13 READING

Learning Objective: skim for the main idea and read for details in an article about natural medicine

- Focus Ss' attention on the article. Tell Ss to look at the title and pictures. Elicit Ss' ideas about what they think they will learn about in the article.

A

- Explain the task. Tell Ss to skim the article for the answer. Point out that they shouldn't worry about any new vocabulary.
- Allow about three minutes for Ss to complete the task. Then Ss check the best description of the article. Elicit the answer.

Answer

The article gives information and facts.

B

- Present or ask Ss to look up key vocabulary from the reading.

TIP

To save time, have Ss look up the vocabulary in a dictionary before class. To encourage peer teaching, assign each S a few words to look up. Then have them teach each other the words in class.

Vocabulary

rain forest: a tropical forest
research: scientific discoveries
appointment: a scheduled meeting with someone, often a dentist or doctor
remedy: a treatment or substance that cures an illness
village: a group of houses and shops that is smaller than a town
gel: a thick substance that is part liquid and is clear, unlike cream

- Explain the task. Then answer the first question and identify the paragraph as a class.
- Ss complete the task individually and compare answers in pairs. Go around the class and check their answers. Help Ss with pronunciation as needed.

Answers

1. C 2. D 3. B 4. C 5. D 6. B

- ***Option:*** Ss read the article again and underline any words they still don't know. Explain the words.

C *Group work*

- Ss discuss the question in small groups. Go around the class and help with vocabulary as needed. Then elicit Ss' answers. (Possible answers: They're a source of oxygen, wood, rubber, and food. They're a home for many animals.)

End of Cycle 2

See the Supplementary Resources chart at the beginning of this unit for additional teaching materials and student activities related to this Cycle and for assessment tools.

13 READING

A Skim the article. Then check the best description of the article.

- ☐ The article gives the author's opinion about the subject.
- ☐ The article gives information and facts.
- ☐ The article tells a story about a scientist.

Toothache?

Visit the rain forest!

acmella oleracea

A Nobody likes having a toothache, and not many people enjoy visiting the dentist's office. Exciting new research suggests that there is a different way to treat a toothache – one that doesn't need an appointment with a dentist.

B Scientists say that a very rare red and yellow plant from the Amazon rain forest could stop a toothache. It's more powerful than taking pain medicine, and it's more effective than most treatments you get in the dentist's chair. The plant, named *acmella oleracea,* has been used as a remedy for toothaches by the Keshwa Lamas, a Peruvian community, for many years.

C Dr. Françoise Barbira Freedman is an anthropologist – a scientist who studies humans. She learned about the plant 30 years ago on a trip to Peru. One day, she got a terrible toothache. The people in the village where she was living gave her the remedy and her pain disappeared.

D Now this amazing plant has been made into a gel. Many tests show that it really helps with the pain of toothaches and even helps babies who are getting their first teeth. To thank the Keshwa Lamas for this remedy, there is a plan to give some of the money from the gel back to the community. So it's good news for everyone.

B Read the article. Then answer these questions. Write the letter of the paragraph where you find the answers.

1. ______ When did Dr. Freedman learn about the plant?
2. ______ What has the plant been made into?
3. ______ What is the plant's scientific name?
4. ______ Who gave Dr. Freedman the remedy?
5. ______ What will be given back to the Keshwa Lamas?
6. ______ Where can you find the plant?

C **GROUP WORK** What are some other reasons why rain forests are important?

Units 11–12 Progress check

SELF-ASSESSMENT

How well can you do these things? Check (✓) the boxes.

I can . . .	Very well	OK	A little
Understand descriptions of towns and cities (Ex. 1)	☐	☐	☐
Get useful information about towns and cities (Ex. 1, 2)	☐	☐	☐
Describe towns and cities (Ex. 2)	☐	☐	☐
Ask for and make suggestions (Ex. 2, 3, 4)	☐	☐	☐
Ask and answer questions about experiences (Ex. 3, 4)	☐	☐	☐
Ask for and give advice about problems (Ex. 4)	☐	☐	☐

1 LISTENING So, you're from Hawaii?

A Listen to Megan talk about Honolulu. What does she say about these things? Complete the chart.

1. size of city ______	**3.** prices of things ______
2. weather ______	**4.** Waikiki Beach ______

B Write sentences comparing Honolulu with your hometown. Then discuss with a partner.

Honolulu isn't too big, but Seoul is really big.

2 ROLE PLAY My hometown

Student A: Imagine you are planning to visit Student B's hometown. Ask questions to learn more about the place. Use the questions in the box and your own ideas.

Student B: Answer Student A's questions about your hometown.

A: What's your hometown like?
B: It's very interesting, but it's crowded and polluted.

Change roles and try the role play again.

possible questions

What's your hometown like?
How big is it?
What's the weather like?
Is it expensive?
What should you see there?
What can you do there?

Units 11–12 Progress check

SELF-ASSESSMENT

Learning Objectives: reflect on one's learning; identify areas that need improvement

- Ask: "What did you learn in Units 11 and 12?" Elicit Ss' answers.
- Ss complete the Self-assessment. Encourage them to be honest, and point out they will not get a bad grade if they check (✓) *A little.*
- Ss move on to the Progress check exercises. You can have Ss complete them in class or for homework, using one of these techniques:
  1. Ask Ss to complete all the exercises.
  2. Ask Ss: "What do you need to practice?" Then assign exercises based on their answers.
  3. Ask Ss to choose and complete exercises based on their Self-assessment.

1 LISTENING

Learning Objective: demonstrate one's ability to listen to and understand a description of a city and compare it to one's hometown using adjectives, adverbs, and conjunctions

A *[CD 3, Track 22]*

- Set the scene and explain the task. Megan is talking about Honolulu, her hometown. Ss listen and write the size of the city, weather, prices of things, and what she says about Waikiki Beach in their chart.
- Play the audio program once or twice. Ss listen and complete the chart.

Audio script

Man So, you're from Hawaii, Megan?
Megan That's right.
Man Where in Hawaii?
Megan I'm from Honolulu – on the island of Oahu.
Man Wow! Honolulu! That's a fairly big city, isn't it?
Megan No, not really. It's not too big.
Man The weather is great, though. Right?
Megan Oh, yes. It is. It's very comfortable the whole year. Warm, but not too hot.
Man I've heard that Honolulu is an expensive city. Is that true?
Megan Well, yes, it is pretty expensive. Rents are high and food is expensive, too. That's because everything comes in from the mainland.
Man What's that beach in Honolulu?
Megan Well, Waikiki Beach is really famous. That's where all the tourists go.
Man Yeah, that's it. Waikiki Beach.

- Go over answers with the class.

Answers

1. size of city	not too big
2. weather	very comfortable; warm but not too hot
3. prices of things	pretty expensive
4. Waikiki Beach	really famous

B

- Explain the task. Ss write sentences comparing Honolulu with their hometowns. Point out the conjunction, adjectives, and adverbs in the example.
- Ss write sentences individually. Then they compare their sentences in pairs.

2 ROLE PLAY

Learning Objectives: demonstrate one's ability to ask questions about hometowns; demonstrate one's ability to describe one's hometown and give suggestions for sightseeing

- Explain the task. Ss work in pairs. Student A is planning to visit Student B's hometown and asks questions about it. Student B answers the questions.
- Go over the possible questions. Model the example conversation with a S.
- Ss practice the role play in pairs. Then they change roles and practice again. Go around the class and give help as needed.

3 DISCUSSION

Learning Objective: demonstrate one's ability to ask for and give suggestions and advice

A *Group work*

- Explain the task and model the example conversation with two Ss.
- Ss write advice and remedies for the problems individually. Go around the class and give help as needed.
- Ss compare their ideas in small groups. Encourage Ss to use expressions of advice (e.g., *it's useful to, it's helpful to, you should*).
- Go around the room and check Ss' use of adjective + infinitive and noun + infinitive.

B *Group work*

- Read the questions and explain the task.
- Ss discuss the questions in small groups. Encourage them to add follow-up questions.

4 SPEAKING

Learning Objective: demonstrate one's ability to give advice

A *Group work*

- Set the scene. The three problems are from an advice column.
- Ss read the problems silently. Then elicit or explain any new vocabulary.
- Explain the task. In small groups, Ss suggest advice for each problem and choose the best advice. Model the example conversation with two Ss.
- Ss complete the task.

B *Class activity*

- Ask different Ss to share their group's advice.

WHAT'S NEXT?

Learning Objective: become more involved in one's learning

- Focus Ss' attention on the Self-assessment again. Ask: "How well can you do these things now?"
- Ask Ss to underline one thing they need to review. Ask: "What did you underline? How can you review it?"
- If needed, plan additional activities or reviews based on Ss' answers.

3 DISCUSSION Medicines and remedies

A GROUP WORK Write your suggestions for these common problems and then discuss your ideas in groups.

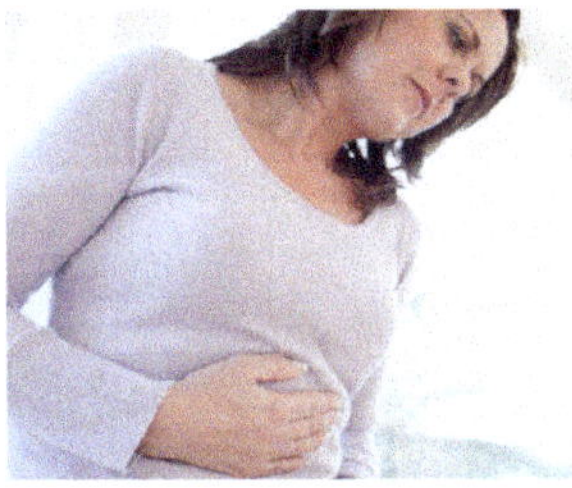

a stomachache

an insect bite

the hiccups

a nosebleed

For a stomachache, it's a good idea to . . .

A: What can you do for a stomachache?
B: I think it's helpful to drink herbal tea.
C: Yes. And it's a good idea to see a doctor.

B GROUP WORK What health problems do you visit a doctor for? go to a drugstore for? use a home remedy for? Ask for advice and remedies.

4 SPEAKING What's your advice?

A GROUP WORK Read these people's problems. Suggest advice for each problem. Then choose the best advice.

I'm visiting the United States. I'm staying with a family while I'm here. What small gifts can I get for them?

My co-worker always talks loudly to his friends during work hours. I can't concentrate! What can I do?

Our school wants to buy some new gym equipment. Can you suggest some good ways to raise money?

A: Why doesn't she give them some flowers? They're always nice.
B: That's a good idea. Or she could bring chocolates.
C: I think she should . . .

B CLASS ACTIVITY Share your group's advice for each problem with the class.

WHAT'S NEXT?

Look at your Self-assessment again. Do you need to review anything?

Unit 13 Supplementary Resources Overview

	After the following SB exercises	You can use these materials in class	Your students can use these materials outside the classroom
CYCLE 1	1 **Snapshot**		**DW** Unit 13 Vocabulary 1
	2 **Conversation**		
	3 **Grammar Focus**		**SB** Unit 13 Grammar plus, Focus 1 **DW** Unit 13 Grammar 1, 3
	4 **Pronunciation**	**TR** Unit 13 Extra Worksheet	**WB** Unit 13 exercises 1–3
CYCLE 2	5 **Word Power**	**TR** Unit 13 Vocabulary Worksheet	**DW** Unit 13 Vocabulary 2
	6 **Conversation**		
	7 **Grammar Focus**	**TR** Unit 13 Grammar Worksheet	**SB** Unit 13 Grammar plus, Focus 2 **DW** Unit 13 Grammar 2, 4–7
	8 **Role Play**		
	9 **Listening**	**TR** Unit 13 Listening Worksheet	
	10 **Interchange 13**		
	11 **Writing**	**TR** Unit 13 Writing Worksheet	
	12 **Reading**	**TR** Unit 13 Project Worksheet **VID** Unit 13 **VRB** Unit 13	**DW** Unit 13 Reading 1–2 **DW** Unit 13 Listening 1–2 **DW** Unit 13 Video 1–2 **WB** Unit 13 exercises 4–8

Key **SB:** Student's Book **DW:** Digital Workbook **TR:** Teacher's Resources
VID: Video (DW/TR) **VRB:** Video Resource Book (TR) **WB:** Print Workbook

My Plan for Unit 13

Use the space below to customize a plan that fits your needs.

With the following SB exercises	I am using these materials in class	My students are using these materials outside the classroom

With or instead of the following SB section	I am using these materials for assessment

13 What would you like?

- Agree and disagree about food preferences
- Order food in a restaurant

1 SNAPSHOT

Favorite Foods

apple pie

☐ brought to North America from Europe in the 17th century

chocolate

☐ originally prepared as a drink by the Olmec people in Mexico over 3,000 years ago

french fries

☐ first made in Belgium around 1680

hamburger

☐ created around 1900 in the U.S. as a quick and inexpensive meal

ice-cream cone

☐ created at the 1904 World's Fair in the U.S. by a Syrian chef, Ernest Hamwi

pasta

☐ first written about in a Greek recipe from the 1st century CE

the sandwich

☐ named for the English Earl of Sandwich in the 1760s

sushi

☐ modern style sushi first made in Japan in the 1820s

What are these foods made of? Put the foods in order from your favorite (1) to your least favorite (8). What are three other foods you enjoy? Which have you eaten recently?

2 CONVERSATION I'm tired of shopping.

A Listen and practice.

Simon: Hey, do you want to get something to eat?
Kristin: Sure. I'm tired of shopping.
Simon: So am I. What do you think of Thai food?
Kristin: I love it, but I'm not really in the mood for it today.
Simon: Yeah. I'm not either, I guess. It's a bit spicy.
Kristin: What about Japanese food?
Simon: Fine by me! I love Japanese food.
Kristin: So do I. There's a great restaurant on the first floor. It's called Kyoto Garden.
Simon: Perfect. Let's go try it.

B Listen to the rest of the conversation. What do they decide to do after eating? Is there something they don't want to do?

13 What would you like?

Cycle 1, Exercises 1–4

In Unit 13, students agree and disagree about food preferences and order food in a restaurant. By the end of Cycle 1, students will be able to agree and disagree about food preferences using *so, too, neither,* and *either.* By the end of Cycle 2, students will be able to use *would* and *will* to order food at a restaurant.

1 SNAPSHOT

Learning Objective: discuss food and food preferences

- Books closed. Write these foods on the board:

apple pie	ice-cream cone
chocolate	pasta
french fries	the sandwich
hamburger	sushi

- Ask Ss to guess where each food item is from.
- Books open. Ss check their answers with the Snapshot.
- Ask different Ss to read the facts. Elicit or explain any new vocabulary.

Vocabulary
around: about that time
CE: common era
earl: a British man of high social rank

- Point out that the Earl of Sandwich's real name was John Montague, and he loved to play cards. He created the first sandwich so he could eat neatly during card games.
- Ask: "Does any information in the Snapshot surprise you?" Elicit Ss' answers.
- Explain the tasks. Then Ss complete the tasks in pairs. Go around the class and give help as needed.

2 CONVERSATION

Learning Objective: use *so, too, neither,* and *either* in a conversation about deciding where to go for dinner

A *[CD 3, Track 23]*

- Books closed. Set the scene. Simon and Kristin are discussing where to go for dinner. Write these focus questions on the board:
  1. *What two kinds of food do they talk about?*
  2. *What kind of food do they decide to eat?*
- Play the audio program. Then elicit the answers. (Answers: 1. Thai and Japanese 2. Japanese)
- Books open. Play the audio program again. Ss listen and read silently.
- Elicit or explain any new vocabulary.

Vocabulary
I'm not in the mood for: I don't really want
a bit: a little
spicy: with a hot or strong flavor, like pepper or curry

- Ss practice the conversation in pairs. Then ask Ss to role-play the conversation for the class.

! For a new way to practice this Conversation, try ***Say It with Feeling!*** – download it from the website.

B *[CD 3, Track 24]*

- Explain the task and read the focus questions. Then play the audio program. Elicit the answers.

Audio script

Simon Wow, that was delicious, but I'm full!
Kristin So am I. I'm in the mood for something relaxing. What about a movie?
Simon Good idea. What do you want to see?
Kristin Anything, really. We can see what's playing.
Simon OK, but no romance! I promised to see the new Ryan Gosling movie with my sister. One romance movie is enough.
Kristin [*chuckles*] You're a good brother.
Simon It's her birthday next week. That's the only reason why!

Answers

They decide to see a movie. They don't want to see a romance movie.

3 GRAMMAR FOCUS

Learning Objective: agree and disagree about food preferences using *so, too, neither,* and *either*

[CD 3, Track 25]

- Focus Ss' attention on the Grammar Focus box. Ask: "Which statements are positive? Which statements are negative?" (Answers: The top three statements are positive (*I'm crazy about/I can/I like*), and the bottom three statements are negative (*I'm not in the mood/I can't stand/I don't like*).)

So *and* too

- Focus Ss' attention on the first three responses in the second column. Point out that we can use *so* or *too* to agree with a positive statement.
- Write these responses on the board:

  So am I.   *So can I.*   *So do I.*

  Ask: "When do we use each response?" Elicit or explain the rule. (Answer: The verb in each response matches that of the sentence before it.)
- Focus Ss' attention on the difference between *so* and *too*. Point out that *so* is at the beginning of the response and *too* is at the end:
  So + *am/can/do* + *I.*
  I + *am/can/do,* + ***too***.
- Ask Ss to find responses in the third column that disagree with positive statements. (Answers: Oh, I'm not./Really? I can't./Oh, I don't.)
- Play the audio program for the first column.
- ***Option:*** Drill *So am I, So can I,* or *So do I* responses. Read a list of ten positive statements to the class (e.g., I am smart. I can speak English. I live near here.). Ss respond chorally and then individually.

Neither *and* either

- Focus Ss' attention on the last three responses in the second column of the Grammar Focus box. Elicit the rules for agreeing with a negative statement:
  Neither + *am/can/do* + *I.*
  I'm ***not****/I* ***can't****/I* ***don't*** + ***either***.
- Point out different ways to disagree with negative statements (e.g., *Really? I am./Oh, I love it!/Oh, I like it a lot.*).
- Play the audio program for the second column.
- ***Option:*** Drill *Neither am I, Neither can I,* or *Neither do I* responses. Read a list of ten negative statements to the class (e.g., *I'm not hungry. I can't cook French food./I don't like fish ice cream.*). Ss respond chorally and then individually.

A

- Ask different Ss to read the adjectives describing food. Help with pronunciation as needed.
- Explain the task. Ss write responses to show agreement with the statements. Point out that each statement has two correct responses.
- Read the first two statements and elicit Ss' responses. Write correct responses on the board.
- Ss complete the task individually. Then they compare answers in pairs. Go over answers with the class.

Possible answers

1. Neither am I./I'm not either.
2. So can I./I can, too.
3. So do I./I do, too.
4. Neither can I./I can't either.
5. Neither do I./I don't either.
6. So am I./I am, too.
7. So am I./I am, too.
8. Neither do I./I don't either.
9. So do I./I do, too.
10. Neither can I./I can't either.

B *Pair work*

- Explain the task. Ss work in pairs. They take turns reading the statements in part A and responding with their own opinions.
- Go around the class and check Ss' use of grammar.

For more practice, play ***Concentration*** – download it from the website. Ss match cards with the same meaning (e.g., *So do I.* and *I do, too.*).

C

- Elicit different ways to say *I like* and *I don't like.* Write them on the board:

I like	I don't like
I really like	I don't really like
I'm in the mood for	I'm not in the mood for
I like . . . very much	I don't like . . . very much
I'm crazy about	I'm not crazy about
I love	I hate

- Explain the task. Model the first example by writing two sentences on the board.
- Ss complete the task individually. Don't ask Ss to compare statements at this time. They will do this in Exercise 4.

3 GRAMMAR FOCUS

So, too, neither, either

	Agree	Disagree
I'**m** crazy about Italian food.	**So am** I./I **am, too**.	Oh, I'**m not**.
I **can** eat really spicy food.	**So can** I./I **can, too**.	Really? I **can't**.
I **like** Japanese food a lot.	**So do** I./I **do, too**.	Oh, I **don't (like it very much)**.
I'**m not** in the mood for Indian food.	**Neither am** I./I'**m not either**.	Really? I **am**.
I **can't** stand fast food.	**Neither can** I./I **can't either**.	Oh, I **love** it!
I **don't like** salty food.	**Neither do** I./I **don't either**.	Oh, I **like** it a lot.

GRAMMAR PLUS *see page 144*

bland

delicious

greasy

healthy

rich

salty

spicy

A Write responses to show agreement with these statements. Then compare with a partner.

1. I'm not crazy about Italian food. __________
2. I can eat any kind of food. __________
3. I think Indian food is delicious. __________
4. I can't stand greasy food. __________
5. I don't like salty food. __________
6. I'm in the mood for something spicy. __________
7. I'm tired of fast food. __________
8. I don't enjoy rich food very much. __________
9. I always eat healthy food. __________
10. I can't eat bland food. __________

B **PAIR WORK** Take turns responding to the statements in part A again. Give your own opinion when responding.

C Write statements about these things. (You will use the statements in Exercise 4.)

1. two kinds of food you like
2. two kinds of food you can't stand
3. two kinds of food you would like to eat today

4 PRONUNCIATION Stress in responses

A Listen and practice. Notice how the last word of each response is stressed.

I do, **too**.	So do **I**.	I don't **either**.	Neither do **I**.
I am, **too**.	So am **I**.	I'm not **either**.	Neither am **I**.
I can, **too**.	So can **I**.	I can't **either**.	Neither can **I**.

B **PAIR WORK** Read and respond to the statements your partner wrote for Exercise 3, part C. Pay attention to the stress in your responses.

5 WORD POWER Food categories

A Complete the chart. Then add one more word to each category.

bread	fish	mangoes	peas	shrimp
chicken	grapes	octopus	potatoes	strawberries
corn	lamb	pasta	rice	turkey

Fruit	Vegetables	Grains	Meat	Seafood

B **GROUP WORK** What's your favorite food in each category? Are there any you haven't tried?

6 CONVERSATION May I take your order?

A Listen and practice.

Server: May I take your order?

Customer: Yes, please. I'd like the veggie burger.

Server: All right. And would you like soup or salad with your burger?

Customer: What's the soup of the day?

Server: It's chicken soup. We also have cream of potato soup and onion soup.

Customer: I'll have the onion soup, please.

Server: And would you like anything to drink?

Customer: Yes, I'd like a lemonade, please.

B Listen to the server talk to the next customer. What does he order?

4 PRONUNCIATION

Learning Objective: sound more natural when responding with *so, too, either,* and *neither*

A *[CD 3, Track 26]*

- Explain the task. Then play the audio program. Point out the stress by clapping your hands on the last word of each response.
- Play the audio program again. Ss listen and practice.

B ***Pair work***

- Explain the task. Then Ss complete the task in pairs. Go around the class and check Ss' pronunciation.

End of Cycle 1

See the Supplementary Resources chart at the beginning of this unit for additional teaching materials and student activities related to this Cycle.

Cycle 2, Exercises 5–12

5 WORD POWER

Learning Objective: categorize food items

A

- Explain the task. Explain what the different food categories are and any new vocabulary.
- Ss complete the chart individually.
- Draw the chart on the board. Ask different Ss to complete the chart.

Answers

Fruit	Vegetables	Grains	Meat	Seafood
grapes	corn	bread	chicken	fish
mangoes	peas	pasta	lamb	octopus
strawberries	potatoes	rice	turkey	shrimp
apples	*broccoli*	*cereal*	*beef*	*salmon*
bananas	*spinach*	*muffin*	*hot dog*	*ceviche*

(Note: Possible answers are italicized.)

B ***Group work***

- Read the questions and explain the task.
- Ss discuss the questions in small groups. Encourage them to add follow-up questions.

6 CONVERSATION

Learning Objective: use *would* and *will* in a conversation to order food at a restaurant

A *[CD 3, Track 27]*

- Ss cover the text. Elicit ideas and vocabulary from the picture. Ask: "What kind of restaurant is this? What kinds of food do they serve?"
- Set the scene. A server is taking a customer's order. Write this summary sentence on the board:

  The customer orders a veggie burger / chicken burger and cream of potato soup / onion soup, and an iced tea / lemonade.
- Play the audio program. Ss listen for the correct answers. Ask different Ss to circle the correct answers on the board. (Answers: veggie burger, onion soup, lemonade)
- Ss uncover the text. Play the audio program again. Ss listen and read silently.
- Ss practice the conversation in pairs.

B *[CD 3, Track 28]*

- Explain the task and read the focus question. Then play the audio program. Elicit the answer.

Audio script

Server Are you ready to order?
Man Yes, I think so . . . I'd like the chicken curry, please.
Server Would you like today's special, chicken curry and mango salad?
Man Yes, I'll have the curry and salad, please.
Server OK. Anything to drink?
Man Yeah. I'll have a large orange juice, please.
Server And how about some dessert? We have pie, cake, and ice cream.
Man No dessert for me, thanks.

Answers

He orders chicken curry and a mango salad. To drink, he orders a large orange juice.

7 GRAMMAR FOCUS

Learning Objective: use *would* and *will* to order food at a restaurant

[CD 3, Track 29]

***Modal verbs* would *and* will**

- Write these sentences on the board:

  1. And do you <u>want</u> soup or salad with your burger?
  2. And do you <u>want</u> anything to drink?
  3. I <u>want</u> the onion soup, please.
  4. I <u>want</u> a lemonade, please.

  Explain that people don't usually say *want* in formal situations.
- Focus Ss' attention on the Conversation on page 88. Ss find and underline sentences and questions with the same meaning as those on the board. Ask different Ss to write them on the board. (Answers: 1. And would you like soup or salad with your burger? 2. And would you like anything to drink? 3. I'll have the onion soup, please. 4. I'd like a lemonade, please.)
- Focus Ss' attention on the Grammar Focus box. Elicit the structure for making Wh- and yes/no questions with *would*:
  Wh-question + *would* + subject + verb?
  Would + subject + verb?

  Point out that the word *would* does not have strong stress.
- Elicit or explain that we can order in a restaurant with *I'd like* or *I'll have*. Point out the contractions. Play the audio program.
- Explain the task and model the first two lines of the conversation. Ss complete the conversation individually. Then they compare answers in pairs.
- Go over answers by asking different Ss to read the conversation.

Answers

Server:	What **would** you like to order?
Customer:	I**'ll** have the spicy fish.
Server:	**Would** you like salad or potatoes?
Customer:	I**'d** like potatoes, please.
Server:	OK. And **would** you like anything to drink?
Customer:	I**'ll** just have a glass of water.
Server:	Would you **like** anything else?
Customer:	No, that's all for now, thanks.
(*Later*)	
Server:	Would you **like** dessert?
Customer:	Yes, I**'d** like ice cream.
Server:	What flavor **would** you like?
Customer:	Hmm. I**'ll** have mint chocolate chip, please.

! For a new way to practice the conversations in this Grammar Focus, try the ***Substitution Dialog*** – download it from the website. Ss replace the food and drink items with their own ideas.

8 ROLE PLAY

Learning Objective: use *would* and *will* to order food at a restaurant

- Ss work in pairs. Set the scene and explain the task. Student A is a customer in a coffee shop. Student B is a server. Student A orders lunch and Student B takes the order. If possible, Student A sits at a table and Student B stands. Model the pronunciation of the food items if needed.
- Model taking the order with a S. Show how to add follow-up questions (e.g., *Would you like dressing on your salad? Would you like anything else?*). Ss complete the role play in pairs.
- Provide useful feedback. Then ask Ss to change roles and use their own information. Go around the class and encourage Ss to ask follow-up questions.
- ***Option:*** Ss complete the role play in small groups. One S is the server and the other Ss are customers.

TIP

To make role plays more authentic, bring props to class. For example, in a restaurant role play you can bring real menus, pens, and notepads.

! For a new way to practice this Role Play, try ***Time Out!*** – download it from the website.

7 GRAMMAR FOCUS

Modal verbs *would* and *will* for requests

What **would** you **like**?	**I'd like** the veggie burger. **I'll have** a mango salad.	**Contractions** **I'll** = I will **I'd** = I would
What kind of soup **would** you **like**?	**I'd like** onion soup, please. **I'll have** the soup of the day.	
What **would** you **like** to drink?	**I'd like** a lemonade. **I'll have** a large orange juice.	
Would you **like** anything else?	Yes, please. **I'd like** some coffee. That's all, thanks.	

GRAMMAR PLUS *see page 144*

Complete this conversation. Then practice with a partner.

Server: What ______________ you like to order?
Customer: I ______________ have the spicy fish.
Server: ______________ you like salad or potatoes?
Customer: I ______________ like potatoes, please.
Server: OK. And ______________ you like anything to drink?
Customer: I ______________ just have a glass of water.
Server: Would you ______________ anything else?
Customer: No, that's all for now, thanks.

Later

Server: Would you ______________ dessert?
Customer: Yes, I ______________ like ice cream.
Server: What flavor ______________ you like?
Customer: Hmm. I ______________ have mint chocolate chip, please.

8 ROLE PLAY At a coffee shop

Student A: You are a customer at a coffee shop. Order what you want for lunch.
Student B: You are the server. Take your customer's order.

TODAY'S LUNCH SPECIALS

Cheeseburger with onion rings
Spicy shrimp and rice
Chicken salad sandwich
Lamb curry and potatoes
Sushi plate with miso soup
Vegetarian pizza and salad

Drinks

Coffee
Tea
Soda
Fresh juice
Sparkling water

Desserts

Ice cream
Chocolate cake
Lemon pie
Fresh fruit salad

Change roles and try the role play again.

9 LISTENING Working late

A Steven and Sarah are working late. Listen as their boss asks what they would like for dinner. What do they order? Fill in their choices.

Steven	Sarah
___________ pizza	___________ pizza
Salad with ___________	Salad with ___________ dressing
Drink: ___________ with ___________	Drink: ___________ with ___________
Dessert: a piece of ___________	Dessert: a slice of ___________

B Listen to their conversation after the food arrives. Choose the two items that are missing from the order.

10 INTERCHANGE 13 Planning a food festival

Create a menu to offer at a food festival. Go to Interchange 13 on page 128.

11 WRITING A restaurant review

A Have you eaten out recently? Write a review of a restaurant, café, or food truck. Choose at least five questions from the list. Answer these questions and add ideas of your own.

What's the name of the place?
When did you go there?
What time did you go?
Who did you go with?
What did you have to eat?
What did you have to drink?
Did you order dessert?
What did you like about the place?
What didn't you like about it?
Would you recommend it? Why? Why not?

B **GROUP WORK** Take turns reading your reviews. Which place would you like to try?

9 LISTENING

Learning Objective: listen for details about a food order

A [CD 3, Track 30]

- Set the scene and explain the task.
- Play the audio program. Ss fill in the chart individually.
- Ss compare answers in pairs. Play the audio program again if needed. Then go over answers with the class.

! For a new way to practice this Listening, try ***Prediction Bingo*** – download it from the website.

Audio script

Luis Sarah! Steven! Thanks for working late tonight, guys. I'm going to order dinner for you from City Table restaurant.
Steven Wow, thanks, Luis!
Sarah Yeah, thanks!
Luis I emailed you a link to their online menu. Open it up and have a look. What would you like?
Steven I don't even need to look. I love their sausage pizza. I'd like a small one.
Sarah And I'd like a small pizza with peppers, please.
Luis OK, great. The pizzas come with salads. What kind of dressing would you like?
Sarah I'll have Italian dressing.
Steven I'd like vinaigrette, please.
Luis Great. Now, what would you like to drink? Some coffee, maybe?
Steven That sounds good. I'll have a coffee.
Luis OK. How do you take it?
Steven With cream and sugar.
Sarah I'd like an iced tea with lemon, please.
Luis Perfect. Have you looked at the desserts? They're really good.
Sarah Are they? Well, then, I'd like a slice of blueberry pie.
Luis And how about you, Steven?
Steven Hmm. I don't usually eat dessert.
Luis Are you sure? Remember, I'm paying.
Steven Well, OK. I'll have a piece of chocolate cake.
Luis Good choice! That's my favorite. OK, I'll order everything online. The food will probably be here in 30 minutes.

Answers

Steven: sausage pizza, salad with vinaigrette
Drink: coffee with cream and sugar
Dessert: a piece of chocolate cake
Sarah: pepper pizza, salad with Italian dressing
Drink: iced tea with lemon
Dessert: a slice of blueberry pie

B [CD 3, Track 31]

- Ask: "Has a server ever made a mistake with your order? What happened?" Elicit Ss' answers.
- Play the audio program. Ss complete the task individually. Then go over answers with the class.

Audio script

Luis OK, guys. Here's the food from City Table.
Sarah That was quick!
Steven Wow, it smells so good.
Luis Let's see. . . . Two small pizzas, one sausage and one with peppers.
Sarah Thanks. The one with peppers is mine.
Luis OK. And two salads, one with Italian dressing and one with vinaigrette.
Steven The one with vinaigrette is mine.
Luis OK. And there's a coffee and an iced tea.
Sarah The iced tea is mine, and the coffee is his.
Steven Umm, this has sugar in it, but no cream. Is there any in the bag?
Luis Let me see. Maybe it's in the bottom of the bag. . . . No, I don't see any cream.
Steven Well, that's all right. I think we have some in the office kitchen.
Luis Oh, that's good. And finally, a piece of chocolate cake. That's everything.
Sarah Oh, but I ordered a slice of blueberry pie.
Luis Hmm. It's not on the receipt. Sorry, Sarah! I think I forgot to order it.
Sarah Oh well, that's OK.
Steven Would you like some of my chocolate cake, Sarah? This piece is huge.
Sarah Really? Thanks, Steven! That's so nice of you.

Answers

The missing items are Steven's cream and Sarah's blueberry pie.

10 INTERCHANGE 13

See page T-128 for teaching notes.

11 WRITING

Learning Objective: write a restaurant review

A

- Explain the task and read the questions. Ss read the example review silently. Ss then discuss the questions in pairs.
- Ss complete the task individually in class or for homework.

! For a new way to teach this Writing, try ***Mind Mapping*** – download it from the website.

B *Group work*

- Explain the task. Ss read their reviews in small groups. Then they choose a restaurant they would like to try.
- ***Option:*** Put the reviews on the walls around the class. Ss read them and choose one they would like to try.

12 READING

Learning Objectives: scan for specific information; make inferences from context in a reading about tipping in the United States

- Focus Ss' attention on the picture. Ask: "Where are these people? What are they doing?" Elicit Ss' answers and explain new vocabulary. (Answers: They are customers at a restaurant. The customers are paying for the meal/paying the bill/paying the check.)
- Explain that this article is about tipping around the world. Ss read the first paragraph silently. Ask: "What is a 'tip'?" (Possible answer: extra money you pay to say thank you)

A

- Explain the task and read the questions. Ss scan the article for the answers.
- Go over answers with the class. Ask: "What helped you find the answers?" (Possible answers: Scanning for 15–20% and negative words like "isn't")

Answers

15–20% tip on food: United States
Tipping unnecessary: Japan

- ***Option:*** Ask Ss if they ever tip at home or when traveling.

! For a new way to teach this Reading, try ***Running Dictation*** – download it from the website. Use the first paragraph only.

B

- Explain the task. Encourage Ss to guess the answers by choosing the meaning of each word that best fits the sentence in the article.
- Ss complete the task individually. Then they compare answers in pairs.
- Go over answers with the class. Elicit or explain any new vocabulary.

Vocabulary

slang: informal spoken language
service: help that someone gives a customer
bellhop: hotel employee who carries your bags for you

Answers

1. change
2. need
3. regular pay for a job
4. difficult to understand
5. usual
6. giving more than enough

C

- Explain the task. Ss complete the task individually and compare answers in pairs.
- Ask different Ss to write the answers on the board. Then ask the class to correct the answers if needed.

Answers

1. not checked – You leave about 11–12%.
2. checked
3. not checked – You don't usually tip in Japan.
4. checked
5. checked

D *Group work*

- Ss discuss the questions in small groups. Then they share their information with the class.

End of Cycle 2

See the Supplementary Resources chart at the beginning of this unit for additional teaching materials and student activities related to this Cycle.

12 READING

A Scan the article. In which country do people usually leave a 15–20% tip on food? In which country is tipping unnecessary?

TO TIP OR NOT TO TIP?

WHAT'S A TIP?

The verb *to tip* means to give money, and the noun *tip* is the money that you give to someone. It's a slang word from Old English. Around the world, many people give tips to people who provide a service for them. It's a way of saying thank you. But did you know that tipping customs around the world *vary* a lot?

WHO AND WHERE TO TIP

In some countries, like the United States, it's common to give a tip in a lot of different places. Almost everybody gives tips to servers in restaurants and cafés. Servers *rely on* those tips to add to the low *wages* they get paid for their jobs. People also tip taxi drivers and hairstylists. If an airport worker or a hotel bellhop helps you with a heavy suitcase, you tip them as well. In Japan, though, it's a very different story. In Japan, tipping isn't part of the culture, so it rarely happens. In fact, a tip might be *confusing* to the server. And in France, a "service charge" is included on all restaurant checks, so in fact, you've already tipped your server.

HOW MUCH TO TIP?

The amount people tip in the United States varies between 15 and 20% on restaurant checks. So, for example, if a restaurant total is $40, people give the server around $6–8. That seems like a lot of money for some visitors who come from countries where tipping isn't *customary*. According to one news source, the average tip in a New York restaurant is 19.1% of the total, but in London it's 11.8%. That's a big difference.

WHO'S THE BEST TIPPER?

A millionaire named Benjamin Olewine probably wins the prize for giving the world's most *generous* tip. Mr. Olewine paid for his server's nursing school fees as a tip! The waitress, Melissa, was working in a restaurant to save money for school. One day, she served breakfast to Mr. Olewine. The check was $3.45. The tip was more than $20,000!

B Read the article. Find the words in italics, then check (✓) the correct meaning of each word.

1. *vary*
   - ☐ change
   - ☐ stay the same
2. *rely on*
   - ☐ ask for
   - ☐ need
3. *wages*
   - ☐ regular pay for a job
   - ☐ tips received for a job
4. *confusing*
   - ☐ unnecessary
   - ☐ difficult to understand
5. *customary*
   - ☐ usual
   - ☐ unusual
6. *generous*
   - ☐ very rich
   - ☐ giving more than enough

C Check (✓) the statements that describe correct tipping behavior. For the items you don't check, what is acceptable?

- ☐ **1.** You're eating at a restaurant in London. You leave a 25% tip.
- ☐ **2.** You give your New York server a 15% tip.
- ☐ **3.** You give a large tip after your meal in Tokyo.
- ☐ **4.** Your bellhop in Chicago helps you carry your suitcase. You give him a tip.
- ☐ **5.** You pay your check in Paris and don't leave a tip.

D **GROUP WORK** Is tipping customary in your country? If it is, who do you tip and how much? If it isn't, what do you think about tipping?

Unit 14 Supplementary Resources Overview

	After the following SB exercises	You can use these materials in class	Your students can use these materials outside the classroom
CYCLE 1	1 Word Power		DW Unit 14 Vocabulary 1–2
	2 Conversation		
	3 Grammar Focus	TR Unit 14 Vocabulary Worksheet	SB Unit 14 Grammar plus, Focus 1 DW Unit 14 Grammar 1–3, 5
	4 Pronunciation	TR Unit 14 Grammar Worksheet	
	5 Speaking		
	6 Listening		
	7 Interchange 14		WB Unit 14 exercises 1–5
CYCLE 2	8 Snapshot		
	9 Conversation		
	10 Grammar Focus	TR Unit 14 Extra Worksheet TR Unit 14 Listening Worksheet	SB Unit 14 Grammar plus, Focus 2 DW Unit 14 Grammar 4, 6
	11 Writing	TR Unit 14 Writing Worksheet	
	12 Reading	TR Unit 14 Project Worksheet VID Unit 14 VRB Unit 14	DW Unit 14 Reading 1–2 DW Unit 14 Listening 1–2 DW Unit 14 Video 1–2 WB Unit 14 exercises 6–8

With or instead of the following SB section	You can also use these materials for assessment
Units 13–14 Progress Check	**TESTING PROGRAM** Units 13–14 Oral Quiz **TESTING PROGRAM** Units 13–14 Written Quiz

Key **SB:** Student's Book **DW:** Digital Workbook **TR:** Teacher's Resources
VID: Video (DW/TR) **VRB:** Video Resource Book (TR) **WB:** Print Workbook

My Plan for Unit 14

Use the space below to customize a plan that fits your needs.

With the following SB exercises	I am using these materials in class	My students are using these materials outside the classroom

With or instead of the following SB section	I am using these materials for assessment

14 It's the coldest city!

- Describe and compare different places in the world
- Describe temperatures, distances, and measurements

1 WORD POWER Places around the world

A Match the words from the list to the letters in the picture. Then compare with a partner.

1. beach ______
2. desert ______
3. forest ______
4. hill ______
5. island ______
6. lake ______
7. mountain ______
8. ocean ______
9. river ______
10. valley ______
11. volcano ______
12. waterfall ______

B **PAIR WORK** What other geography words can you think of? Do you see any of these places in the picture above?

C **GROUP WORK** Try to think of famous examples for each item in part A.

A: A famous beach is Shirahama Beach in Japan.

B: And the Sahara is a famous . . .

14 It's the coldest city!

Cycle 1, Exercises 1–7

In Unit 14, students describe and compare different places in the world and describe temperatures, distances, and measurements. By the end of Cycle 1, students will be able to describe geography using comparative and superlative forms of adjectives. By the end of Cycle 2, students will be able to describe distances and measurements, and ask and answer questions with *how*.

1 WORD POWER

Learning Objective: give examples of types of geographical features

A

- ***Option:*** Bring in a world map, globe, or atlas to class.
- Explain that this unit is about world geography.
- Explain the task. Ss label the picture with words from the list. Go around the class and give help as needed.
- Ss compare their pictures in pairs. Elicit or explain any new vocabulary or pronunciation.

Answers

1. i	2. e	3. f	4. d	5. l	6. h
7. a	8. j	9. c	10. b	11. k	12. g

B *Pair work*

- Ss brainstorm to see how many words they can think of that relate to geography. Ask different Ss to write their words on the board under these headings:

Water-related words	Land-related words
Climate-related words	Other

- Go over the words and ask Ss to copy them into their vocabulary notebooks.

Possible answers

Water-related: sea, stream, coast, pond, coral reef
Land-related: continent, plateau, canyon, rain forest
Climate-related: weather, storm, rain, snow, cloud, fog
Other: country, city, town, village

TIP
Create a Vocabulary Box. As a new word is taught, a S writes the word on a slip of paper and puts it in the box. Review words as a warm-up activity in future classes, or use them in games.

- ***Option:*** Review vocabulary with ***Odd Man Out***. List geography words, and ask Ss to find which word is different from the others (e.g., *hill, mountain, volcano, ocean*; ocean is the only water-related word).

C *Group work*

- Explain the task. Read the example conversation. Tell Ss that the words *Mount* (for names of mountains) and *Lake* come before the name (e.g., ***Mount*** *Fuji*, ***Lake*** *Victoria*). The other terms come after the name (e.g., *Waikiki* ***Beach***, *the Nile* ***River***, *the Sahara* ***Desert***).
- Ss work in small groups to think of other examples. Ask groups to share their examples with the class.
- Point out that seas, rivers, and mountain ranges (but not most lakes) use the definite article (e.g., *the Black Sea, the Rhine River, the Himalayas*), but bring this up only if Ss ask you.

Possible answers

beach – Waikiki, Copacabana, Maho
desert – Sahara, Atacama, Gobi
forest – Black Forest, Sherwood Forest
hill – Capitol Hill, Bunker Hill, Beverly Hills
island – Puerto Rico, Java, Hokkaido
lake – Michigan, Superior, Baikal
mountain – Aconcagua, Everest, Kilimanjaro
ocean – Atlantic, Indian, Arctic
river – Amazon, Rhine, Mekong
valley – Silicon, Loire, Death
volcano – Cotopaxi, Etna, Pinatubo
waterfall – Angel Falls, Iguaçú Falls, Niagara Falls

! For a new way to practice this vocabulary, try ***Picture Dictation*** – download it from the website. Describe a scene similar to the one in the picture.

2 CONVERSATION

Learning Objectives: use comparative and superlative adjectives in a conversation about geography

A *[CD 3, Track 32]*

- Set the scene. Claire is asking Steve some questions from a geography quiz. Point out that Steve might get some answers wrong.
- Play the audio program. Ss listen to Steve's answers and underline them in the conversation.
- Ask: "How many questions do you think Steve got right? One? Two? Three? All four?"

B *[CD 3, Track 33]*

- Play the audio program. Ss listen for the correct answers to the geography quiz. (Answers: Australia, the Amazon, Malta, Hong Kong)
- Ask: "How many answers did Steve get right?"

Audio script

Claire So, let's see how you did on this quiz. The first question: Which is larger, Mexico or Australia? You said . . .
Steve Australia.
Claire And you're right! Both are large, but Australia is larger. Next: What's the longest river in the world? You said the Nile. Sorry, that's wrong. It's the Amazon.
Steve Oh, of course. I knew that!
Claire This next question I didn't know. Malta *is* more crowded than England.
Steve So I got it right? I remember hearing that Malta is the most crowded country in Europe.
Claire And finally, you said that Paris is the most expensive city.
Steve Yeah, and it is, right?
Claire Sorry, Steve. Actually, Hong Kong is the most expensive of the three!
Steve Really? Wow, I guess I didn't do so well – two right, but two wrong!
Claire: No, come on. You did OK!

Answer

He got two questions right.

3 GRAMMAR FOCUS

Learning Objective: ask and answer questions using comparisons with adjectives

[CD 3, Track 34]

Comparative and superlative forms of adjectives

- Focus Ss' attention on the Conversation in Exercise 2. Ask Ss to identify the first two questions that compare things. (Answers: Which country is larger, Mexico or Australia? What's the longest river in the world?)
- Ask Ss to make sentences comparing two things in their country (e.g., mountains, rivers, cities). If necessary, review comparative adjectives using Exercise 10 in Unit 3.
- Draw a chart on the board, like this:

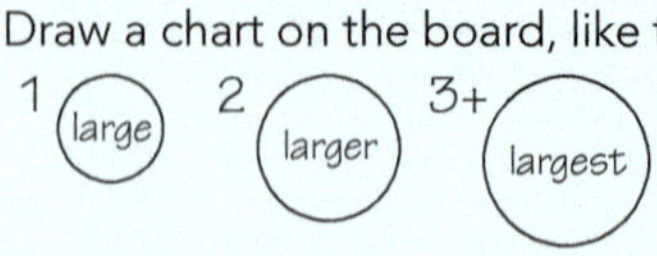

- Explain the reasons for the numbers 1, 2, 3+ (e.g., *3+ is used when we are comparing three or more things*).
- Elicit or explain the rules for forming the superlative:
  1. use the definite article (e.g., ***the*** *largest country*)
  2. when the adjective has only one syllable or two syllables ending in *y*, use: *the* + adjective + *-est* + noun (e.g., *the long**est** river, the pretti**est** lake*)
  3. when the adjective has two or more syllables, use: *the most* + adjective + noun (e.g., *the **most** crowded country*)
- Refer Ss to the appendix in the back of their book (page T–151 of the Teacher's Edition) for spelling rules. Go over with the class.
- Give Ss a list of adjectives. Ss write comparative and superlative forms in the circles on the board.
- Point to the examples in the Grammar Focus box. Play the audio program.

A

- Go over the task. Ss complete the sentences individually. Then they ask and answer the questions in pairs.
- Elicit the Ss' answers.

Answers

1. Which country is **smaller**, Monaco or Vatican City?
2. Which waterfall is **higher**, Niagara Falls or Victoria Falls?
3. Which city is **more crowded**, Hong Kong or Cairo?
4. Which lake is **larger**, Lake Michigan or Lake Baikal?
5. Which is **the highest**: Mount Aconcagua, Mount Everest, or Mount Fuji?
6. What is **the longest** river in the Americas: the Mississippi, the Colorado, or the Amazon?
7. Which city is **the most expensive**: London, Tokyo, or Moscow?
8. What is **the deepest** ocean in the world: the Pacific, the Atlantic, or the Arctic?

(Note: Answers to questions are underlined.)

B ***Class activity***

- Explain the task. Ss write four questions and take turns asking them around the class.

2 CONVERSATION I love quizzes!

A Listen and practice.

Claire: This is one of the best airline magazines I've ever read. Oh, look! A quiz! "Our world – How much do you know?"
Steve: Oh, I love quizzes! Ask me the questions.
Claire: Sure. First question: Which country is larger, Mexico or Australia?
Steve: I know. Australia is larger than Mexico.
Claire: OK, next. What's the longest river in the world?
Steve: That's easy. It's the Nile!
Claire: All right. Here's a hard one. Which country is more crowded, Malta or England?
Steve: I'm not sure. I think Malta is more crowded.
Claire: Really? OK, one more. Which city is the most expensive: Hong Kong, London, or Paris?
Steve: Oh, that's easy. Paris is the most expensive.

B Listen to the rest of the conversation. How many questions did Steve get right?

3 GRAMMAR FOCUS

Comparisons with adjectives

Which country is **larger**, Australia or Mexico?
Australia is **larger than** Mexico.
Which country is **the largest** in the world?
Russia is **the largest** country.
Which is **more crowded**? Malta or England?
Malta is **more crowded than** England.
Malta is **the most crowded** country in Europe.

Adjective	Comparative	Superlative
long	longer	the longest
large	larger	the largest
dry	drier	the driest
big	bigger	the biggest
beautiful	more beautiful	the most beautiful
crowded	more crowded	the most crowded
expensive	more expensive	the most expensive
good	better	the best
bad	worse	the worst

GRAMMAR PLUS see page 145

A Complete questions 1 to 4 with comparatives and questions 5 to 8 with superlatives. Then ask and answer the questions.

1. Which country is ______________, Monaco or Vatican City? (small)
2. Which waterfall is ______________, Niagara Falls or Victoria Falls? (high)
3. Which city is ______________, Hong Kong or Cairo? (crowded)
4. Which lake is ______________, Lake Michigan or Lake Baikal? (large)
5. Which is ______________: Mount Aconcagua, Mount Everest, or Mount Fuji? (high)
6. What is ______________ river in the Americas, the Mississippi, the Colorado, or the Amazon? (long)
7. Which city is ______________: London, Tokyo, or Moscow? (expensive)
8. What is ______________ ocean in the world, the Pacific, the Atlantic, or the Arctic? (deep)

B **CLASS ACTIVITY** Write four questions like those in part A about your country or other countries. Then ask your classmates the questions.

4 PRONUNCIATION Questions of choice

A Listen and practice. Notice how the intonation in questions of choice drops, then rises, and then drops again.

Which city is more crowded, Hong Kong or Cairo?

Which city is the most expensive: London, Tokyo, or Moscow?

B **PAIR WORK** Take turns asking these questions. Pay attention to your intonation. Do you know the answers?

Which desert is bigger, the Gobi or the Atacama?
Which city is higher, Bogotá or La Paz?
Which ocean is the smallest: the Arctic, the Indian, or the Atlantic?
Which mountains are the highest: the Andes, the Rockies, or the Himalayas?

5 SPEAKING Travelers' tips

GROUP WORK Imagine these people are planning to visit your country. What would they enjoy doing? Agree on a recommendation for each person.

"I like all kinds of outdoor activities, especially hiking and bike riding. I can't stand crowded and polluted cities."

"I enjoy visiting museums, trying local food, and shopping at small stores. I don't like boring tourist places."

"I love nightlife. My favorite activity is going dancing and meeting new people! I really don't like small towns."

6 LISTENING Quiz Show!

Listen to three people on a TV quiz show. Check (✓) the correct answers.

1.	☐ the Eiffel Tower	☐ the Statue of Liberty	☐ the Panama Canal
2.	☐ Victoria Falls	☐ Niagara Falls	☐ Angel Falls
3.	☐ gold	☐ butter	☐ all
4.	☐ the Arctic Ocean	☐ the Southern Ocean	☐ the Indian Ocean
5.	☐ São Paulo	☐ Mexico City	☐ Seoul
6.	☐ Africa	☐ Antarctica	☐ Australia

4 PRONUNCIATION

Learning Objective: sound more natural when asking questions of choice

A *[CD 3, Track 35]*

- Point out that intonation changes in questions of choice. Play the audio program.
- ***Option:*** Model the intonation by humming. Ss repeat.
- Play the audio program again. Ss listen and practice.

B *Pair work*

- Explain the task. Then Ss complete the task in pairs. Go around the class and check Ss' pronunciation.
- Check the answers as a class by having pairs model the intonation of each question and then give their answer.

Answers

the Gobi, La Paz, the Arctic, the Himalayas

5 SPEAKING

Learning Objective: give recommendations using comparisons with adjectives

Group work

- Set the scene. Ss imagine that three people are planning to visit their country.
- Ask a S to read Jana's statement. Elicit recommendations from the class. Ask: "Where do you think Jana should go? What should she do?"

TIP

Discussions are difficult for many Ss. Allow Ss time to plan what they are going to say.

- Ss from the same countries should work in groups if possible. Ss discuss where the visitors should go and why. Go around the class and give help as needed.

6 LISTENING

Learning Objective: listen for details about geographical facts

[CD 3, Track 36]

- Set the scene. Explain that Ss are going to hear three people on a TV quiz show.
- Write these focus questions on the board:

  1. Which is the ______?
  2. What is the ______ waterfall in the world?
  3. Which is the ______?
  4. Which of the world's oceans is the ______?
  5. Which city has the ______ population?
  6. Which continent is the ______?

- Play the audio program. Ss listen for the quiz show questions and fill in the blanks. (Answers: oldest, tallest, heaviest, smallest, largest, driest)
- Play the audio program again. Ss check their answers.

Audio script

Hostess [*music and applause*] Our contestants this evening are Joshua, Rachel, and Andrew. And now, contestants, let's get right to our first question. Question number one: Which is the oldest: the Statue of Liberty, the Eiffel Tower, or the Panama Canal? Joshua?

Joshua I think the Statue of Liberty is the oldest. I'm pretty sure they built the Eiffel Tower and the Panama Canal later.

Hostess That's correct! [*applause*] Question number two: What is the tallest waterfall in the world? Is it Niagara Falls, Angel Falls, or Victoria Falls? Rachel.

Rachel Angel Falls is the highest. It's over 1,000 meters high.

Hostess That's right! [*applause*] Question number three: Which is the heaviest: a pound of gold, a pound of butter, or a pound of feathers? Andrew.

Andrew They all weigh the same.

Hostess Yes! [*applause*] Question number four: Which of the world's oceans is the smallest: the Southern Ocean, the Arctic Ocean, or the Indian Ocean? Nobody knows? Does anybody want to guess? Joshua.

Joshua Uh . . . the Indian Ocean is the smallest.

Hostess No, sorry!

Joshua Oh, shoot!

Hostess Andrew.

Andrew The Arctic Ocean is the smallest.

Hostess Correct! [*applause*] Question number five: Which city has the largest population: Seoul, São Paulo, or Mexico City? Rachel.

Rachel São Paulo has the largest population.

Hostess Very good! [*applause*] Question number six: Which continent is the driest, meaning which gets the least rain: Africa, Antarctica, or Australia? Rachel.

Rachel Antarctica is the driest of the three.

Hostess That's right! [*applause*] OK, contestants, the winner is . . .

Answers

1. the Statue of Liberty
2. Angel Falls
3. They all weigh the same.
4. the Arctic Ocean
5. São Paulo
6. Antarctica

7 INTERCHANGE 14

See page T-129 for teaching notes.

End of Cycle 1

See the Supplementary Resources chart at the beginning of this unit for additional teaching materials and student activities related to this Cycle.

Cycle 2, Exercises 8–12

8 SNAPSHOT

Learning Objective: read and discuss facts about the world

- Books closed. As a warm-up, ask some questions about items in the Snapshot (e.g., *What's the hottest place in the world?*). Ss guess the answers in teams.
- Books open. Ss read the Snapshot individually. Help Ss with vocabulary.
- Read the questions to the class. Have a brief class discussion.
- ***Option:*** Ss underline all the superlative forms of adjectives in the Snapshot. (Answers: *hottest, largest, coldest, windiest, most watched, largest, most popular, highest, best-selling, most, largest)*

9 CONVERSATION

Learning Objective: use questions with *how* in a conversation about temperatures and distances

A *[CD 3, Track 37]*

- Books closed. Ask: "What do you know about Toronto, Canada? What do you know about Fairbanks, Alaska? Which city do you think is colder?" Ss work in small groups to discuss the questions.
- Play the audio program. Ss listen for information about the weather in Toronto and Fairbanks. (Answer: Fairbanks is colder.)
- Write these focus questions on the board:

  1. Where is Alberto going in January?
  2. Where is Lily from?
  3. How far is Fairbanks from Toronto?

- Books open. Play the audio program again. Ss read the conversation silently. They write down the answers. (Answers: 1. Toronto, Canada 2. Fairbanks, Alaska, U.S.A. 3. about 3,000 miles/4,800 kilometers)
- Ss practice the conversation in pairs.

! For a new way to practice this Conversation, try ***Look Up and Speak!*** – download it from the website.

B *[CD 3, Track 38]*

- Write the following on the board:

northern lights	large university	ice hockey
ice fishing	24-hour sunlight	snowboarding
good skiing	volcanoes	baseball games

- Play the audio program. Ss listen to find the things mentioned in the conversation.
- Elicit answers from around the class. Then have a brief follow-up discussion. Ask: "Would you like to visit Fairbanks? Why or why not?"

Audio script

Alberto	Tell me a little more about Fairbanks, Lily.
Lily	Well, it's one of the biggest cities in Alaska. We have a large university, the University of Alaska Fairbanks, and the people there love ice hockey.
Alberto	I can imagine! What other winter sports are there?
Lily	Well, there's good skiing in Fairbanks. Lots of people go there to ski.
Alberto	Cool! I really like skiing.
Lily	And in the summer there's the famous Midnight Sun baseball game. In June, it's still sunny at midnight!
Alberto	Wow! Sun at midnight? That sounds amazing.
Lily	Yeah, it is! Also, you should definitely try to see the northern lights between August and April.
Alberto	I'd love to do that. That sounds so beautiful.
Lily	So, that's Fairbanks. But don't forget the low temperatures . . .
Alberto	You know, Fairbanks sounds perfect. I think I should spend a month there. Well, maybe not in January . . .

Possible answers

No, Fairbanks is one of the biggest cities in Alaska. She mentions the University of Alaska Fairbanks, ice hockey, skiing, the Midnight Sun baseball game, the northern lights, and the low temperatures.

7 INTERCHANGE 14 How much do you know?

You probably know more than you think! Take a quiz. Go to Interchange 14 on page 129.

8 SNAPSHOT

8 Surprising Facts

1 The hottest place in the world is Death Valley, California. The temperature there has reached 134°F (56.7°C).

2 Antarctica is the largest desert on Earth. It is 5.4 million square miles (14 million square kilometers). It's also the coldest, windiest continent.

3 *NCIS* is the world's most watched TV show. Over 55 million people across the world have watched it.

4 The largest cat in the world is the Siberian tiger. At 700 pounds (320 kilos), it is bigger than a lion.

5 France is the most popular country to visit. It gets over 80 million visitors a year.

6 The highest price for a car at an auction was just over $38 million for a 1962 Ferrari. The auction happened in 2014.

7 The best-selling music album of all time is Michael Jackson's *Thriller*. The 1982 album has sold around 65 million copies.

8 The planet in our Solar System with the most moons, 67 total, is Jupiter. The largest one, Ganymede, is the ninth largest object in the Solar System.

Which facts do you find surprising? Why?
What are some facts about your country? What's the tallest building? the busiest airport? the most popular city to visit?

9 CONVERSATION That's freezing!

A Listen and practice.

Alberto: Hi, Lily. You're from Canada, right? I'm going to Toronto in January.
Lily: Actually, I'm from the U.S., but I went to school in Toronto. Winter there can be pretty cold.
Alberto: How cold is it on average?
Lily: Um, I think the average in January is around 20° or maybe 25°.
Alberto: Twenty-five degrees? But that's warm!
Lily: Twenty-five degrees Fahrenheit. That's about . . . minus 3 or 4 Celsius.
Alberto: Minus 3 or 4? That's freezing!
Lily: Oh, come on, that's not *so* cold, at least not where I'm from.
Alberto: Really? Where are you from?
Lily: Well, I live in Fairbanks, Alaska, around 3,000 miles from Toronto. That's . . . let me check on my phone . . . Yes, that's about 4,800 kilometers.
Alberto: Wow. . . . So, is it colder than Toronto?
Lily: It's much colder than Toronto. It's the coldest city in the United States!

B Listen to the rest of the conversation. Is Fairbanks a small town? What else does Lily say about it?

10 GRAMMAR FOCUS

Questions with *how*

How cold is Toronto in the winter?	It gets down to minus 25° Celsius.	(-13° Fahrenheit)
How hot is Fairbanks in the summer?	It gets up to about 20° Celsius.	(68° Fahrenheit)
How far is Toronto from Fairbanks?	It's about 4,800 kilometers.	(3,000 miles)
How big is Seoul?	It's 605 square kilometers.	(233.6 square miles)
How high is Mount Everest?	It's 8,848 meters **high**.	(29,028 feet)
How long is the Mississippi River?	It's about 3,700 kilometers **long.**	(2,300 miles)
How deep is the Grand Canyon?	It's about 1,828 meters **deep**.	(6,000 feet)

GRAMMAR PLUS *see page 145*

A Write the questions to these answers. Then practice with a partner.

1. **A:** ____?
   B: Niagara Falls is 52 meters (170 feet) high.
2. **A:** ____?
   B: California is about 423,970 square kilometers (163,670 square miles).
3. **A:** ____?
   B: The Nile is 6,670 kilometers (4,145 miles) long.
4. **A:** ____?
   B: Osaka is about 400 kilometers (250 miles) from Tokyo.
5. **A:** ____?
   B: Mexico City gets up to about 28° Celsius (82° Fahrenheit) in the summer.

B **GROUP WORK** Think of five questions with *how* about places in your country or other countries you know. Ask and answer your questions.

11 WRITING An article about a place

A Write an article about a place in your country or in another country that you think tourists would like to visit. Describe a place from the list.

a beach
a desert
an island
a lake
a mountain
a river
a volcano
a waterfall

B **PAIR WORK** Read your partner's article. Ask questions to get more information.

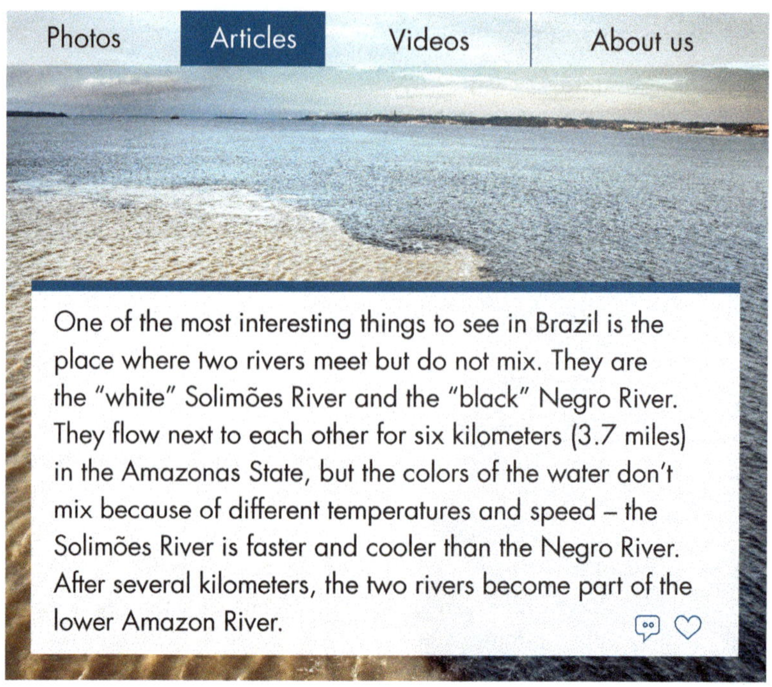

One of the most interesting things to see in Brazil is the place where two rivers meet but do not mix. They are the "white" Solimões River and the "black" Negro River. They flow next to each other for six kilometers (3.7 miles) in the Amazonas State, but the colors of the water don't mix because of different temperatures and speed – the Solimões River is faster and cooler than the Negro River. After several kilometers, the two rivers become part of the lower Amazon River.

10 GRAMMAR FOCUS

Learning Objective: ask and answer questions with *how*

[CD 3, Track 39]

How + *adjective*

- ***Option:*** Find out which systems Ss are familiar with for distances (e.g., meters and kilometers or feet and miles) and for temperature (Celsius or Fahrenheit). Use the most suitable system during the class.
- Write this on the board:

How far is Toronto from Fairbanks?	It's 8,848 meters high.
How big is Seoul?	It's about 1,828 meters deep.
How high is Mount Everest?	It's about 4,800 kilometers.
How deep is the Grand Canyon?	It's 605 square kilometers.

- Ask Ss to match the questions with the correct answers. Ss check their answers in the Grammar Focus box.
- Point out the use of *how* + adjective (e.g., how far, how big) in questions. Elicit more examples. Ask Ss to write them on the board in visual form:

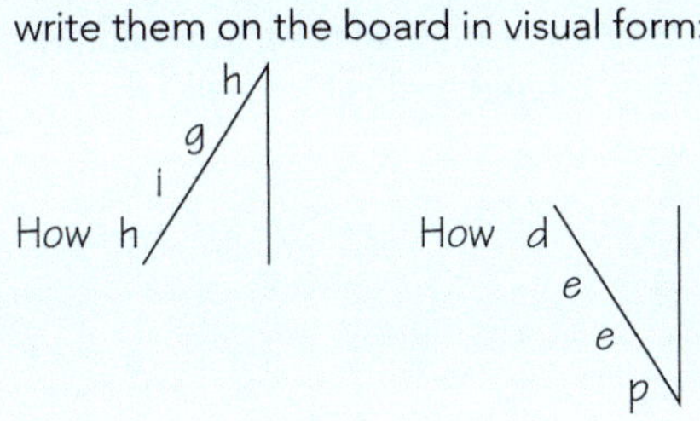

TIP
Visual and spatial Ss find structures and vocabulary easier to remember if they store the language in a pictorial form.

- Focus Ss' attention on the answers in the Grammar Focus box. Ask: "What is different about *high*, *deep*, and *long*?" (Answer: They are repeated in the answer.)
- Use the audio program to present the questions and answers.
- ***Option:*** Give your Ss practice with large numbers by having them repeat the answers line by line.

A

- Explain the task. Ss complete the task individually. Check Ss' answers before they work in pairs to practice the conversations.

Answers

1. How high is Niagara Falls?
2. How big is California?
3. How long is the Nile?
4. How far is Osaka from Tokyo?
5. How hot is Mexico City in the summer?

B *Group work*

- ***Option:*** Ss can find facts in advance of this activity from the Internet, an atlas, or a guidebook.
- Explain the task. Elicit an example question. Ss write five questions with *how*.
- Ss work individually to write the questions. Go around the class and give help as needed.
- Ss ask and answer questions in groups.
- ***Option:*** Organize the class into teams and prepare a class quiz show using the Ss' questions.

11 WRITING

Learning Objective: write an article recommending a place to tourists

A

- ***Option:*** Ss check the Internet or other sources for information about their country. Tell Ss to look at real examples of country websites.
- Explain the task. Ss will write about their country and places to visit.
- Ss read the example article silently. Elicit the topics included in the article.
- Ss choose a place in their country to write about. Brainstorm with the class details to include in the articles (e.g., location, landscape, weather, history, how to get there, and when to go).
- Ss compose their first drafts. Then ask Ss to correct their grammar and spelling after writing the content.
- ***Option:*** Ss prepare attractive articles and display them on the wall for others to read.

B *Pair work*

- Explain the task. Ss work in pairs. They exchange articles and read them silently. Then the reader asks questions to get more information (e.g., *What else is it famous for?*).
- Encourage Ss to give each other helpful peer feedback. Then Ss revise their articles.

12 READING

Learning Objectives: make inferences about an author's intent; read for specific information in an article about three places

A

- Books closed. Write these questions on the board:

  Where in the world is the cleanest lake?
  Where in the world is the cleanest air?
  Where in the world is the cleanest city?

- Ss discuss the questions in pairs. Encourage students to guess general areas, continents, and countries.
- Books open. Explain that this article is about the Earth's cleanest places. Ss look at the pictures and guess why these places are so clean. Help Ss with vocabulary.

B

- Explain the task. Ss read the article. Then they check what the goal of the article is.
- Elicit or explain any new vocabulary.
- Ask a few Ss to tell you the reason for their answers. Then go over the answer with the class.

Vocabulary
exist: to be real
pure: clean and healthy
strict: a rule or law that must be obeyed
fine: money you have to pay when you break a rule or law
respect: to show something is important

Answer

to inform people

C

- Explain the task. Read aloud the first question in part C. Ask: "Where should we look for the answer?" (Answer: the section about Lake Vostok)
- Ss continue the task individually. Go over answers with the class.

Possible answers

1. People discovered Lake Vostok in 1956.
2. It's been hidden for fifteen million years.
3. It's famous for its clean air and water.
4. The Roaring Forties bring clean air and water.
5. About 5.7 million people live in Singapore.
6. They have to pay fines.

D *Group work*

- Ss work in groups to discuss the questions. Go around the class and give help as needed.
- Groups share their descriptions with the class.

End of Cycle 2

See the Supplementary Resources chart at the beginning of this unit for additional teaching materials and student activities related to this Cycle and for assessment tools.

12 READING

A Look at the title of the article and the pictures. Why do you think these places are so clean?

Earth's Cleanest Places

Lake Vostok, Antarctica

About four kilometers (2.5 miles) under a large area of ice in Antarctica, there's a lake named Lake Vostok. It covers 15,690 square kilometers (6,058 square miles) and is 800 meters (2,625 feet) deep in some places. Lake Vostok is prehistoric – millions of years old – but until 1956, no one even knew it existed. It's a fresh water lake, and it has been hidden from sunlight for 15 million years. What this means is that the water is some of the cleanest, purest water on Earth.

Cape Grim, Australia

We all know that air pollution is a problem all around the world, so where do you go if you want really clean air? Well, Cape Grim in Tasmania, Australia is probably the best idea. Cape Grim has some of the cleanest air on Earth. Cape Grim also has beautiful, clean water. Why is this? Wind! Special winds called "The Roaring Forties" cross the Southern Ocean, bringing with them wonderfully clean water and air. In fact, in Cape Grim, people are allowed to put rain water into bottles and sell it. That's how clean it is!

Singapore

The tiny island of Singapore has a population of about 5.7 million people. It also has very strict rules about the way its people behave. Singapore is one of the cleanest cities on the planet because of these rules. People are not allowed to chew gum unless it's from a doctor, and all used chewing gum has to go in a trash can. That means that you don't find gum on the sidewalks. In fact, no one drops trash in the street.There are big fines for people who don't respect the rules, but most people are happy to keep their city clean and healthy.

B Read the article. What is the main goal of the article? Check (✓) the correct answer.

☐ to entertain people ☐ to inform people ☐ to persuade people to do something

C Read the article and answer the questions.

1. When did people discover Lake Vostok? ______________________
2. How long has Lake Vostok been hidden? ______________________
3. What two things is Cape Grim famous for? ______________________
4. What's the main reason that Cape Grim is so clean? ______________________
5. About how many people live in Singapore? ______________________
6. What happens when people break the rules in Singapore? ______________________

D **GROUP WORK** What do you think is the cleanest place in your country? Why is it so clean? How would you describe it to a friend?

Units 13–14 Progress check

SELF-ASSESSMENT

How well can you do these things? Check (✓) the boxes.

I can . . .	Very well	OK	A little
Say what I like and dislike (Ex. 1)	☐	☐	☐
Agree and disagree with other people (Ex. 1)	☐	☐	☐
Understand a variety of questions in a restaurant (Ex. 2)	☐	☐	☐
Order a meal in a restaurant (Ex. 3)	☐	☐	☐
Describe and compare things, people, and places (Ex. 4, 5)	☐	☐	☐
Ask questions about distances and measurements (Ex. 5)	☐	☐	☐

1 SPEAKING Survey: food preferences

A Answer these questions. Write your responses under the column "My answers." Then add one more question to the chart.

	My answers	Classmate's name
What food are you crazy about?		
What food can't you stand?		
Do you like vegetarian food?		
Can you eat very spicy food?		
How often do you go out to eat?		
What restaurant do you like a lot?		
______________		

B CLASS ACTIVITY Go around the class. Find someone who has the same opinions or habits.

A: I'm crazy about Japanese food.
B: I am, too./So am I. OR Oh, I'm not. I'm crazy about . . .

2 LISTENING In a restaurant

Listen to six requests in a restaurant. Check (✓) the best response.

1. ☐ Yes. This way, please.
   ☐ Yes, please.
2. ☐ No, I don't.
   ☐ Yes, I'll have tea, please.
3. ☐ I'd like the fish, please.
   ☐ Yes, I would.
4. ☐ I'll have a green salad.
   ☐ Italian, please.
5. ☐ Broccoli, please.
   ☐ Yes, I would.
6. ☐ Yes, I'd like more water.
   ☐ No, I don't think so.

Units 13–14

Progress check

SELF-ASSESSMENT

Learning Objectives: reflect on one's learning; identify areas that need improvement

- Ask: "What did you learn in Units 13 and 14?" Elicit Ss' answers.
- Ss complete the Self-assessment. Encourage them to be honest, and point out they will not get a bad grade if they check (✓) *A little*.
- Ss move on to the Progress check exercises. You can have Ss complete them in class or for homework, using one of these techniques:
  1. Ask Ss to complete all the exercises.
  2. Ask Ss: "What do you need to practice?" Then assign exercises based on their answers.
  3. Ask Ss to choose and complete exercises based on their Self-assessment.

1 SPEAKING

Learning Objective: demonstrate one's ability to agree and disagree about likes and dislikes

A

- Ss write answers to the questions in the *My answers* column individually. Then they add one more question to the chart.

B *Class activity*

- Explain the task. Then model the example conversation with a few Ss. Point out that the S begins the conversation by making a statement.
- Elicit how to make statements from the remaining questions in the chart.
- Explain that Ss write the name of a classmate with the same opinion or habit in the *Classmate's name* column. Then they move on and talk to another classmate.
- Ss complete the task. Encourage them to respond with expressions of agreement or disagreement (e.g., *So am I. Oh, I'm not.*).
- Go around the class and note any grammar, vocabulary, or pronunciation errors.

2 LISTENING

Learning Objective: demonstrate one's ability to understand questions asked in a restaurant

[CD 3, Track 40]

- Explain the task. Ss listen to restaurant requests and check (✓) the correct responses.
- Play the audio program once or twice. Ss complete the task individually.
- Go over answers with the class.

Audio script

1. Could we have a table for two, please?
2. Can I get you anything to drink?
3. What would you like for dinner?
4. What kind of dressing would you like?
5. What vegetable would you like?
6. Would you like dessert?

Answers

1. Yes. This way, please.
2. Yes, I'll have tea, please.
3. I'd like the fish, please.
4. Italian, please.
5. Broccoli, please.
6. No, I don't think so.

3 ROLE PLAY

Learning Objective: demonstrate one's ability to order a meal in a restaurant

- Set the scene and explain the task. Ss work in pairs. Student A is a server in a restaurant and Student B is a hungry customer. Student B orders a meal and Student A writes the order on the check.
- Ss practice the role play in pairs. Then they change roles.
- Go around the class and check Ss' use of *would* and *will*.

4 SPEAKING

Learning Objective: demonstrate one's ability to describe a place using comparative and superlative adjectives

A *Pair work*

- Explain the task and read the example fact and question.
- Ss write six facts and six related Wh-questions in pairs. Encourage Ss to use comparisons with adjectives.

B *Group work*

- Explain the task. Each pair joins another pair. Ss take turns asking and answering their questions. Tell each pair to write down how many questions the other pair answers correctly.
- Ss complete the task in groups. Go around the class and check Ss' use of comparisons with adjectives. Then ask which pair got the most correct answers.
- ***Option:*** Ask Ss to share their facts. Find out who has the most unusual facts.

5 GAME

Learning Objective: demonstrate one's ability to make comparative statements and ask questions using comparatives

A

- Explain the task and ask different Ss to read the example statements.
- Point out that all the statements can be answers for Wh- or *how* questions. Elicit possible questions (e.g., *Which are the coldest months in our city? Which desert is drier, the Atacama or the Sahara? How far is your house from the school?*).
- Ss complete the task. Go around the class and give help as needed.

B *Class activity*

- Explain the task and model the example conversation with a S.
- Ss play the game as a class.

WHAT'S NEXT?

Learning Objective: become more involved in one's learning

- Focus Ss' attention on the Self-assessment again. Ask: "How well can you do these things now?"
- Ask Ss to underline one thing they need to review. Ask: "What did you underline? How can you review it?"
- If needed, plan additional activities or reviews based on Ss' answers.

3 ROLE PLAY May I take your order?

Student A: Imagine you are a server and Student B is a customer. Take his or her order and write it on the check.

Student B: Imagine you are a hungry customer at any restaurant you choose. Student A is a server. Order a meal.

Change roles and try the role play again.

....
....
....
....
....
THANK YOU TOTAL: ....

4 SPEAKING Your hometown quiz

A PAIR WORK Write down six facts about your town or city using comparatives or superlatives. Then write six *Wh*-questions based on your facts.

1. The longest street is Independence Street.
What's the longest street in our city?

B GROUP WORK Join another pair. Take turns asking the other pair your questions. How many can they answer correctly?

5 GAME What's the question?

A Think of three statements that can be answered with *how* questions or *Wh*-questions with comparatives and superlatives. Write each statement on a separate card.

June and July are the coldest months in our city.

B CLASS ACTIVITY Divide into Teams A and B. Shuffle the cards together. One student from Team A picks a card and reads it to a student from Team B. That student tries to make a question for it.

A: The Atacama is drier than the Sahara.
B: Which desert is drier, the Atacama or the Sahara?

Keep score. The team with the most correct questions wins.

The Atacama is drier than the Sahara.

It's about two kilometers from my house to the school.

WHAT'S NEXT?

Look at your Self-assessment again. Do you need to review anything?

Unit 15 Supplementary Resources Overview

	After the following SB exercises	You can use these materials in class	Your students can use these materials outside the classroom
CYCLE 1	1 **Snapshot**		
	2 **Conversation**		
	3 **Grammar Focus**		**SB** Unit 15 Grammar plus, Focus 1 **DW** Unit 15 Grammar 1–3, 5
	4 **Word Power**	**TR** Unit 15 Vocabulary Worksheet	**DW** Unit 15 Vocabulary 1–2
	5 **Role Play**		
	6 **Interchange 15**	**TR** Unit 15 Listening Worksheet	**WB** Unit 15 exercises 1–6
CYCLE 2	7 **Conversation**	**TR** Unit 15 Extra Worksheet	
	8 **Grammar Focus**	**TR** Unit 15 Grammar Worksheet	**SB** Unit 15 Grammar plus, Focus 2 **DW** Unit 15 Grammar 4, 6
	9 **Writing**	**TR** Unit 15 Writing Worksheet	
	10 **Pronunciation**		
	11 **Listening**		
	12 **Role Play**		
	13 **Reading**	**TR** Unit 15 Project Worksheet **VID** Unit 15 **VRB** Unit 15	**DW** Unit 15 Reading 1–2 **DW** Unit 15 Listening 1–2 **DW** Unit 15 Video 1–2 **WB** Unit 15 exercises 7–11

Key **SB:** Student's Book **DW:** Digital Workbook **TR:** Teacher's Resources
VID: Video (DW/TR) **VRB:** Video Resource Book (TR) **WB:** Print Workbook

My Plan for Unit 15

Use the space below to customize a plan that fits your needs.

With the following SB exercises	I am using these materials in class	My students are using these materials outside the classroom

With or instead of the following SB section	I am using these materials for assessment

15 What are you doing later?

- Discuss future activities and plans
- Give messages

1 SNAPSHOT

HOW TO DECLINE AN INVITATION POLITELY

A friend has invited you to go out, but you can't make it. Follow our advice and learn how you can decline an invitation politely and keep your friend.

To thank your friend, you can say:
"Thanks so much for asking me. It sounds like a lot of fun."
"Thanks so much for the invite."

To apologize and explain why you can't accept, you can say:
"Sorry, but I already have plans."
"Sorry, but I have something else going on that day."
"I'm so sorry, but I can't make it. I'm really busy these days."

To offer another time to do something together, you can say:
"This week is crazy, but let's shoot for next week."
"Maybe another time? I'm free next week."
"Can I take a rain check?"

Do you feel comfortable declining friends' invitations? Why? Why not?
What polite excuses have you used? Which are effective? Which are not?
What is the best tip, in your opinion? Why?

2 CONVERSATION Are you doing anything tomorrow?

A Listen and practice.

Alicia: Hey, Mike, what are you doing tonight? Do you want to go see the new photo exhibit?
Mike: Thanks so much for asking me, but I can't. I'm going to have dinner with my parents.
Alicia: Oh, well, maybe some other time.
Mike: Are you doing anything tomorrow? We could go then.
Alicia: Tomorrow sounds fine. I have class until four.
Mike: So let's go around five.
Alicia: OK. Afterward, maybe we can get some dinner.
Mike: Sounds great.

B Listen to the rest of the conversation. Where are Alicia and Mike going to have dinner? Who are they going to meet for dinner?

15 What are you doing later?

Cycle 1, Exercises 1–6

In Unit 15, students discuss future activities and plans, and give messages. By the end of Cycle 1, students will be able to discuss future activities and plans using the present continuous, *be going to*, and time expressions. By the end of Cycle 2, students will be able to give messages using *tell* and *ask*.

1 SNAPSHOT

Learning Objective: discuss common excuses for declining invitations

- Books closed. Write the following excuses on the board. Ask Ss to guess what this Snapshot is about. Elicit or explain that these are all excuses.

  I'm sorry, I can't. *Thanks, but I'm busy that night.*
  I'm not feeling well. *Maybe another time? I have to work.*

- Books open. Call on Ss to read the polite excuses.
- Elicit or explain any new vocabulary.

Vocabulary
shoot for: (slang) to try to do something
take a rain check: a saying when you can't accept an invitation and would like to do it at another time

- Explain the task. Ss work in pairs to discuss the questions. Go around the class and give help as needed.
- Ask Ss for feedback on the second question. Which excuses are effective? Which ones are not?
- Elicit Ss' opinions for the third question and their reasons.

2 CONVERSATION

Learning Objective: use the present continuous and *be going to* in a conversation about making plans

A *[CD 3, Track 41]*

- Ask Ss to look at the picture and invent a story about the two people. To guide Ss, ask: "Who are they? Where are they? What is their relationship? What is she asking him? What is he saying?"

For more practice with vocabulary, play ***Picture It!*** – download it from the website.

- Set the scene. Alicia and Mike are college students. Alicia is asking Mike out on a date./Alicia is asking Mike to hang out.
- Books closed. Write these focus questions on the board:

  1. *What is Alicia inviting Mike to do?*
  2. *Why can't Mike go?*
  3. *When are they going to meet?*

- Play the audio program. Then elicit the answers. (Answers: 1. go to a photo exhibit 2. He's going to have dinner with his parents. 3. tomorrow at five)
- Books open. Play the audio program again. Ss listen and read along silently.

For a new way to practice this Conversation, try ***Say It with Feeling!*** – download it from the website.

B *[CD 3, Track 42]*

- Read the focus questions aloud. Ask Ss to guess the answers. Write some of their ideas on the board.
- Play the audio program. Ss work individually. Then go over answers with the class.

Audio script

Alicia After the exhibit, do you want to go to the Korean House for dinner?
Mike Sure. I love their food. We can go around 7:00. Look, there's Garrett! Maybe he can join us.
Alicia Yeah. Hey, Garrett! What are you doing tomorrow after class? Do you want to go to a photo exhibit with me and Mike – then dinner at the Korean House? We're meeting at 5:00.
Garrett Oh, I have class till 6:30. But why don't I meet you for dinner later? Can you text me the address?
Alicia Sure.

Answers

They are going to have dinner at the Korean House. They are going to meet their friend Garrett for dinner.

- ***Option:*** Have a brief class discussion. Ask: "Do young people go on dates in your country? Where do people usually go on dates? What do friends do when they hang out?"

3 GRAMMAR FOCUS

Learning Objective: use the present continuous and *be going to* to discuss future activities and plans

[CD 3, Track 43]

Present continuous with future meaning

- Focus Ss' attention on the Conversation on page 100. Write these sentences on the board:

  Alicia: What ________ you ________ tonight?
  Mike: ________ you ________ anything tomorrow?
- Call on Ss to fill in the blanks. (Answers: are/doing, Are/doing) Ask: "Do you recognize this tense?"
- Explain that earlier we used this tense to talk about what is happening right now. Now we are going to use it to talk about the future.
- Point to the first column in the Grammar Focus box. Elicit the rule for forming the present continuous: Question: (Wh-question +) *be* + subject + verb + *-ing*? Statement: Subject + *be* + verb + *-ing*.

Be going to

- Explain that we can also use *be going to* + verb for future plans. Focus Ss' attention on the second column in the Grammar Focus box.
- Draw a calendar for the week, and point to today's date. Ask questions like these:

  T: Are you going to do anything on Friday? (pointing to Friday)
  S1: Yes. I'm going to study.
  T: What about you, Pablo? What are you doing on Friday?
- Play the audio program. Ask Ss to repeat or mouth the words as they hear them.

A

- Explain the task. Model the first answer in both columns.
- Ss complete the conversations individually. Ask early finishers to write their answers on the board.

Answers

1. What **are** you **doing** tonight? Would you like to go out?
2. **Are** you **doing** anything on Friday night? Do you want to see a movie?
3. We**'re having** friends over for a barbecue on Sunday. Would you and your parents like to come?
4. **Are** you **staying** in town next weekend? Do you want to go for a hike?

a. I**'m going to be** here on Saturday, but not Sunday. Let's try to go on Saturday.
b. Well, my father **is going to visit** my brother at college. But my mother and I **are going to be** home. We'd love to come!
c. Sorry, I can't. I**'m going to work** late tonight. How about tomorrow night?
d. Can we go to a late show? I**'m going to stay** at the office till 7:00.

B

- Explain the task. Ss match the invitations to the responses. Go over answers with the class.

Answers

1. c 2. d 3. b 4. a

- Ss practice the invitations in pairs.

4 WORD POWER

Learning Objective: discuss types of free-time activities

A

- Explain the task. Model with several activities from the list.
- Ss work in pairs. Go around the class, giving help with vocabulary.
- Ss add one more example to each category. To check answers, write the chart on the board.

Answers

Sports and games

a soccer game	a video game tournament
a car race	a baseball game
a football game	

Friends and family

a birthday party	a class reunion
a barbecue	a wedding
a beach party	

Art and performances

a rock concert	a musical
a film festival	a hip-hop dance performance
an opera	

(Note: Additional examples are italicized.)

B *Pair work*

- Explain the task. Ss talk about the activities in pairs. Go around the class and give help as needed.

To review the vocabulary in this Word Power, play ***Vocabulary Tennis*** – download it from the website.

3 GRAMMAR FOCUS

Future with present continuous and *be going to*

With present continuous	With *be going to* + verb	Time expressions
What **are** you **doing** tonight?	What **is** she **going to do** tomorrow?	tonight
I**'m going** to a party.	She**'s going to see a play.**	tomorrow
Are you **doing** anything tomorrow?	**Are** they **going to see** the photo exhibit?	on Friday
No, I**'m** not (**doing** anything).	Yes, they **are** (**going to see** it).	this weekend
		next week

GRAMMAR PLUS see page 146

A Complete the invitations in column A with the present continuous used as future. Complete the responses in column B with *be going to*.

A

1. What ______________ you ______________ (do) tonight? Would you like to go out?
2. ______________ you ______________ (do) anything on Friday night? Do you want to see a movie?
3. We ______________ (have) friends over for a barbecue on Sunday. Would you and your parents like to come?
4. ______________ you ______________ (stay) in town next weekend? Do you want to go for a hike?

B

a. I ______________ (be) here on Saturday, but not Sunday. Let's try to go on Saturday.
b. Well, my father ______________ (visit) my brother at college. But my mother and I ______________ (be) home. We'd love to come!
c. Sorry, I can't. I ______________ (work) late tonight. How about tomorrow night?
d. Can we go to a late show? I ______________ (stay) at the office till 7:00.

B Match the invitations in column A with the responses in column B. Then practice with a partner.

4 WORD POWER Free-time activities and events

A Complete the chart with words and phrases from the list. Then add one more example to each category.

a rock concert	a barbecue	a wedding	a hip-hop dance performance
a soccer game	a film festival	a musical	a video game tournament
a birthday party	a class reunion	a car race	a baseball game

Sports and games	Friends and family	Art and performances

B **PAIR WORK** Are you going to do any of the activities in part A? When are you doing them? Talk with a partner.

5 ROLE PLAY Accept or refuse?

Student A: Choose an activity from Exercise 4 and invite a partner to go with you. Be ready to say where and when the activity is.

A: So, are you doing anything on . . . ? Would you like to . . . ?

Student B: Your partner invites you out. Either accept the invitation and ask for more information or say you can't go and give an excuse.

Accept	**Refuse**
B: OK. That sounds fun. Where is it?	**B:** Oh, I'm sorry, I can't. I'm . . .

Change roles and try the role play again.

6 INTERCHANGE 15 Weekend plans

Find out what your classmates are going to do this weekend. Go to Interchange 15 on page 130.

7 CONVERSATION Can I take a message?

A Listen and practice.

CAITLIN Hello?

JAKE Hi, Caitlin. It's Jake. Are you busy?

CAITLIN No, I'm having coffee with Brittney. Where are you? Class is going to start soon.

JAKE That's the problem. I don't think I'm going to make it tonight.

CAITLIN Why not? What's the matter?

JAKE My bus is stuck in traffic. Nobody is moving.

CAITLIN Oh, no! What are you going to do?

JAKE I don't know. Could you tell Mr. Eaton that I'm going to miss class?

CAITLIN No problem. I'll give him the message.

JAKE Oh, and could you ask Brittney to take pictures of the whiteboard for me?

CAITLIN Sure. But I can take the pictures.

JAKE Um, thanks, but the last time you took a picture of the board all I could see was the wall!

B Listen to three other phone calls. Write the callers' names.

5 ROLE PLAY

Learning Objectives: invite someone to go to a free-time event; accept or refuse an invitation

- Divide the class into groups A and B. Ask Students B to look at the excuses in the Snapshot on page 100 while you explain the task to Students A.
- Explain the task to Students A. Model the example questions. Elicit additional questions that Ss can use to invite someone out (e.g., *What are you doing on . . .? Are you busy on . . .?*). Write these cues on the board for Students A to use in their invitations:

  activity/event   day/date/time   place

- While Students A plan their invitations, explain the task to Students B. Model how to accept or refuse an invitation. Elicit more examples from Ss (e.g., *Wow! That sounds great! Thanks, I've really wanted to do that!*).
- Model the role play with Ss. Show Ss how to ask for more information and use their own words.
- Ss work in pairs to do the role play. Remind Ss to use the cues in the book and on the board.
- Provide feedback. Then Ss change roles and do the activity again.

6 INTERCHANGE 15

See page T-130 for teaching notes.

End of Cycle 1

See the Supplementary Resources chart at the beginning of this unit for additional teaching materials and student activities related to this Cycle.

Cycle 2, Exercises 7–13

7 CONVERSATION

Learning Objective: use *tell* and *ask* in a conversation about making requests over the phone

A *[CD 3, Track 44]*

- Ask Ss to cover the text. Have Ss describe the picture. Then ask: "Have you ever taken a message? Who for? What information did you get?"
- Write this focus question on the board:

  What are Jake's two messages?

- Play the audio program. Then elicit the answers. (Answers: I'm not going to make it to class tonight. Could Brittney take pictures of the whiteboard?)
- Ask Ss to uncover the text. Play the audio program again. Ss read the conversation silently.
- Ss practice the conversation in pairs. Tell Ss to sit back to back.

B *[CD 3, Track 45]*

- Explain the task. Ss listen to find out the names of the three callers. Play the audio program.
- Elicit answers from around the class.

Audio script

1.
Caitlin Hello?
Vanessa Hi Caitlin, it's Vanessa. Are you in class yet?
Caitlin No, not yet. Is everything OK?
Vanessa I think I have the flu. I can't go to class today.
Caitlin Oh, I'm sorry! You need to rest!
Vanessa Could you tell Mr. Eaton that I'm sick?
Caitlin Of course. I'm sure he'll understand. Feel better, Vanessa!

2.
Caitlin Hello?
Scott [*coughs*] Caitlin, it's Scott.
Caitlin Oh, no. Are you sick, too?
Scott Yeah, I feel terrible. I'm not going to class.
Caitlin Well, you're not the only one.
Scott Hey, Rob isn't answering his phone. Would you ask him to call me after class? He has my book.
Caitlin Of course. Feel better, Scott!

3.
Caitlin Hello?
Danny Hey, Caitlin!
Caitlin Hi, Danny! Don't tell me that you're sick, too.
Danny No, I feel fine!
Caitlin Great! So, what's going on?
Danny I'm having car trouble, so I'm running late to class. Can you tell Mr. Eaton that I'm going to be about 20 minutes late?
Caitlin Oh, good! I'm not going to be the only one in class. Sure, I'll tell him!

Answers

Vanessa, Scott, Danny

8 GRAMMAR FOCUS

Learning Objective: give messages using *tell* and *ask*

[CD 3, Track 46]

Tell *with statements*

- Focus Ss' attention on the "statement" part of the Grammar Focus box. Ask these four questions:
  1. "What is the message?" (I'm going to miss class tonight.)
  2. "Do we use *tell* or *ask* with statements?" (*tell*)
  3. "Does the message change when we use *tell*?" (no)
  4. "What are three ways to ask someone to relay a message?" (Please tell X . . . /Could you tell him/her . . . ?/Would you tell him/her . . . ?)
- Elicit the rule for forming messages with a statement: *Tell* + person + (*that*) + the statement.

Ask *with requests*

- Repeat the above steps for requests with the "request" part of the Grammar Focus box.
  1. "What is the message?" (Could she take a picture of the board?)
  2. "Do we use *tell* or *ask* with requests?" (*ask*)
  3. "Does the message change when we use *ask*?" (no, but we use *to*)
  4. "What are three ways to ask someone to relay a message?" (Please ask X . . . /Could you ask him/her . . . ?/Would you ask him/her . . . ?)
- Elicit the rule for forming messages with a request: *Ask* + person + *to* + the request.
- Focus Ss' attention on the Conversation on page 102. Ask: "What structures does Jake use when he gives his two messages?" (Answers: Could you tell Mr. Eaton that . . . ? Could you ask Brittney to . . . ?)
- Use the audio program to present the language.

A

- Present messages 1–6. Model how to unscramble the first sentence. Point out that both statements and requests begin with the words *please, could,* or *would.*
- Ss complete the task individually.
- ***Option:*** If Ss have difficulty with the patterns for *tell* and *ask*, ask them to read each message and find the *ask* examples (2, 5, 6). Ask Ss: "Are these requests?" (yes)
- Ss compare messages in pairs. Then elicit and check Ss' answers around the class.

Answers

1. Please tell Haru that the barbecue is on Saturday.
2. Could you ask Caitlin to call me at 4:00?
3. Could you tell Mia that the dance performance is tonight?
4. Would you tell Casey that the picnic is in the park?
5. Would you ask Maika to meet me at the stadium?
6. Please ask Garrett to bring the tickets to the rock concert.

B *Pair work*

- Explain the task and model the example conversation.
- Have pairs of students sit back to back to complete the task.

9 WRITING

Learning Objective: write texts with requests

A *Pair work*

- Explain the task. Ask Ss to read the example messages silently. Using the example messages, demonstrate writing "texts" on a piece of paper with a S.

TIP

For timed activities such as this one, tell Ss to write quickly and not worry about correcting their text.

- Give Ss three minutes to write their messages. Ss write their messages.
- ***Option:*** Ss can text their messages to their partner using their phones.

B *Class activity*

- Explain the task and read the example dialogue with a S.
- Ss exchange their notes with a partner. Then everyone gets up to deliver each message.
- ***Option:*** Ss can use the messages on their phones to tell the other Ss the message.

8 GRAMMAR FOCUS

Formal and informal messages with *tell* and *ask*

Statements	Messages with a statement: *tell*	
I'm going to miss class tonight.	(Please) **Tell him (that)** I'm going to miss class. **Could you tell him (that)** I'm going to miss class? **Would you tell him (that)** I'm going to miss class?	informal ↓ formal
Requests	**Messages with a request: *ask***	
Could she take a picture of the board?	(Please) **Ask her** to take a picture of the board. **Could you ask her** to take a picture of the board? **Would you ask her** to take a picture of the board?	informal ↓ formal

GRAMMAR PLUS *see page 146*

A Unscramble these messages. Then compare with a partner.

1. tell / that / is / please / Haru / the barbecue / on Saturday
   ______________________________.
2. call me / at / 4:00 / you / Caitlin / could /ask / to
   ______________________________?
3. is / that / Mia / tonight / could / you / the dance performance / tell
   ______________________________?
4. tell / is / Casey / in the park / would / you / that / the picnic
   ______________________________?
5. meet me / to / you / would / Maika / ask / at the stadium
   ______________________________?
6. ask / to the rock concert / please / bring / Garrett / to / the tickets
   ______________________________.

B **PAIR WORK** Imagine that you are far from school and cannot come to class. "Call" your partner and ask him or her to give a message to your teacher and to one of the students in your group.

A: Could you tell Ms. Clark that . . . And could you ask Joel to . . .

9 WRITING Text message requests

A **PAIR WORK** "Text" your partner. Write messages to each other with requests for your classmates. Write as many messages as you can in three minutes.

> A: Hi, Sandra. Would you ask Marcella to have dinner with us after class?
>
> B: OK, Chris. And could you tell Jules that we have a test tomorrow?

B **CLASS ACTIVITY** Give the messages to your classmates.

A: Hi, Jules. I have a message from Sandra. We have a test tomorrow.

B: Hi, Marcella. I have a message from Chris. Would you like to have dinner with us after class?

10 PRONUNCIATION Reduction of *could you* and *would you*

A Listen and practice. Notice how **could you** and **would you** are reduced in conversation.

[cʊdʒə]
Could you tell him I'm going to miss class?

[wʊdʒə]
Would you ask him to call me after class?

B **PAIR WORK** Practice these questions with reduced forms.

Could you tell them I'm in bed with a cold?
Would you ask her to be on time?
Could you ask her to return my dictionary?
Would you tell him there's a food festival tomorrow?

11 LISTENING I'm going to be late.

Listen to four people leaving messages. Who is the message from? Who is it for? What is the message? Complete the chart.

1
Message from: ____________________
Message for: ____________________
Message: ____________________
____

2
Message from: ____________________
Message for: ____________________
Message: ____________________
____

3
Message from: ____________________
Message for: ____________________
Message: ____________________
____

4
Message from: ____________________
Message for: ____________________
Message: ____________________
____

12 ROLE PLAY Who's calling?

Student A: You have a computer repair store. A client, Sophie Green, has left her laptop at your store. Call her to tell her this:

The computer needs a new motherboard. It's going to cost $250.
She can buy a used motherboard for $90. Could she please call you before 5:00?

Student B: Someone calls for your mother, Sophie Green. She isn't at home. Take a message for her.

useful expressions

Caller
May I speak to . . . ?
Can I leave a message?

Receiver
Sorry, but . . . isn't here.
Can I take a message?
I'll give him/her the message.

Change roles and try another role play.

Student A: You are a receptionist at Techniware Industries. Someone calls for your boss, Mr. Yun. He isn't in. Take a message for him.

Student B: Call Mr. Yun at Techniware Industries to tell him this:

You can't make your lunch meeting at 12:00 next Wednesday. You would like to meet at 12:30 at the same place instead. Could he please call you to arrange the new time?

10 PRONUNCIATION

Learning Objective: sound more natural using *could you* and *would you* in reduced forms in questions

A ***[CD 3, Track 47]***

- Play the audio program. Model the consonant sounds *d* + *y* in *could you* and *would you*. Ss repeat.
- Call on different Ss to try the reductions.

B ***Pair work***

- Read out the four questions for the class. Ask Ss to repeat.

! For a new way to practice this Pronunciation, try ***Walking Stress*** – download it from the website.

11 LISTENING

Learning Objective: listen for details in messages

[CD 3, Track 48]

- Explain the task. Read the questions and point out the different parts of the messages.
- Play the audio program. Ss listen and write down the messages. Then Ss compare answers with a partner.
- Play the audio program again. Pause after every few lines to give Ss time to complete the messages.

Audio script

1.
Fatima Hi, John. Where are you? Class is starting soon!
John I know. I missed the bus, so I'm going to be late.
Fatima But we're giving our class presentation today.
John Don't worry! Would you tell the teacher that I'm going to be late? We can do our presentation at the end of class.
Fatima OK, but hurry up!

2.
William Hi, Samantha.
Samantha Hi, William. Martin asked me to call him today, but he's not answering his phone. Is he in the office?
William Yes, but he's in an important meeting.
Samantha Oh, . . . Well, when he's free, would you ask him to call me?
William Yes, of course.
Samantha Thank you, William.

3.
Amanda Hi, Ryan. Where are you?
Ryan Hi, Amanda. We're on Main Street. We just passed the high school.
Amanda The high school? Oh, you've gone too far.
Ryan Sorry. Jennifer's never driven to your house before.
Amanda No problem. Could you tell her to turn around and turn left on Summer Street?
Ryan OK, Amanda, no problem. See you soon.

4.
Brandon Hi, Brittany. What's up?
Brittany Hi, Brandon. I'm calling to see if you and Emily would like to come to our house for dinner tomorrow night.
Brandon Thanks! I'd love to go, but Emily might be working late tomorrow.
Brittany Well, when you see her, could you tell her that I invited you both?
Brandon Sure. I hope we can come.

- Call on Ss to write their answers on the board.

Answers

1. Message from: John
   Message for: the teacher
   Message: John is going to be late.
2. Message from: Samantha
   Message for: Martin
   Message: Call Samantha when you're free.
3. Message from: Amanda
   Message for: Jennifer
   Message: Turn around and turn left on Summer St.
4. Message from: Brittany
   Message for: Emily
   Message: Brittany invited you and Brandon to dinner tomorrow.

12 ROLE PLAY

Learning Objective: leave and take messages

- Divide the class into pairs and assign A/B roles. Explain the roles and go over the A/B cues. Elicit or explain that a *motherboard* is the main part that makes a computer function.
- Model the role play with a S. Have Ss sit back to back. Change roles if necessary.
- ***Option:*** Before starting the activity, tell Ss to reread the Conversation on page 102. Or Ss can listen again to the audio program in Exercise 11 to review phone language. Ask Students A to find expressions callers use and Students B to find expressions receivers use.
- Ss do the first role play, sitting back to back. Provide feedback after they finish.
- Explain the second role play and go over the A/B cues. Pairs change roles and do the new role play.

TIP
To maintain interest, it's best to ask only one pair to demonstrate the role play to the class.

13 READING

Learning Objectives: develop skills in summarizing; read for specific information in an article about cell phone accidents

A

- Books closed. To set the scene, ask Ss to brainstorm mistakes that cell phone users make while using their phones (e.g., *They bump into people. They talk too loudly about personal things.*).
- Books open. Call on a S to read the title aloud.
- Read the focus question. Tell Ss to read the cell phone article quickly to find the answer to the question. (Answer: The map app on the phone led to the wrong address.)

B

- Explain the task. Ss read the article silently. Remind Ss to try to guess the meanings of any words they don't know.
- Elicit or explain any new vocabulary.

Vocabulary

embarrassing: something that makes you feel ashamed or shy
accident: something bad that happens (not on purpose)
security camera: a camera, often hidden, that is meant to keep people safe
capture: get
throw: (irr., past tense *threw*) to push something out of your hand and through the air
track: the metal rails a train or subway moves along
lamppost: a tall post with a light on top to light roads and sidewalks
reaction: how you respond to something that has happened

! For a new way to teach the vocabulary in this Reading, try ***Vocabulary Mingle*** – download it from the website.

- Ss choose the best summary. Then go over the answer with the class. (Answer: 2)

C

- Explain the task. Ss check (✓) the facts that are in the article.
- Ss complete the task individually. Then they compare answers with a partner.
- Go over answers with the class.

Answers

2, 3, 5, 7, and 8 should be checked.

D *Pair work*

- Explain the task. Ss work in pairs to discuss the first question. Then they discuss advice they would give to a child about using a cell phone. Have pairs share their best stories and advice with the class.

End of Cycle 2

See the Supplementary Resources chart at the beginning of this unit for additional teaching materials and student activities related to this Cycle.

13 READING

A Scan the article. Why did some people go to the wrong address?

Home News Technology Lifestyle Fashion Politics Food

Cell Phone Trouble!

Have you ever had an embarrassing time because of your cell phone? If you have, you're not alone. Check out this selection of cell phone "accidents."

Security cameras in a fancy hotel captured a video of a well-dressed woman, about 30 years old, texting on her phone. There's nothing unusual about that, is there? Well, yes, this time there is. The woman was so busy on her phone that she walked right into a pool of water in the hotel lobby . . . fully dressed! Nobody knows who the woman is or where the watery adventure happened, but almost half a million people have watched the video on the Internet!

A New Yorker was riding the subway home from work one evening. He was very excited by the video game he was playing on his smartphone. When he won the game, he threw his arms in the air in excitement . . . At that moment, the subway doors opened to let people on and off the train. The problem is that the man threw his phone right out of the subway car and on to the tracks below. Oops! No more video games for a while!

A lot of people are so busy looking at their smartphones that they often walk into lampposts and hurt themselves. The problem is so big that Brick Lane in London is now a "safe text" zone. Every lamppost in the street is covered in soft padding just in case somebody walks into it.

Most of us use map apps on our phones to get to the places we want to go. But sometimes, these apps get a little confused. A demolition company (a company that tears down buildings) used a map app to find a house. So far so good, right? Well, no. The map led the workers to the wrong house, a house one block away from the correct house in a town in Texas. The workers tore the house down. Imagine the owner's reaction when she arrived back home later that day!

B Read the article. Which advice best summarizes the article?

1. London is a great place to visit if you like using cell phones.
2. Be careful when you use your cell phone.
3. Lampposts and water are extremely dangerous.

C Check the facts that are mentioned in the article.

- ☐ **1.** A woman on a subway fell into some water while she was using her phone.
- ☐ **2.** Many people have watched a video of a woman falling into water.
- ☐ **3.** A man on a subway lost his phone.
- ☐ **4.** The man on the subway didn't like the video game he was playing.
- ☐ **5.** London has an area where you can text more safely.
- ☐ **6.** Every lamppost in London is padded.
- ☐ **7.** A demolition company tore down someone's home.
- ☐ **8.** The torn down building was in Texas.

D **PAIR WORK** Have you ever had a cell phone "accident?" What happened? What advice about cell phone safety would you give to a child?

Unit 16 Supplementary Resources Overview

	After the following SB exercises	You can use these materials in class	Your students can use these materials outside the classroom
CYCLE 1	**1 Snapshot**		**DW** Unit 16 Vocabulary 1
	2 Conversation		
	3 Grammar Focus		**SB** Unit 16 Grammar plus, Focus 1 **DW** Unit 16 Grammar 1, 3, 6
	4 Listening	**TR** Unit 16 Listening Worksheet **TR** Unit 16 Extra Worksheet	
	5 Word Power		**DW** Unit 16 Vocabulary 2 **WB** Unit 16 exercises 1–5
CYCLE 2	**6 Conversation**		
	7 Grammar Focus	**TR** Unit 16 Vocabulary Worksheet **TR** Unit 16 Grammar Worksheet	**SB** Unit 16 Grammar plus, Focus 2 **DW** Unit 16 Grammar 2, 4–5, 7
	8 Pronunciation		
	9 Interchange 16		
	10 Speaking		
	11 Writing	**TR** Unit 16 Writing Worksheet	
	12 Reading	**TR** Unit 16 Project Worksheet **VID** Unit 16 **VRB** Unit 16	**DW** Unit 16 Reading 1–2 **DW** Unit 16 Listening 1–2 **DW** Unit 16 Video 1–2 **WB** Unit 16 exercises 6–10

With or instead of the following SB section	You can also use these materials for assessment
Units 15–16 Progress Check	**TESTING PROGRAM** Units 15–16 Oral Quiz **TESTING PROGRAM** Units 15–16 Written Quiz **TESTING PROGRAM** Units 9–16 Test

Key **SB:** Student's Book **DW:** Digital Workbook **TR:** Teacher's Resources
VID: Video (DW/TR) **VRB:** Video Resource Book (TR) **WB:** Print Workbook

My Plan for Unit 16

Use the space below to customize a plan that fits your needs.

With the following SB exercises	I am using these materials in class	My students are using these materials outside the classroom

With or instead of the following SB section	I am using these materials for assessment

16 How have you changed?

- Describe life changes
- Describe plans for the future

1 SNAPSHOT

LIFE-CHANGING EXPERIENCES

Change schools	Graduate from college	Fall in love
Move to a new house	Get a job	Get married
Turn 18	Move to a new city	Have children
Get a driver's license	Travel abroad	Retire

Which of these events are the most important changes? Why?
What changes have you gone through in the last year? Which do you expect to happen soon?
What other things bring about change in our lives?

2 CONVERSATION I haven't seen you in ages.

A Listen and practice.

Hayden: Hey, Thomas! I haven't seen you since you changed schools! How have you been?

Thomas: Not bad. How about you? Have you finished college?

Hayden: Yeah. I majored in business administration, and I've just started a new job. How about you? Are you still in college?

Thomas: Oh, no, I finished school. I majored in drama. Actually, I'm in a play right now.

Hayden: No kidding! What's the name of the play? I'd love to see it!

Thomas: I'm acting in *A Change for the Better* at the Atlas Theater.

Hayden: Cool! You know, you look different. Have you changed your hair?

Thomas: Yeah, it's longer now. My character has long hair. And I wear contacts.

Hayden: Well, you look fantastic!

Thomas: Thanks, so do you!

B Listen to the rest of the conversation. What are some other changes in Hayden's life?

16 How have you changed?

Cycle 1, Exercises 1–5

In Unit 16, students describe life changes and describe plans for the future. By the end of Cycle 1, students will be able to describe changes in their lives using the comparative and present, past, and present perfect tenses. By the end of Cycle 2, students will be able to describe plans for the future using verb + infinitive.

1 SNAPSHOT

Learning Objective: discuss life-changing experiences in one's life

- Books closed. Explain that this unit is about important changes in our lives.
- Ss brainstorm things that change our lives (e.g., *get married, have a child, change schools*). Help with vocabulary as needed.
- Books open. Ss compare their ideas with those in the Snapshot.
- Elicit or explain any new vocabulary.

Vocabulary

driver's license: a document that proves you are legally allowed to drive a car
graduate: complete your studies
abroad: to a foreign country
retire: to stop working, usually because one is old

- Explain the tasks. Ss discuss the questions in pairs or small groups. Remind Ss they don't have to share personal information. They can respond by saying "I prefer not to talk about that."
- Have a brief class discussion about changes that have occurred in Ss' lives.

2 CONVERSATION

Learning Objective: use the comparative and present, past, and present perfect tenses in a conversation about changes in one's life

A *[CD 3, Track 49]*

- Set the scene. Two old friends run into each other and "catch up" on changes in their lives.
- Books closed. Play the audio program. Ask: "Has Thomas's life changed for the better or for the worse?" (Answer: for the better)
- Write these focus questions on the board:

  True or false?
  1. Thomas is still in school.
  2. His hair is longer than before.
  3. He's in a band.
- Play the audio program again. Then elicit the answers. (Answers: 1. false 2. true 3. false) For the false ones, ask Ss what really happened. (Answers: He finished school. He's in a play.)
- Books open. Play the audio program again. Ss listen and read along silently. Elicit or explain any new vocabulary.

Vocabulary

business administration: the study of how to run a business
drama: plays and acting
contacts: short for contact lenses

! For a new way to practice this Conversation, try ***Say It With Feeling!*** – download it from the website.

- Ss practice the conversation in pairs. Go around the class and give help as needed.
- ***Option:*** Ss write their own conversation, based on the one in the book. They practice the new conversation in pairs.

B *[CD 3, Track 50]*

- Play the audio program once or twice. Ss listen to find out how Hayden has changed.
- Ss compare answers in small groups. Then go over answers with the class.

Audio script

Thomas So tell me, Hayden, what else have you been up to?
Hayden Well, let's see. I've just bought an apartment on Market Street, near the park. It's less noisy than downtown.
Thomas Really? That's a very nice area. So you don't live with your sister anymore?
Hayden Oh, yes, I still do. I'm going to move into my new place in two months.
Thomas Are you going to live alone?
Hayden No, actually, I got engaged to Paul. We're going to get married in July.
Thomas Wow! That's great news! Congratulations!

Answers

Hayden bought an apartment and got engaged. She's going to get married in July.

3 GRAMMAR FOCUS

Learning Objective: use the comparative and present, past, and present perfect tenses to describe changes in one's life

[CD 3, Track 51]

- ***Option:*** Ask Ss to bring in some old photos that show how they have changed. Ss can show each other their photos and discuss them.
- Write these four categories on the board:

  Present tense　　Present perfect
  Past tense　　Comparative

- Focus Ss' attention on the Conversation on page 106. Ask Ss to find examples in each category. Call on Ss to write them on the board.
- ***Option:*** Divide the class into four groups and assign each group a different tense.

Possible answers

Present tense
Are you still in college?
Actually, I'm in a play right now.
What's the name of play?
You look different.
My character has long hair.
And I wear contacts.
Well, you look fantastic!

Present perfect
I haven't seen you since you changed schools!
How have you been?
Have you finished college?
I've just started a new job.
Have you changed your hair?

Past tense
I majored in business administration/drama.
I finished school.

Comparative
It's longer now.

- Play the audio program to present the grammar. Then ask Ss to describe the changes to the woman in the picture (e.g., *She wears different clothes now. Her hairstyle is different now.*).
- ***Option:*** If needed, review the tenses. For the past tense, see Unit 7; for the present perfect, see Unit 10; and for comparatives, see Unit 14.

A

- Explain the task. Ss check (✓) true statements and correct any false statements. Put this example on the board:

  (✓) 1. I dress differently now.
  2. I've changed my hairstyle.　　My hairstyle is the same.

- Ss complete the task individually. Go around the class and give help as needed.

B *Pair work*

- Explain the task. Then Ss work in pairs to compare their part A responses. Ask the class: "Who has changed in similar ways?"

C *Group work*

- Explain the task. Ss work individually. They write five sentences describing other changes in their lives.
- Ss work in groups to compare answers. Allow about five minutes for discussion. Remind Ss to decide who in the group has changed the most.

4 LISTENING

Learning Objective: listen for details about changes in people's lives

[CD 3, Track 52]

- Set the scene. Madison and Zachary are looking through online photo albums and discussing how they have changed over the years.
- Play the audio program. Ss listen and take notes on three changes they hear. Go over answers with the class.

Audio script

Madison What are you looking at, Zachary?
Zachary Oh, just one of our online photo albums.
Madison Oh, look – it's our wedding picture.
Zachary Yeah. Just think, we'll be celebrating our fifth wedding anniversary this month.
Madison Yeah, and I remember we didn't get along so well when we first met. But a year later, we fell in love and got married.
Zachary And here's a picture of our honeymoon. Wow! We sure look different now, don't we?
Madison Yes. My hair is much shorter now. And you wore glasses back then. Oh, and look. Here's a picture of the day we brought Maggie home from the hospital.
Zachary She's so cute. And now we have two kids. Who would have guessed?
Madison Yeah. We're just lucky that they look like me.

Possible answers

They didn't get along when they first met.
They're married now.
Madison's hair is shorter.
Zachary doesn't wear glasses.
They have two kids now.

3 GRAMMAR FOCUS

Describing changes

With the present tense

I'**m not** in school anymore.

I **wear** contacts now.

With the past tense

I **majored** in business administration.

I **got** engaged.

With the present perfect

I'**ve** just **started** a new job.

I'**ve bought** a new apartment.

With the comparative

It's **less noisy** than downtown.

My hair is **longer** now.

GRAMMAR PLUS *see page 147*

A How have you changed in the last five years? Check (✓) the statements that are true for you. If a statement isn't true, give the correct information.

- ☐ **1.** I dress differently now.
- ☐ **2.** I've changed my hairstyle.
- ☐ **3.** I've made some new friends.
- ☐ **4.** I got a pet.
- ☐ **5.** I've joined a gym.
- ☐ **6.** I moved into my own apartment.
- ☐ **7.** I'm more outgoing than before.
- ☐ **8.** I'm not in high school anymore.
- ☐ **9.** My life is easier now.
- ☐ **10.** I got married.

B **PAIR WORK** Compare your responses in part A. Have you changed in similar ways?

C **GROUP WORK** Write five sentences describing other changes in your life. Then compare in groups. Who in the group has changed the most?

4 LISTENING Online photo albums

Madison and Zachary are looking through online photo albums. Listen to their conversation. How have they changed? Write down three changes.

Changes

____

____

____

5 WORD POWER Changes

A Complete the word map with phrases from the list. Then add two more examples to each category.

dye my hair
get a bank loan
get a credit card
get a pay raise
grow a beard
improve my English vocabulary
learn a new sport
learn how to dance
open a savings account
pierce my ears
start a new online course
wear contact lenses

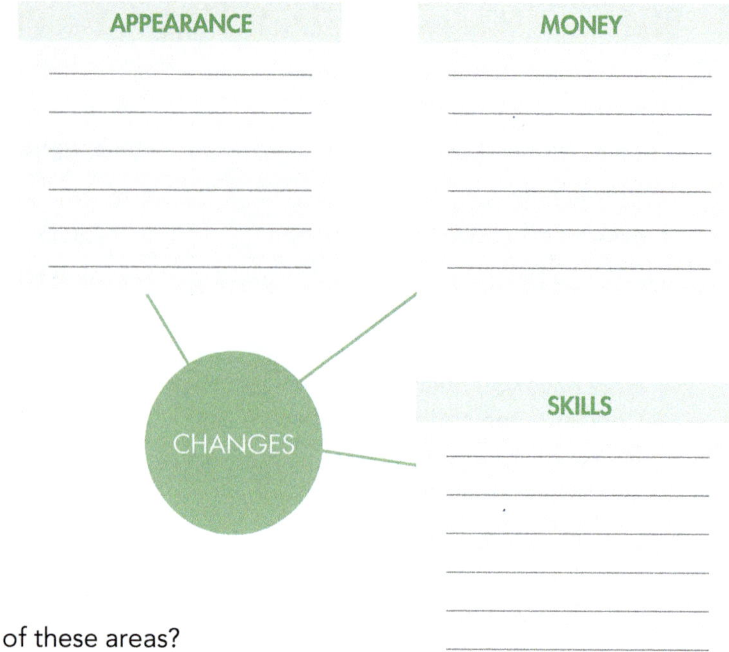

B **PAIR WORK** Have you changed in any of these areas? Tell your partner about a change in each category.

A: I started an Italian cooking class last month. I've always loved Italian food.
B: I've improved my English vocabulary a lot. I always watch movies with English subtitles now.

6 CONVERSATION Planning your future

A Listen and practice.

Matt: So, what are you going to do this year? Any New Year's resolutions?
Robin: Well, I'd love to learn how to play the guitar, so I plan to take lessons.
Matt: That sounds great. I don't have any musical talents, but I'd like to learn how to dance. Maybe I can learn to salsa!
Robin: Why not? I hope to learn to play some Latin music, too.
Matt: I know! We can take a trip to Puerto Rico and spend a month learning guitar and dancing. How about that?
Robin: Uh . . . Matt? I don't have any money. Do you?
Matt: I don't either, but I hope to get a new job soon.
Robin: Have you started looking?
Matt: Not yet, but I plan to start right after the holidays.

B Listen to the rest of the conversation. What kind of job does Matt want? What other plans does Robin have for the new year?

5 WORD POWER

Learning Objective: discuss types of life changes

A

- Explain the task. Ss complete the word map with phrases from the list.
- Call on Ss to read the phrases. Explain any vocabulary.
- Ss complete the word map. Remind them to add two more examples to each category.
- Draw the word map on the board. Ask Ss to write answers and add more examples to each category.

Answers

Appearance	Money	Skills
dye my hair	get a bank loan	improve my English vocabulary
grow a beard	get a credit card	learn a new sport
pierce my ears	get a pay raise	learn how to dance
wear contact lenses	open a savings account	start a new online course
get a haircut	*get a mortgage*	*learn how to paint*
dress better	*support a charity*	*take an art class*

(Note: Additional examples are italicized.)

B Pair work

- Explain the task and model the example with a S. Elicit additional responses and write them on the board.
- Ss discuss their changes in each category.

End of Cycle 1

See the Supplementary Resources chart at the beginning of this unit for additional teaching materials and student activities related to this Cycle.

Cycle 2, Exercises 6–12

6 CONVERSATION

Learning Objective: use verb + infinitive in a conversation about planning for the future

A *[CD 3, Track 53]*

- Have Ss cover the text. Use the picture to set the scene. Ask: "What's happening? What do you think they are discussing?" Elicit ideas.
- Write this chart on the board (without the answers). Ask Ss to listen for three future plans for each person.
  Future plans
  Robin: play the guitar, take guitar lessons, learn to play Latin music
  Matt: learn how to dance salsa, take a trip to Puerto Rico, get a new job
- Play the audio program. Ss write their answers. Ss compare answers in pairs. Then go over answers with the class. Have Ss fill in the chart on the board.
- Have Ss uncover the text. Play the audio program again. Ss read the conversation silently.
- Elicit or explain any new vocabulary. A *resolution* is something a person "resolves" or intends to do in the future. Resolutions are often made for the new year.
- Ss practice the conversation in pairs.

B *[CD 3, Track 54]*

- Play the audio program. Ss listen to find out the answers to the focus questions.
- Elicit answers from around the class.

Audio script

Robin So, what kind of job are you looking for?
Matt Um, I've thought about it a lot. I have a minor in computer science, so I hope to get a job with a big computer company.
Robin Well, good luck!
Matt Thanks. Do you have any other plans for the new year, Robin?
Robin Well, I'd like to travel around the United States a bit. There are so many places that I've never seen. I guess the guitar will have to wait a couple of months.
Matt Well, don't forget to take lots of pictures and post them online.
Robin Don't worry, I won't. And I hope you get the job.
Matt Me, too!

Answers

Matt wants to get a job with a big computer company. Robin would like to travel around the United States.

7 GRAMMAR FOCUS

Learning Objective: use verb + infinitive to ask and answer questions about plans for the future

[CD 3, Track 55]

- Books closed. Write these sentences on the board:
  Robin: I'd ________ ________ learn how to play the guitar.
  Robin: I ________ ________ take lessons.
  Matt: I'd ________ ________ learn how to dance.
  Matt: I ________ ________ get a new job soon.
- Books open. Focus Ss' attention on the Conversation on page 108. Call on Ss to find the answers and to fill in the blanks on the board. (Answers: *love to, plan to, like to, hope to*)
- Ask Ss to look at the Grammar Focus box.
- Ask: "What do these structures have in common? What other structures follow this pattern?" (Answers: They are verb + infinitive; *going to, want to*)
- Play the audio program. Then have Ss make sentences of their own (e.g., *I don't plan to get married this year.*).

For more practice with verb + infinitive, play ***Line Up!*** – download it from the website. Ss line up according to the age when they hope to marry, how many children they hope to have, etc.

A

- Explain the task. Tell Ss to write true information about themselves. Encourage Ss to use each verb from the Grammar Focus box at least once.
- Ss work individually to complete the sentences. Remind Ss to add two more statements for numbers 9 and 10. Go around the class and give help. (Note: Don't check Ss' answers until the end of part B.)

B *Pair work*

- Ss work in pairs to discuss their responses. Tell pairs to check (✓) the statements on their lists that are the same and to put an *X* next to the ones that are different.
- Elicit some "same" and "different" responses from pairs.

C *Group work*

- Explain the task. Call on Ss to read the questions. Check for correct intonation.
- Ss work in small groups. They take turns asking and answering the questions. Tell Ss to ask the questions in any order they want. Also encourage Ss to ask follow-up questions and to respond to group members' plans.
- ***Option:*** Encourage Ss to use all of the Wh-words as follow-up questions at least once: *Why, Where, When, Who,* and *How.*

8 PRONUNCIATION

Learning Objective: recognize the differences in pronunciation in words spelled with *o*

A *[CD 3, Track 56]*

- Explain that words spelled with *o* are pronounced in different ways in English. Point out the two examples in the book.
- Play the audio program and let Ss listen to the two sounds and practice.
- Elicit more words that contain the two sounds (e.g., *grow, oh, son, from*).
- ***Option:*** If Ss are having problems, ask them to find words spelled with *o* in the unit. Say the words, and ask Ss which have the /oʊ/ sound, which have the /ʌ/ sound, and which have some other sound.

For more practice with this Pronunciation, play ***Bingo*** – download it from the website.

B *[CD 3, Track 57]*

- Explain the task. Model the first word.
- Play the audio program. Ss check (✓) the sound they hear.
- ***Option:*** Ss first check (✓) the sound they think is represented by the letter *o*. Then play the audio program. Ss check if their guesses were right or wrong.
- Check Ss' answers on the board.

Answers

/oʊ/	both	cold	home	over
/ʌ/	come	honey	money	mother

- ***Option:*** Ss work in pairs. They write a conversation with at least five words from part A or B. Then Ss practice the conversation.

TIP
Each week, select a "sound of the week" and focus specifically on that (or, in this case, the two sounds).

7 GRAMMAR FOCUS

Verb + infinitive

What **are** you **going to do** this year?

I'm (not) **going to take** a trip to the Caribbean.	I **hope to get** a new job.
I (don't) **plan to take** guitar lessons.	**I'd like to travel** around the United States.
I (don't) **want to learn** to dance.	**I'd love to play** the guitar.

GRAMMAR PLUS see page 147

A Complete these statements so that they are true for you. Use verb + infinitive as shown in the grammar box. Then add two more statements of your own.

1. I ______________ travel abroad.
2. I ______________ live with my parents.
3. I ______________ get married.
4. I ______________ have a lot of children.
5. I ______________ make a lot of money!
6. I ______________ become famous.
7. I ______________ buy a sports car.
8. I ______________ learn another language.
9. ______________________________
10. ______________________________

B PAIR WORK Compare your responses with a partner. How are you the same? How are you different?

C GROUP WORK What are your plans for the future? Take turns asking and answering these questions.

What are you going to do after this English class is over?
Do you plan to study English again next year?
What other languages would you like to learn?
What countries would you like to visit? Why?
Do you want to get a (new) job in a few years?
What other changes do you hope to make in your life? Why?

8 PRONUNCIATION Vowel sounds /oʊ/ and /ʌ/

A Many words spelled with *o* are pronounced /oʊ/ or /ʌ/. Listen to the difference and practice.

/oʊ/ = don't	smoke	go	loan	own	hope
/ʌ/ = month	love	some	does	young	touch

B Listen to these words. Check (✓) the correct pronunciation.

	both	cold	come	home	honey	money	mother	over
/oʊ/	☐	☐	☐	☐	☐	☐	☐	☐
/ʌ/	☐	☐	☐	☐	☐	☐	☐	☐

9 INTERCHANGE 16 Our possible future

Imagine you could do anything, go anywhere, and meet anybody.
Go to Interchange 16 on page 131.

10 SPEAKING An English course abroad

A **GROUP WORK** You want to take an English course abroad in an English-speaking country. Groups get special discounts, so your whole group has to agree on a trip. Talk about these details and take notes on your group's decisions.

1. Where you'd like to study (choose an English-speaking country and city)
2. When you'd like to travel (choose month of the year)
3. How long you want to stay there
4. Where you'd like to stay (choose one): a family home, a dorm, a hostel, an apartment, a hotel
5. Courses you plan to take (choose two): grammar, writing, pronunciation, conversation, business English
6. Tourist places you hope to see

A: Where would you like to study?
B: How about Australia?
C: Australia is great, but it's going to be too expensive. I'd love to go to London. I've never been there.
D: When do you want to go? I think May and June are the best months.

B **CLASS ACTIVITY** Present your ideas to the class. If the whole class agrees on one trip, you can get a bigger discount.

11 WRITING Travel plans

A **GROUP WORK** Work with the same group from Exercise 10. As a group, write to your teacher about your plans for the class trip abroad.

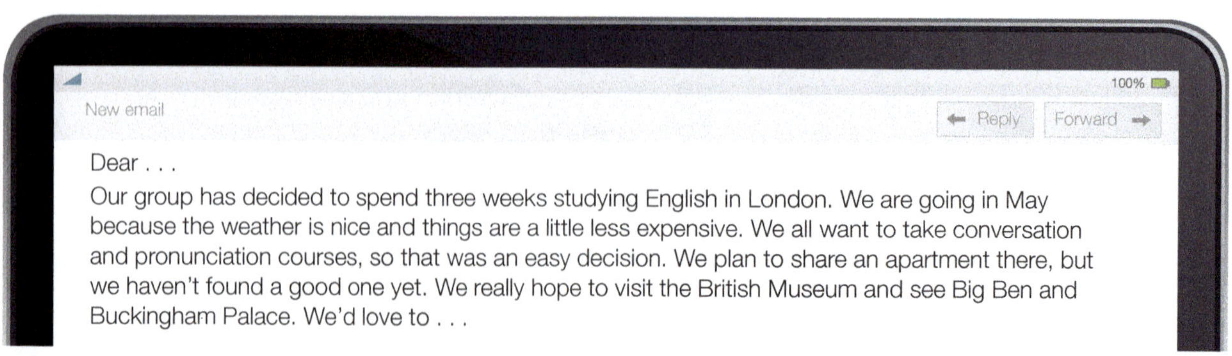

Dear . . .

Our group has decided to spend three weeks studying English in London. We are going in May because the weather is nice and things are a little less expensive. We all want to take conversation and pronunciation courses, so that was an easy decision. We plan to share an apartment there, but we haven't found a good one yet. We really hope to visit the British Museum and see Big Ben and Buckingham Palace. We'd love to . . .

B **PAIR WORK** Get together with a student from another group and read each other's messages. Do you have similar plans?

9 INTERCHANGE 16

See page T-131 for teaching notes.

10 SPEAKING

Learning Objective: describe plans about a future trip

A *Group work*

- Explain the task. Groups make plans to take an English course abroad. The whole group has to agree on the destination. Go over the details they need to think about (e.g., *place, time, length, housing, coursework, tourist places to visit*). Model the conversation with three Ss.
- Encourage Ss to use a variety of verb + infinitive forms.
- Ss work in small groups to discuss their plans. Set a time limit of about ten minutes. Tell groups to choose one person to take notes.

TIP
If you notice that you always monitor groups in the same order (e.g., you always start at the front of the class), change your routine. Try starting from another direction so that some Ss do not get ignored.

B *Class activity*

- Explain the task.
- Groups present their plans to the class. Encourage the whole class to try to agree on one of the trips.

11 WRITING

Learning Objective: write about plans for a class trip abroad

A *Group work*

- Explain the task. Ask Ss to read the example plan silently. Ss write a similar plan, based on their discussion in Exercise 10.
- Ss form the same small groups as in Exercise 10. They write their plan for an English course abroad. Go around the groups and give help as needed. Each S should write their group's plan.

B *Pair work*

- Ss pair up with a S from another group and read each other's trip ideas.
- Pairs discuss how their trips are similar.

12 READING

Learning Objectives: make inferences about audience; read for specific information in an article about a person's goals

A

- Go over the question. Ask Ss to read the article to find out what it is about.
- Ss read the article individually. Then have Ss tell you what the article was generally about.

Answer

An important invention

B

- Explain the task. Ss read the article silently. Remind Ss to try to guess the meanings of any words they don't know.
- Ask: "Who do you think the article was written for?" Go over the answer with the class.

Answer

People who care about the environment

- Elicit or explain any remaining new vocabulary.

Vocabulary

benefit: to help someone or something else
accomplish: achieve; to get something done or make something happen
garbage: unwanted things that are thrown away
plastic: a light, artificial substance, such as is used to make water bottles
century: 100 years
extraordinary: very special or unusual
donate: to give money, goods, or services freely, without being paid

C

- Read aloud the questions in part C. Then ask Ss to look for the answers. (Encourage Ss to look for the information quickly, without reading the whole article again.) Give Ss a time limit.
- Ss compare answers in pairs or groups. Have the Ss who finish first write their responses on the board.

Answers

1. He was on vacation in Greece.
2. He left school to start The Ocean Cleanup.
3. It takes centuries to break down.
4. He asked people to donate money online.
5. He hopes the oceans will be clean in 20 or 30 years.

D *Group work*

- Explain the task. Ss work in pairs to discuss a personal goal that they've achieved or a goal that someone else has achieved. Have a few Ss share their goals with the class.

End of Cycle 2

See the Supplementary Resources chart at the beginning of this unit for additional teaching materials and student activities related to this Cycle and for assessment tools.

12 READING

A Read the article. What is it about? Check (✓) the correct answer.

☐ Students in the Netherlands ☐ An important invention ☐ Vacations near the ocean

A Goal Accomplished

Boyan Slat has one huge goal. It's a goal that could benefit people and animals all over the world. Amazingly, it looks like he's going to accomplish it.

When he was 16, Dutch engineering student Boyan Slat was on vacation in Greece, and he started to think about all the garbage that gets washed up on beaches. The oceans around the world are full of plastic – millions of tons of plastic. Unfortunately, plastic doesn't just disappear. It takes centuries to break down. Slat wanted to do something to change all that. So he made it a personal goal to clean up the garbage in the world's oceans.

Slat started with an idea for an extraordinary machine to "catch" the plastic floating in the water using the natural energy of the ocean. He left school in 2013 to begin work on his project, which he called The Ocean Cleanup.

A year later, he was leading a team of 100 scientists and engineers working on the invention. Slat needed money for this, so he started asking people to donate to his project online and raised over $2 million!

Soon after, Slat was named a "Champion of the Earth" by the United Nations. It's the most important title the UN gives to people helping the environment. The Ocean Cleanup also won several awards for having one of the best inventions of 2015. But the dream goes on for Boyan Slat. He hopes that the oceans will be free of plastic in about twenty or thirty years.

B Who do you think this article was written for? Choose (✓) the correct answer.

☐ People who care about the environment
☐ College students who want to be inventors
☐ People on vacation who hate garbage

C Read the article and answer the questions.

1. Where was Boyan Slat when he had his big idea?
2. Why did Slat leave school?
3. What is the problem with plastic?
4. How did Slat get the money for his project?
5. When does Slat hope the oceans will be clean?

D **GROUP WORK** Have you had a personal goal that you achieved? Or do you know someone who achieved an amazing personal goal? What was the goal?

Units 15–16 Progress check

SELF-ASSESSMENT

How well can you do these things? Check (✓) the boxes.

I can . . .	Very well	OK	A little
Discuss future plans and arrangements (Ex. 1)	☐	☐	☐
Make and respond to invitations (Ex. 2)	☐	☐	☐
Understand and pass on telephone messages (Ex. 3)	☐	☐	☐
Ask and answer questions about changes in my life (Ex. 4)	☐	☐	☐
Describe personal goals (Ex. 5)	☐	☐	☐
Discuss and decide how to accomplish goals (Ex. 5)	☐	☐	☐

1 DISCUSSION The weekend

A **GROUP WORK** Find out what your classmates are doing this weekend. Ask for details about each person's plans.

Name	Plans	Details

A: What are you going to do this weekend?
B: I'm watching a soccer game on Sunday.
C: Who's playing?

B **GROUP WORK** Whose weekend plans sound the best? Why?

2 ROLE PLAY Inviting a friend

Student A: Invite Student B to one of the events from Exercise 1. Say where and when it is.

Student B: Student A invites you out. Accept and ask for more information, or refuse and give an excuse.

Change roles and try the role play again.

Units 15–16

Progress check

SELF-ASSESSMENT

Learning Objectives: reflect on one's learning; identify areas that need improvement

- Ask: "What did you learn in Units 15 and 16?" Elicit Ss' answers.
- Ss complete the Self-assessment. Encourage them to be honest, and point out they will not get a bad grade if they check (✓) *A little*.
- Ss move on to the Progress check exercises. You can have Ss complete them in class or for homework, using one of these techniques:
    1. Ask Ss to complete all the exercises.
    2. Ask Ss: "What do you need to practice?" Then assign exercises based on their answers.
    3. Ask Ss to choose and complete exercises based on their Self-assessment.

1 DISCUSSION

Learning Objective: demonstrate one's ability to discuss future plans

A *Group work*

- Explain the task. Ss work in groups of four. Each S writes the names of the other three Ss in the first column. Ss then ask each other about their weekend plans. Encourage them to ask follow-up questions to find out details. Model the example with two Ss.
- Ss complete the task. Go around the class and check their use of the present continuous and *be going to.*

B *Group work*

- Explain the task. Ss discuss the questions in groups and share their results with the class.

2 ROLE PLAY

Learning Objective: demonstrate one's ability to make and accept or decline invitations

- Elicit different ways to make invitations, accept invitations, refuse invitations, and make excuses. Write them on the board.
- Explain the task. Ss work in pairs. Student A invites Student B to an event from Exercise 1. Student B accepts or refuses.
- Model the role play with a S.
- Ss complete the role play in pairs. Then they change roles and practice again. Go around the class and give help as needed.

3 LISTENING

Learning Objective: demonstrate one's ability to take phone messages

[CD 3, Track 58]

- Set the scene and explain the task. Ss will hear two telephone calls. They listen and write the name of the person the message is for, the caller, and the message.
- Play the audio program once or twice. Ss listen and complete the messages.

Audio script

1.

Mr. Daniels	Hello?
Alyssa	Hi, Mr. Daniels. This is Alyssa Jenkins. Is Matthew there? I've tried calling his cell, but he's not answering.
Mr. Daniels	I'm sorry, Alyssa. Matthew isn't here. May I take a message?
Alyssa	Oh, um. Sure. Would you tell him to meet me at the theater at 7:00? The play starts at 7:30.
Mr. Daniels	OK, let me just write this down. So, you want him to meet you at the theater at 7:00, right?
Alyssa	That's right.
Mr. Daniels	And the play is at 7:30, right?
Alyssa	Yes, that's right. Thanks so much.
Mr. Daniels	No problem. Have a good time!

2.

Man	Hello.
Kayla	Hi. Jacob?
Man	No, sorry. Jacob isn't here right now. Can I take a message?
Kayla	Yes, thanks. Do you have a pen?
Man	Yeah. Go ahead.
Kayla	OK. This is Kayla. Could you tell him that I'm still at the barbecue? Please ask him to pick me up here. Not at home.
Man	OK. So, you're still at the barbecue, right?
Kayla	Yes, that's right.
Man	And he should pick you up there. Not at home. Right?
Kayla	That's right. Thanks.
Man	No problem.

- Go over answers with the class.

Possible answers

1. Message for: Matthew
   Caller: Alyssa
   Message: Meet her at theater at 7:00. The play is at 7:30.
2. Message for: Jacob
   Caller: Kayla
   Message: Pick her up at barbecue, not at home.

4 SURVEY

Learning Objective: demonstrate one's ability to ask and answer questions about changes in one's life

A *Class activity*

- Explain the task and go over the chart. Explain any new vocabulary. Then elicit how to make questions with the phrases in the chart (e.g., *Do you not wear glasses anymore?*).
- Set a time limit of about ten minutes. Ss complete the task. Go around the class and note any grammar or vocabulary errors.

B *Class activity*

- Ss compare their information as a class. Ask: "Who has changed the most?"

5 SPEAKING

Learning Objectives: demonstrate one's ability to set goals; demonstrate one's ability to decide how best to accomplish goals

- Ss check (✓) the goals they want to accomplish individually. Then they add two more goals.
- Explain the task. Each S chooses one goal. Then they plan how to achieve the goal in pairs.
- Model the example conversation with a S. Then Ss complete the task in pairs. Go around the class and check their use of verb + infinitive.

WHAT'S NEXT?

Learning Objective: become more involved in one's learning

- Focus Ss' attention on the Self-assessment again. Ask: "How well can you do these things now?"
- Ask Ss to underline one thing they need to review. Ask: "What did you underline? How can you review it?"
- If needed, plan additional activities or reviews based on Ss' answers.

3 LISTENING Matthew isn't here.

Listen to the phone conversations. Write down the messages.

1

Message for: ______________________

Caller: ______________________

Message: ______________________

____

____

2

Message for: ______________________

Caller: ______________________

Message: ______________________

____

____

4 SURVEY Changes

A CLASS ACTIVITY Go around the class and find this information. Write a classmate's name only once. Ask follow-up questions.

Find someone who . . .	Name
1. doesn't wear glasses anymore	
2. goes out more often these days	
3. got his or her hair cut last month	
4. got married last year	
5. has changed schools recently	
6. has gotten a part-time job recently	
7. has started a new hobby	
8. is happier these days	

B CLASS ACTIVITY Compare your information. Who in the class has changed the most?

5 SPEAKING Setting goals

Check (✓) the goals you have and add two more. Then choose one goal. Plan how to accomplish it with a partner.

- ☐ get into a good school
- ☐ have more free time
- ☐ have more friends
- ☐ move to a new city
- ☐ own my own apartment
- ☐ travel a lot more
- ☐ live a long time
- ☐ ______________________
- ☐ ______________________

A: I'd like to have more free time.
B: How are you going to do that?

WHAT'S NEXT?

Look at your Self-assessment again. Do you need to review anything?

Interchange activities

INTERCHANGE 1

Learning Objective: interview classmates to learn more about their backgrounds

A *Class activity*

- As a warm-up, ask a S: "What's your name? What city are you from?"
- Go over the questions in the chart. Help Ss with vocabulary and pronunciation. If necessary, review hobbies and the months of the year.
- Explain the task. Model the questions with a S. Point out that Ss will write one more question and then interview three classmates.
- Ss complete the task. Go around the class and give help as needed. Write down any grammar or vocabulary errors and go over them after Ss complete the task.

B *Group work*

- Explain the task. Go over the questions and review the vocabulary if needed. Ask, "Who has a long first name?" Have a S answer.
- Ss discuss the questions as a group.
- ***Option:*** Elicit interesting information that Ss found out about their classmates.

Interchange activities

INTERCHANGE 1 Getting to know you

A CLASS ACTIVITY Add one more question to the chart. Go around the class and interview three classmates. Complete the chart.

	Classmate 1	Classmate 2	Classmate 3
What's your first name?			
What's your last name?			
What city are you from?			
When's your birthday?			
What's your favorite color?			
What are your hobbies?			

B GROUP WORK Compare your information. Then discuss these questions.

Who . . . ?

has a long first name	has the next birthday
has a long last name	likes orange or brown
is not from a big city	has an interesting hobby

114 Interchange 1

INTERCHANGE 2 What we have in common

A **CLASS ACTIVITY** Add one more question to the chart. Answer these questions about yourself. Then interview two classmates. Write their names and the times they do each thing.

What time do you . . . ?	Me	Name ______	Name ______
get up during the week			
get up on weekends			
have breakfast			
leave for school or work			
get home during the week			
have dinner			
go to bed during the week			
______			

B **PAIR WORK** Whose schedule is similar to yours? Tell your partner.

A: Amir and I have similar schedules. We both get up at 7:00 and have breakfast at 7:30.
B: I leave for work at 7:30, but Nikki leaves for school at . . .

useful expressions
We both . . . at . . .
We . . . at different times.
My schedule is different from my two classmates' schedules.

Interchange 2 115

INTERCHANGE 2

Learning Objective: survey classmates to learn more about their routines

A *Class activity*

- Focus Ss' attention on the pictures at the bottom of the page. Ask: "What does the man do every day? What time does he do each thing?"
- Go over any new vocabulary in the list. Teach or review how to write and say times.
- Explain the first part of the task. Ask Ss: "What time do you get up during the week?" Ss complete the first line in the *Me* column. Then they complete the rest of the column individually. Allow about three minutes. Go around the class and give help as needed.
- Explain the rest of the task. Ss go around the class and interview two classmates. They write each classmate's name at the top of the column and ask the questions in the chart. They write a time for each response.
- Model the task with a S.
- Set a time limit of about 15 minutes. Then Ss complete the task. Go around the class and give help as needed. Write down any errors you hear for Ss to correct later.

TIP
At beginning levels, sometimes instructions are difficult to understand. It is much more effective to model the task than to explain it.

B *Pair work*

- Explain the task. Go over the useful expressions and model the example conversation with a S.
- Ss complete the task in pairs. Encourage them to explain why their schedules are similar.
- Elicit answers from the class.

INTERCHANGE 3

Learning Objective: talk more fluently when asking about prices of items for sale

A

- Point out the title. Explain that a *flea market* is a place where people sell used things. Sellers have an "asking price," but people bargain.
- Ask: "Are there flea markets in your country? Do people bargain for better prices?" Encourage discussion.
- Focus Ss' attention on the pictures on both pages. Ask: "What do you see here? What are these people doing?"
- Divide the Ss into pairs and assign pages A and B. Explain the task.
- Focus Ss' attention on the tablet. Ask: "What is a good price for a used tablet?" Tell Ss with page A to choose an "asking price" and write it down. Then focus Ss' attention on the mugs. Ask: "What is a good price for mugs?" Tell Ss with page B to choose an "asking price" and write it down.
- Ss work individually to make up prices for the remaining items.

> **TIP**
> If Ss have difficulty with a specific task, try a different grouping for the task. For example, have them work in small groups instead of pairs.

B *Pair work*

- Explain the task. Ss work in pairs. Students A and B take turns as buyer and seller. The buyers choose three things they want to buy from their partner's page. Buyers decide on a good price for each thing.

INTERCHANGE 3 Flea market

STUDENT A

A You want to sell these things. Write your "asking price" for each item.

- Model the example conversation with a few Ss, showing that A is the buyer and B is the seller. Remind the class to vary the conversation and to bargain.
- Give Ss a time limit of about ten minutes. Explain that partners need to take turns starting the conversation so that each S is both buyer and seller.
- Continue until both partners buy and sell at least three things. Tell the Ss to write down the prices they bought the things for.
- Go around the class and give help as needed.

STUDENT B

A You want to sell these things. Write your "asking price" for each item.

MUGS
asking price: ______
sold for: ______

PRINTER
asking price: ______
sold for: ______

ELECTRIC GUITAR
asking price: ______
sold for: ______

TREADMILL
asking price: ______
sold for: ______

STUDENTS A AND B

B **PAIR WORK** Now choose three things you want to buy. Get the best price for each one. Then write what each item "sold for" on the price tag.

A: How much is the tablet computer?
B: It's only $70.
A: Wow! That's expensive!
B: Well, how about $35?
A: No. That's still too much. I'll give you $30 for it.
B: Sold! It's yours.

C **GROUP WORK** Compare your earnings in groups. Who made the most money at the flea market?

- ***Option:*** Ask a pair of Ss to perform their role play for the class. Alternatively, Ss can change partners and try the activity again.
- ***Option:*** Ss make a list of six to eight things to sell at a flea market. They can also bring in two or three things and role-play a sale at a flea market.

C *Group work*

- Ss look at the "sold for" part of their page and add up the amount of money they made individually.
- Ss work in groups to take turns comparing who made the most money at the flea market. Go around the room and encourage Ss to talk about their sales with useful expressions from Unit 3.
- ***Option:*** Elicit the best bargains Ss got.

INTERCHANGE 4

Learning Objective: speak more fluently when making plans

A

- Explain the task. Ss read the directions. Ss write three things they need to do and three things they want to do this weekend and the days and times. Model an example for *need to* and *want to* for the class.
- Ss complete the task individually.

B *Pair work*

- Explain the task. Model the example with a S. Review invitations and polite refusals if necessary. Point out that Ss should give a reason if they decline an invitation.
- Ss work in pairs to agree on two activities to do together.

C *Group work*

- Explain the task. Pairs work with another pair to take turns making and responding to invitations.
- Go around the room and encourage Ss to respond politely.

D *Class work*

- Explain the task. Read the example. Groups share their choices with the class.
- ***Option:*** Elicit interesting refusals that Ss made.

INTERCHANGE 4 Are you free this weekend?

A Write three things you need to do and three things you want to do this weekend. Include the days of the week and the times.

I need to . . .	I want to . . .

B **PAIR WORK** Invite your partner to do things on the weekend. Accept or decline invitations. If you decline an invitation, explain why. Agree on two activities to do together.

A: Would you like to see a movie on Saturday at 8:00 P.M.?
B: I'd like to, but I need to study for a test. Would you like to go to the park on Sunday at 10:00 A.M.?
A: Yes, I would. And would you like to . . . ?

C **GROUP WORK** Get together with another pair. Can you agree on two things to do together?

D **CLASS WORK** Explain your group's choices to the class.
"Eu-jin wanted to go to the park on Sunday at 10 A.M., but Serhat needs to visit his aunt on Sunday morning, so we're going out for lunch on Sunday at . . ."

INTERCHANGE 5 Is that true?

CLASS ACTIVITY Go around the class telling your classmates three activities that members of your family are doing these days. Two activities have to be true, but one needs to be false! Can your classmates guess which activity is false with only two questions?

A: My brother is working in Berlin and his wife is studying German there. My niece is learning three languages at school: German, English, and Spanish.
B: Is your brother really working in Berlin?
A: Yes, he is.
B: Is your niece really learning Spanish?
A: No, she's not! She's learning German and English, but she isn't learning Spanish.

INTERCHANGE 5

Learning Objective: speak more fluently when asking and answering questions about family members

Class activity

- Focus Ss' attention on the pictures. Explain the task. Point out that Ss can use the pictures to say what their family members are doing these days. Two things they say will be true and one will be false.
- Model the dialogue with a S. Point out that Ss can only ask two questions to guess which statement is false.
- Set a time limit of 10 to 15 minutes. Ss complete the activity with at least three other classmates, taking turns to speak and guess.
- Go around the room. Note any errors, but don't point them out.
- Have Ss share what they learned about their classmates' family members. Go over any errors you noticed by writing them on the board and asking Ss to correct them.

INTERCHANGE 6

Learning Objective: speak more fluently about free-time activities

A *Class activity*

- Focus Ss' attention on the chart. Read through the list of items. Explain any unfamiliar vocabulary.
- Have Ss add two of their own ideas to the chart.
- Explain the task. Ss ask each other who does these activities, how often they do them, and how well they do them. Point out that Ss must try to find one person who does each thing. Also, they cannot use the same name twice.
- Model the task with a S at the front of the class, using the example conversation.
- Set a time limit of 10 to 15 minutes. Ss go around the room and complete the activity.

B *Group work*

- Focus Ss' attention on the picture. Ask: "What is a fundraiser?" Elicit ideas. If needed, explain that it is an event where people raise money to get something or to benefit a charity or other organization. Sometimes people make things or perform services to get the money.
- Explain the task. Tell Ss to imagine the class is participating in a fundraiser. Ss choose three people from the class to help raise money at the fundraiser. Ask: "What will each person do for the fundraiser? Why?"

INTERCHANGE 6 What's your talent?

A CLASS ACTIVITY Add two items to the chart. Does anyone in your class do these things? How often and how well? Go around the class and find one person for each activity.

	Name	How often?	How well?
bake cookies			
cook			
cut hair			
do card tricks			
fix things			
play an instrument			
sing			
do yoga			

A: Do you bake cookies?
B: Yes, I do.
A: How often do you bake cookies?
B: Once a month.
A: Really? And how well do you bake?

B GROUP WORK Imagine there's a fundraiser to buy new books for the school library this weekend. Who do you think can help? Choose three people from your class. Explain your choices.

A: Let's ask Lydia to help with the fundraiser.
B: Why Lydia?
A: Because she bakes cookies very well.
C: Yes, she really does. And Mariana is very good at fixing things. Let's ask her, too!

120 Interchange 6

- Model the conversation with two Ss. Then Ss complete the task in small groups.
- Ask the groups to share and explain their choices with the class. Have the class agree on the three people.

INTERCHANGE 7 Memories

GROUP WORK Play the board game. Follow these instructions.

1. Write your initials on small pieces of paper. These are your game pieces.
2. Take turns by tossing a coin: If the coin lands face up, move two spaces. If the coin lands face down, move one space.
3. When you land on a space, answer the question. Answer any follow-up questions.
4. If you land on "Free question," another player asks you any question.

A: I'll go first. OK, one space. Last night, I met my best friend.
B: Oh, yeah? Where did you go?
A: We went to the movies.

Interchange 7 121

INTERCHANGE 7

Learning Objective: speak more fluently about past events using the simple past

Group work

- Focus Ss' attention on the board game and read the instructions. Show Ss how to write their initials on small pieces of paper and use them as markers.
- ***Option:*** Ss can use other small items as markers (e.g., pen caps or erasers).
- Show Ss how to toss a coin. Point out which side is face up and which side is face down.
- Have different Ss read the questions in each space. Explain that a "free question" can be any question another player wants to ask you. Remind Ss they can make up an answer if they don't want to answer truthfully.
- Then ask two Ss to model the example conversation. Point out that Ss should ask follow-up questions.
- Show how to play the game with a group of three Ss.

TIP
In low-level classes, it is more effective to model a game or activity than to explain it.

- Ss play the game in small groups. Go around the class and encourage Ss to ask follow-up questions.
- ***Option:*** Ask Ss to share any interesting information they learned about their classmates.

INTERCHANGE 8

Learning Objective: describe places in a neighborhood with *there is/there are* and quantifiers

Class activity

- Explain that Ss will play a guessing game. Read the locations. Elicit or explain any location meanings.
- Read the instructions. Put Ss into two teams, A and B. Explain that each team will choose a location and keep it secret for now.
- Explain that one S from each team will go to the front of the class. Those two Ss will guess the other team's location.
- Teams then show the opposite team the location but keep it secret from that team's guesser. Teams take turns giving clues to the other team's guesser. Point out that Ss will use *there is/ there are* and quantifiers. Model an example: "There are a lot of people waiting at this place." is one clue, and "There are a lot of planes." is a second clue.
- Explain that teams can give up to ten clues. The teams try to guess the location in as few guesses as possible. Each clue is worth one point. Teams don't want many points.
- Have three Ss model the example conversation at the bottom of the page.
- Show how to play the game with a group of three Ss.

TIP
In low-level classes, it is more effective to model a game or activity than to explain it.

- Put the class into two teams to play. Listen to make sure that Ss use *there is/there are* + quantifiers. Give help as needed.

INTERCHANGE 8 Where are we?

CLASS ACTIVITY Play a guessing game. Follow these instructions.

1. Get into two teams, A and B.
2. Each team chooses one of the locations below. Keep it a secret!
3. Each team chooses a teammate to guess the other team's location. He or she is the guesser.
4. Show your location to all the students on the other team, except their guesser.
5. Take turns giving your guessers one clue at a time until they guess the location. Use *There is/ There are* plus a quantifier. You cannot give more than 10 clues. Your team can get 1 to 10 points, depending on how many clues you need to give your guesser (1 clue = 1 point) before he or she guesses the right location. Remember: you don't want to get many points!
6. At the end of the game, the team with fewer points wins.

A: There is a lot of food here. Where are we?
B: You're in a grocery store.
C: No. There aren't any walls here. This isn't a building.
B: You're at an outdoor market!
A: Correct! We're at an outdoor market.

122 Interchange 8

INTERCHANGE 9A Find the differences

STUDENT A

A **PAIR WORK** How many differences can you find between your picture here and your partner's picture? Ask questions like these to find the differences.

How many people are standing / sitting / wearing . . . / holding a drink? Who?
What color is . . . 's T-shirt / sweater / hair?
Does . . . wear glasses / have a beard / have long hair?
What does . . . look like?

B **CLASS ACTIVITY** How many differences are there in the pictures?
"In picture 1, Daniel's T-shirt is . . . In picture 2, it's . . ."

Interchange 9a 123

INTERCHANGE 9A

Learning Objective: speak more fluently about people's appearance

A *Pair work*

- Ss work in pairs. One S looks at Interchange 9A and the other S looks at Interchange 9B.
- Explain the task. Both Ss have pictures of a party, but there are some differences in the pictures. Ss ask each other questions to find the differences without looking at their partner's picture.
- Ask different Ss to read the questions at the top of the page. Point out that Ss can use these questions to find the differences.
- Model the task with one pair. Ask: "What is Daniel wearing in Picture 1? in Picture 2?" Elicit answers. (Answers: Student A: In Picture 1, Daniel is wearing a blue shirt. Student B: In Picture 2, he's wearing a light brown/beige shirt.)

TIP
With information gap activities, tell Ss to sit across from their partners and put a textbook between them. That way, they can hear each other but not see each other's pictures.

- Ss complete the task in pairs. Go around the class and give help as needed.

B *Class activity*

- Tell pairs to look over their answers (i.e., the differences between the two pictures) and to choose one to write on the board. Encourage them to come to the board quickly by making it a rule that no answer can be written twice.
- To check the answers written on the board, ask the pair who wrote an answer to read it aloud for the class. Then find out if other Ss agree. If they do agree, go on to the next answer until all of them have been checked. If Ss don't agree, ask the class to look at both pictures again to check it.

INTERCHANGE 9B

Possible answers

1. In Picture 1, Dave is wearing a blue shirt. In Picture 2, he's wearing a light brown/ beige shirt.
2. In Picture 1, Dave has blond hair. In Picture 2, he has brown hair.
3. In Picture 1, Joanna's hair is short. In Picture 2, it's long.
4. In Picture 1, Joanna is standing. In Picture 2, she's sitting.
5. In Picture 1, Joanna is wearing pants and sneakers. In Picture 2, she's wearing a dress and shoes.
6. In Picture 1, Leon is wearing an orange shirt and shorts. In Picture 2, he's wearing a denim jacket and jeans.
7. In Picture 1, Isla's T-shirt is yellow. In Picture 2, it's red.
8. In Picture 1, Isla has short blond hair. In Picture 2, she has long light brown hair.
9. In Picture 1, Megan has long curly red hair. In Picture 2, she has short curly red hair.
10. In Picture 1, Megan is wearing a long dress. In Picture 2, she's wearing a short dress.
11. In Picture 1, Elliott is wearing a green shirt and long pants. In Picture 2, he's wearing a gray shirt and shorts.

INTERCHANGE 9B Find the differences

STUDENT B

A PAIR WORK How many differences can you find between your picture here and your partner's picture? Ask questions like these to find the differences.

How many people are standing / sitting / wearing . . . / holding a drink? Who?
What color is . . .'s T-shirt / sweater / hair?
Does . . . wear glasses / have a beard / have long hair?
What does . . . look like?

B CLASS ACTIVITY How many differences are there in the pictures?
"In picture 1, Daniel's shirt is . . . In picture 2, it's . . ."

124 Interchange 9b

INTERCHANGE 10 Fun survey

A **PAIR WORK** How much fun does your partner have? Interview him or her. Write the number of points using this scale.

never = 1 point	4–7 times = 3 points
1–3 times = 2 points	8 or more times = 4 points

Home Posts News Contact us Log in

SURVEY

HOW MANY TIMES HAVE YOU . . .	POINTS
1. watched a really good movie or TV show in the last two months?	
2. listened to your favorite kind of music in the last week?	
3. talked to your best friend in the last two weeks?	
4. read something interesting that wasn't for work or school in the last month?	
5. eaten your favorite foods in the last three weeks?	
6. had a really fun weekend in the last three months?	
7. spent at least one hour doing something you like in the last three days?	
8. taken a relaxing vacation in the last year?	
9. had a good laugh in the last 24 hours?	
10. told yourself "This is fun!" in the last 12 hours?	

B **GROUP WORK** Add up your partner's points. Tell the group how much fun your partner has and why.

10–19 = You don't have enough fun. You should try to do things you enjoy more often! Stop and smell the roses!
20–29 = You have fun sometimes, but you need to do it more often. Continue to take time to do the things that you like.
30–40 = You know how to have fun! You know how to have a good time and enjoy life. Keep it up!

"Ellen has fun sometimes. She watches her favorite TV show once a week and takes a vacation twice a year. But she never reads anything she really likes – only the things she has to read for school."

C **CLASS ACTIVITY** Do you think your partner needs to have more fun? In what way?

"I think Ellen needs to have more fun in her life. She needs to spend more time doing things she likes. And she needs to eat her favorite foods more often. She also . . ."

Interchange 10 125

INTERCHANGE 10

Learning Objective: speak more fluently about one's lifestyle

A *Pair work*

- Focus S's attention on the survey. Ask a few Ss to say what they think is fun and how many times they've done something fun in the last week.
- Explain the task. Then Ss read the questions silently. Elicit or explain any new vocabulary.
- Model the activity by asking a S the first interview question. Explain that the S should answer with the number of times he or she has done the thing asked about.
- Show how to use the chart at the top to calculate the number of times into points. Based on Ss' responses, show where to write the number of points.
- Ss complete the survey in pairs. Go around the class and give help as needed.
- ***Option:*** To make Ss listen more carefully, tell them to ask the questions in a different order.

B *Group work*

- Explain the task and demonstrate how to add up the points. Then ask a few Ss to read the results chart and the example reading. Point out that Ss will use the results chart to create their own explanation about how much fun their partner has.
- Ss use their surveys to make notes about how much fun their partner has.
- In groups, Ss take turns talking about how much fun their partner has.

C *Class activity*

- Explain the task and read the example.
- Ask the class: "Who knows how to have fun? Why? Who needs to have more fun? In what way?" Elicit Ss' answers.

INTERCHANGE 11

Learning Objective: speak more fluently when giving suggestions about one's city

A *Pair work*

- Ask: "What are some fun and exciting places and things for tourists to do in your city?" Elicit Ss' answers.

> **TIP**
> To get Ss' attention, give them instructions from different places. Sometimes give them from the back of the classroom; other times give them from the middle of the classroom.

- Explain the task. Ss make a city guide for tourists, such as for a travel website. Have them choose their own city or a city they know well.
- Focus Ss' attention on the photos and the text. Point out that this guide is from a city's website. Go over the text. Point out that the photos provide ideas about topics to write about. Elicit or explain any new vocabulary. Explain that a *reasonable price* is one that isn't too expensive.
- Ss complete the guide in pairs in class or for homework.

B *Class activity*

- Explain the task. Ask different Ss to read the follow-up questions aloud. Then elicit additional questions and ask a S to write them on the board.
- Ss compare their city guides in small groups. (If possible, Ss should work with classmates who wrote about different cities.)
- Go around the class and encourage Ss to ask follow-up questions.

INTERCHANGE 11 Welcome to our city!

A PAIR WORK You want to attract more visitors to your city or town. Complete the sentences below and add one more sentence to write a guide for tourists.

WELCOME TO OUR CITY!

LOGIN / REGISTER

It's a really ________ place and you will find ________ to do here.
The weather is ________ and the best times of the year to visit are ________ and ________.
You can ________, ________, and ________, and you shouldn't miss the famous ________!
Don't forget to try our local food! ________ can be a little expensive, though, but you can have a good meal for a reasonable price at ________.
Also, ________.

Enjoy your stay and come back soon!

B CLASS ACTIVITY Read your guide to the class.
Ask follow-up questions to learn more.

What is the first place you should visit?
What is an exciting place to have fun on a Saturday night?
What is a relaxing place to visit on a Sunday morning?
What is a quiet place to study or do some work?
What is a really beautiful area that you shouldn't miss?
What is a dangerous area that you should avoid?
What places are usually too crowded?
Where can you exercise outdoors?
What fun things can you do for free?
Where's a popular place to meet?

C CLASS ACTIVITY Which are your two favorite guides? Which details did you find especially interesting about them?

126 Interchange 11

C *Class activity*

- Ask groups to share their favorite guides and give examples of details they found interesting. Have the class choose their favorite guides overall.

INTERCHANGE 12 What should I do?

A **GROUP WORK** Play the board game. Follow these instructions.

1. Write your initials on small pieces of paper. These are your game pieces.
2. Take turns by tossing a coin: If the coin lands face up, move two spaces. If the coin lands face down, move one space.
3. When you land on a space, ask two others in your group for advice.
4. The first person to cross the finish line is the winner.

A: I have the hiccups, Hiroto. What should I do?
B: Well, it's sometimes useful to hold your breath.
A: Thanks. What about you, Erica? What's your advice?
C: You should drink some water. That always works for me.

useful expressions
You should . . .
You could . . .
It's a good idea to . . .
It's important to . . .
I think it's useful to . . .

B **CLASS ACTIVITY** Who gave the best advice in your group? Tell the class.

INTERCHANGE 12

Learning Objective: speak more fluently about health problems and medical advice

A *Group work*

- Focus Ss' attention on the board game and read the instructions. Show Ss how to write their initials on small pieces of paper and use them as markers.
- ***Option:*** Ss can use other small items as markers (e.g., pen caps or erasers).
- Show Ss how to toss a coin. Point out which side is face up and which side is face down.
- Have different Ss read the problems in each space. Elicit or explain any vocabulary. Then ask three Ss to model the example conversation.
- Show how to play the game with a group of three Ss.

TIP
In low-level classes, it is more effective to model a game or activity than to explain it.

- Ss play the game in small groups. Go around the class and encourage Ss to use the expressions in the useful expressions box.

B *Class activity*

- Read the question. Elicit information from each group. Encourage them to give examples.

INTERCHANGE 13

Learning Objective: speak more fluently about types of food

A *Pair work*

- Set the scene and explain the task. Explain that a *food truck* usually has a theme or specific type of food it sells, such as only foods made with bacon, or a combination of Indian curry and tacos, or savory cupcakes. They usually offer fewer dishes than a regular restaurant menu.
- Ask the class about any food trucks they have seen or eaten from. Elicit possible themes and foods for a food truck from the class. Encourage Ss to be creative and to think of their favorite foods.
- Ss complete the task in pairs. Ss choose a name for their food truck and write it at the top of the menu. To help Ss think of ideas, ask these questions: "What kind of food truck is it? What's special about it?" Then they complete the menu.
- Go around the class and give help with vocabulary, spelling, or prices.

B *Group work*

- Read the instructions and explain the task. Pairs trade menus with another pair and order food and drinks from each other's menu.
- Then pairs make suggestions about the other pair's menu. Tell Ss they may want to make suggestions about the prices, the most interesting dish, the healthiest dish, and the name of the food truck.
- Elicit answers from the class. Encourage Ss to explain their reasons.

INTERCHANGE 13 Planning a food festival

A **PAIR WORK** Imagine your class is organizing a food festival with different food trucks. You and your classmate are responsible for one of the trucks. Choose a name for your truck. Write it at the top of the menu. Then, write the food and drinks you'd like to sell at your truck. Then write the prices.

B **GROUP WORK** Trade your menus with another pair. Order food and drinks from their menu, and then leave some suggestions about the menu on the message board.

128 Interchange 13

INTERCHANGE 14 How much do you know?

A PAIR WORK Take turns asking and answering these questions. Check (✓) the answer you think is correct for each question. Then write two more questions and answers.

World Knowledge Quiz

1. Which place is the wettest?	☐ Kaua'i, Hawai'i	☐ Manaus, Brazil	☐ Emei Shan, China
2. Which country is the hottest?	☐ Algeria	☐ Libya	☐ Somalia
3. Which country is closest to the equator?	☐ Colombia	☐ India	☐ Malaysia
4. Which animal is the biggest?	☐ a bison	☐ an elephant	☐ a blue whale
5. Which animal lives the longest?	☐ an elephant	☐ a tortoise	☐ a green iguana
6. Which mountain range is the longest?	☐ the Andes	☐ the Himalayas	☐ the Rockies
7. Which planet is the smallest?	☐ Earth	☐ Mercury	☐ Venus
8. Which planet is the largest?	☐ Jupiter	☐ Neptune	☐ Saturn
9. Which city is the oldest?	☐ Beijing, China	☐ Luxor, Egypt	☐ Rome, Italy
10. Which metal is the heaviest?	☐ aluminum	☐ gold	☐ silver
11. ______	______	______	______
12. ______	______	______	______

B PAIR WORK Check your answers. You and your partner get a point for every correct answer.

C CLASS ACTIVITY Ask your classmates your two questions. Get a point for every question nobody can answer correctly.

Interchange 14 129

INTERCHANGE 14

Learning Objective: speak more fluently about general knowledge facts

A Pair work

- Write these subjects on the board:

  biology *geography*
  science *history*
  chemistry *foreign languages*

- As a warm-up, ask: "Do you watch quiz shows on TV? How well would you do with these subjects?" Encourage discussion.
- Explain the task. Model the first question with its three choices. Point out the photos that refer to the question.
- Call on Ss to read through the list of questions and their choices. (It's best not to explain new words at this time as this might give away the answer.)
- Model this possible conversation with a S:

  T: Look at question 1. Which place is the wettest: Kaua'i, Hawai'i; Manaus, Brazil; or Emei Shan, China?

  S: I think Kaua'i, Hawai'i, is the wettest.

  T: Hmm. I think Manaus, Brazil, is the wettest.

  S: I don't agree. Actually, I think Emei Shan, China, is the wettest.

  T: OK, I guess we disagree here. So I'll check Kaua'i, Hawai'i, and you check Emei Shan, China. We'll find out later who got the correct answer for this one.

  S: Now it's my turn. Let's go on to question 2. Which country . . . ?

- Ss work in pairs. Ss take turns asking and answering the questions. Tell Ss to cover the answers.
- After pairs have completed the quiz, they write two more questions and three answer choices for each.
- Then pairs correct their incorrect answers.
- Allow five to ten minutes for the activity.

B Pair work

- Explain the task. Pairs check their answers at the bottom of the quiz. They get one point for every correct answer they had originally.
- Ask the class which pair got the most points.

C Class activity

- Explain the task. Pairs ask the class their two questions. If the class can't answer a question, the pair gets a point.
- Have pairs report their total points at the end.

INTERCHANGE 15

Learning Objective: speak more fluently about weekend plans

Class activity

- As a warm-up, ask: "What are you doing this weekend?"
- ***Option:*** Let the class ask you about your weekend plans.
- Ask Ss to look at the items in the chart. Elicit or explain any new vocabulary. Call on Ss to form the questions from the phrases (e.g., *Are you going to go to a party this weekend?*).
- Model by asking different Ss: "Are you going to go out of town this weekend?" When a S says "no," go on to the next person until you find someone who says "yes." Write that person's name in the chart, and ask at least two follow-up questions. Write the details in the *Notes* column.
- Ask two Ss to model the conversation.
- Model how to react to hearing about someone's plans (e.g., *Really? That sounds great! Wow! That sounds like fun!*). Ss practice the expressions.
- Ss move around the class to do the activity.

TIP

It's best not to interrupt Ss during a fluency exercise. For this type of activity, communication of real information is more important than grammatical or lexical accuracy.

- After the activity, go over any common errors.

INTERCHANGE 15 Weekend plans

CLASS ACTIVITY What are your classmates' plans for the weekend? Add two activities to the list. Then go around the class and find people who are going to do these things. For each question, ask for more information and take notes.

Find someone who's going to . . .	Name	Notes
go to a party		
go out of town		
go shopping		
see a live performance		
see/watch a movie		
see/watch a game		
meet friends		
visit relatives		
clean the house		
study for a test		

A: Samira, are you going to a party this weekend?
B: Yes, I am.
A: Where is the party going to be?
B: At my friend Lila's place. She's having a party to celebrate her birthday.

130 Interchange 15

INTERCHANGE 16 Our possible future

A **PAIR WORK** Talk with your partner and complete this chart with two ideas for each question – your idea and your partner's idea.

What is . . .	You	Your partner
something you plan to do next year?		
something you aren't going to do next year?		
something you hope to buy in the next year?		
something you would like to change about yourself?		
something you would like to learn?		
a place you would like to visit someday?		
a city you would like to live in someday?		
a job you would like to have?		
a goal you hope to achieve?		

A: What is something you plan to do next year?
B: Well, I'm going to travel to Morocco.
A: Oh, really? Where in Morocco?
B: I'm not sure yet! What about you? What do you plan to do next year?
A: I'd like to get my own place.
B: Oh, really? Are you planning to rent an apartment?
A: No, actually I'm going to buy one.
B: Good for you!

B **GROUP ACTIVITY** Compare your information with another pair. Explain your goals and plans.

A: What are two things you plan to do next year?
B: Well, I'm going to visit Morocco, and Helena is going to get her own place.
C: That's right. I'm going to buy a small apartment. And you?
A: Well, I . . .

Interchange 16 131

INTERCHANGE 16

Learning Objective: speak more fluently about possibilities for the future

A *Pair work*

- Focus Ss' attention on the picture. Elicit what kind of dreams and plans the person has.
- Explain the task and that Ss will discuss their answers in pairs. Direct Ss' attention to the first question in the chart. Model the example conversation at the bottom with a S.
- ***Option:*** Have Ss ask you the questions in the chart. Reply with your own information. If there are any problems with pronunciation or intonation of questions, review briefly.
- Then in pairs, Ss take turns asking and answering the questions from the chart. They record their own and their partner's answers on the chart. Encourage them to ask follow-up questions.
- Go around the class and give help as needed.

B *Group activity*

- Explain the task. Model the example conversation with two Ss.
- Pairs join another pair and take turns explaining their possible future plans.
- ***Option:*** Ask each group to choose the most interesting or unusual future plans that someone talked about. Then that S tells the rest of the class about his or her plans.

Grammar plus

UNIT 1

1 Statements with *be*; possessive adjectives page 3

■ Don't confuse contractions of *be* with possessive adjectives: **You're** a student. **Your** class is English 1. (NOT: ~~You're class is English 1.~~) **He's** my classmate. **His** name is Ricardo. (NOT: ~~He's name is Ricardo.~~)

Choose the correct words.

1. This (is) / **are** Dulce Castelo. **She's** / **Her** a new student from Santo Domingo.
2. My name **am** / **is** Sergio. **I'm** / **He's** from Brazil.
3. My brother and I **is** / **are** students here. **Our** / **We're** names are Nate and Chad.
4. **He's** / **His** Kento. **He's** / **His** 19 years old.
5. **They're** / **Their** in my English class. **It's** / **Its** a big class.

2 Wh-questions with *be* page 4

■ Use *What* to ask about things: **What's** in your bag? Use *Where* to ask about places: **Where's** your friend from? Use *Who* to ask about people: **Who's** your teacher? Use *What . . . like?* to ask for a description: **What's** your friend **like**?

Match the questions with the answers.

1. Who's that? __f__
2. Where's your teacher? ____
3. What are your friends like? ____
4. Where's she from? ____
5. Who are they? ____
6. What's his name? ____

a. They're really nice.
b. She's from South Korea.
c. They're my brother and sister.
d. His name is Daniel.
e. He's in class.
f. That's our new classmate.

3 Yes/No questions and short answers with *be* page 5

■ Use short answers to answer yes/no questions. Don't use contractions with short answers with Yes: **Are you** from Mexico? Yes, **I am**. (NOT: ~~Yes, I'm.~~)

Complete the conversations.

1. **A:** __Are they__ in your class?
   B: No, ________. They're in English 2.
2. **A:** Hi! ________ in this class?
   B: Yes, ________. I'm a new student here.
3. **A:** ________ from the United States?
   B: No, ________. We're from Calgary, Canada.
4. **A:** Hi, Monica. ________ free?
   B: No, ________. I'm on my way to class.
5. **A:** That's the new student. ________ from Paraguay?
   B: No, ________. He's from Uruguay.
6. **A:** ________ from Indonesia?
   B: Yes, ________. She's from Jakarta.

UNIT 2

1 Simple present Wh-questions and statements page 10

Statements

- Verbs with *he/she/it* end in *–s*: He/She **walks** to school. BUT I/You/We/They **walk** to school.
- *Have*, *go*, and *do* are irregular with *he/she/it*: She **has** a class at 1:00. He **goes** to school at night. She **does** her homework before school.

Wh-questions

- Use *does* in questions with *he/she/it* and *do* with all the others: Where does he/she/it live? Where do I/you/we/they live?
- Don't add *–s* to the verb: Where does she **live**? (NOT: ~~Where does she lives~~?)

Complete the conversations with the correct form of the verbs in parentheses.

1. A: I ___*have*___ (have) good news! Mona ______________ (have) a new job.
   B: How ______________ she ______________ (like) it?
   A: She ______________ (love) it. The hours are great.
   B: What time ______________ she ______________ (start)?
   A: She ______________ (start) at ten and ______________ (finish) at four.
2. A: What ______________ you ______________ (do)?
   B: I'm a teacher.
   A: What ______________ you ______________ (teach)?
   B: I ______________ (teach) Spanish and English.
   A: Really? My sister ______________ (teach) English, too.

2 Time expressions page 12

- Use *in* with *the morning/afternoon/evening*. Use *at* with *night*: He goes to school **in** the afternoon and works **at** night. BUT: **on** Friday night.
- Use *at* with clock times: She gets up **at** 7:00.
- Use *on* with days: He gets up early **on** weekdays. She has class **on** Mondays.

Complete the conversation with time expressions from the box.
You can use some words more than once.

at   early   in   on   until

A: How's your new job?
B: I love it, but the hours are difficult. I start work ______________ 6:30 A.M., and I work ______________ 3:30.
A: That's interesting! I work the same hours, but I work ______________ night. I start ______________ 6:30 ______________ the evening and finish ______________ 3:30 ______________ the morning.
B: Wow! What time do you get up?
A: Well, I get home ______________ 4:30 and go to bed ______________ 5:30. And I sleep ______________ 2:00. But I only work ______________ weekends, so it's OK. What about you?
B: Oh, I work ______________ Monday, Wednesday, and Friday. And I get up ______________ – around 5:00 A.M.

UNIT 3

1 Demonstratives; *one, ones* page 17

- With singular nouns, use *this* for a thing that is nearby and *that* for a thing that is not nearby: How much is **this** hat here? How much is **that** hat over there?
- With plural nouns, use *these* for things that are nearby and *those* for things that are not nearby: How much are **these** earrings here? How much are **those** earrings over there?
- Use *one* to replace a singular noun: I like the red hat. I like the red **one**. Use *ones* to replace plural nouns: I like the green bags. I like the green **ones**.

Choose the correct words.

1. **A:** Excuse me. How much are **this** / **these** shoes?
   B: **It's** / **They're** $279.
   A: And how much is **this** / **that** bag over there?
   B: **It's** / **They're** only $129.
   A: And are the two gray **one** / **ones** $129, too?
   B: No. **That** / **Those** are only $119.
   A: Oh! **This** / **That** store is really expensive.
2. **A:** Can I help you?
   B: Yes, please. I really like **these** / **those** jeans over there. How much **is it** / **are they**?
   A: Which **one** / **ones**? Do you mean **this** / **these**?
   B: No, the black **one** / **ones**.
   A: Let me look. Oh, **it's** / **they're** $35.99.
   B: That's not bad. And how much is **this** / **that** sweater here?
   A: **It's** / **They're** only $9.99.

2 Preferences; comparisons with adjectives page 20

- For adjectives with one syllable or adjectives of two syllables ending in *–y*, add *–er* to form the comparative:
  cheap → cheaper; nice → nicer; big → bigger, pretty → prettier.
- For adjectives with two syllables not ending in *–y* or adjectives of three or more syllables, use *more* + adjective to form the comparative: stylish → more stylish, expensive → more expensive.

A Write the comparatives of these adjectives.

1. attractive *more attractive*
2. happy ____________
3. exciting ____________
4. friendly ____________
5. interesting ____________
6. reasonable ____________
7. sad ____________
8. warm ____________

B Answer the questions. Use the first word in the parentheses in your answer. Then write another sentence with the second word.

1. Which pants do you prefer, the cotton ones or the wool ones? (wool / attractive)
   I prefer the wool ones. They're more attractive than the cotton ones.
2. Which ring do you like better, the gold one or the silver one? (silver / interesting)
   ____
3. Which one do you prefer, the silk blouse or the cotton blouse? (silk / pretty)
   ____
4. Which ones do you like more, the black shoes or the purple ones? (purple / cheap)
   ____

UNIT 4

1 Simple present questions; short answers page 23

- Use *do* + base form for yes/no questions and short answers with *I/you/we/they*: **Do** I/you/we/they **like** rock? Yes, I/you/we/they **do**. No, I/you/we/they **don't.**
- Use *does* in yes/no questions and short answers with *he/she/it*: **Does** he/she **like** rock? Yes, he/she **does**. No, he/she **doesn't.**
- Use *don't* and *doesn't* + base form for negative statements: I **don't** like horror movies. He **doesn't like** action movies.
- Remember: Don't add *–s* to the base form: Does she **like** rock? (NOT: ~~Does she likes rock~~?)
- Subject pronouns (*I, you, he, she, it, we, they*) usually come before a verb. Object pronouns (*me, you, him, her, it, us, them*) usually come after a verb: He likes **her**, but she doesn't like **him**.

A Complete the questions and short answers.

1. **A:** Do you play (play) a musical instrument?
   B: Yes, I do. I play the guitar.
2. **A:** ____________ (like) Carrie Underwood?
   B: No, ____________. John doesn't like country music.
3. **A:** ____________ (like) talk shows?
   B: Yes, ____________. Lisa is a big fan of them.
4. **A:** ____________ (watch) the news on TV?
   B: Yes, ____________. Kevin and I watch the news every night.
5. **A:** ____________ (like) hip-hop?
   B: No, ____________. But I love R&B.
6. **A:** ____________ (listen to) jazz?
   B: No, ____________. But my parents listen to a lot of classical music.

B Complete the sentences with object pronouns.

1. We don't listen to hip-hop because we really don't like it.
2. We love your voice. Please sing for ________.
3. These sunglasses are great. Do you like ________?
4. Who is that man? Do you know ________?
5. Beth looks great in green. It's a really good color for ________.

2 *Would*; verb + *to* + verb page 26

- Don't use a contraction in affirmative short answers with *would*: **Would** you **like to go to** the game? Yes, I **would**. (NOT: ~~Yes, I'd~~.)

Unscramble the questions and answers to complete the conversation.

A: tonight / to see / would you like / with me / a movie
____?

B: I would. / yes, / what / to see / would you like
____?

A: the new Matt Damon movie / to see / I'd like
____.

B: OK. That's a great idea!

UNIT 5

1 Present continuous page 32

- Use the present continuous to talk about actions that are happening now: What **are** you **doing (these days)**? **I'm studying** English.
- The present continuous is present of *be* + *–ing*. For verbs ending in *e*, drop the *e* and add *–ing*: have → having, live → living.
- For verbs ending in vowel + consonant, double the consonant and add *–ing*: sit → sitting.

Write questions with the words in parentheses and the present continuous. Then complete the responses with short answers or the verbs in the box.

live study take ✓ teach work

1. **A:** (what / your sister / do / these days) *What's your sister doing these days?*
   B: *She's teaching* English.
   A: Really? (she / live / abroad) ______________________
   B: Yes, ____________. She ____________ in South Korea.
2. **A:** (how / you / spend / your summer) ______________________
   B: I ____________ part-time. I ____________ two classes also.
   A: (what / you / take) ______________________
   B: My friend and I ____________ photography and Japanese. We like our classes a lot.

2 Quantifiers page 34

- Use *a lot of, all, few, nearly all* before plural nouns: **A lot of/All/Few/Nearly all** families are small. Use *no one* before a verb: **No one** gets married before the age of 18.
- *Nearly all* means "almost all."

Read the sentences about the small town of Monroe. Rewrite the sentences using the quantifiers in the box. Use each quantifier only once.

a lot of all few nearly all ✓ no one

1. In Monroe, 0% of the people drive before the age of 16.
   In Monroe, no one drives before the age of 16.
2. Ninety-eight percent of students finish high school.
   ____
3. One hundred percent of children start school by the age of six.
   ____
4. Eighty-nine percent of couples have more than one child.
   ____
5. Five percent of families have more than four children.
   ____

UNIT 6

1 Adverbs of frequency

page 37

- Adverbs of frequency (*always, almost always, usually, often, sometimes, hardly ever, almost never, never*) usually come before the main verb: She **never plays** tennis. I **almost always eat** breakfast. BUT Adverbs of frequency usually come after the verb *be*: I**'m always** late.
- *Usually* and *sometimes* can begin a sentence: **Usually** I walk to work. **Sometimes** I exercise in the morning.
- Some frequency expressions usually come at the end of a sentence: *every day, once a week, twice a month, three times a year:* Do you exercise **every day**? I exercise **three times a week**.

Put the words in order to make questions. Then complete the answers with the words in parentheses.

1. you what weekends usually do do on
   Q: *What do you usually do on weekends?*
   A: I ____________________ (often / play sports)
2. ever you go jogging do with a friend
   Q: ____________________
   A: No, ____________________ (always / alone)
3. you play do basketball how often
   Q: ____________________
   A: I ____________________ (four times a week)
4. do you what in the evening usually do
   Q: ____________________
   A: My family and I ____________________ (almost always / go online)
5. go how often you do to the gym
   Q: ____________________
   A: I ____________________ (never)

2 Questions with *how*; short answers

page 40

- Don't confuse *good* and *well*. Use the adjective *good* with *be* and the adverb *well* with other verbs: How **good** are you at soccer? BUT How **well** do you play soccer?

Complete the questions with *How* and a word from the box. Then match the questions and the answers.

good long often well

1. __________ do you lift weights? _____
2. __________ do you play basketball? _____
3. __________ are you at volleyball? _____
4. __________ do you spend at the gym? _____

a. Not very well, but I love it.
b. About six hours a week.
c. Not very often. I prefer martial arts.
d. Pretty good, but I hate it.

UNIT 7

1 Simple past page 45

- Use *did* with the base form – not the past form – of the main verb in questions: How **did** you **spend** the weekend? (NOT: ~~How did you spent~~ . . .?)
- Use *didn't* with the base form in negative statements: We **didn't go** shopping. (NOT: ~~We didn't went shopping.~~)

Complete the conversation.

A: ___Did___ you ___have___ (have) a good weekend?
B: Yes, I ________ . I ________ (have) a great time. My sister and I ________ (go) shopping on Saturday. We ________ (spend) all day at the mall.
A: ________ you ________ (buy) anything special?
B: I ________ (buy) a new laptop. And I ________ (get) some new clothes, too.
A: Lucky you! What clothes ________ you ________ (buy)?
B: Well, I ________ (need) some new boots. I ________ (get) some great ones at Great Times Department Store. What about you? What ________ you ________ (do) on Saturday?
A: I ________ (not, do) anything special. I ________ (stay) home and ________ (work) around the house. Oh, but I ________ (see) a really good movie on TV. And then I ________ (make) dinner with my mother. I actually ________ (enjoy) the day.

2 Past of *be* page 47

Present		Past
am/is	→	**was**
are	→	**were**

Rewrite the sentences. Find another way to write each sentence using *was, wasn't, were,* or *weren't* and the words in parentheses.

1. Bruno didn't come to class yesterday. (in class)
   Bruno wasn't in class yesterday.
2. He worked all day. (at work)
   ____
3. Bruno and his co-workers worked on Saturday, too. (at work)
   ____
4. They didn't go to work on Sunday. (at work)
   ____
5. Did Bruno stay home on Sunday? (at home)
   ____
6. Where did Bruno go on Sunday? (on Sunday)
   ____
7. He and his brother went to a baseball game. (at a baseball game)
   ____
8. They stayed at the park until 7:00. (at the park)
   ____

UNIT 8

1 *There is, there are; one, any, some* page 51

- Don't use a contraction in a short answer with *Yes*: Is there a hotel near here? Yes, **there is**. (NOT: ~~Yes, there's~~.)
- Use *some* in affirmative statements and *any* in negative statements: There are **some** grocery stores in my neighborhood, but there aren't **any** restaurants. Use *any* in most questions: Are there **any** nice stores around here?

Complete the conversations. Choose the correct words.

1. **A:** **Is** / **Are** there any supermarkets in this neighborhood?
   B: No, there **isn't** / **aren't**, but there are **one** / **some** on Main Street.
   A: And **is** / **are** there a post office near here?
   B: Yes, **there's** / **there is**. It's across from the bank.
2. **A:** **Is** / **Are** there a gas station around here?
   B: Yes, **there's** / **there are** one behind the shopping center.
   A: Great! And are there **a** / **any** coffee shops nearby?
   B: Yes, there's a good **one** / **some** in the shopping center.

2 Quantifiers; *how many* and *how much* page 54

- Use *a lot* with both count and noncount nouns: Are there many traffic lights on First Avenue? Yes, there are **a lot**. Is there much traffic? Yes, there's **a lot**.
- Use *any* – not *none* – in negative statements: How much traffic is there on your street? There **isn't any**. = There**'s none**. (NOT: ~~There isn't none~~.)
- Use *How many* with count nouns: **How many books** do you have?
- Use *How much* with noncount nouns: **How much traffic** is there?

A Complete the conversations. Choose the correct words.

1. **A:** Is there **many** / **much** traffic in your city?
   B: Well, there's **a few** / **a little**.
2. **A:** Are there **many** / **much** Wi-Fi hotspots around here?
   B: No, there aren't **many** / **none**.
3. **A:** **How many** / **How much** restaurants are there in your neighborhood?
   B: There **is** / **are** a lot.
4. **A:** **How many** / **How much** noise **is** / **are** there in your city?
   B: There's **much** / **none**. It's very quiet.

B Write questions with the words in parentheses. Use *much* or *many*.

1. **A:** *Is there much pollution in your neighborhood?* (pollution)
   B: No, there isn't. My neighborhood is very clean.
2. **A:** ______________________________ (parks)
   B: Yes, there are. They're great for families.
3. **A:** ______________________________ (crime)
   B: There's none. It's a very safe part of the city.
4. **A:** ______________________________ (laundromats)
   B: There aren't any. A lot of people have their own washing machines.

UNIT 9

1 Describing people page 59

- Use *have* or *is* to describe eye and hair color: I **have** brown hair. = My hair **is** brown. He **has** blue eyes. = His eyes **are** blue.
- Don't confuse *How* and *What* in questions: **How** tall are you? (NOT: ~~What tall are you?~~) **What** color is your hair? (NOT: ~~How color is your hair?~~)

Unscramble the questions. Then write answers using the phrases in the box.

blond	brown eyes	contact lenses
✓ tall and good-looking	6 foot 2	26 – two years older than me

A: brother like look what your does
What does your brother look like?
B: *He's tall and good-looking.*
A: tall is how he
____
B: _______________
A: he does glasses wear
____
B: _______________
A: what hair color his is
____
B: _______________
A: he does blue have eyes
____
B: _______________
A: old he how is
____
B: _______________

2 Modifiers with participles and prepositions page 62

- Don't use a form of *be* in modifiers with participles: Sylvia is the woman **standing** near the window. (NOT: ~~Sylvia is the woman is standing near the window.~~)

Rewrite the conversations. Use the words in parentheses and *one* or *ones*.

1. **A:** Who's Carla? — **A:** *Which one is Carla?* (which)
   B: She's the woman in the red dress. — **B:** _______________ (wearing)
2. **A:** Who are your neighbors? — **A:** _______________ (which)
   B: They're the people with the baby. — **B:** _______________ (walking)
3. **A:** Who's Jeff? — **A:** _______________ (which)
   B: He's the man wearing glasses. — **B:** _______________ (with)

UNIT 10

1 Present perfect; *already, yet* page 65

- Use the present perfect for actions that happened some time in the past.
- Use *yet* in questions and negative statements: Have you checked your email **yet**? No, I haven't turned on my computer **yet**. Use *already* in affirmative statements: I've **already** checked my email.

A Complete the conversations with the present perfect of the verbs in parentheses and short answers.

1. **A:** ___Has___ Leslie ___called___ (call) you lately?
   B: No, she ________ (not call) me, but I ________ (get) some emails from her.
2. **A:** ________ you and Jan ________ (have) lunch yet?
   B: No, we ________. We're thinking of going to Tony's. ________ you ________ (try) it yet? Come with us.
   A: Thanks. I ________ (not eat) there yet, but I ________ (hear) it's pretty good.

B Look at things Matt said. Put the adverb in the correct place in the second sentence.

1. I'm very hungry. I haven't eaten ^yet. (yet)
2. I don't need any groceries. I've gone shopping. (already)
3. What have you done? Have you been to the zoo? (yet)
4. I called my parents before dinner. I've talked to them. (already)

2 Present perfect vs. simple past page 66

- Don't mention a specific time with the present perfect: I'**ve been** to a jazz club. Use the simple past to say when a past action happened: I **went** to a jazz club **last night**.

Complete the conversation using the present perfect or the simple past of the verbs in parentheses and short answers.

1. **A:** ___Did___ you ___see___ (see) the game last night? I really ________ (enjoy) it.
   B: Yes, I ________. It ________ (be) an amazing game. ________ you ever ________ (go) to a game?
   A: No, I ________. I ________ never ________ (be) to the stadium. But I'd love to go!
   B: Maybe we can go to a game next year.
2. **A:** ________ you ever ________ (be) to Franco's Restaurant?
   B: Yes, I ________. My friend and I ________ (eat) there last weekend. How about you?
   A: No, I ________. But I ________ (hear) it's very good.
   B: Oh, yes – it's excellent!

3 *For* and *since* page 67

- Use *for* + a period of time to describe how long a present condition has been true: We've been in New York **for two months**. (= We arrived two months ago.)
- Use *since* + a point in time to describe when a present condition started: We've been here **since August**. (= We've been here from August to now.)

Choose the correct word.

1. I bought my car almost 10 years ago. I've had it **for** / **since** almost 10 years.
2. The Carters moved to Seattle six months ago. They've lived there **for** / **since** six months.
3. I've wanted to see that movie **for** / **since** a long time. It's been in theaters **for** / **since** March.

UNIT 11

1 Adverbs before adjectives page 73

- Use *a/an* with (adverb) + adjective + singular noun: It's **a very modern city**. It's **an expensive city**. Don't use *a/an* with (adverb) + adjective: It's **really interesting**. (NOT: ~~It's a really interesting~~.)

Read the sentences. Add *a* or *an* where it's necessary to complete the sentences.

1. Brasília is ^an extremely modern city.
2. Seoul is very interesting place.
3. Santiago is pretty exciting city to visit.
4. Montreal is beautiful city, and it's fairly old.
5. London has really busy airport.

2 Conjunctions page 73

- Use *and* for additional information: The food is delicious, **and** it's not expensive.
- Use *but, though,* and *however* for contrasting information: The food is delicious, **but** it's very expensive./The food is delicious. It's expensive, **though/however**.

Choose the correct word.

1. Spring in my city is pretty nice, **and** / **but** it gets extremely hot in summer.
2. There are some great museums. They're always crowded, **and** / **however**.
3. There are a lot of interesting stores, **and** / **but** many of them aren't expensive.
4. There are many amazing restaurants, **and** / **but** some are closed in August.
5. My city is a great place to visit. Don't come in summer, **but** / **though**!

3 Modal verbs *can* and *should* page 75

- Use *can* to talk about things that are possible: Where **can** I get some nice souvenirs? Use *should* to suggest things that are good to do: You **should** try the local restaurants.
- Use the base form with *can* and *should* – not the infinitive: Where **can I get** some nice souvenirs? (NOT: ~~Where can I to get . . .?~~) **You should try** the local restaurants. (NOT: ~~You should to try . . .~~)

Complete the conversation with *can, can't, should,* or *shouldn't*.

A: I ___can't___ decide where to go on vacation. ______ I go to Costa Rica or Hawaii?
B: You ______ definitely visit Costa Rica.
A: Really? What can I see there?
B: Well, San Jose is an exciting city. You ______ miss the Museo del Oro. That's the gold museum, and you ______ see beautiful animals made of gold.
A: OK. What else ______ I do there?
B: Well, you ______ visit the museum on Mondays. It's closed then. But you ______ definitely visit the rain forest. It's amazing!

UNIT 12

1 Adjective + infinitive; noun + infinitive

page 79

■ In negative statements, *not* comes before the infinitive: With a cold, it's important **not to exercise** too hard. (NOT: ~~With a cold, it's important **to don't exercise** too hard.~~)

Rewrite the sentences using the words in parentheses. Add *not* when necessary.

1. For a bad headache, you should relax and close your eyes. (a good idea)
   It's a good idea to relax and close your eyes when you have a headache.
2. You should put some cold tea on that sunburn. (sometimes helpful)
   ______
3. For a backache, you should take some pain medicine. (important)
   ______
4. For a cough, you shouldn't drink milk. (important)
   ______
5. For a cold, you should take a hot bath. (sometimes helpful)
   ______
6. When you feel stressed, you shouldn't drink a lot of coffee. (a good idea)
   ______

2 Modal verbs *can, could,* and *may* for requests; suggestions

page 81

■ In requests, *can*, *could*, and *may* have the same meaning. *May* is a little more formal than *can* and *could*.

Number the lines of the conversation. Then write the conversation below.

______ Hi. Yes, please. What do you suggest for itchy skin?
______ Here you are. Can I help you with anything else?
______ Sure I can. You should see a dentist!
__1__ Hello. May I help you?
______ You should try this lotion.
______ Yes. Can you suggest something for a toothache?
______ OK. And could I have a bottle of pain medicine?

A: *Hello. May I help you?*
B: ______
A: ______
B: ______
A: ______
B: ______
A: ______

UNIT 13

1 *So, too, neither, either* page 87

- Use *so* or *too* after an affirmative statement: I'm crazy about sushi. **So** am I./I am, **too**.
- Use *neither* or *not either* after a negative statement: I don't like fast food. **Neither** do I./I don't **either**.
- With *so* and *neither*, the verb comes before the subject: **So am I.** (NOT: ~~So I am~~.) **Neither do I.** (NOT: ~~Neither I do~~.)

A Choose the correct response to show that B agrees with A.

1. **A:** I'm in the mood for something salty.
   B: **I am, too.** (circled) / **I do, too.**
2. **A:** I can't stand fast food.
   B: **Neither do I. / I can't either.**
3. **A:** I really like Korean food.
   B: **So do I. / I am, too.**
4. **A:** I don't eat French food very often.
   B: **I do, too. / I don't either.**
5. **A:** I'm not crazy about chocolate.
   B: **I am, too. / Neither am I.**

B Write responses to show agreement with these statements.

1. **A:** I'm not a very good cook.
   B: ______________________________
2. **A:** I love french fries.
   B: ______________________________
3. **A:** I can't eat very spicy food.
   B: ______________________________
4. **A:** I never eat bland food.
   B: ______________________________
5. **A:** I can make delicious desserts.
   B: ______________________________

2 Modal verbs *would* and *will* for requests page 89

- Don't confuse *like* and *would like*. *Would like* means "want."
- You can also use *I'll have . . .* when ordering in a restaurant to mean *I will have . . .*

Complete the conversation with *would*, *I'd*, or *I'll*.

A: ___Would___ you like to order now?
B: Yes, please. __________ have the shrimp curry.
A: __________ you like noodles or rice with that?
B: Hmm, __________ have rice.
A: And __________ you like a salad, too?
B: No, thanks.
A: __________ you like anything else?
B: Yes, __________ like a cup of green tea.

UNIT 14

1 Comparisons with adjectives page 93

- Use the comparative form (adjective + *-er* or *more* + adjective) to compare two people, places, or things: Which river is **longer**, the Nile or the Amazon? The Nile is **longer than** the Amazon. Use the superlative form (*the* + adjective + *-est* or *the most* + adjective) to compare three or more people, places, or things: Which river is **the longest**: the Nile, the Amazon, or the Mississippi? The Nile is **the longest** river in the world.
- You can use a comparative or superlative without repeating the noun: Which country is **larger**, Canada or China? Canada is **larger**. What's the highest waterfall in the world? Angel Falls is **the highest**.

Write questions with the words. Then look at the underlined words, and write the answers.

1. Which desert / dry / the Sahara or <u>the Atacama</u>?
   Q: *Which desert is drier, the Sahara or the Atacama?*
   A: *The Atacama is drier than the Sahara.*
2. Which island / large / <u>Greenland</u>, New Guinea, or Honshu?
   Q: ____________________
   A: ____________________
3. Which island / small / New Guinea or <u>Honshu</u>?
   Q: ____________________
   A: ____________________
4. Which U.S. city / large / Los Angeles, Chicago, or <u>New York</u>?
   Q: ____________________
   A: ____________________
5. Which ocean / deep / the Atlantic or <u>the Pacific</u>?
   Q: ____________________
   A: ____________________

2 Questions with *how* page 96

- Use *high* to describe mountains and waterfalls: How **high** is Mount Fuji? Angel Falls is 979 meters **high**. Use *tall* to describe buildings: How **tall** is the Empire State Building? (NOT: ~~How high is the Empire State Building?~~)

Complete the questions with the phrases in the box. There is one extra phrase.

How big	How cold	✓ How deep	How high	How tall

1. **Q:** *How deep* is Lake Baikal? **A:** It's 1,642 meters (5,387 feet) at its deepest point.
2. **Q:** ______ is Alaska? **A:** It's 1,717,900 square kilometers (663,300 square miles).
3. **Q:** ______ is Denali? **A:** It's 6,190 meters (20,310 feet) high.
4. **Q:** ______ is the Tokyo Skytree? **A:** It is 634 meters (2,080 feet) tall.

UNIT 15

1 Future with present continuous and *be going to* page 101

- Use the present continuous to talk about something that is happening now: What **are** you **doing**? I'**m studying**. You can also use the present continuous with time expressions to talk about the future: What **are** you **doing tomorrow**? I'**m working.**
- Use *be going to* to talk about the future: I'**m going to** see an old school friend tomorrow.

A Read the sentences. Are they present or future? Write **P** or **F**.

1. Why are you wearing shorts? It's cold. ___P___
2. What are you wearing to the party on Friday? ______
3. What are you doing this weekend? ______
4. What are you doing? Can you please see who's at the door? ______
5. Are you going to see a movie tonight? ______

B Complete the conversations. Use *be going to*.

1. **A:** What ___are___ you and Tony going to ___do___ (do) tonight?
   B: We __________ (try) the new Chinese restaurant. Do you want to come?
   A: I'd love to. What time __________ you __________ (go)?
   B: We __________ (meet) at Tony's house at 7:00. And don't forget an umbrella. The weather forecast says it __________ (rain) tonight.
2. **A:** Where __________ you __________ (go) on vacation this year?
   B: I __________ (visit) my cousins in Paris. It __________ (be) great!
   A: Well, I __________ (not go) anywhere this year. I __________ (stay) home.
   B: That's not so bad. Just think about all the money you __________ (save)!

2 Messages with *tell* and *ask* page 103

- In messages with a request, use the infinitive of the verb: Please ask her **to meet** me at noon. (NOT: ~~Please ask her meet me at noon~~.)
- In messages with negative infinitives, *not* goes before *to* in the infinitive: Could you ask him **not to be** late? (NOT: ~~Could you ask him to don't be late~~?)

Read the messages. Ask someone to pass them on. Use the words in parentheses.

1. Message: Patrick – We don't have class tomorrow. (please)
   Please tell Patrick that we don't have class tomorrow.
2. Message: Ana – Wait for me after class. (would)
   ____
3. Message: Alex – The concert on Saturday has been canceled. (would)
   ____
4. Message: Sarah – Don't forget to return the book to the library. (could)
   ____

UNIT 16

1 Describing changes page 107

- You can use several tenses to describe change – present tense, past tense, and present perfect.

A Complete the sentences with the information in the box. Use the present perfect of the verbs given.

buy a house | **change her hairstyle** | **join a gym** | **start looking for a new job**

1. Chris and Brittany ____________________. Their apartment was too small.
2. Josh ____________________. The one he has now is too stressful.
3. Shawna ____________________. Everyone says it's more stylish.
4. Max ____________________. He feels healthier now.

B Rewrite the sentences using the present tense and the words in parentheses.

1. Holly doesn't wear jeans anymore. *She wears dresses.* (dresses)
2. They don't live in the city anymore. ____________________ (in the suburbs)
3. Jackie isn't so shy anymore. ____________________ (more outgoing)
4. I don't eat greasy food anymore. ____________________ (healthier food)

2 Verb + infinitive page 109

- Use the infinitive after a verb to describe future plans or things you want to happen: I **want to learn** Spanish.

Complete the conversation with the verbs in parentheses in the correct form.

A: Hey, Zach. What *are you going to do* (go / do) after graduation?
B: Well, I ____________________ (plan / stay) here in the city for a few months.
A: Really? I ____________________ (want / go) home. I'm ready for my mom's cooking.
B: I understand that, but my boss says I can keep my job for the summer. So I ____________________ (want / work) a lot of hours because I ____________________ (hope / make) enough money for a new car.
A: But you don't need a car in the city.
B: I ____________________ (not plan / be) here for very long. In the fall, I ____________________ (go / drive) across the country. I really ____________________ (want / live) in California.
A: California? Where in California ____________________ (like / live)?
B: In Hollywood, of course. I ____________________ (go / be) a movie star!

Grammar plus answer key

Unit 1

1 Statements with *be*; possessive adjectives

1. This **is** Dulce Castelo**.** **She's** a new student from Santo Domingo.
2. My name **is** Sergio. **I'm** from Brazil.
3. My brother and I **are** students here. **Our** names are Nate and Chad.
4. **He's** Kento. **He's** 19 years old.
5. **They're** in my English class. **It's** a big class.

2 Wh-questions with *be*

2. e 3. a 4. b 5. c 6. d

3 Yes/No questions and short answers with *be*

1. A: Are they in your class?
   B: No, **they're not** / **they aren't**. They're in English 2.
2. A: Hi! **Are you** in this class?
   B: Yes, **I am**. I'm a new student here.
3. A: **Are you** from the United States?
   B: No, **we're not** / **we aren't**. We're from Calgary, Canada.
4. A: Hi, Monica. **Are you** free?
   B: No, **I'm not**. I'm on my way to class.
5. A: That's the new student. **Is he** from Paraguay?
   B: No, **he's not** / **he isn't**. He's from Uruguay.
6. A: **Is she** from Indonesia?
   B: Yes, **she is**. She's from Jakarta.

Unit 2

1 Simple present Wh-questions and statements

1. A: I **have** good news! Mona **has** a new job.
   B: How **does** she **like** it?
   A: She **loves** it. The hours are great.
   B: What time **does** she **start**?
   A: She **starts** at ten and **finishes** at four.
2. A: What **do** you **do**?
   B: I'm a teacher.
   A: What **do** you **teach**?
   B: I **teach** Spanish and English.
   A: Really? My sister **teaches** English, too.

2 Time expressions

B: I love it, but the hours are difficult. I start work **at** 6:30 A.M., and I work **until** 3:30.
A: That's interesting! I work the same hours, but I work **at** night. I start **at** 6:30 **in** the evening and finish **at** 3:30 **in** the morning.
B: Wow! What time do you get up?
A: Well, I get home **at** 4:30 and go to bed **at** 5:30. And I sleep **until** 2:00. But I only work **on** weekends, so it's OK. What about you?
B: Oh, I work **on** Monday, Wednesday, and Friday. And I get up **early** – around 5:00 A.M.

Unit 3

1 Demonstratives; *one, ones*

1. A: Excuse me. How much are **these** shoes?
   B: **They're** $279.
   A: And how much is **that** bag over there?
   B: **It's** only $129.
   A: And are the two gray **ones** $129, too?
   B: No. **Those** are only $119.
   A: Oh! **This** store is really expensive.
2. A: Can I help you?
   B: Yes, please. I really like **those** jeans over there. How much **are they**?
   A: Which **ones**? Do you mean **these**?
   B: No, the black **ones**.
   A: Let me look. Oh, **they're** $35.99.
   B: That's not bad. And how much is **this** sweater here?
   A: **It's** only $9.99.

2 Preferences; comparisons with adjectives

A

2. happier
3. more exciting
4. friendlier
5. more interesting
6. more reasonable
7. sadder
8. warmer

B

2. I like the silver one (better). It's more interesting.
3. I prefer the silk one. It's prettier.
4. I like the purple ones (more). They're cheaper.

Unit 4

1 Simple present questions; short answers

A

2. A: **Does John like** Carrie Underwood?
   B: No, **he doesn't**. John doesn't like country music.
3. A: **Does Lisa like** talk shows?
   B: Yes, **she does**. Lisa is a big fan of them.
4. A: **Do you / you and Kevin watch** the news on TV?
   B: Yes, **we do**. Kevin and I watch the news every night.
5. A: **Do you like** hip-hop?
   B: No, **I don't**. But I love R&B.
6. A: **Do your parents listen to** jazz?
   B: No, **they don't**. But my parents listen to a lot of classical music.

B

2. us 3. them 4. him 5. her

2 *Would*; verb + *to* + verb

A: Would you like to see a movie with me tonight?
B: Yes, I would. What would you like to see?
A: I'd like to see the new Matt Damon movie.

Unit 5

1 Present continuous

1. A: Really? **Is she living abroad?**
   B: Yes, **she is**. She**'s living** / **is living** in South Korea.
2. A: **How are you spending your summer?**
   B: **I'm working** part-time. **I'm taking** two classes also.
   A: **What are you taking?**
   B: My friend and I **are studying** photography and Japanese. We like our classes a lot.

2 Quantifiers

2. Nearly all students finish high school.
3. All children start school by the age of six.
4. A lot of couples have more than one child.
5. Few families have more than four children.

Unit 6

1 Adverbs of frequency

1. A: **I often play sports.**
2. Q: **Do you ever go jogging with a friend?**
   A: No, **I always jog / go jogging alone.**
3. Q: **How often do you play basketball?**
   A: **I play (basketball) four times a week.**
4. Q: **What do you usually do in the evening?**
   A: My family and I **almost always go online.**
5. Q: **How often do you go to the gym?**
   A: I **never go (to the gym).**

2 Questions with *how*; short answers

1. **How often** do you lift weights? c
2. **How well** do you play basketball? a
3. **How good** are you at volleyball? d
4. **How long** do you spend at the gym? b

Unit 7

1 Simple past

B: Yes, I **did**. I **had** a great time. My sister and I **went** shopping on Saturday. We **spent** all day at the mall.
A: **Did** you **buy** anything special?
B: I **bought** a new laptop. And I **got** some new clothes, too.
A: Lucky you! What clothes **did** you **buy**?
B: Well, I **needed** some new boots. I **got** some great ones at Great Times Department Store. What about you? What **did** you **do** on Saturday?
A: I **didn't do** anything special. I **stayed** home and **worked** around the house. Oh, but I **saw** a really good movie on TV. And then I **made** dinner with my mother. I actually **enjoyed** the day.

2 Past of *be*

2. He was at work all day.
3. Bruno and his co-workers were at work on Saturday, too.
4. They weren't at work on Sunday.
5. Was Bruno at home on Sunday?
6. Where was Bruno on Sunday?
7. He and his brother were at a baseball game.
8. They were at the park until 7:00.

Unit 8

1 *There is, there are; one, any, some*

1. A: **Are** there any supermarkets in this neighborhood?
   B: No, there **aren't**, but there are **some** on Main Street.
   A: And **is** there a post office near here?
   B: Yes, **there is**. It's across from the bank.
2. A: **Is** there a gas station around here?
   B: Yes, **there's** one behind the shopping center.
   A: Great! And are there **any** coffee shops nearby?
   B: Yes, there's a good **one** in the shopping center.

2 Quantifiers; *how many* and *how much*

A

1. A: Is there **much** traffic in your city?
   B: Well, there's a **little**.
2. A: Are there **many** Wi-Fi hotspots around here?
   B: No, there aren't **many**.
3. A: **How many** restaurants are there in your neighborhood?
   B: There **are** a lot.
4. A: **How much** noise **is** there in your city?
   B: There's **none**. It's very quiet

B

2. A: Are there many parks (in your neighborhood)?
3. A: Is there much crime (in your neighborhood)?
4. A: Are there many laundromats (in your neighborhood)?

Unit 9

1 Describing people

A: How tall is he?
B: He's 6 foot 2.
A: Does he wear glasses?
B: No, he doesn't. He wears contact lenses.
A: What color is his hair?
B: He has blond hair.
A: Does he have blue eyes?
B: No, he has brown eyes.
A: How old is he?
B: He's 26 – two years older than me.

2 Modifiers with participles and prepositions

1. B: She's the one wearing a red dress.
2. A: Which ones are your neighbors?
   B: They're the ones walking with the baby.
3. A: Which one is Jeff?
   B: He's the one with glasses.

Unit 10

1 Present perfect; *already, yet*

A

1. B: No, she **hasn't called** me, but I**'ve gotten** some emails from her.
2. A: **Have** you and Jan **had** lunch yet?
   B: No, we **haven't**. We're thinking of going to Tony's. **Have** you **tried** it yet? Come with us.
   A: Thanks. I **haven't eaten** there yet, but I**'ve heard** it's pretty good.

B

2. I've **already** gone shopping.
3. Have you been to the zoo **yet**?
4. I've **already** talked to them./I've talked to them **already**.

2 Present perfect vs. simple past

1. A: Did you see the game last night? I really **enjoyed** it.
   B: Yes, I **did**. It **was** an amazing game. **Have** you ever **gone** to a game?
   A: No, I **haven't**. I**'ve** never **been** to the stadium. But I'd love to go!
   B: Maybe we can go to a game next year.
2. A: **Have** you ever **been** to Franco's Restaurant?
   B: Yes, I **have**. My friend and I **ate** there last weekend. How about you?
   A: No, I **haven't**. But I**'ve heard** it's very good.
   B: Oh, yes – it's excellent!

3 *For* and *since*

1. I've had it **for** almost 10 years.
2. They've lived there **for** six months.
3. I've wanted to see that movie **for** a long time. It's been in theaters **since** March.

Unit 11

1 Adverbs before adjectives

2. Seoul is **a** very interesting place.
3. Santiago is **a** pretty exciting city to visit.
4. Montreal is **a** beautiful city, and it's fairly old.
5. London has **a** really busy airport.

2 Conjunctions

1. Spring in my city is pretty nice, **but** it gets extremely hot in summer.
2. There are some great museums. They're always crowded, **however**.
3. There are a lot of interesting stores, **and** many of them aren't expensive.
4. There are many amazing restaurants, **but** some are closed in August.
5. My city is a great place to visit. Don't come in summer, **though**!

3 Modal verbs *can* and *should*

A: I **can't** decide where to go on vacation. **Should** I go to Costa Rica or Hawaii?
B: You **should** definitely visit Costa Rica.
A: Really? What can I see there?
B: Well, San Jose is an exciting city. You **shouldn't** miss the Museo del Oro. That's the gold museum, and you **can** see beautiful animals made of gold.
A: OK. What else **can** / **should** I do there?
B: Well, you **can't** visit the museum on Mondays. It's closed then. But you **should** definitely visit the rain forest. It's amazing!

Unit 12

1 Adjective + infinitive; noun + infinitive

Possible answers:

2. For a sunburn, **it's sometimes helpful to put** some cold tea on it.
3. For a backache, **it's important to take** some pain medicine.
4. For a cough, **it's important not to drink** milk.
5. For a cold, **it's sometimes helpful to take** a hot bath.
6. When you feel stressed, **it's a good idea not to drink** a lot of coffee.

2 Modal verbs *can, could,* and *may* for requests; suggestions

2. Yes, please. What do you suggest for itchy skin?
3. You should try this lotion.
4. OK. And could I have a bottle of pain medicine?
5. Here you are. Can I help you with anything else?
6. Yes. Can you suggest something for a toothache?
7. Sure I can. You should see a dentist!

Unit 13

1 ***So, too, neither, either***

A

2. B: I can't either.
3. B: So do I.
4. B: I don't either.
5. B: Neither am I.

B

1. B: I'm not either./Neither am I.
2. B: I do, too./So do I.
3. B: I can't either./Neither can I.
4. B: I don't either./Neither do I.
5. B: I can, too./So can I.

2 **Modal verbs *would* and *will* for requests**

B: I'll
A: Would
B: I'll
A: would
A: Would
B: I'd

Unit 14

1 **Comparisons with adjectives**

2. Q: Which island is the largest: Greenland, New Guinea, or Honshu?
   A: Greenland is the largest.
3. Q: Which island is smaller, New Guinea or Honshu?
   A: Honshu is smaller than New Guinea.
4. Q: Which U.S. city is the largest: Los Angeles, Chicago, or New York?
   A: New York is the largest.
5. Q: Which ocean is deeper, the Atlantic or the Pacific?
   A: The Pacific is deeper than the Atlantic.

2 **Questions with *how***

2. How big
3. How high
4. How tall

Unit 15

1 **Future with present continuous and *be going to***

A

2. F
3. F
4. P
5. F

B

1. B: We**'re going to try** the new Chinese restaurant. Do you want to come?
   A: I'd love to. What time **are** you **going to go**?
   B: We**'re going to meet** at Tony's house at 7:00. And don't forget an umbrella. The weather forecast says it**'s going to rain** tonight.
2. A: Where **are** you **going to go** on vacation this year?
   B: I**'m going to visit** my cousins in Paris. It**'s going to be** great!
   A: Well, I**'m not going to go** anywhere this year. I**'m going to stay** home.
   B: That's not so bad. Just think about all the money you**'re going to save**!

2 **Messages with *tell* and *ask***

2. Would you ask Ana to wait for me after class?
3. Would you tell Alex (that) the concert on Saturday has been canceled?
4. Could you tell Sarah not to forget to return the book to the library?

Unit 16

1 **Describing changes**

A

1. Chris and Brittany **have bought a house**.
2. Josh **has started looking for a new job**.
3. Shawn **has changed her hairstyle**.
4. Max **has joined a gym**.

B

2. They live in the suburbs.
3. Jackie/She is more outgoing.
4. I eat healthier food now.

2 **Verb + infinitive**

B: Well, I **plan to stay** here in the city for a few months.
A: Really? I **want to go** home. I'm ready for my mom's cooking.
B: I understand that, but my boss says I can keep my job for the summer. So I **want to work** a lot of hours because I **hope to make** enough money for a new car.
A: But you don't need a car in the city.
B: I **don't plan to be** here for very long. In the fall, I**'m going to drive** across the country. I really **want to live** in California.
A: California? Where in California **would you like to live**?
B: In Hollywood, of course. I**'m going to be** a movie star!

Appendix

Countries, nationalities, and languages

This is a partial list of countries, nationalities, and languages, many of which are presented in this book.

Countries	Nationalities
Argentina	Argentine
Australia	Australian
Austria	Austrian
Bolivia	Bolivian
Brazil	Brazilian
Canada	Canadian
Chile	Chilean
China	Chinese
Colombia	Colombian
Costa Rica	Costa Rican
Ecuador	Ecuadorian
Egypt	Egyptian
England	English
France	French

Countries	Nationalities
Germany	German
Greece	Greek
Hungary	Hungarian
India	Indian
Indonesia	Indonesian
Ireland	Irish
Italy	Italian
Japan	Japanese
Lebanon	Lebanese
Malaysia	Malaysian
Mexico	Mexican
Morocco	Moroccan
New Zealand	New Zealander
Peru	Peruvian

Countries	Nationalities
the Philippines	Filipino
Poland	Polish
Russia	Russian
Saudi Arabia	Saudi Arabian
Singapore	Singaporean
South Korea	Korean
Spain	Spanish
Switzerland	Swiss
Thailand	Thai
Turkey	Turkish
the United Kingdom (the U.K.)	British
the United States (the U.S.)	American
Uruguay	Uruguayan
Vietnam	Vietnamese

Irregular verbs

Present	Past	Participle
(be) am/is, are	was, were	been
bring	brought	brought
buy	bought	bought
come	came	come
cut	cut	cut
do	did	done
drink	drank	drunk
drive	drove	driven
eat	ate	eaten
fall	fell	fallen
feel	felt	felt
fly	flew	flown
get	got	gotten
give	gave	given
go	went	gone
grow	grew	grown
have	had	had
hear	heard	heard
keep	kept	kept
lose	lost	lost

Present	Past	Participle
make	made	made
meet	met	met
put	put	put
quit	quit	quit
read	read	read
ride	rode	ridden
run	ran	run
see	saw	seen
sell	sold	sold
set	set	set
sit	sat	sat
sleep	slept	slept
speak	spoke	spoken
spend	spent	spent
take	took	taken
teach	taught	taught
tell	told	told
think	thought	thought
wear	wore	worn
write	wrote	written

Comparative and superlative adjectives

Adjectives with *-er* and *-est*

big	deep	heavy	nice	small
busy	dirty	high	old	tall
cheap	dry	hot	pretty	thin
clean	easy	large	quiet	ugly
cold	fast	light	safe	warm
cool	friendly	long	short	wet
dark	funny	new	slow	young

Adjectives with *more* and *most*

attractive	dangerous	expensive	outgoing
beautiful	delicious	famous	popular
boring	difficult	important	relaxing
crowded	exciting	interesting	stressful

Irregular adjectives

good → better → the best
bad → worse → the worst

1 Language summary

VOCABULARY

Nouns
School subjects
biology
business
chemistry
English
geography
history
literature
math
physical education
physics

Other
actor
birthday
brother
city
class
classmate
college
family
friend
hobby
moon
name
parents
person
planet
semester
sister
space
star
student
teacher
vacation

Pronouns
Subject pronouns
I
you
he
she
it
we
they

Titles
Mr.
Mrs.

Adjectives
Possessives
my
your
his
her
its
our
their

Other
beautiful
cool
exciting
famous
favorite
friendly
good
great
interesting
next
nice
old
popular
same
trendy
unique
unusual

Articles
a
an
the

Verbs
am
are
has
is
love
spell

Adverbs
Responses
no
yes

Other
actually
here
(over) there
not
now
pretty/really/very (+ adjective)

Prepositions
at (2:00/City College)
from (Seoul/South Korea)
in (the morning/the same class)

Conjunctions
and
but
or

EXPRESSIONS

Saying hello
Good morning.
Hey.
Hello.
Hi.
How are you?/How's it going?
(I'm) fine, thanks.
Great.
Pretty good.
OK.
What's up?

Saying good-bye
Bye.
Good-bye.
Good night.
Have a good day.
See you later.
See you tomorrow.
Talk to you later.

Exchanging personal information
What's your name?
I'm . . . /My name is . . .
What's your first/last name?
It's . . .
When's your birthday?
It's . . .
What's . . . like?
He's/She's/It's . . .
What are . . . like?
They're . . .
Where are you from?
I'm/We're from . . .

Introducing someone
This is . . . /These are . . .
Nice to meet you.

Asking about someone
Who's that?
That's . . .
His/Her name is . . .
Who are they?
They're . . .
Their names are . . . and . . .
Where's your friend?
He's/She's . . .

Thanking someone
Thanks.
Thank you.

Checking information
How do you spell . . . ?
Sorry, what's your (first/last) name again?
It's . . .
What do people call you?
Everyone calls me . . .
Please call me . . .

Making suggestions
Let's . . .

Apologizing
(I'm) sorry.

Agreeing
OK.
Sure.
That's right.

2 Language summary

VOCABULARY

Nouns

Jobs/Professions

accountant
babysitter
carpenter
cashier
chef
cook
dancer
dentist
doctor
engineer
fashion designer
firefighter
fitness instructor
flight attendant
front desk clerk
graphic designer
lawyer
mechanic
musician
nurse
office assistant
office manager
pilot
police officer
receptionist
reporter
restaurant host
sales associate
salesperson
security guard
server
singer
social media assistant
social media manager
sociologist
software engineer
taxi driver
teacher
tour guide
tutor
vendor
web designer

Types of jobs

entertainment business
food service
office work
travel industry

Workplaces

(computer) company
hospital
office
restaurant
school
store
university

Other

app
clothes
dessert
dinner
fabrics
fashion design
food
job
lunch
meeting
music
phone
piano
posts
schedule
snack
social media
thing
time
work

Adjectives

boring
different
difficult
exciting
fantastic
favorite
full-time
great
incredible
part-time

Verbs

answer
behave
cook
do
exercise
get (home/up/fit)
go (to bed/to school/
to work)
have (a job/lunch)
know
leave (work/for work)
like
sleep
start
stay up
study
take (care of)
teach
track
wake up
wear
work (in a hospital/
in the afternoon)
write

Adverbs

Response

yeah

Other

a lot
early
exactly
home
late
usually

Prepositions

after (midnight)
around/about (10:00/noon)
at (6:00/night/midnight)
at (a school)
before (noon)
in (a restaurant)
in (the morning/the
afternoon/the evening)
like (= for example)
on (weekdays/Fridays)
until (midnight)

EXPRESSIONS

Talking about school/work

What do you do (exactly/there)?
I'm a/an . . .
Where does he work?
He works in/at/for . . .
How do you like your job/classes?
I like it/them a lot.
I love it/them.
Where do you go to school?
I go to . . .
What's your favorite . . .?
My favorite . . . is . . .

Asking for more information

What time . . .?
Which . . .?
Why?

Talking about daily schedules

What time do you go to work?
I start work at . . .
When do you get home?
I usually get home at . . .

Expressing interest

That's cool.
Really?

Expressing surprise

Wow!

Starting a sentence

Well, . . .
Oh, . . .
So, . . .

3 Language summary

VOCABULARY

Nouns

Clothes and jewelry
backpack
bag
belt
boots
bracelet
dress
earrings
flip-flops
jacket
jeans
ring
shirt
sneakers
socks
suit
sunglasses
sweater
tie
T-shirt
watch

Materials*
cotton
gold
leather
plastic
rubber
silk
silver
wool

Other
acre
armchair
bid
birthday
cent(s)
certificate
(sales) clerk
customer
design
dollar
electric guitar
flea market
headphones
item
land
mug
notebook
opinions
pet rock
phone
present
price
printer
skateboard
style
tablet
(price) tag
treadmill

Pronouns
one
ones

Adjectives

Colors
black
blue
brown
gray
green
orange
pink
purple
red
white
yellow

Other
attractive
boring
cheap
confident
crazy
creative
digital
each
expensive
extraordinary
friendly
happy
hopeful
huge
jealous
light
loving
nice
online
perfect
powerful
pretty
reasonable
sad
stylish
truthful

Verbs

Modal
can

Other
ask
buy
compare
cost
help
look (= seem)
look (at/for)
mean
pay (for)
prefer
say
try (it on)

Adverbs
more
(shop) online

*Names of materials can be used as nouns or adjectives.

EXPRESSIONS

Talking about prices
How much is this/that T-shirt?
  It's . . .
That's not bad.
How much are these/those sneakers?
  They're . . .
That's expensive.

Comparing
It's nicer/more stylish than the black one.

Getting someone's attention
Excuse me.

Offering help
Can I help you?

Identifying things
Which one?
  The blue one.
Which ones?
  The gray ones.

Talking about preferences
Which one do you prefer?
  I prefer the . . . one.
Which ones do you like better/more?
  I like the . . . ones better/more.

Making and declining an offer
Would you like to . . . ?
  Oh, no. That's OK.

Thanking someone
Thanks anyway.
You're welcome.

Expressing doubt
Hmm.

Pausing to think
Let's see . . .

4 Language summary

VOCABULARY

Nouns

Movies
action
horror
musical
science fiction

TV programs
game show
reality show
soap opera
talk show

Music*
classical
country
electronic
funk
hip-hop
jazz
Latin
pop
rap
R&B (rhythm and blues)
reggae
rock
salsa
soul

Musical instruments
guitar
piano
violin

Entertainers
actor
actress
athlete
band
group
musician
performer
rapper
singer
songwriter

Other
album
award
clothing designer
concert
contract
date
fan
hurricane
inauguration
(musical) instrument
kind (of)
(text) message
platinum
record
ticket
victim
video game

Pronouns

Object pronouns
me
you
him
her
it
us
them

Adjectives

free (= not have plans)
million

Verbs

Modal
would

Other
chill out
come
go (out/platinum)
have to (+ verb)
know
meet
need to (+ verb)
play (an instrument)
visit
want to (+ verb)
win

Adverbs

just
never
tomorrow
(not) very much

Prepositions

about
for (dinner)
from . . . to . . .
with (me)

*Names of musical styles can be used as nouns or adjectives.

EXPRESSIONS

Talking about likes and dislikes
Do you like . . . ?
Yes, I do. I like . . . a lot./I love . . .
No, I don't. I don't like . . . very much.
What kind of . . . do you like?
Who's/What's your favorite . . . ?

Inviting someone
Would you like to . . . ?
Do you want to . . . ?
Let's . . .

Accepting an invitation
Yes, I would.
Thanks. I'd love to.

Refusing an invitation
I'd like to, but I have to . . .
I'd like to, but I need to . . .
I'd like to, but I want to . . .

Asking about events
When is it?
Where is it?
What time does it start/end?

5 Language summary

VOCABULARY

Nouns

Family/Relatives
aunt
brother
children
cousin
dad
daughter
father
grandfather
grandmother
husband
mom
mother
nephew
niece
sister
sister-in-law
son
uncle
wife

Other
age
attention
barbecue
college
couple
effort
email
fact
family tree
foreign language
housework
only child
(medical aid)
 organization
people
percent
population
(birthday) present
women

Pronoun

no one

Adjectives

Quantifiers
a lot of
all
few
many
most
nearly all
not many
some

Other
dear (+ name)
lonely
married
old
only (child)
related
rural
stay-at-home (dad)

Verbs

enjoy
get (married)
raise (money)
spend (time)
tell
travel
vote
wait

Adverbs

Time expressions
always
regularly
right now
these days
this year

Other
alone
together

Preposition

of

Conjunction

because

EXPRESSIONS

Asking about family
Do you have any brothers and sisters?
 I have . . . brother(s) and . . . sister(s).
 I'm an only child.
How old is your brother?

Exchanging information about the present
Are you living at home?
 Yes, I am./No, I'm not.
What is your brother doing?
 He's traveling in . . .
What are you/your friends doing these days?
 I'm . . . /They're . . .

Expressing interest
What an interesting . . .

Expressing sincerity
I'm serious!

6 Language summary

VOCABULARY

Nouns

Sports and fitness activities

baseball
basketball
bike riding
bowling
football
golf
ice hockey
jogging
martial arts
Pilates
running
soccer
swimming
tennis
volleyball
walking
weight training/lifting
yoga

Other

athlete
couch potato
country
energy
fitness
fitness freak
free time
fundraiser
gym
gym rat
junk food
serving (= portion of food)
sports nut
talent
teen (= teenager)
tip
treadmill
vitamin

Pronoun

nothing

Adjectives

active
average
fit
good at (something)
healthy
middle-aged
real
regular
tired

Verbs

chat
do (yoga/card tricks)
eat
exercise
keep (fit)
lift weights
play (a sport)
relax
sing
spend (time)
work out

Adverbs

Frequency

almost always
almost never
always
every . . .
hardly ever
never
not very often/much
often
once a . . .
sometimes
three times a . . .
twice a . . .
usually

Other

sometime
well

Prepositions

in (my free time/great shape)
like (that)

EXPRESSIONS

Talking about routines

How often do you . . . ?
Every . . .
Once/Twice/Three times a . . .
Not very often.
Do you ever . . . ?
Yes, I often/sometimes . . .
No, I never/hardly ever . . .
How long do you spend . . . ?
Thirty minutes a day./Two hours a week.

Talking about abilities

How well do you . . . ?
Pretty well.
About average.
Not very well.
How good are you at . . . ?
Pretty good./OK.
Not so good.

Asking for more information

What else . . . ?

Expressing surprise/disbelief

Seriously?

Agreeing

All right.
No problem.

7 Language summary

VOCABULARY

Nouns
architect
building
cable car
chore
cloud
desert
engineer
guide
homework
lake
land art
laundry
(open) market
monument
mountain
neighbor
noise
party
satellite
snorkeling
spaghetti
surfing
swimming
test
tour
town
trip
vacation
waves
weather

Pronouns
anything
something

Adjectives
amazing
breathtaking
broke
ceramic
cloudy
cold
cool
excellent
free-time
giant
handmade
incredible
lucky
manmade
prehistoric
special
spectacular
tiring
whole
windy

Verbs
call
cook
disappear
drive
forget
happen
invite
make (a phone call)
read
stay (home)
stop
take (a day off/photos)
worry

Adverbs
Time expressions
all day/weekend
as usual
last night/week/weekend
the whole time
today
yesterday

Other
also
anywhere
downtown
unfortunately

Prepositions
on (business/vacation)
over (the weekend)

EXPRESSIONS

Asking about past activities
Did you go anywhere last weekend?
  Yes, I did. I . . .
  No, I didn't.
How did you spend . . . ?
How long were you . . . ?
What did you do . . . ?
What time did you . . . ?
Where did you . . . ?
Who did you . . . with?

Giving opinions about past experiences
How did you like . . . ?/How was . . . ?
  It was . . .
What was the best thing about . . . ?
Was the . . . OK?

8 Language summary

VOCABULARY

Nouns

Neighborhood/ Recreational facilities

airport
apartment (building)
ATM
avenue
bank
bookstore
boutique
café
(college) campus
clothing store
coffee shop
concert hall
department store
district
drugstore
electronics store
gas station
grocery store
hair salon
hospital
hotel
laundromat
library
(shopping) mall
(outdoor) market
movie theater
museum
newsstand
park
post office
school
shopping center
stadium
suburbs
theater
(public) transportation
venue
Wi-Fi hot spot
zoo

Other

crime
fashion
festival
haircut
(traffic) light
nightlife
parking
pollution
price
traffic
trash

Adjectives

convenient
creative
expensive
hip
indie (music/movies)
industrial
live (music)
locally made
narrow
perfect
safe

Verbs

check out
drive
dry
wash

Adverb

too (= also)

Prepositions

across from/opposite
around (the world)
between
in back of/behind
in front of
near/close to
next to
on
on the corner of

Conjunction

so

EXPRESSIONS

Asking for and giving locations

Is there a/an . . . near here?
  No, there isn't, but there's one . . .
Are there any . . . around here?
  Yes, there are. There are some . . .
  No, there aren't, but there are some . . .
  No, there aren't any . . . around here.

Asking about quantities

Are there many . . . ?
  Yes, there are a lot.
  Yes, there are a few.
  No, there aren't many.
  No, there aren't any.
  No, there are none.
Is there much . . . ?
  Yes, there's a lot.
  Yes, there's a little.
  No, there isn't much.
  No, there isn't any.
  No, there's none.
How many . . . are there?
  There are . . .

Adding information

By the way, . . .

9 Language summary

VOCABULARY

Nouns
appearance
app/application
astronaut
beard
belt
(baseball) cap
celebrity
centimeter
contact lenses
couple
eye(s)
fashion
foot
girlfriend
glasses
hair
height
hipster
inch
(basketball) jersey
length
logo
looks
meter
mustache
outfit
picture
print
psychologist
selfie
streetwear
window

Adjectives
baggy
bald
blond
boho
casual
classic
comfortable
curly
dark
elderly
flattering
floral
flowy
good-looking
handsome
khaki
leather
long
medium
middle-aged
pastel
physical
preppy
pretty
rude
short
skinny
straight
tall
trendy
young

Verbs
control
describe
learn
orbit
sit
wear

Adverbs
fairly (+ adjective)
pretty (+ adjective)
so (+ adjective)

Prepositions
behind
in (a T-shirt/jeans/her thirties)
next to
on (the couch)
to the left/right of
with (brown hair)

EXPRESSIONS

Asking about appearance

What does she look like?
She's tall.
She has brown hair.
How old is she?
She's about 32.
She's in her thirties.
How tall is she?
She's 1 meter 78.
About 5 foot 10, I suppose.
How long is her hair?
It's pretty short.
What color is his hair?
It's dark/light brown.
Does he wear glasses?
Yes, he does.
No, he wears contacts.

Identifying someone

Who's Diego?
He's the man wearing a blue shirt/talking to Brooke.
Which one is Paula?
She's the one in jeans/near the window.
Which ones are the Harrisons?
They're the people/the ones on the couch.

10 Language summary

VOCABULARY

Nouns
alligator
bathtub
blue cheese
burglar alarm
charity
costume
donation
engine
event
hairstyle
iced coffee
ID (= identification)
jazz club
lines
motorcycle
octopus
shopping
sleepwalk
space center
sports car
sushi
theme park
(traffic) ticket
truck
truffle
uniform
wedding

Adjectives
asleep
awake
current
important
live (concert)
several
valuable

Verbs
be engaged (to someone)
bet
clean
cut
hear
invent
kill
lose
raise
ride
sail
show
take it easy
taste
try

Adverbs
ago
already
extremely
in the past (week)
recently
underground
yet

Prepositions
for (six months/two years)
since (6:45/last weekend/ elementary school)

EXPRESSIONS

Talking about past experiences
Have you ever . . . ?
Have you . . . recently/this week?
Yes, I have./No, I haven't.
Have you/they . . . yet?
Yes, I have. I've (already) . . .
No, they haven't. They haven't . . . (yet).
How many times have you . . . ?
I've . . . once/a couple of times.
How long have you lived here?
I've lived here for/since . . .
How long did you live there?
I lived there for . . .

Expressing uncertainty
I can't decide.

Apologizing
I'm sorry (I'm late).

11 Language summary

VOCABULARY

Nouns
bargain
beach
bike path
canoe
capital
church
crafts
district
(city) guide
harbor
hometown
island
landmark
mangrove
nightclub
plaza
pyramid
salsa (steps)
scenery
subway
tapas
taxi
tourist
town
visitor

Pronoun
you (= anyone)

Adjectives
best
clear
crowded
dangerous
delicious
historic
lively
noisy
polluted
reasonable
safe
spacious
stressful
ugly
walled (city/area)

Verbs
Modal
should

Other
miss
move away
plan to (+ verb)
recommend
rent
tell (someone) about (something)
use

Adverbs
all year
anytime
definitely
easily
extremely (+ adjective)
fairly (+ adjective)
pretty (+ adjective)
really (+ adjective)
somewhat (+ adjective)
too (+ adjective)
very (+ adjective)

Preposition
in (town)

Conjunctions
however
though

EXPRESSIONS

Describing something
What's . . . like?
It's . . . and . . .
It's . . . , but (it's not) . . .
It's . . . It's not (too) . . . , though.
It's . . . It's not (too) . . . , however.

Asking for information
Can you tell me about . . . ?

Talking about advisability
What can I do . . . ?
You can . . .
You can't . . .

Asking for and giving suggestions
What should I . . . ?
You should . . .
You shouldn't . . .

12 Language summary

VOCABULARY

Nouns

Health problems
backache
burn
cold
cough
dry skin
earache
fever
(the) flu
headache
(the) hiccups
insect bite
insomnia
itchy eyes
nosebleed
sore muscles/throat
stomachache
sunburn
toothache
upset stomach

Containers
bag
bottle
box
can
jar
pack
stick
tube

Pharmacy items
bandages
breath mints
cough drops
cream
deodorant
eyedrops
face cream
heating pad
lotion
medication
(pain) medicine
pills
shaving cream
tissues
toothpaste
vitamin C

Other
advice
anthropologist
appointment
chamomile (tea)
community
dentist
energy
garlic (tea)
gel
idea
liquid
medicine cabinet
muscle
plant
rain forest
remedy
research
rest
throat
village

Adjectives
effective
helpful
hungry
itchy
powerful
sick
sore
stressed
terrible
useful

Verbs

Modal
could
may

Other
boil
chop up
concentrate
disappear
get (some rest)
put (= apply directly, as ointment)
rest
see (a doctor/dentist)
suggest
take (medicine/ something for . . .)
treat
work (= succeed)

Prepositions
in (bed)
under (cold water)

EXPRESSIONS

Talking about health problems
Are you all right?
  Not really.
That's too bad.

Offering and accepting assistance
Can/May I help you?
  Yes, please.
Can/Could/May I have . . . ?

Asking for and giving advice
What should you do . . . ?
  It's important/helpful/a good idea to . . .
What do you suggest/have for . . . ?
  Try/I suggest/You should/You could . . .

Expressing dislike
Yuck!

Agreeing
You're right.

13 Language summary

VOCABULARY

Nouns

Food and beverages

bread
(veggie) burger
cake
cheeseburger
chicken
chocolate
corn
curry
dessert
dressing
fish
flavor
french fries
fruit
grains
grapes
hamburger
ice cream
ice-cream cone
lamb
lemon
lemonade
mangoes
meat
miso
octopus
onion (rings/soup)
pasta
peas
(apple) pie
pizza
potatoes
rice
salad
sandwich
seafood
shrimp
soup
strawberries
sushi
turkey
vegetable
water

Other

bellhop
coffee shop
custom
hairstylist
menu
order
review
server
service
slang
tip
wages
waitress

Adjectives

bland
confusing
crispy
customary
delicious
fresh
generous
greasy
healthy
rich
salty
spicy
vegetarian

Verbs

Modals

will
would

Other

order
rely on
take (an order)
tip
vary

Adverbs

a bit (+ adjective)
either
neither
too

EXPRESSIONS

Expressing feelings

I'm (not) crazy about . . .
I'm (not) in the mood for . . .
I can't stand . . .

Agreeing and disagreeing

I'm crazy about . . .
    So am I./I am, too.
    Oh, I'm not.
I can . . .
    So can I./I can, too.
    Really? I can't.
I like . . .
    So do I.
    Oh, I don't (like it very much).
I'm not in the mood for . . .
    Neither am I./I'm not either.
    Really? I am.
I can't . . .
    Neither can I./I can't either.
    Oh, I love it.
I don't like . . .
    Neither do I./I don't either.
    Oh, I like it a lot.

Ordering in a restaurant

May I take your order?
What would you like (to . . .)?
    I'd like/I'll have a/an/the . . .
What kind of . . . would you like?
    I'd like/I'll have . . . , please.
Would you like anything else?
    Yes, please. I'd like . . .
    No, thank you.
    That's all, thanks.

14 Language summary

VOCABULARY

Nouns

Geography

beach
canal
continent
desert
Earth
(the) falls
forest
hill
island
lake
mountain
ocean
river
valley
volcano
waterfall
world

Distance and measurements

degree (Celsius/ Fahrenheit)
(square) kilometer
meter
(square) mile
pound

Other

airport
auction
feather
fine
million
planet
(air) pollution
population
quiz
tower
winter

Adjectives

clean
cold
crowded
deep
dry
far
high
hot
pure
strict

Verbs

exist
get down (to)
get up (to)
respect

Prepositions

in (the summer/the world/the Americas)
on (the planet/sidewalks)

EXPRESSIONS

Talking about distances and measurements

How cold is . . . in the winter?
  It gets down to . . . degrees.
How hot is . . . in the summer?
  It gets up to . . . degrees.
How far is . . . from . . .?
  It's about . . . kilometers.
How big is . . .?
  It's . . . square kilometers.
How high is (are) . . .?
  It's (They are) . . . meters high.
How long is . . .?
  It's . . . kilometers long.
How deep is . . .?
  It's . . . meters deep.

Making comparisons

Which country is larger, . . . or . . .?
  . . . is larger than . . .
Which country is the largest in the world?
  Russia is the largest country.
Which country is more crowded, . . . or . . . ?
  . . . is more crowded than . . .
  . . . is the most crowded country in . . .

15 Language summary

VOCABULARY

Nouns

Leisure activities
barbecue
(rock) concert
(film) festival
(baseball/soccer) game
musical
(dance) performance
picnic
play
(car) race
(class) reunion
(video game) tournament

Other
accident
address
cell (phone)
excuse
invitation
lamppost
meeting
message
motherboard
reaction
request
security camera
smartphone
statement
track

Adjectives
embarrassing
fancy
late

Verbs
accept
capture
give
refuse
return
speak
throw

Adverbs
afterward
late
on time

EXPRESSIONS

Talking about plans
What are you doing tonight?
  I'm going . . .
Are you doing anything tomorrow?
  No, I'm not (doing anything).
What is she going to do tomorrow?
  She's going to . . .
Are they going to . . . ?
  Yes, they are (going to . . .).

Apologizing and giving reasons
Thanks for asking me, but I can't. I . . .
Sorry, but I already have plans.

Making a call
May I speak to . . . ?
  Sorry, but . . . isn't here.
Can I take/leave a message?
  I'll give . . . the message.

Leaving a message
Can I take a message?
  Please tell . . . (that) . . .
  Please ask . . . to . . .
  Could you tell . . . (that) . . . ?
  Could you ask . . . to . . . ?
  Would you tell . . . (that) . . . ?
  Would you ask . . . to . . . ?

16 Language summary

VOCABULARY

Nouns
(savings) account
(photo) album
century
change
contacts/contact lenses
course
credit card
drama
experience
garbage
goal
hairstyle
(driver's) license
life
(bank) loan
plastic
(pay) raise
resolution
subtitle
vocabulary

Adjectives
extraordinary
outgoing
own
personal
possible

Verbs
accomplish
achieve
become
benefit
bring about
catch
change
donate
dress
dye
fall (in love)
get (engaged/married)
graduate
hope (+ verb)
improve
join
pierce
plan (+ verb)
retire

Adverbs
abroad
differently
less

Prepositions
in (ages/a few years)
into (my own apartment)

EXPRESSIONS

Describing changes
I'm not in school anymore.
I wear contacts now.
I majored in business administration.
I got engaged.
I've just started a new job.
I've bought a new apartment.
It's less noisy than downtown.
My hair is longer now.

Talking about future plans
What are you going to do?
I'm (not) going to . . .
I (don't) plan/want to . . .
I hope to . . .
I'd like/love to . . .

Workbook answer key

1 Where are you from?

Exercise 1
Answers will vary.

Exercise 2
2. A: What's your teacher's name?
3. A: Where is your teacher from?
4. A: What are your friends' names?
5. A: What are your classmates like?

Responses will vary.

Exercise 3
2. A: My name is Bill Matory.
   B: Nice to meet you, Bill.
3. A: Hello. I'm a new student here.
   B: Welcome.
4. A: I'm sorry. What's your name again?
   B: Eun-ha Park.
5. A: How do you spell your first name?
   B: A-K-I-R-A.
6. A: What do people call you?
   B: Everyone calls me Angie.

Exercise 4
2. *Agent:* What's your last name?
   Silvia: My last name's Garcia.
3. *Agent:* Who's that?
   Silvia: That's my husband.
4. *Agent:* What's his name?
   Silvia: His name is Gustavo.
5. *Agent:* Where are you from?
   Silvia: We're from Venezuela.
6. *Agent:* Who are they?
   Silvia: They're my children.

Exercise 5
2. I'm from Barcelona, Spain. It is a beautiful city.
3. Excuse me. What's your last name again?
4. They're my classmates. Their names are Jill and Tae-min.
5. My name is Naoko. Please call me Nao.
6. This is Ellen's husband. His name is Tim.
7. My parents are on vacation. They are in Australia.
8. We have English at 10:00. Our classroom number is 108-C.

Exercise 6
Amber: Who are the men over there, Ethan?
Ethan: Oh, they are/'re on my baseball team. Let me introduce you. Hi, Pablo, this is Amber Fox.
Pablo: Nice to meet you, Amber.
Amber: Nice to meet you, too. Where are you from?
Pablo: I am/'m from Cuba.
Ethan: And this is Marco. He is/'s from Brazil.
Lisa: Hi, Marco.

Exercise 7
A

	Name	Where from	Languages	Sports
1.	Rafael	Puebla, Mexico	Spanish, French	volleyball
2.	Fatima	Tunis, Tunisia	Arabic and French	no sports
3.	Su-yin	Wuhan, China	English and Chinese	volleyball
4.	Arun	Chennai, India	Hindi and English	soccer

B
Answers will vary.

Exercise 8
Stacey: Hello, I'm Stacey.
Omar: Hi, Stacey. I'm Omar. How are you?
Stacey: Pretty good, thanks. Are you a student here?
Omar: Yes, I am. I'm an exchange student from Egypt.
Stacey: Welcome. Do you like it here? What's your favorite subject?
Omar: I really like biology.
Stacey: Oh, really? Is Ben Jones in your class?
Omar: Yes, he is. We're in Biology 300. Is he your friend?
Stacey: No, he's my brother! Actually, I have to go meet him now. Nice to meet you, Omar.
Omar: You, too. Talk to you later.

Exercise 9
Alex: Hello. I'm Alex Robles. And this is my sister Celia.
Paola: Hi. I'm Paola Vieira.
Celia: Are you from South America, Paola?
Paola: Yes, I am. I'm from Brazil. Where are you both from?
Alex: We're from Puerto Rico.
Paola: Are you from San Juan?
Celia: No, we aren't/we're not. We're from Ponce. By the way, are you in English 101?
Paola: No, I'm not. I'm in English 102.

Exercise 10
2. A: What's your favorite school subject?
   B: My favorite school subject is history.
3. A: Are you from Germany?
   B: No, we're not from Germany. We're from Switzerland.
4. A: Do you like your [literature] class?
   B: Yes, it's an interesting class.
5. A: Are Mary and Yuka in your class?
   B: Yes, Mary and Yuka are in my class.
6. A: What's Ryan like?
   B: Ryan is funny and friendly.
7. A: Is Ms. Rogers your English teacher?
   B: No, Ms. Rogers isn't my English teacher. She's my math teacher.

Exercise 11

		Hello	Good-bye
1.	How are you?	✓	
2.	See you tomorrow.		✓
3.	Good night.		✓
4.	Good morning.	✓	
5.	Talk to you later.		✓
6.	How's it going?	✓	
7.	Have a good day.		✓
8.	What's up?	✓	

Exercise 12
Answers will vary.
1. Yes, I am. *or* No, I'm not.
2. Yes, he/she is. *or* No, he's/she's not./No, he/she isn't.
3. Yes, it is. *or* No, it's not./No, it isn't.
4. Yes, it is. *or* No, it's not./No, it isn't.
5. Yes, I am. *or* No, I'm not.
6. Yes, I am. *or* No, I'm not.

2 What do you do?

Exercise 1

2. c
3. e
4. a
5. f
6. b

Exercise 2

2. She's a cook. She cooks food. She works in a restaurant.
3. She's a math teacher. She teaches math to students. She works in a school.
4. He's a taxi driver. He drives a car. He takes people to places they want to go.

Exercise 3

2. She's ***an*** office manager. She works for ***a*** large company. It's ***an*** interesting job.
3. He works in ***a*** restaurant. He's ***a*** server. He's also ***a*** part-time student. He takes ***a*** business class in the evening.
4. She works for ***a*** travel company. She arranges tours. She's ***a*** travel agent.
5. He has ***a*** difficult job. He's ***a*** flight attendant. He works on ***an*** airplane.

Exercise 4

Answers will vary.

Exercise 5

Tiffany: What does your brother do, exactly?
Kate: He works for the city. He's a firefighter.
Tiffany: How does he like it?
Kate: It's an interesting job. He likes it very much. But he works long hours. And what do you do?
Tiffany: I'm a student. I study geography.
Kate: Oh, really? Where do you to go to school?
Tiffany: I go to Matthews University. My brother goes there, too.
Kate: Really? And what does he study?
Tiffany: He studies graphic design.
Kate: That sounds interesting.

Exercise 6

Tom: Where do you work?
Ray: I work for Brady Corporation.
Tom: And what do you do there?
Ray: I'm an accountant.
Tom: An accountant? How do you like it?
Ray: I like numbers, so it's a great job. And what do you do?
Tom: I'm a teacher.
Ray: Really? What do you teach?
Tom: I teach accounting!

Exercise 7

1. He is a flight attendant.
2. He works on the international flight from Miami to Recife, Brazil.
3. He carries his dictionary everywhere he goes.
4. She is a security guard.
5. She works at Matthews University.
6. The hardest part of her job is when she has to stop people from breaking the rules.

Exercise 8

Answers will vary. Possible answers:
2. Where does he work?
3. When does he go to work?
4. How does he like his job?

Exercise 9

Everyone knows Patricio at the hospital. Patricio is a part-time nurse. He works at night on weekends. *On* Saturdays and Sundays, Patricio sleeps most of the day and wakes up a little before nine in the evening, usually at 8:45 or 8:50. He has breakfast very late, around 9:30 or 10:00 P.M.! He watches television until eleven o'clock, and then starts work at midnight. Early in the morning, usually around 5:00 A.M., he leaves work, has a little snack, goes home, goes to bed, and sleeps late. It's a perfect schedule for Patricio. He's a pre-med student on weekdays at a local college.

Exercise 10

2. Stella goes to bed after midnight.
3. Bonnie gets up early in the morning.
4. What does your sister do?
5. Roland starts work at 8:00 A.M.
6. My brother works in a bookstore. He sells books and magazines.
7. The Havana Garden restaurant serves good Cuban food.
8. Dan does his school work on his new computer.
9. Nunu writes about 30 emails a day.
10. David is a receptionist. He answers the phone and greets people.
11. Miguel works in a restaurant.

Exercise 11

2. What does he do?
3. She cares for people's pets.
4. He goes to the university.
5. She stays up late.
6. He works part-time.

Exercise 12

1. Larry's Diner needs *servers*. Work during the day or at night, weekdays or weekends, full-time or part-time. Call (901) 555–1977.
2. Interesting job for a language student. Take people on tours. Evenings only. Need good English and Japanese skills. Email Brenda at Brenda44@cup.org.
3. We need a great office manager! Work Monday through Friday, no weekends. Start work at 9:00 in the morning.

3 How much are these?

Exercise 1

James: Look at those pants, Linda.
Linda: Which ones?
James: The yellow ones over there. They're nice.
Linda: Yes. But I don't really like yellow.
James: Hmm. Well, what about that sweater? It's perfect for you.
Linda: Which one?
James: This blue one.
Linda: Well, I like it, but it's expensive.
James: Hey, let me buy it for you. It's a present!
Linda: Oh, James. Thank you very much.

Exercise 2

2. A: How much are those glasses over there?
B. They're $87.
3. A: How much are these sneakers right here?
B: They're $79.99.
4. A: How much is that cat over there?
B: That's *my* cat, and he's not for sale!

Exercise 3

2. gloves
3. parties
4. boys
5. ties
6. boxes
7. scarves
8. blouses
9. T-shirts
10. hairbrushes
11. computers
12. dresses

Exercise 4

Answers will vary.

Exercise 5

1. *Shirley:* I like *those* earrings over there.
Clerk: Which ones?
Shirley: The small gold ones.
Clerk: They're $399.
Shirley: Oh, they're expensive!
2. *George:* Excuse me. How much are those pants?
Clerk: They're only $65.
George: And how much is this shirt?
Clerk: Which one? They're all different.
George: This green one.
Clerk: It's $47.
3. *Clerk:* Good afternoon.
Martina: Oh, hi. How much is this watch?
Clerk: It's $195.
Martina: And how much is that one?
Clerk: It's $255.
Martina: Oh, really? Well, thanks anyway.

Exercise 6

Cotton	*Gold*	*Leather*	*Plastic*	*Silk*	*Wool*
gloves	bracelet	belt	bracelet	gloves	boots
jacket	button	boots	button	jacket	gloves
pants	necklace	gloves	hairbrush	pants	jacket
shirt	ring	jacket	ring	shirt	pants

Exercise 7

1. A: Hey, look at these silver earrings! They're nice. And they're *cheaper than* those gold earrings.
B: But they're smaller than the gold ones.
A: Well, yeah. The gold ones are bigger than the silver ones. But four hundred dollars is a lot of money!
2. A: This leather coat is more attractive than the wool one.
B: Yes, but the wool one is warmer.
3. A: This orange shirt is an interesting color!
B: Yes, but the color is prettier than the design.
A: The design isn't bad.
B: I think the pattern on that gray shirt is better than the pattern on this orange one.
4. A: These cotton dresses are nice.
B: Yes, but the silk ones are nicer.
A: They're also more expensive.

Exercise 8

Clothing	*Electronics*	*Jewelry*
boots	MP3 player	bracelet
dress	tablet	earrings
pants	television	necklace
T-shirt	smartphone	ring

Exercise 9

Answers will vary.
2. I like the . . . more.
3. I like the . . . more.
4. I prefer the . . . gloves.
5. I like the . . . ones better.

Exercise 10

A

1. b
2. d
3. a
4. c

B

1. True
2. True
3. False
4. False

C

Answers will vary.

4 Do you play the guitar?

Exercise 1

A

Answers will vary.

B

Answers will vary.

Exercise 2

Answers will vary.

Exercise 3

1. Hope Solo is an athlete.
2. Fall Out Boy are a pop group.
3. Chris Hemsworth is an actor.
4. Luke Bryan is a singer.

Exercise 4

1. *Ken:* Do you like pop music, Janet?
   Janet: Yes, I like it a lot. I'm a big fan of Beyoncé.
   Ken: Oh, does she play the guitar?
   Janet: No, she doesn't, but she's a great dancer.
2. *Alice:* What kind of music do your parents like, Jack?
   Jack: They like country music.
   Alice: Who do they like? Jason Aldean?
   Jack: No, they don't like him very much. They prefer Carrie Underwood.
3. *Harold:* Kelly, who's your favorite female singer? Do you like Selena Gomez?
   Kelly: No, I don't. I can't stand her. I like Etana.
   Harold: I don't know her. What kind of music does she sing?
   Kelly: She sings reggae. She's really great!

Exercise 5

Answers to questions will vary.

1. What kinds of movies do you like?	I like . . .
2. What is your favorite movie?	My favorite . . .
3. What kinds of movies do you dislike?	I dislike . . .
4. What kinds of TV shows do you like?	I like . . .
5. Who is your favorite actor or actress?	My favorite . . .
6. What is your favorite song?	My favorite . . .
7. What is your favorite rock band?	My favorite . . .
8. What is your favorite video game?	My favorite . . .

Exercise 6

Answers will vary.

Exercise 7

A

Answers may vary. Possible answers:

listen to	***play***	***watch***
music	the drums	a basketball game
R&B	the guitar	a movie
the radio	the piano	videos

B

Answers will vary.

Exercise 8

A

1. *Ahead of Time*: science fiction
2. *House of Laughs*: comedy
3. *Coming Up for Air*: crime thriller

B

Answers will vary. Possible answers:

1. *future*, travel, century, time, adventures
2. different, funny, laugh, funnier
3. action, catch, thief, gold, surprise

Exercise 9

2. A: Do you like jazz music?
   B: I can't stand it.
3. A: There's a soccer game tonight.
   B: Great. Let's go.
4. A: Would you like to see a movie this weekend?
   B: That sounds great!

Exercise 10

A

Accept?	***Yes***	***No***
2. Thanks, but I don't really like animated films.		✓
3. That sounds great. Where is it?	✓	
4. I'd love to, but I have to work until midnight.		✓
5. Thanks. I'd really like to. When do you want to meet?	✓	

B

Answers will vary.

Exercise 11

1. *Eva:* Do you like pop music, Anita?
   Anita: Yes, I do. I like it a lot.
   Eva: There's a Justin Bieber concert on Friday. Would you like to go with me?
   Anita: Yes, I'd love to! Thanks.
2. *Marco:* There's a baseball game on TV tonight. Would you like to come over and watch it?
   Tony: I'd like to, but I have to study tonight.
   Marco: Well, do you like basketball?
   Tony: Yes, I do. I love it!
   Marco: There's a game on TV tomorrow at 3:00. Would you like to watch that with me?
   Tony: I'd love to. Thanks!

Exercise 12

2. Chad can't stand country music.
3. I love soap operas!
4. Celia isn't/is not a fan of new age music.
5. Would you like to go to a soccer match?

5 What an interesting family!

Exercise 1

Males	*Females*
brother	aunt
father	daughter
husband	mother
nephew	niece
son	sister
uncle	wife

Exercise 2

Jan: You look tired, Monica. Are you studying late at night these days?
Monica: No, I'm not. My brother and sister are staying with me right now. They keep me up late every night.
Jan: Really, both of them? What are they doing this summer? Are they taking classes, too?
Monica: No, they aren't. My brother is on vacation now, but he is looking for a part-time job here.
Jan: What about your sister? Is she working?
Monica: Yes, she is. She has a part-time job at the university. What about you, Jan? Are you in school this summer?
Jan: Yes, I am. I'm studying two languages.
Monica: Oh, are you taking Korean and Spanish again?
Jan: Well, I'm taking Korean again, but now I'm starting Portuguese classes.
Monica: Really? That's exciting!

Exercise 3

2. Ann is John's wife.
3. My aunt is a teacher.
4. We have a son and a daughter.
5. My mother-in-law is from Mexico.
6. Brooke is Willie and Mabel's granddaughter.

Exercise 4

Kathy: Are you still living in Miami, Martin?
Martin: No, I'm not. I'm living in Singapore now.
Kathy: Wow! Do you like it?
Martin: Yes, I do. I like it a lot.
Kathy: And is your brother still working in Seoul?
Martin: Yes, he is. He loves it there.
Kathy: And how about your parents? Are they still living in Florida?
Martin: No, they aren't. They're living in Atlanta now. How about you and your family, Kathy? Are you still living here?
Kathy: Yes, we are. We really love Miami.

Exercise 5

1. This is my cousin Martin. He *lives* in Houston, but he is visiting/'s visiting Peru this summer. He is taking/'s taking cooking classes there.
2. And these are my parents. They are working/'re working in Paris. They are/'re on vacation right now.
3. Here's a photo of my grandparents. They are not working/aren't working now. They are/'re retired.
4. This is my sister-in-law, Amanda. She wants to start her own company. She is studying/'s studying business in Australia right now.
5. And this is my nephew, George. He goes to high school. He likes history, but he does not like/doesn't like chemistry.

Exercise 6

Answers will vary.

Exercise 7

A

Answers will vary.

B

1. False. "Boomerang kids" are college graduates who go back to live in their parents' home.
2. True.
3. False. College graduates who live at home are trying to save money for the future.
4. True.
5. False. Parents want their kids to help around the house.
6. False. Parents and kids have different ideas about rules and expectations, and this causes tension.

Exercise 8

1. all
2. nearly all
3. most
4. many
5. some
6. few
7. no

Exercise 9

1. Most *children go to public schools*. Few children go to private schools.
2. Many young people go to college after they finish high school. Some young people look for work.
3. Not many people over 65 like to play soccer. A lot of people over 65 like to spend time on a hobby. Nearly all people over 65 like to talk to family and friends.

Exercise 10

In my country, some *couples* get married fairly young. Not many marriages break up, and nearly all divorced people remarry. Elderly couples often live at home and take care of their grandchildren.

Exercise 11

Answers will vary.

6 How often do you run?

Exercise 1

Sports	*Fitness activities*
baseball	jogging
basketball	Pilates
football	walking
soccer	weight training
volleyball	yoga

Exercise 2

2. Does Ryan ever do yoga?
3. How often do you go swimming?
4. I almost never go jogging.
5. They hardly ever play basketball.
6. What do you usually do on Sundays?

Exercise 3

2. A: What do you usually do after work?
B: Well, I usually do martial arts or watch TV after work.
3. A: Do you ever play sports on weekends?
B: Yes, I sometimes play sports on weekends – usually soccer.
4. A: How often do you exercise?
B: I don't exercise very often at all.
5. A: Do you ever go to the gym on Saturdays?
B: No, I never go to the gym on Saturdays.
6. A: How often do you go jogging?
B: I usually go jogging four times a week.

Exercise 4

A

Answers will vary.

B

Answers will vary.

Exercise 5

Kelly: What time do you go swimming *in* the morning?
Neil: I always go swimming ***at*** 7:00. How about you, Kelly?
Kelly: I usually go swimming ***around*** noon. I swim ***for*** about 30 minutes.
Neil: And do you also play sports ***in*** your free time?
Kelly: No, I usually go out ***with*** my classmates. What about you?
Neil: I go to the gym ***on*** Mondays and Wednesdays. And sometimes I go jogging ***on*** weekends.
Kelly: Wow! You really like to stay in shape.

Exercise 6

2. How often do you do martial arts?
3. I like to stay in shape. I play sports every day.
4. Jeff does weight training every evening. He lifts 50-pound weights.
5. Arturo goes jogging twice a week. He usually runs about three miles.
6. Miho often watches TV in the evening.
7. Maria is on the soccer team at her high school. She's good at passing the ball.
8. Judy never goes swimming when the water is cold.
9. Kyle often goes bike riding on weekends.
10. I run on the treadmill at the gym three times a week.
11. In Canada, many people like to play ice hockey outside in the winter.

Exercise 7

A

Answers will vary.

B

	Capoeira	*Hurling*	*Bashi*
1. hit a ball backwards			✓
2. run very fast		✓	
3. know what your opponent is thinking	✓		
4. get a ball in a net		✓	
5. move with music	✓		
6. hit a ball over a net			✓

Exercise 8

2. A: How long do you spend on the golf course?
B: About four hours.
3. A: And how well do you play?
B: I'm about average.
4. A: How good are you at other sports?
B: Not very good, actually.

Exercise 9

2. A: How good are you at playing football?
B: I'm pretty good at it. I'm on the school team.
3. A: How often do you go for a walk?
B: Almost every day. I really enjoy it.
4. A: How (well) do you like baseball?
B: Baseball? Pretty well, I guess. Yeah, I like it a lot.
5. A: How long do you spend jogging? / How much time do you spend jogging?
B: I spend about an hour jogging.

Exercise 10

2. Tamara doesn't exercise very often.
3. Patty tries to stay in shape.
4. Ricardo often works out at the gym.
5. I always go jogging after work.
6. How well do you play tennis?

Exercise 11

Answers will vary.

7 We went dancing!

Exercise 1

A

2. played
3. invited
4. arrived
5. studied
6. hurried
7. traveled
8. washed
9. looked

B

2. do
3. meet
4. see
5. sleep
6. spend
7. drive
8. go

C

Answers will vary.

Exercise 2

2. I met a famous artist.
3. I bought a new pair of jeans.
4. We liked the movie a lot./We liked it a lot.
5. They spent their vacation in the country./They spent it in the country.
6. We got home a little after 1:00.

Exercise 3

Answers will vary.

Exercise 4

A: How *did you spend the weekend*?
B: I spent the weekend with my sisters.
A: What did you do (on Saturday)?
B: Well, on Saturday, we went shopping.
A: That sounds like fun! What did you buy?
B: I bought a new pair of shoes and a new purse.
A: Where did you go on Sunday?
B: We went to an amusement park.
A: Oh, how did you like it?
B: We had a great time. In fact, we stayed there all day.
A: Really? What time did you get home?
B: We got home very late, around midnight.

Exercise 5

2. A: Beth left work at 2:00 yesterday afternoon. Did you go home early, too?
   B: No, I didn't. I worked all day until six o'clock.
3. A: I watched TV all weekend. Did you spend the weekend at home, too?
   B: No, I didn't. I went out with friends.
4. A: I saw you and Amy at the library on Saturday. Did you work together on Sunday, too?
   B: No, we didn't. We finished the project on Saturday.
5. A: Giovanni drove me to work yesterday morning. Did you drive to work?
   B: No, I didn't. I took the bus.
6. A: Sandy went to the baseball game last night. Did you and Martin go to the game?
   B: No, we didn't. We watched it on TV.

Exercise 6

2. c
3. b
4. e
5. a
6. d

Exercise 7

A

Olivia went to Bangkok for the first time.

B

	Joseph	*Olivia*
2. visited the floating market		✓
3. bought fruit	✓	✓
4. saw some historic ruins		✓
5. traveled on the river	✓	
6. loved the food the most	✓	
7. enjoyed everything		✓

Exercise 8

A: How was your vacation in Thailand, Rich?
B: It was great. I really enjoyed it.
A: How long were you there?
B: We were there for two weeks.
A: Were you in Bangkok the whole time?
B: No, we weren't. We were in the mountains for a few days.
A: And how was the weather? Was it good?
B: No, it wasn't good at all! In fact, it was terrible. The city was very hot, and the mountains were cold and rainy!

Exercise 9

A: *How was your vacation in South America?*
B: It was a great trip. I really enjoyed Brazil and Argentina.
A: How long were you in Brazil?
B: I was in Brazil for ten days.
A: And how long were you in Argentina?
B: For about eight days.
A: Wow, that's a long time! How was the weather?
B: It was hot and sunny the whole time.
A: And what was the best part?
B: It was definitely the beaches in Brazil. Oh, and we learned the tango in Argentina!

Exercise 10

1. We took a trip to Egypt last summer.
2. My brothers played video games at home all weekend.
3. I worked really hard in Germany last week. I was there on business.
4. I'm sorry I was late. I had to make a phone call.
5. I stayed home last night and did the laundry.

Exercise 11

A

Answers will vary.

B

Answers will vary.

8 How's the neighborhood?

Exercise 1

A

2. college campus
3. gas station
4. grocery store
5. hair salon
6. movie theater
7. post office
8. shopping mall
9. Wi-Fi hot spot

B

2. A: I want to buy some new clothes. Is there a shopping mall near here?
B: No, there isn't, but there's one in Center City.
3. A: I need to mail this package. Is there a post office around here?
B: Yes, there's one next to the bank.
4. A: I want to see a movie tonight. Is there a movie theater around here?
B: Yes, there's one in the shopping mall.
5. A: We need some gas. Are there any gas stations on this street?
B: No, there aren't, but there are a couple on Second Avenue.
6. A: We need to buy some cereal and some apples. Is there a grocery store near here?
B: Yes, there's one near the gym on Brown Street.

Exercise 2

Answers will vary. Possible answers:

3. There's a laundromat on the corner of 1st Street and Oak in Springfield, but there isn't one in Riverside. There's a hospital.
4. There's a grocery store on Elm between 1st Street and 2nd Street in Riverside, but there isn't one in Springfield.
5. There's a restaurant on the corner of Oak and 3rd Street in Springfield, but there isn't one in Riverside. There's a drugstore.
6. There's a bank on the corner of Oak and 2nd Street in Springfield, but there isn't one in Riverside. There's a department store.
7. There's a post office next to the hotel on 3rd Street in Springfield, but there isn't one in Riverside. There's a movie theater.
8. There's a gas station on the corner of 2nd Street and Elm in Springfield, but there isn't one in Riverside.
9. There are houses between 3rd Street and 4th Street in Springfield, but there aren't any in Riverside. There are apartments.
10. There's a hair salon on 4th Street in Springfield, but there isn't one in Riverside. There's a coffee shop.

Exercise 3

2. Yes. There's one on the corner of Lincoln Street and 3rd Avenue.
3. There's one across from the gas station on 2nd Avenue.
4. Yes. There's one on Lincoln Street near the gym.
5. Yes. There's one between the gym and the hotel.
6. Yes. There's one in the hotel on 2nd Avenue.

Exercise 4

Answers will vary.

Exercise 5

A

Charles would like to live in a small town.
Arlene would like to live downtown.

B

	Advantages	*Disadvantages*
Downtown	convenient	noisy
	near shopping center	streets full of people
	near bus station	terrible traffic
	safe	parking is a problem
Small town	nice	no privacy
	great square	everyone knows what you're doing
	social events	not many interesting people
	music on summer evenings	too quiet
	safe place to raise children	not enough action

C

Answers will vary.

D

Answers will vary.

Exercise 6

Count nouns	Noncount nouns
bank	crime
hospital	noise
library	parking
people	pollution
school	traffic
theater	water

Exercise 7

2. How many buses are there? There aren't any./There are none.
3. How much traffic is there? There's a lot.
4. How many bicycles are there? There are many./There are a lot.
5. How many police officers are there? There are a few.
6. How much crime is there? There isn't any./There is none.

Exercise 8

Andrea: Are there any coffee shops around here, Carlos?
Carlos: Sure. There are a lot. There's a coffee shop across from the Daily Market, but it's expensive.
Andrea: Well, are there any others?
Carlos: Yeah, there are a few. There's a nice one near here. It's called Morning Joe.
Andrea: That's perfect! Where is it, exactly?
Carlos: It's on Third Avenue, between the National Bank and the Chinese restaurant.
Andrea: So let's go!

Exercise 9

1. I'm going to the grocery store to get some food.
2. We're taking a long drive. We need to stop at the gas station.
3. I live on the 8th floor of my apartment building.
4. Our apartment is in the center of the city. We live downtown.

9 What does she look like?

Exercise 1

2. curly / straight
3. short / tall
4. long / short
5. elderly / young

Exercise 2

A

2. fairly long
3. good-looking
4. middle-aged
5. dark brown

B

2. A: What does he look like?
B: He's good-looking.
3. A: What color is his hair?
B: It's dark brown.
4. A: How long is his hair?
B: It's fairly long.
5. A: How old is he?
B: He's middle-aged.

Exercise 3

Marta: Let's find Arturo. I need to talk to him.
Alli: *What does he look like?*
Marta: He's very handsome, with curly brown hair.
Alli: And how long is his hair?/how long is it?
Marta: It's medium length.
Alli: How tall is he?/Is he tall?
Marta: He's fairly tall.
Alli: And how old is he?
Marta: He's in his early twenties.
Alli: What is he wearing?/What does he usually wear?
Marta: Well, he usually wears jeans.
Alli: I think I see him over there. Is that him?

Exercise 4

Answers will vary.

Exercise 5

Answers may vary. Possible answers:

1. He isn't young. He's elderly. He doesn't have curly hair. He's bald.
2. Her hair isn't long. It's short. She isn't wearing sneakers. She's wearing boots.
3. She isn't/She's not tall. She's short. She isn't wearing a scarf and a skirt. She's wearing a jacket and pants.

Exercise 6

Formal	***Casual***
dress	boots
high heels	cap
jewelry	jeans
necktie	shorts
shirt	sneakers
suit	T-shirt

Exercise 7

Answers may vary. Possible answers:

2. Angela is the one talking to the man.
3. Li Na is the young woman carrying a jacket.
4. Tiffany and Matt are the ones wearing sunglasses.
5. Rodrigo is the short man wearing a suit and tie.

Exercise 8

2. Eduardo is the one standing behind the couch.
3. Keith and Lauren are the ones eating pizza.
4. Jennifer is the woman sitting on the couch.
5. Ken is the man with the short black hair.

Exercise 9

2. A: Which ones are the servers? Who are the servers?
B: They're the ones in the red polo shirts. They're the ones wearing red polo shirts.
3. A: Which one is Naomi? Who's Naomi?
B: She's the one on the couch next to Lisa. She's the one sitting next to Lisa.

Exercise 10

Ruby: I'm glad you brought me to this party, Bill. I'm *looking* for someone here named Jeff.
Bill: Yeah, I don't know too many people here. But let's try to find him. Is he one of those guys playing football? What about the guy with black hair and wearing the dark T-shirt?
Ruby: Hmm, no. That's not Jeff.
Bill: How about the one using the music system over there, in the white T-shirt.
Ruby: No, I know him. That's Ken.
Bill: Hmm. Oh, is that Jeff sitting at the table and talking to the two women? It looks like they're already eating.
Ruby: No, not him, either. Gee, I wonder if Jeff even came to the party?
Bill: Well, he can't be the chef, right? The guy cooking vegetables at the grill?
Ruby: That's him! Hey, Jeff!

Exercise 11

2. A: Where's Samantha?
B: She couldn't make it.
3. A: Is Avery the one wearing glasses?
B: That's right.
4. A: How tall is she?
B: Pretty short.

10 Have you ever been there?

Exercise 1

2. e
3. h
4. b
5. i
6. d
7. j
8. f
9. c
10. a

Exercise 2

2. A: How many times have you gone to the gym this month?
   B: Actually, not at all. Let's go later today!
3. A: How many phone calls have you made today?
   B: I made two calls – both to you!
4. A: Have you done your homework yet?
   B: Yes, I have. I did it after class.
5. A: Have you eaten at the new Italian restaurant?
   B: Yes, we already have. It's very good but a little expensive.
6. A: How long have you had those boots?
   B: I bought them on Monday.

Exercise 3

A

Answers will vary.

B

Answers will vary.

Exercise 4

2. I have been a teacher for several years.
3. I haven't had this much fun since I was a kid!
4. I'm so sleepy. I've been awake since 4:00 this morning.
5. Kyoko was an exchange student in Peru for a whole semester.
6. Marcus has lived in Dubai since 2010.
7. How are you? I haven't seen you since high school.
8. Where have you been? I've been here for over an hour!
9. Mr. and Mrs. Lopez have been married for nearly 50 years.

Exercise 5

Answers will vary.

Exercise 6

A

The first blogger went to Mexico City. She wanted to get a better look at a statue behind some ropes.
The second blogger went to Athens. He wanted to go for a walk before dinner.

B

1 and 2 went to a foreign country
1 got lost
1 and 2 got help from someone
2 stayed at a hotel
1 went underground
1 and 2 made a mistake
2 went on the trip alone

C

Answers will vary.

Exercise 7

2. A: Have you ever seen a rugby match?
   B: Actually, I saw a rugby match last week on TV. It was awesome!
3. A: Have you ever eaten sushi?
   B: Yes, I love sushi.
4. A: Have you ever been to Houston?
   B: No, I haven't. But my uncle lives in Houston.
5. A: Have you ever visited an amusement park?
   B: Yes, I visited an amusement park last month.
6. A: Have you ever been camping?
   B: No, I haven't. I don't think I would like camping.
7. A: Have you ever ridden a motorcycle?
   B: Yes, I have. I once rode my aunt's motorcycle.

Exercise 8

Answers will vary

Exercise 9

A: *Have* you ever *lost* anything valuable?
B: Yes, I lost my cell phone last month.
A: Have you found it yet?
B: No. Actually, I've already bought a new one. Look!
A: Oh, that's nice. Where did you buy it?
B: I got it at the mall last weekend. What about you? Have you ever lost anything valuable?
A: Well, I left my leather jacket in a coffee shop a couple of months ago.
B: Oh, no! Did you go back and look for it?
A: Well, I called them, but it was gone.

Exercise 10

2. A: Are you having a good time?
   B: Yes, really good.
3. A: How long did Theresa stay at the party?
   B: For two hours.
4. A: Have you had breakfast?
   B: Yes, I've already eaten.
5. A: How many times has Tony lost his keys?
   B: Twice.
6. A: Do you want to see that new movie?
   B: Sure. I hear it's great.
7. A: Have you been here long?
   B: No, just a few minutes.
8. A: Have you seen Sara today?
   B: Yes, I saw her this morning.

11 It's a really nice city.

Exercise 1

2. Chicago has amazing skyscrapers right next to a gorgeous lake. It's a really beautiful city.
3. My hometown is not an exciting place. The nightlife there is pretty boring.
4. Some parts of our city are fairly dangerous. It's not very safe late at night.
5. The streets in this city are always full of people, cars, and buses. It's a very crowded city.

Exercise 2

A: *What's your hometown like?*
B: My hometown? It's a pretty nice place, and the people are very friendly.
A: Is it big?
B: No, it's fairly small, but it's not too small.
A: What's the weather like?
B: The winter is wet and really cold. It's very nice in the summer, though.
A: Is the nightlife exciting?
B: No! It's really boring. There are no good restaurants or nightclubs.

Exercise 3

2. Dubai is a very nice place. The summers are terribly hot, though.
3. Hong Kong is an exciting city, and it's a fun place to sightsee.
4. My hometown has some great restaurants, but it's not a good place for shopping.
5. Our hometown is somewhat ugly. It has some beautiful old homes, however.

Exercise 4

2. Restaurants are very cheap in Ecuador. (no change)
3. ✓ Brisbane is ***a*** clean city.
4. The buildings in Florence are really beautiful. (no change)
5. Apartments are very expensive in Hong Kong. (no change)
6. ✓ Sapporo is ***a*** very cold city in the winter.
7. Beijing's museums are really excellent. (no change)
8. ✓ Mumbai is ***an*** exciting place to visit.

Exercise 5

Paris is France's biggest city. It is a very lively city with an interesting history. It is a city of interesting buildings and churches, and it has many beautiful parks. It also has some of the best museums in the world. Paris has nice weather most of the year, but it is pretty cold in the winter. It is a popular city with foreign tourists and has millions of visitors a year. The city is famous for its fashion and has many excellent stores. Paris has convenient trains and buses that cross the city, so it is easy for tourists to get around.

Exercise 6

A

Seoul is in South Korea.
Quito is in Ecuador.
Rabat is in Morocco.

B

City	*Date founded*	*Population*	*Attractions*
Seoul	18 BCE	10.5 million	115 museums, many monuments, parks and music festivals
Quito	1534	2.6 million	downtown center, walking in the mountains, visit a volcano
Rabat	1146	580,000	the music festival Mawazine, the Kasbah fortress, outdoor markets

C

1. Seoul and Rabat have music festivals.
2. Rabat is the capital city with the smallest population.
3. Seoul is the oldest capital city.
4. Ecuador has the capital city with the highest altitude.

Exercise 7

2. You shouldn't stay near the airport. It's too noisy.
3. You shouldn't miss the museum. It has some new exhibits.
4. You can take a bus tour of the city if you like.
5. You shouldn't walk alone at night. It's too dangerous.
6. You can get a taxi if you're out late.

Exercise 8

A: I'm taking my vacation in Japan. What *should I* do there?
B: You shouldn't miss Kyoto, the old capital city. There are a lot of beautiful old buildings. For example, you should see the Ryoanji Temple.
A: Sounds great. Hakone is very popular, too. Should I go there?
B: Yes, you should. It's very interesting, and the hot springs are fantastic.
A: Should I take a lot of money with me?
B: No, you shouldn't. You can use the ATMs in Japan.
A: So when should I go there?
B: In the spring or the fall. You can see the cherry blossoms or the fall colors.

Exercise 9

Answers will vary.

Exercise 10

2. You shouldn't miss the new aquarium.
3. Apartments are extremely expensive in my country.
4. This neighborhood is very quiet.
5. When is a good time to visit the city?

12 It's important to get rest.

Exercise 1

A

2. go to bed and rest
3. put it under cold water
4. take some pain medicine
5. apply anti-itch cream
6. use some ointment

B

A: What should you do for a bad cold?
B: It's important/It's sometimes helpful/It's a good idea to go to bed and rest.
A: What should you do for a burn?
B: It's important/It's sometimes helpful/It's a good idea to put it under cold water.
A: What should you do for a headache?
B: It's important/It's sometimes helpful/It's a good idea to take some pain medicine.
A: What should you do for an insect bite?
B: It's important/It's sometimes helpful/It's a good idea to apply anti-itch cream.
A: What should you do for sore muscles?
B: It's important/It's sometimes helpful/It's a good idea to use some ointment.

Exercise 2

2. For a sore throat, it's important/it's a good idea/it's sometimes helpful not to talk too much.
3. For a burn, it's important/it's a good idea/it's sometimes helpful not to put ice on it.
4. For insomnia, it's important/it's a good idea/it's sometimes helpful not to drink coffee at night.
5. For a fever, it's important/it's a good idea/it's sometimes helpful not to get out of bed.

Exercise 3

Answers will vary.

Exercise 4

A

Laughter has important health benefits for your body.

B

1. True
2. True
3. False
4. True
5. False

C

Answers will vary.

Exercise 5

A

Bottle	*Box*	*Tube*	*Can*
eyedrops	herbal tea	anti-itch cream	insect spray
pain medicine	bandages	muscle ointment	shaving cream

B

2. He should buy a bottle of pain medicine.
3. She should buy a tube of muscle ointment.
4. She should buy a can of insect spray/a tube of anti-itch cream.
5. He should buy a box of bandages.
6. She should buy a tube of anti-itch cream.
7. He should buy a can of shaving cream.
8. She should buy a bottle of eyedrops.

Exercise 6

1. *Pharmacist:* Can I help you?
Customer: Yes. Can I have a bottle of pain medicine?
Pharmacist: Here you are.
Customer: And what do you have for a sunburn?
Pharmacist: I suggest this lotion.
Customer: Thanks.
2. *Pharmacist:* Hi. Can I help you?
Customer: Yes. Could I have something for sore muscles?
Pharmacist: Sure. Try this ointment.
Customer: Thanks. And what do you suggest for the flu?
Pharmacist: Try some of these tablets. They really work.
Customer: OK, thanks. I'll take them. And could I have a box of tissues?
Pharmacist: Sure. Here you are.

Exercise 7

A: Wow, you don't look very good! Do you feel OK?
B: No, I think I'm getting a cold. What should I do <u>for</u> it?
A: You should stay <u>at</u> home and go <u>to</u> bed.
B: You're probably right. I've got a really bad cough, too.
A: Try drinking some hot tea <u>with</u> honey. It really helps.
B: Anything else?
A: Yeah, I suggest you get a big box <u>of</u> tissues!

Exercise 8

Answers will vary.

13 What would you like?

Exercise 1

2. A: I really like Mexican food.
   B: So do I.
3. A: I'm in the mood for Italian food.
   B: I am, too.
4. A: I can't stand spicy food.
   B: Neither can I.
5. A: I don't like greasy food very much.
   B: I don't either.
6. A: I want to eat healthy food for lunch.
   B: I do, too.

Exercise 2

A

Answers will vary.

B

Answers will vary.

Exercise 3

A

1. Carlota: Fantastic!! (★★★★★)
2. Adam: Awful! (★)
3. Luka: Pretty good. (★★★)

B

	Carlota	*Luka*	*Luka's wife*	*Adam*
Ordered:	grilled salmon with baby asparagus and baked potato	sushi with rice and a cucumber salad, chocolate cake	lamb curry with spicy vegetables and garlic bread, chocolate cake	quinoa burger and almond milkshake
Problems:	no	yes	yes	yes
Recommends:	yes	yes	yes	no

Exercise 4

2. sushi
3. ice cream
4. pork
5. bread
6. a cookie

Exercise 5

Server: May I take your order?
Customer: Yes, I'll have the salmon.
Server: What kind of dressing would you like on your salad – French, blue cheese, or vinaigrette?
Customer: I'd like French, please.
Server: And would you like something to drink?
Customer: Yes, I'll have iced coffee.
Server: With milk and sugar?
Customer: Yes, please.
Server: Anything else?
Customer: No, thank you. That'll be all.

Exercise 6

2. A: Would you like soup or salad?
   B: I'd like soup, please.
3. A: What would you like on your pizza?
   B: I'll have pepperoni.
4. A: Would you like anything to drink?
   B: No, thanks.
5. A: What flavor ice cream would you like?
   B: Vanilla, please.
6. A: Would you like anything else?
   B: That'll be all, thanks.

Exercise 7

2. In a restaurant, the server takes your order.
3. Many people like dressing on their salad.
4. Some people rarely cook with spices. They prefer food to be bland.
5. Strawberry is a popular ice cream flavor.

Exercise 8

Maria: I feel tired tonight. I really don't want to cook.
Courtney: Neither do I. Let's order out. Do you like Chinese food?
Maria: It's delicious! I like it a lot!
Courtney: I do, too. It's my favorite kind of food. Let's call Beijing Express for home delivery.
Maria: Great idea! Their food is always good. I eat there a lot.
Courtney: So do I. Well, what would you like tonight?
Maria: I'm in the mood for some soup.
Courtney: So am I. And I think I'll have orange chicken and fried rice.
Maria: OK, let's order. Oh, wait. They don't take credit cards, and I don't have any cash on me.
Courtney: Neither do I. Too bad! What should we do?
Maria: Well, let's look in the refrigerator. Hmm. Do you like boiled eggs?
Courtney: I can't stand them!
Maria: Actually, neither can I.

14 It's the coldest city!

Exercise 1

A

2. a (desert)
3. b (valley)
4. c (lake)
5. c (waterfall)
6. b (forest)

B

2. Amazon River
3. Grand Canyon
4. Atlantic Ocean
5. Mojave Desert
6. Niagara Falls
7. Mediterranean Sea
8. Mount Everest

Exercise 2

2. cooler, the coolest
3. friendlier, the friendliest
4. heavier, the heaviest
5. nicer, the nicest
6. noisier, the noisiest
7. older, the oldest
8. safer, the safest
9. smaller, the smallest
10. wetter, the wettest

Exercise 3

Keegan: So where did you go for your vacation, Kathy?
Kathy: Japan.
Keegan: How exciting! Did you have a good time?
Kathy: It was terrific! I think Japan is *the most exciting* country in Asia.
Keegan: Well, it certainly has some of the most interesting cities in the world – Tokyo, Osaka, and Kyoto.
Kathy: Yeah. I had the best time in Kyoto. It's the most beautiful city I've ever seen. Of course, it's also one of the most popular tourist attractions. It was the most crowded city I visited this summer.
Keegan: I've always wanted to visit Japan. What's it like in the winter?
Kathy: Actually, I think that's the worst time to visit because I don't like cold weather. However, I think the Sapporo Snow Festival is the most fascinating festival in the world.

Exercise 4

3. Mount Waialeale in Hawaii gets 1,170 centimeters (460 inches) of rain a year. It is the wettest place on Earth!
4. Canada and Russia are the largest countries in the world.
5. Russia is larger than Canada.
6. The highest waterfall in the world is in Venezuela.
7. The Atacama Desert in Chile is the driest place in the world.
8. The hottest capital city in the world is Muscat, Oman.
9. The continent of Antarctica is colder than any other place in the world.
10. The Himalayas are some of the most dangerous mountains to climb.
11. Mont Blanc in the French Alps is higher than the Matterhorn in the Swiss Alps.
12. The Pacific Ocean is deeper than the Atlantic Ocean. At one place, the Pacific Ocean is 11,033 meters (36,198 feet) deep.

Exercise 5

A

Answers may vary. Possible answers:
It's different because it's the coldest and windiest place on Earth. It is mostly covered in ice. Scientists work in Antarctica to study the effects of climate change.

B

1. True
2. False
3. False
4. True
5. False
6. True
7. False

Exercise 6

2. How long is the Yangtze River?
a. It's 6,300 kilometers (3,917 miles) long.
3. How cold is Antarctica?
b. It gets down to –88.3 degrees Celsius.
4. How far is it from Australia to New Zealand?
a. It's about 2,000 kilometers (1,200 miles).
5. How big is the Amazon Rain Forest?
a. It's 6 million square kilometers (2.5 million square miles).
6. How deep is the Grand Canyon?
b. It's about 1.6 kilometers deep.

Exercise 7

Answers will vary.

Exercise 8

2. i
3. o
4. a
5. j
6. g
7. l
8. b
9. p
10. m
11. c
12. h
13. e
14. d
15. n
16. k

15 What are you doing later?

Exercise 1

2. birthday party
3. car race
4. class reunion
5. medical appointment
6. rock concert
7. tennis match

Exercise 2

2. On Monday, Joe is going to attend the managers' meeting at work.
3. On Tuesday at 6:00 P.M., Joe is going to see a movie with Angela.
4. On Wednesday night, Joe is going to watch the soccer match with Annie and Bob.
5. On Thursday at noon, Joe is going to have lunch with Paco.
6. On Friday evening, Joe is going to go to the rock concert with friends.
7. On Saturday, Joe is going to stay home and do laundry.

Exercise 3

Stacey: What are you going to do this weekend, Hannah?
Hannah: I'm going to go to a jazz concert on Saturday.
Stacey: That sounds interesting.
Hannah: Yeah. There's a free concert in the park. What about you, Stacey?
Stacey: Well, Ryan and I are going to see a baseball game in the afternoon.
Hannah: And what are you going to do in the evening?
Stacey: Ryan is going to visit his mother in the hospital. But I'm not going to do anything really.
Hannah: Well, I'm going to have some friends over for a barbecue. Would you like to come?
Stacey: Thanks, I'd love to!

Exercise 4

2. A: Would you like to have dinner at Bella's Bistro tonight?
   B: Yes, that sounds great! But it's my turn to pay.
3. A: Do you want to go hiking tomorrow?
   B: Sure, I'd love to.
4. A: How about going to a movie on Saturday?
   B: Oh, I'm sorry. I can't.

Exercise 5

Answers will vary.

Exercise 6

Answers will vary.

Exercise 7

A

Hannah is moving into a new apartment and has a few heavy things to move.

B

1. b (Eliana has a bicycle race.)
2. f (Richard has to study.)
3. a (Daichi has to drive his sister around.)
4. d (Pablo is going to the beach.)
5. c (Kalil is going to work all weekend.)
6. g (Lien is going to a baseball tournament.)
7. e (Rachel is going to visit her grandmother.)

Exercise 8

Answers will vary. Possible answers:

2. Please tell Mr. Rodriguez that we need the report by noon. Could you ask him to call Ms. Brady as soon as possible?
3. Please tell Mr. Welch that the new laptop is ready. Could you ask him to pick it up this afternoon?

Exercise 9

Answers will vary. Possible answers:

1. Could you tell Michael not to come/go to the airport until midnight?
2. Please ask Lucy not to forget the tickets.
3. Could you tell Chris that the surprise party starts at noon?

Exercise 10

Receptionist: Hello. McKenzie Corporation.
Mr. Brown: May I speak to Mr. Scott Myers, please?
Receptionist: I'm sorry. He's not in. Can I take a message?
Mr. Brown: Yes, please. This is Mr. Brown. Would you tell him that I have to reschedule our meeting? My phone number is (303) 555-9001. Could you ask him to call me?
Receptionist: OK, Mr. Brown. I'll give him the message.
Mr. Brown: Thank you very much. Good-bye.

Exercise 11

2. Could I ask her to call you back?
   Yes. My number is (303) 555-3241.
3. Who's calling, please?
   This is John. John Abrams.
4. Would you like to come to a party?
   Sure, I'd love to come. Thanks.
5. Could I speak to Tiffany, please?
   Let me see if she's in.
6. Why don't we eat at Sam's Steak House tonight?
   Oh, no. I don't eat meat.

16 How have you changed?

Exercise 1

2. A: I haven't seen you for ages.
   B: I know. How have you been?
3. A: You know, I have three kids now.
   B: Wow, I can't believe it!
4. A: How are you?
   B: I'm doing really well.

Exercise 2

1. JoAnn has gotten two pay raises this year. Now she has enough money to buy a house.
2. Irvin has started an online course. He's studying to become a graphic designer.
3. Gisela and Russ have fallen in love. They're going to get married in December.

Exercise 3

2. Sara grew a lot/is tall now.
3. Ella cut her hair/has short hair now.
4. Ron lost weight/is thinner now.

Exercise 4

2. Raquel is heavier now.
3. Ben changed schools.
4. Helen and George aren't married anymore.
5. Traci eats healthier food now.
6. We don't go to the gym anymore.

Exercise 5

A

1. Diane had an interesting job two years ago.
2. Krystina had money problems two years ago.
3. Rafael was a student two years ago.

B

1. c
2. a
3. b

C

Answers may vary. Possible answers:
Rafael: I dress up now, and my hair is shorter.
Diane: I got married six months ago! We're taking classes several nights a week.
Krystina: I work as a computer programmer for an international company. I've moved to Seoul.

Exercise 6

2. I'd like to be successful in my first job. Then I can get a better job and a raise.
3. I go to school, and I have a family and a part-time job. I have a lot of responsibilities.
4. After graduation, Amelia and Lee plan to look for jobs.
5. Max lost his job. Now he's broke, and he can't pay his rent.
6. What career are you most interested in pursuing?

Exercise 7

Mariko: What do you plan to do this summer, Brian?
Brian: I want to get a summer job. I'd like to save money for a vacation.
Mariko: Really? Where would you like to go?
Brian: I'd love to travel to Latin America. What about you, Mariko?
Mariko: Well, I'm not going to get a job right away. First, I want to go to Spain and Portugal.
Brian: Sounds great, but how are you going to pay for it?
Mariko: I hope to borrow some money from my brother. I have a good excuse. I plan to take courses in Spanish and Portuguese.
Brian: Oh, I'm tired of studying!
Mariko: I love to study. I also hope to take people on tours to Latin America. Why don't you come on my first tour?
Brian: Count me in!

Exercise 8

Answers will vary.

Exercise 9

2. This job is more stressful than my last job.
3. After graduation, Kira plans to work for an international company.
4. Stephanie's salary is much lower than before. She had to take a pay cut.
5. I hope to buy a house soon. I need to get a bank loan.
6. Neil and Kelly got engaged last summer. The wedding will be in April.

Exercise 10

Answers will vary.

CREDITS

The authors and publishers acknowledge the following sources of copyright material and are grateful for the permissions granted. While every effort has been made, it has not always been possible to identify the sources of all the material used, or to trace all copyright holders. If any omissions are brought to our notice, we will be happy to include the appropriate acknowledgements on reprinting and in the next update to the digital edition, as applicable.

Key: E = Exercise, T = Top, B = Below, TR = Top Right, TL = Top Left, BR = Below Right, BL = Below Left, C = Center, CR = Center Right, CL = Center Left, L = Left, R = Right, BC = Below Center, B/G = Background.

Illustrations

337 Jon (KJA Artists): 17 (T); **Mark Duffin**: 17 (B), 80; **Thomas Girard** (Good Illustration): 50, 64, 66, 78 (B), 108, 116–117; **Daniel Gray-Barnett**: 51, 57, 92; **Quino Marin** (The Organisation): 17 (C), 18, 56, 70, 120; **Gavin Reece** (New Division): 2, 3, 5, 61, 123, 124; **Paul Williams** (Sylvie Poggio Artists): 60, 78 (T).

Photos

Back cover (woman with whiteboard): Jenny Acheson/Stockbyte/GettyImages; Back cover (whiteboard): Nemida/GettyImages; Back cover (man using phone): Betsie Van Der Meer/Taxi/GettyImages; Back cover (woman smiling): PeopleImages.com/DigitalVision/GettyImages; Back cover (name tag): Tetra Images/GettyImages; Back cover (handshake): David Lees/Taxi/GettyImages; screenshots on p. x from Interchange 5e Self-Study, Jack C. Richards with Jonathan Hull and Susan Proctor; screenshots on pp. xi–xiv from Interchange 5e Student's Book 1, Jack C. Richards with Jonathan Hull and Susan Proctor; screenshots on p. xv and p. xvi (T) from Interchange 5e Self-Study, Jack C. Richards with Jonathan Hull and Susan Proctor; screenshot on p. xvi (B) from Interchange 5e Games, Jack C. Richards with Jonathan Hull and Susan Proctor; screenshots on p. xvii from Interchange 5e Workbook 1, Jack C. Richards with Jonathan Hull and Susan Proctor; screenshot on p. xviii from Interchange 5e Teacher's Edition 1, Jack C. Richards with Jonathan Hull and Susan Proctor; screenshot on p. xviii from Interchange 5e Complete Assessment Program, Jack C. Richards with Jonathan Hull and Susan Proctor; p. xix (woman with whiteboard): Jenny Acheson/Stockbyte/GettyImages; p. xix (whiteboard): Nemida/GettyImages; screenshots on p. xix from Interchange 5e Student's Book 1, Jack C. Richards with Jonathan Hull and Susan Proctor; screenshot on p. xx (L) from Interchange 5e Supplementary Resources Overviews, Jack C. Richards with Jonathan Hull and Susan Proctor; screenshot on p. xx (R) from Interchange 5e Teacher's Resource Worksheets, Jack C. Richards with Jonathan Hull and Susan Proctor; p. xxiii: Caiaimage/Chris Ryan/GettyImages; p. 2 (header), p. iv (Unit 1): M G Therin Weise/Photographer's Choice RF/GettyImages; p. 4 (photo 1): Hill Street Studios/Tobin Rogers/Blend Images/GettyImages; p. 4 (photo 2): Steve Debenport/E+/GettyImages; p. 4 (photo 3): Monty Rakusen/Cultura/GettyImages; p. 4 (photo 4): Jose Luis Pelaez Inc/Blend Images/GettyImages; p. 4 (photo 5): Peter Cade/Iconica/GettyImages; p. 4 (photo 6): Sofia Bagdasarian/EyeEm/GettyImages; p. 4 (photo 7): Jon Feingersh/Blend Images/GettyImages; p. 4 (photo 8): Echo/Cultura/GettyImages; p. 6 (T): Caiaimage/Sam Edwards/Caiaimage/GettyImages; p. 6 (B): DragonImages/iStock/Getty Images Plus/GettyImages; p. 7 (T): Jamie McCarthy/Getty Images Entertainment/GettyImages; p. 7 (B): Pool/Samir Hussein/WireImage/GettyImages; p. 8 (header), p. iv (Unit 2): Hero Images/GettyImages; p. 8 (babysitter): Jonas unruh/E+/GettyImages; p. 8 (fitness instructor): Jutta Klee/Canopy/GettyImages; p. 8 (office assistant): Sturti/E+/GettyImages; p. 8 (sales associate): Matthias Tunger/DigitalVision/GettyImages; p. 8 (social media assistant): Tim Robberts/Taxi/GettyImages; p. 8 (tutor): Prasit photo/Moment/GettyImages; p. 9 (T): Hero Images/GettyImages; p. 9 (C): Westend61/GettyImages; p. 9 (B): Westend61/GettyImages; p. 10: Steve Debenport/E+/GettyImages; p. 11 (T): Marc Romanelli/Blend Images/GettyImages; p. 11 (B): Yellow Dog Productions/Iconica/GettyImages; p. 11 (taxi driver): Monty Rakusen/Cultura/GettyImages; p. 11 (Kristina): Yellow Dog Productions/Iconica/GettyImages; p. 13 (Danny): tulpahn/iStock/Getty Images Plus/GettyImages; p. 13 (Carla): Image Source/DigitalVision/GettyImages; p. 13 (Nico): Golero/E+/GettyImages; p. 13 (Lisa): Portishead1/E+/GettyImages; p. 14: Fabrice LEROUGE/ONOKY/GettyImages; p. 15 (engineer): B Busco/Photographer's Choice/GettyImages; p. 15 (caregiver): Maskot/GettyImages; p. 15 (electrician): Pamela Moore/E+/GettyImages; p. 15 (IT worker): Echo/Cultura/GettyImages; p. 15 (B): i love images/Cultura/GettyImages; p. 16 (header), p. iv (Unit 3): John Fedele/Blend Images/GettyImages; p. 16 (white mug): Steve Gorton/Dorling Kindersley/GettyImages; p. 16 (blue mug): Dorling Kindersley/GettyImages; p. 16 (green mug): Denis Gladkiy/iStock/Getty Images Plus/GettyImages; p. 16 (yellow mug): serggn/iStock/Getty Images Plus/GettyImages; p. 16 (orange mug): Markus Guhl/Stockbyte/GettyImages; p. 16 (red mug): ampols/iStock/Getty Images Plus/GettyImages; p. 16 (pink mug): Pavlo Vakhrushev/Hemera/Getty Images Plus/GettyImages; p. 16 (purple mug): Ozii45/iStock/Getty Images Plus/GettyImages; p. 16 (brown mug): spaxiax/iStock/Getty Images Plus/GettyImages; p. 16 (black mug): DaddyBit/iStock/Getty Images Plus/GettyImages; p. 16 (gray mug): ambassador806/iStock/Getty Images Plus/GettyImages; p. 17 (B): londoneye/E+/GettyImages; p. 17: Nick David/Iconica/GettyImages; p. 17: londoneye/Vetta/GettyImages; p. 19 (tie): Phil Cardamone/E+/GettyImages; p. 19 (bracelet): Elnur Amikishiyev/Hemera/Getty Images Plus/GettyImages; p. 19 (ring): frender/iStock/Getty Images Plus/GettyImages; p. 19 (shirt): gofotograf/iStock/Getty Images Plus/GettyImages; p. 19 (belt): clark_fang/iStock/Getty Images Plus/GettyImages; p. 19 (earrings): Tarzhanova/iStock/Getty Images Plus/GettyImages; p. 19 (flip-flops): subjug/E+/GettyImages; p. 19 (socks): Gary Ombler/Dorling Kindersley/GettyImages; p. 19 (B): Klaus Vedfelt/Iconica/GettyImages; p. 20 (jacket): White Packert/The Image Bank/GettyImages; p. 20 (coat): Steve Gorton/Dorling Kindersley/GettyImages; p. 20 (orange sweater): ARSELA/iStock/Getty Images Plus/GettyImages; p. 20 (grey sweater): popovaphoto/iStock/Getty Images Plus/GettyImages; p. 20 (gold rings): Tarek El Sombati/E+/GettyImages; p. 20 (silver rings): Burazin/Photographer's Choice/GettyImages; p. 21 (TR): Ivo Peer/EyeEm/GettyImages; p. 21 (TL): martinedoucet/E+/GettyImages; p. 21 (BR): Richard Boll/Photographer's Choice/GettyImages; p. 21 (BL): Al Freni/The LIFE Images Collection/GettyImages; p. 22 (header), p. iv (Unit 4): Westend61/GettyImages; p. 22 (T): Philip Othberg/EyeEm/GettyImages; p. 23 (T): Mark Metcalfe/Getty Images Entertainment/GettyImages; p. 23 (C): Leon Bennett/WireImage/GettyImages; p. 23 (Seth): Halfpoint/iStock/Getty Images Plus/GettyImages; p. 23 (Leanne): Caiaimage/Martin Barraud/Caiaimage/GettyImages; p. 23 (B): Ollie Millington/WireImage/GettyImages; p. 24 (Adele): Joern Pollex/Getty Images Entertainment/GettyImages; p. 24 (Steph Curry): TPG/Getty Images Entertainment/GettyImages; p. 24 (Star Wars): Bravo/NBCUniversal/GettyImages; p. 24 (Top chef): Atlaspix/Alamy; p. 25 (Alexis): Todor Tsvetkov/E+/GettyImages; p. 25 (Jacob): Neustockimages/E+/GettyImages; p. 25 (Tyler): fotostorm/E+/GettyImages; p. 25 (Andrew): panic_attack/iStock/Getty Images Plus/GettyImages; p. 25 (B): Henrik Sorensen/Iconica/GettyImages; p. 25 (Connor): Hero Images/GettyImages; p. 25 (Camila): Tetra Images/Brand X Pictures/GettyImages; p. 27 (B): STAN HONDA/AFP/GettyImages; p. 27 (C): Noel Vasquez/GC Images/GettyImages; p. 27 (T): Michael Tran/FilmMagic/GettyImages; p. 28 (leather jacket): deniztuyel/iStock/Getty Images Plus/GettyImages; p. 28 (wool jacket): Leonid Nyshko/iStock/Getty Images Plus/GettyImages; p. 28 (silk shirt): popovaphoto/iStock/Getty Images Plus/GettyImages; p. 28 (cotton shirt): gofotograf/iStock/Getty Images Plus/GettyImages; p. 28 (laptop): MyImages_Micha/iStock/Getty Images Plus/GettyImages; p. 28 (desktop computer): Ryan McVay/Photodisc/GettyImages; p. 29: Chad Slattery/The Image Bank/GettyImages; p. 30 (header), p. iv (Unit 5): eli_asenova/E+/GettyImages; p. 30 (James): alvarez/E+/GettyImages; p. 30 (Betty): Image Source/GettyImages; p. 30 (Robert): Siri Stafford/Stone/GettyImages; p. 30 (Patricia): Courtney Keating/E+/GettyImages; p. 30 (Deborah): Juanmonino/E+/GettyImages; p. 30 (Arturo): Kevin Dodge/Blend Images/GettyImages; p. 30 (Joseph): Izabela Habur/E+/GettyImages; p. 30 (Keiko): Paul Simcock/Blend Images/GettyImages; p. 30 (Joshua): Liam Norris/Cultura/GettyImages; p. 30 (Nicole): Westend61/Brand X Pictures/GettyImages; p. 30 (Veronica): lukas_zb/iStock/Getty Images Plus/GettyImages; p. 30 (Andrew): BDLM/Cultura/GettyImages; p. 30 (Emily): Robert Daly/Caiaimage/GettyImages; p. 30 (Alyssa): Westend61/GettyImages; p. 30 (Ethan): Compassionate Eye Foundation/Photodisc/GettyImages; p. 31 (Quincy Jones): Jason LaVeris/FilmMagic/GettyImages; p. 31 (Rashida Jones): Barry King/FilmMagic/GettyImages; p. 31 (Ashton Kutcher): JB Lacroix/WireImage/GettyImages; p. 31 (Mila Kunis): Vera Anderson/WireImage/GettyImages; p. 31 (Emma Roberts): Noam Galai/Getty Images North America/GettyImages; p. 31 (Julia Roberts): Dan MacMedan/WireImage/GettyImages; p. 31 (Cameron Diaz): Jason LaVeris/FilmMagic/GettyImages; p. 31 (Nicole Richie): Jeffrey Mayer/WireImage/GettyImages; p. 31 (BL): Vladimir Serov/Blend Images/GettyImages; p. 31 (Max): Flashpop/DigitalVision/GettyImages; p. 31 (Tina): Michael Blann/Iconica/GettyImages; p. 31 (BR): Oliver Strewe/Lonely Planet Images/GettyImages; p. 32 (man calling): Jed Share/Kaoru Share/Blend Images/GettyImages; p. 32 (woman calling): Justin Lambert/DigitalVision/GettyImages; p. 32 (woman chatting): Johnny Greig/iStock/Getty Images Plus/GettyImages; p. 32 (girl chatting): Tim Robberts/The Image Bank/GettyImages; p. 33 (T): Stuart Fox/Gallo Images/GettyImages; p. 33 (B): David Sacks/DigitalVision/GettyImages; p. 33 (C): Aping Vision/STS/Photodisc/GettyImages; p. 33 (Luis): yellowdog/Image Source/GettyImages; p. 33 (Vicky): XiXinXing/GettyImages; p. 34 (T): Robert Daly/Caiaimage/GettyImages; p. 34 (B): Nerida McMurray Photography/DigitalVision/GettyImages; p. 35 (TR): Hero Images/GettyImages; p. 35 (TL): Francesco Ridolfi/Cultura/GettyImages; p. 35 (BR): Compassionate Eye Foundation/Natasha Alipour Faridani/DigitalVision/GettyImages; p. 35 (BL): Edgardo Contreras/Taxi/GettyImages; p. 36 (header), p. iv (Unit 6): Thomas Barwick/DigitalVision/GettyImages; p. 36 (TL): Thomas Barwick/Stone/GettyImages; p. 36 (TR): RuslanDashinsky/iStock/Getty Images Plus/GettyImages; p. 36 (swimming fins): Bluemoon Stock/Stockbyte/GettyImages; p. 36 (shoes): yasinguneysu/E+/GettyImages; p. 36 (golf ball): Duncan Babbage/E+/GettyImages; p. 36 (volleyball): pioneer111/iStock/Getty Images Plus/GettyImages; p. 36 (karate uniform): Comstock/Stockbyte/GettyImages; p. 36 (fitness ball): ayzek/iStock/Getty Images Plus/GettyImages; p. 36 (yoga mat): Serg Myshkovsky/E+/GettyImages; p. 36 (soccer ball): Creative Crop/DigitalVision/GettyImages; p. 36 (bicycle): Comstock/Stockbyte/GettyImages; p. 37 (TR): Mike Kemp/Blend Images/GettyImages; p. 37 (TL): Tim Kitchen/The Image Bank/GettyImages; p. 39 (TR): Jon Bradley/The Image Bank/GettyImages; p. 39 (BR): Studio J Inc/GettyImages; p. 39 (Steph): ATELIER CREATION PHOTO/iStock/Getty Images Plus/GettyImages; p. 39 (Mick): ATELIER CREATION PHOTO/iStock/Getty Images Plus/GettyImages; p. 40 (T): ImagesBazaar/GettyImages; p. 40 (Ex 12.1): Ann Summa/Photolibrary/GettyImages; p. 40 (Ex 12.2): Portra Images/Iconica/GettyImages; p. 40 (Ex 12.3): mediaphotos/E+/GettyImages; p. 40 (Ex 12.4): T.T/Stone/GettyImages; p. 41 (T): Maximilian Stock Ltd./The Image Bank/GettyImages; p. 41 (BR): Gary Burchell/DigitalVision/GettyImages; p. 42: Hero Images/GettyImages; p. 43: Diana Mulvihill/The Image Bank/GettyImages; p. 44 (header), p. iv (Unit 7): edwardolive/iStock/Getty Images Plus/GettyImages; p. 44 (social media): sturti/iStock/Getty Images Plus/GettyImages; p. 44 (go dancing): Tom Merton/Caiaimage/GettyImages; p. 44 (listen to music): Sam Edwards/Caiaimage/GettyImages; p. 44 (play video games): Robert Deutschman/DigitalVision/GettyImages; p. 44 (read): John Lund/Marc Romanelli/Blend Images/GettyImages; p. 44 (relax): SolStock/E+/GettyImages; p. 44 (spend time): Image Source/GettyImages; p. 44 (watch TV): Dan Dalton/Caiaimage/GettyImages; p. 44 (CR): Caiaimage/Paul Bradbury/OJO+/GettyImages; p. 44 (BR): Hero Images/GettyImages; p. 44 (Cara): Caiaimage/Paul Bradbury/OJO+/GettyImages; p. 44 (Neil): Ezra Bailey/Taxi/GettyImages; p. 45: Westend61/GettyImages; screenshot on p. xii from Interchange 5e Student's Book 1, Jack C. Richards with Jonathan Hull and Susan Proctor; p. 46: chinaface/E+/GettyImages; p. 47 (T): AleksandarNakic/E+/GettyImages; p. 47 (B): Songquan Deng/iStock/Getty Images Plus/GettyImages; p. 48: Elena Elisseeva/iStock/Getty Images Plus/GettyImages; p. 49 (T): AYOTOGRAPHY/iStock/Getty Images Plus/GettyImages; p. 49 (C): Gato

Desaparecido/Alamy; p. 49 (B): simon's photo/Moment/GettyImages; p. 50 (header), p. iv (Unit 8): GARDEL Bertrand/hemis.fr/GettyImages; p. 50: Miles Ertman/All Canada Photos/GettyImages; p. 52: Chris Bennett/GettyImages; p. 53 (downtown): Anne Sophie Dhainaut/EyeEm/GettyImages; p. 53 (suburb): Bob O'Connor/Stone/GettyImages; p. 53 (shopping district): Busà Photography/Moment/GettyImages; p. 53 (college campus): Witold Skrypczak/ Lonely Planet Images/GettyImages; p. 53 (business district): Julian Elliott Photography/Photolibrary/GettyImages; p. 53 (theater district): Jerry Driendl/ Stone/GettyImages; p. 53 (industrial district): ULTRA.F/Taxi Japan/GettyImages; p. 53 (small town): Barry Winiker/Photolibrary/GettyImages; p. 53 (BR): UpperCut Images/Stockbyte/GettyImages; p. 53 (Alana): UpperCut Images/ Stockbyte/GettyImages; p. 53 (Barry): franckreporter/E+/GettyImages; p. 54: Guillermo Murcia/Moment/GettyImages; p. 55 (T): Noriko Hayashi/Bloomberg/ GettyImages; p. 55 (C): Alessandra Santorelli/REX/Shutterstock; p. 55 (B): migstock/Alamy; p. 58 (header), p. vi (Unit 9): Tom Merton/Caiaimage/ GettyImages; p. 58 (long hair): Portra Images/DigitalVision/GettyImages; p. 58 (short hair): KidStock/Blend Images/GettyImages; p. 58 (straight hair): Rick Gomez/Blend Images/GettyImages; p. 58 (curly hair): Rainer Holz/Westend61/ GettyImages; p. 58 (bald): wickedpix/iStock/Getty Images Plus/GettyImages; p. 58 (mustache and beard): shapecharge/E+/GettyImages; p. 58 (young): RedChopsticks/GettyImages; p. 58 (middle-aged): Caiaimage/Chris Ryan/ OJO+/GettyImages; p. 58 (elderly): David Sucsy/E+/GettyImages; p. 58 (handsome): Yuri_Arcurs/iStock/Getty Images Plus/GettyImages; p. 58 (good-looking): Wavebreakmedia Ltd/Getty Images Plus/GettyImages; p. 58 (pretty): AntonioGuillem/iStock/Getty Images Plus/GettyImages; p. 58 (short): Ana Abejon/E+/GettyImages; p. 58 (fairly short): DRB Images, LLC/E+/ GettyImages; p. 58 (medium height): 4x6/E+/GettyImages; p. 58 (pretty tall): momentimages/GettyImages; p. 58 (very tall): Photodisc/Stockbyte/ GettyImages; p. 59: Tim Robberts/Taxi/GettyImages; p. 61 (Boho): Christian Vierig/WireImage/GettyImages; p. 61 (Classic): aleksle/E+/GettyImages; p. 61 (Hipster): SeanShot/E+/GettyImages; p. 61 (Streetwear): Peter Muller/Cultura/ GettyImages; p. 63 (TL): Robert Cornelius/Hulton Archive/GettyImages; p. 63 (BL): Dougal Waters/DigitalVision/GettyImages; p. 63 (TR): NASA/Getty Images North America/GettyImages; p. 63 (BR): Tim Stewart News/REX/Shutterstock; p. 64 (header), p. vi (Unit 10): Paul Andrew Lawrence/Visuals Unlimited, Inc./ GettyImages; p. 64 (theme park): Danielle Gali/AWL Images/GettyImages; p. 64 (go dancing): Diverse Images/UIG/GettyImages; p. 64 (space center): Hiroyuki Matsumoto/Photographer's Choice/GettyImages; p. 64 (Cuban food): 424846/ Hemera/Getty Images Plus/GettyImages; p. 64 (alligator): LaDora Sims/ Moment/GettyImages; p. 67: Masaaki Toyoura/The Image Bank/GettyImages; p. 68: Dan Dalton/Caiaimage/GettyImages; p. 69 (TR): Anna_Shepulova/iStock/ Getty Images Plus/GettyImages; p. 69 (CL): James Devaney/WireImage/ GettyImages; p. 69 (CR): Simon Brown NI/Photolibrary/GettyImages; p. 69 (BL): Romilly Lockyer/Photographer's Choice/GettyImages; p. 71: CoCam/iStock/ Getty Images Plus/GettyImages; p. 72 (header), p. vi (Unit 11): Tetra Images/ GettyImages; p. 72 (beautiful): Sylvain Sonnet/GettyImages; p. 72 (ugly): donvictorio/iStock/Getty Images Plus/GettyImages; p. 72 (BR): Jane Sweeney/ AWL Images/GettyImages; p. 73: 2630ben/iStock/Getty Images Plus/ GettyImages; p. 74 (CR): Andrew Bain/Lonely Planet Images/GettyImages; p. 74 (photo 1): Michele Falzone/The Image Bank/GettyImages; p. 74 (photo 2): seng chye teo/Moment/GettyImages; p. 74 (photo 3): WitR/iStock/Getty Images Plus/GettyImages; p. 74 (photo 4): Photo by Hanneke Luijting/Moment/ GettyImages; p. 74 (photo 5): f11photo/iStock/Getty Images Plus/GettyImages; p. 74 (photo 6): Panoramic Images/Panoramic Images/GettyImages; p. 75 (TR): Julius Reque/Moment Mobile/GettyImages; p. 75 (CR): Christian Kober/ robertharding/GettyImages; p. 75 (Jason): svetikd/E+/GettyImages; p. 75 (Claudia): Hill Street Studios/Blend Images/GettyImages; p. 76 (TR): Eric Lo/ Moment/GettyImages; p. 76 (BR): 153photostudio/iStock/Getty Images Plus/ GettyImages; p. 77 (TR): Manfred Gottschalk/Lonely Planet Images/ GettyImages; p. 77 (CL): Jeremy Woodhouse/Photographer's Choice RF/ GettyImages; p. 77 (CR): Kimberley Coole/Lonely Planet Images/GettyImages; p. 78 (header), p. vi (Unit 12): Paul Bradbury/Caiaimage/GettyImages; p. 79 (sore throat): BSIP/UIG/Universal Images Group/GettyImages; p. 79 (fever): Tom Le Goff/DigitalVision/GettyImages; p. 79 (toothache): Eric Audras/ONOKY/ GettyImages; p. 79 (burn): Jurgute/iStock/Getty Images Plus/GettyImages; p. 80: annebaek/E+/GettyImages; p. 81 (TR): Yuri_Arcurs/E+/GettyImages; p. 81 (BR): simarik/E+/GettyImages; p. 82: PeopleImages.com/DigitalVision/ GettyImages; p. 83: rbiedermann/iStock/Getty Images Plus/GettyImages; p. 83 (B/G): Johnny Lye/iStock/Getty Images Plus/GettyImages; p. 85 (stomachache): IAN HOOTON/Science Photo Library/GettyImages; p. 85 (insect bite): BURGER/PHANIE/Canopy/GettyImages; p. 85 (nosebleed): LEA PATERSON/ SCIENCE PHOTO LIBRARY/Science Photo Library/GettyImages; p. 85 (hiccups): Peopleimages/iStock/Getty Images Plus/GettyImages; p. 85 (CL): Image Source/Photodisc/GettyImages; p. 85 (C): Pascal Broze/ONOKY/GettyImages; p. 85 (CR): kali9/E+/GettyImages; p. 86 (header), p. vi (Unit 13): Hero Images/ Hero Images/GettyImages; p. 86 (apple pie): John Montana/StockFood Creative/GettyImages; p. 86 (chocolate): Thomas Francois/iStock/Getty Images Plus; p. 86 (french fries): Rachel Weill/UpperCut Images/GettyImages; p. 86 (hamburger): Westend61/GettyImages; p. 86 (ice-cream cone): Oksana Dzhaketi/EyeEm/EyeEm/GettyImages; p. 86 (pasta): jon whitaker/Dorling Kindersley/GettyImages; p. 86 (sandwich): julie clancy/Moment/GettyImages; p. 86 (sushi): Foodcollection/GettyImages; p. 86 (BR): Cultura RM Exclusive/ Matelly/Cultura Exclusive; p. 87 (bland): powerbeephoto/iStock/Getty Images Plus/GettyImages; p. 87 (delicious): Agnieszka Kirinicjanow/E+/GettyImages; p. 87 (greasy): Foodcollection/GettyImages; p. 87 (healthy): matka_Wariatka/ iStock/Getty Images Plus/GettyImages; p. 87 (rich): Luzia Ellert/StockFood Creative/GettyImages; p. 87 (salty): magnetcreative/iStock/Getty Images Plus/ GettyImages; p. 87 (spicy): Floortje/E+/GettyImages; p. 88 (board): Jon Schulte/E+/GettyImages; p. 88 (B/G): Sonya_illustration/iStock/Getty Images Plus; p. 88 (BR): andresr/E+/GettyImages; p. 89: NicoleArnoldPhotography/ GettyImages; p. 90 (TR): Justin Geoffrey/Iconica/GettyImages; p. 90 (girl): Peopleimages/E+/GettyImages; p. 90 (burger): Yurika Yamada/EyeEm/EyeEm/ GettyImages; p. 91: JGI/Jamie Grill/Blend Images/GettyImages; p. 92 (header), p. vi (Unit 14): Bjarki Reyr/Stone/GettyImages; p. 93: andresr/E+/GettyImages; p. 94 (L): Mint Images – Liesel Bockl/Mint Images RF/GettyImages; p. 94 (C): Celia Peterson/arabianEye/GettyImages; p. 94 (R): Dave and Les Jacobs/ Kolostock/Blend Images/GettyImages; p. 95 (T): Witold Skrypczak/Lonely Planet Images/GettyImages; p. 95 (B): Stuart Westmorland/Photographer's Choice/GettyImages; p. 96: Al Rod/Stockbyte/GettyImages; p. 97 (TR): Canadian Space Agency/RADARSAT/NASA/Science Photo Library; p. 97 (CL): Australian Scenics/Photolibrary/GettyImages; p. 97 (BR): TERADAT SANTIVIVUT/E+/GettyImages; p. 99: itkin_photo/iStock/Getty Images Plus/ GettyImages; p. 100 (header), p. vi (Unit 15): Diverse Images/UIG/Universal Images Group/GettyImages; p. 100 (CR): Westend61/GettyImages; p. 100 (BR): Hero Images/Hero Images/GettyImages; p. 102 (TR): Miroslav Georgijevic/ Vetta/GettyImages; p. 102 (R): Ariel Skelley/Blend Images/GettyImages; p. 102 (Jake): Ariel Skelley/Blend Images/GettyImages; p. 102 (Caitlin): Joan Vicent Canto Roig/E+/GettyImages; p. 103: Robert Daly/Caiaimage/ GettyImages; p. 105 (TR): Todor Tsvetkov/E+/GettyImages; p. 105 (CL): Tony Garcia/Image Source/GettyImages; p. 105 (CR): Getty Images/Staff/Getty Images News/GettyImages; p. 105 (BL): Cultura Exclusive/We Boldly Went/ Cultura Exclusive/GettyImages; p. 106 (header), p. vi (Unit 16): AndreyPopov/ iStock/Getty Images Plus/GettyImages; p. 106 (BR): Westend61/GettyImages; p. 107 (TR): franckreporter/E+/GettyImages; p. 107 (CR): Yagi Studio/ DigitalVision/GettyImages; p. 107 (BR): Catherine Delahaye/Taxi/GettyImages; p. 109 (CR): Peopleimages/E+/GettyImages; p. 109 (BR): Caiaimage/Tom Merton/OJO+/GettyImages; p. 110 (TR): andresr/E+/GettyImages; p. 110 (CR): andresr/E+/GettyImages; p. 111 (TR): Michel Porro/Getty Images News/ GettyImages; p. 111 (B): REMKO DE WAAL/Stringer/AFP/GettyImages; p. 112: Aksonov/Vetta/GettyImages; p. 113: Wavebreakmedia Ltd/Wavebreak Media/ Getty Images Plus/GettyImages; screenshots on pp. T114–131 from Interchange 5e Student's Book 1, Jack C. Richards with Jonathan Hull and Susan Proctor.

Video still on p. xv (B) by Nesson Media Boston Inc.